DIY ON THE LOWER EAST SIDE

DIY ON THE LOWER EAST SIDE

BOOKS, BUILDINGS, AND ART AFTER THE 1975 FISCAL CRISIS

ANDREW STROMBECK

Cover image: *Broken Promises/Falsas Promises*, © John Fekner. Reprinted with permission.

Published by State University of New York Press, Albany

© 2020 State University of New York

All rights reserved

No part of this book may be used or reproduced in any manner whatsoever without written permission. No part of this book may be stored in a retrieval system or transmitted in any form or by any means including electronic, electrostatic, magnetic tape, mechanical, photocopying, recording, or otherwise without the prior permission in writing of the publisher.

For information, contact State University of New York Press, Albany, NY
www.sunypress.edu

Library of Congress Cataloging-in-Publication Data

Name: Andrew Strombeck.
Title: DIY on the Lower East Side: Books, Buildings, and Art after the 1975 Fiscal Crisis / Andrew Strombeck.
Description: Albany : State University of New York Press, [2020] | Includes bibliographical references and index.
Identifiers: ISBN 9781438479811 (hardcover : alk. paper) | ISBN 9781438479804 (pbk. : alk. paper) | ISBN 9781438479828 (ebook)
Further information is available at the Library of Congress.

Library of Congress Control Number: 2020940104

10 9 8 7 6 5 4 3 2 1

Contents

Acknowledgments   vii

Introduction   1

Chapter 1   David Wojnarowicz, Gordon Matta-Clark, and the Fordist Crisis in 1970s New York   29

Chapter 2   The Puerto Rican Working Class and the Literature of Rebuilding   55

Chapter 3   Semiotext(e), Kathy Acker, and the Decline of the Welfare State   85

Chapter 4   The Rise of the Creative Economy: Art, Gentrification, and Narrative   117

Chapter 5   Between Fordism and Post-Fordism: The DIY Literature of *Between C & D*   151

Afterword: ACT UP and the Divergent Possibilities of DIY   179

Notes   189

Works Cited   227

Index   245

Acknowledgments

In researching the culture workers of the Lower East Side of the 1970s and 1980s, I have often been struck by their generosity: the ways that they often commented on, promoted, and collaborated on one another's work. Doing my own work, I have likewise benefited from others' generosity. Some of this generosity came from the writers themselves. Joel Rose and Catherine Texier were especially helpful in sharing their stories, helping me get details right, and understanding the texture of the Lower East Side. Other writers involved in the scene were similarly wonderful, including Lynne Tillman, Chris Kraus, and Darius James. Robert Siegle wrote the original book on these writers, and exchanging emails with Robert established key paradigms for my book early on. From the day I looked her up, Catherine Liu has been an unflinching supporter of this project, and much of the book wouldn't have been possible without the valuable conversations I had with her.

As a researcher who has worked primarily with post-1945 literature, I had scant experience with library archives when I began this project. The staff at Fales Library at New York University made this potentially difficult process feel easy and familiar. While I was at the Fales, talking to Marvin Taylor and David Hobbs helped me reshape questions and find new resources. The staff at the Center for Puerto Rican Studies were similarly fantastic, especially Pedro Juan Hernández. While I never visited the library onsite, the staff at UC San Diego were wonderful as well. All that is to say: research librarians are amazing, and I have never been more grateful for them. Support your local research librarians.

This project received an early, invaluable boost when *Post45 Peer Reviewed* accepted my piece on David Wojnarowicz and Gordon Matta-Clark. I was stunned when someone thought it was acceptable for me to write about art, and I have never looked back. I am grateful to Sean McCann,

Palmer Rampell, Merve Emre, and everyone else involved with Post45. I'm also grateful to Michael LeMahieu and the other editors at *Contemporary Literature*, who, also early on, published a related piece on Rachel Kushner's *The Flamethrowers*. That experience was formative for establishing the themes and problems of this book. (Though we've never met, I'm also grateful to Kushner for writing a novel full of references and paradigms that cleared crucial ground for this study.)

As a scholar working at a regional university, I have sometimes found myself, as some of us do, feeling a bit isolated from the larger field. I cannot express enough how grateful I am to the Association for the Study of Arts of the Present, which has been a welcoming home since I first attended in 2015 in Greenville, SC. At a panel at that first conference, J.D. Connor, Joseph Jeon, and Gloria Fisk showed up with interesting, thoughtful questions for a scholar they'd never heard of, and they have been supportive ever since then. Through ASAP, I've met so many wonderful people whose friendship and intellects have benefited the project, including Sheri Harrison, Lee Konstantinou, Sheila Liming, Theodore Martin, Annie McClanahan, and Min Hyoung Song. Thoughtful conversations with Tyler Bradway, Sarah Broulliette, Leigh Claire La Berge, Diarmuid Hester, Kate Marshall, Andrew Marzoni, Urayoán Noel, Matt Tierney, Jean-Thomas Tremblay, Andrew Lison, and Joshua Clover have also shaped the project. Andrew Hoberek has been simply amazing, promoting the project at every turn, putting me in touch with key people, and generally being a great friend and colleague. Jason Arthur read and gave feedback on multiple drafts of early chapters. Vinnie Haddad has been an ASAP of one here in the Miami Valley.

My career began at the University of California at Davis. I learned to be a scholar under the mentorship of my dissertation advisors David Simpson, Riché Richardson, and Rita Raley. Elizabeth Freeman arrived at Davis too late to be part of my committee, but conversations with her also helped form my intellectual foundations. I would not be where I am today without their guidance, skill, and depth of knowledge, and they have all continued to support my career in ways large and small.

My colleagues at the Department of English Languages and Literatures at Wright State University are a great group. Hope Jennings, Kelli Zeytoun, Lynnette Jones, Annette Oxindine, Carol Mejia LaPerle, and Alpana Sharma have made Wright State a welcoming intellectual community. Deborah Casan told me to keep writing. Chris DeWeese and Heather Christle have helped me understand the avant-garde poetry of the past 40 years from the perspective of brilliant practitioners. Lars Soderland has, alas, moved on to Western Oregon University, but the many Mondays that Lars and I spent sampling bourbons and talking literary theory have left a long mark on the book.

I've also learned from the insights of Wright State's graduate and undergraduate students, especially students in Fall 2017's *Books/Space/Cities/The Present* and the Spring 2016 sections of ENG 3060. Among these students, I need to mention two in particular. Jamal Russell, now writing his own brilliant book at the University of California, Santa Barbara, has been a friend and inspiration since I first had him in class. Dave Shields, too, has inspired me with his intellect and friendship. I appreciate in particular his insights on art and museum curation. Students are amazing. Support your local students.

The College of Liberal Arts at Wright State University provided important research funding for this project in 2014, and allowed me a year of sabbatical in 2016–17. The Wright State chapter of the American Association of University Professors has fought hard both to allow people like me the time to do research, and to keep Wright State as the kind of viable public institution that I discuss in this book. I'll stand alongside them on the picket line through any amount of terrible weather. Unions are amazing. Support your local unions.

I first talked to Rebecca Colesworthy about this project at the Novel conference in Ithaca in 2017. I'm so lucky that I did. From the start, she has been responsive, attentive to the work, encouraging, and, simply, a good person to talk to. She and her colleagues at SUNY Press are the best of their class. I can't imagine this book being anywhere but SUNY. University presses are amazing. Support your local university presses.

Chris Maikels has always been good at getting me to take breaks from all this. I'm grateful for his friendship. I've come to think of writing as including all sorts of activities: walking, cleaning up, going to the library. For this project, it also included playing guitar with Michael Schlaerth, and I'm grateful for his patience with my so-so playing. Jay Lewis has been a rock since I first met him in 1992; I can't imagine my life without him in it. John Beckman and Thomas Heise have encouraged this project from its very early origins at the MLA in 2014, and their friendship over the past twenty years has been one of the very brightest parts of my life.

While working on this project, I'd often joke that it was just an excuse to go to New York. The North Shore neighborhood in Staten Island is quite different from the Lower East Side, but it's come to feel like a second home. Trish Strombeck and Christoph Mayer watched my kids while I worked at

NYU or the Centro, fed me dinner, and talked to me about the art and history of the city. Siblings are amazing. Support your local siblings.

My love of New York City began with my mother, Loraine Strombeck, who grew up at 90th and Amsterdam. Her experiences living there, as one of the few Irish families in a largely Puerto Rican housing project, forms a major underlying inspiration for my work. In some wide sense, this project is about the Duffy family. My father, Paul Strombeck, has been a crucial source of support throughout this path. Parents are amazing. Support your local parents.

I am lucky to be the father and stepfather of three bright, thoughtful teenagers, who surprise and inspire me every day. Soren, Marcela, and Adrian are my in-house philosophers, artists, and historians: this book is theirs as well. Teenagers are amazing. Support your local teenagers.

Every word in this book is half Crystal Lake's. My debt to her is larger than New York City's in 1975, and this project has always been between C(rystal) and D(rew).

Chapter 1 is a revised and extended version of "David Wojnarowicz, Gordon Matta-Clark, and the Fordist Crisis in 1970s New York," *Post45 Peer Reviewed,* October 24, 2016, © 2016 The Post45 Collective. Some elements of chapter 3 appeared previously in "After the Welfare State: Kathy Acker and the American Health Care System," *The Millions,* July 10, 2018, © 2018 The Millions. Some of the ideas in chapter 4 appeared previously in "The Machine, the Garden, and the Hollow," *The Rambling*, October 18, 2018, © 2018 The Rambling.

Introduction

In retrospect, the 1975 New York fiscal crisis changed everything. During the crisis, leaders of finance, leveraging the city's considerable debt, took over the city's management. They cut direct benefits, established tuition at CUNY, raised subway fares, and reduced the city's workforce by tens of thousands. In doing so, they foreshadowed what would soon happen on state, national, and international levels.[1] These leaders told everyone that austerity was the only way forward. The city, they argued, had spent too much, especially on those "peasants," in city commissioner Roger Starr's words, who kept coming to the city looking for work when everyone knew that all the jobs had gone away.[2] That last part was partly true. The city had lost some 500,000 manufacturing jobs in the previous decade, and more losses were coming. The city's housing quality had declined accordingly, and the board had a solution to that as well: cut rent control and let the market do its work.

Particularly in the past twenty years, and more so after the 2008 crisis, this story has become familiar. Reducing benefits, blaming the poor, and letting the market take over the role of government: these are the touchstones of a rising story about the state, its citizenry, and business that would be repeated with increasing frequency for the next forty years.[3] Inevitably, too, public debt has been the lever used by financiers and right-leaning policy makers to break down the broad, if imperfect, safety nets put in place in Western countries during the post–World War II boom. In the 1990s, the International Monetary Fund used debt to reshape the economies of nations like Indonesia, Argentina, and Mexico. After 2008, debt was similarly leveraged against European countries—Ireland, Spain, Italy, Greece, Portugal—to force austerity on these governments as well. In New York, these actions were anticipated by two organizations that acted together as a kind of local IMF: the Municipal Assistance Corporation (MAC), established in June of 1975, and the Emergency Financial Control Board, established in 1978. Both organizations originated with the New York State government, both were intimately tied to the city's lenders and real estate industry, and both shared a mandate to implement austerity and refashion the city's government according to the needs of business. The policies they put in place accentuated the fiscal and social problems that the city had already been facing due to white flight, deindustrialization, and the decline of the city as a major shipping hub. The effects of such problems were felt with particular acuity in lower-income neighborhoods. *DIY on the Lower East Side* focuses on a neighborhood that was, in 1975, struggling, but by the 1990s had changed radically, becoming home to a much more middle- and upper-middle-class population.

The literature written in the city after the crisis records the impacts that changes forced by these boards made on the built environment, the poor, the creative, the entrepreneurial, the queer, the activist. It records the struggles to resist austerity, to build institutions that might supplement government aid. More broadly, it records attempts to make sense of the city's rapid shift away from a model of governance that served all citizens to a model of governance that served the elite. *DIY on the Lower East Side: Books, Buildings, and Art after the 1975 Fiscal Crisis* scrutinizes how the aesthetic productions of the Lower East Side of the 1970s and 1980s refracted the cultural shifts that profoundly shaped, and continue to shape, our current political conditions.

Standing in line for food stamps in June 1975, Kathy Acker heard the man next to her talk about how the federal government would soon close off the cities. She thought to herself that yes, something was up; perhaps the city was returning to the Middle Ages. Writing the introduction to *Nuyorican Poetry*, which would come out the next year, Miguel Algarín praised work that the Dynamite Brothers were doing but that the city was not: rehabilitating homes that had fallen into shameful disrepair. At Columbia, Sylvère Lotringer hosted Gilles Deleuze, Félix Guattari, and Michel Foucault at the "Schizo-Culture" conference for his newly formed journal, *Semiotext(e)*. All three men showed up in part because of the city's reputation for danger. Attending the conference, the therapist Betty Kronsky thought the trio's ecstatic presentations were "glib and bizarre" in the face of "no jobs" and "a city about to default."[4] Somewhere in Times Square, David Wojnarowicz stood in a doorway, talking to a down-and-out woman. He would go on to turn this and similar conversations into a project he called the monologues, works that recorded life as it was lived in the cracks that opened up in the crisis's wake. At Pier 52, Gordon Matta-Clark cut holes into an abandoned warehouse building to create *Day's End*. In the Lower East Side, Adam Purple began his "Garden of Eden," one of many spontaneous gardens appearing throughout the neighborhood amidst the rubble. In Queens, Alanna Heiss prepared to open P.S. 1, a new art center in a school building that had been closed for twelve years. In P.S. 1's inaugural exhibit, *Rooms*, artists like Matta-Clark and Joseph Kosuth would incorporate the dilapidated building into their art, cutting holes in floors and writing on old chalkboards.

The 1975 crisis made bad conditions worse. Decaying buildings and vacant lots proliferated as landlords walked away from properties or had them burned down. For nearly everyone writing the history of the crisis, these buildings serve as potent symbols of social decay and of the city's death. Both Jimmy Carter and Ronald Reagan toured the South Bronx during this era, each using the landscape as a powerful visual metaphor for what had gone wrong in the United States. Terms like "urban decay" and "underclass" became shorthand for falling productivity, the failure of the welfare state, and a general, national *anomie*. For many writers and artists, however, the city's landscape became something different: a site to experiment with new ways of living and new ways of creating.

This body of work produced by these writers reveals how the city's crumbling conditions allowed many to pursue literary projects often at odds with that being produced in creative writing programs at the high point of what Mark McGurl terms the Program Era in American literature. The DIY literature of the Lower East Side documents the shifting networks that made it possible for Acker to live on little money, for Algarín to start the Nuyorican Poets Cafe, for Wojnarowicz to pull himself out of an abusive childhood. At the same time, however, those who found themselves able to create in the ruins of the Lower East Side also closed off their own possibilities. First in SoHo and then in the Lower East Side, lots of people believed that art could bring magic to one of the city's key problems: a lack of middle-class housing. Rents went up accordingly.

Throughout these authors' lives, there's a running thread. They moved to New York, lived in a crummy apartment, wrote constantly, befriended and in some cases became visual artists, and got angry about how the other people living in the neighborhood were treated. They did it themselves—made careers out of limited circumstances—but were frustrated by the conditions that left their neighbors doing it themselves. Before her success, for example,

Acker lived in one terrible apartment in Washington Heights in 1971. After moving around, she ended up in a similar place on East Fifth Street. As her journals from the era detail, her struggles with money were real. At one point, she found herself in Columbia-Presbyterian's emergency room, sick with pelvic inflammatory disease, unable to pay the resulting bills. Acker incorporates these experiences, almost directly, into her early work. In a passage from *Blood and Guts in High School*, Acker's protagonist Janey lives on "a mat on the floor that belongs to the rats and four walls with tiny piles of plaster at the bottom." She encounters "continuous noise" and the smell of "garbage and piss" waft in from the "slums of New York City" while landlords burn their buildings down and the buildings that remain "have no hot water or heat."[5] Sometimes, critics have figured Acker's work as largely nonrepresentational. But Acker's journals from the era show her drawing on lived experience, and the conditions listed in this passage were all real in the Lower East Side, especially after the city's 1975 fiscal crisis.

In the period before the crisis, New York had long, seemingly durable networks that connected its poorest citizens to its richest ones, its art institutions to its commerce, its unions to its government, its government to its citizens. These long networks didn't disappear in 1975. But almost everyone agrees that by a number of measures, those networks became shorter: shorter periods of employment, shorter extensions of the welfare state into neighborhoods, shorter ties binding together neighborhoods.[6] The sociologist Zygmunt Bauman describes this shift as one from the "solid modernity" of the Fordist factory, government bureaucracy, and mandatory union membership to the "liquid modernity" of service work, deregulation, and short-term contracts.[7] Actually, for Bauman, it's a wholesale transformation of social life, from individuals who saw themselves part of—though often trapped in—a rigid hierarchy, to individuals who see themselves as needing to serve their own needs: to do it themselves. The literature of *DIY on the Lower East Side* documents the colliding forms produced by the shift Bauman describes. Often, its attention to such colliding forms produces formal experimentation, as in Wojnarowicz's short monologues, Acker's appropriation, and the New Narrative work of Tillman and Indiana.

As these quick examples suggest, the writers I focus on throughout this study document the aftereffects of the 1975 fiscal crisis. It's true, though, that these aftereffects became clearer over time. As I'll discuss in chapter 4, there's a gulf between Tillman's *Haunted Houses* (1987) and her *No Lease on Life* (1998). The former focuses primarily on the ways that the restrictive gender identities of the suburbs haunt Tillman's protagonists. The latter addresses gentrification and homelessness head on; though set in 1994, it's a post-crisis novel. In the 1980s and 1990s, these writers were often received in terms of an attack on repressive forms of culture. This question is at the core of Robert Siegle's landmark monograph on these writers, *Suburban Ambush: Downtown Writing and the Fiction of Insurgency* (1989).[8] Carefully documenting the literary production of the Lower East Side, Siegle finds the writers and artists working there resisting the constrained lifestyles represented by the suburbs.[9] In 1989, it wasn't possible to see the long view from 1975, the austerity and income inequality that would dominate questions of governance from that point forward. As a result, Siegle draws different conclusions than does my study here. Yet his remarkable research and his *framing* of these writers' insurgency provide invaluable foundations for my work. In 1989, it wasn't fully clear that the ambush could work in reverse. The policies crafted in New York in the late 1970s would come to determine the structures of not just identity, but post-Fordist governance itself. As Richard Florida has ruefully observed, the jarring experiences of austerity, privatization, and income inequality felt by working-class New Yorkers in the 1970s have been increasingly felt in suburbs for the past forty years.[10]

A word about geography: definitions of the Lower East Side are notoriously slippery. In the accounts of real estate developers, geographers, writers, entrepreneurs, and historians, the boundaries of the neighborhood shift and assume new names: The East Village, Loisaida, Alphabet City. I use the term "Lower East Side" to describe the area in Lower Manhattan adjoining the East River below Fourteenth Street, east of the Bowery/Third Avenue, and roughly north of Canal Street.[11] While I invoke "the East Village" a few times in describing the neighborhood's art galleries, I tend to avoid this term because of the way it was used by real estate developers in the 1980s to make the neighborhood seem more acceptable to middle-class whites. "Alphabet City" was used in opposite ways but toward something of the same end, to depict the neighborhood as a lawless zone nevertheless full of thrills for nonresidents. While I praise the use of "Loisaida" by Puerto Rican writers, activists, and artists in chapter 2, this term was not widely used by the other culture workers I discuss here. "Lower East Side" is, then, at once an expansive and relatively neutral term for the geographical area I cover here.

Do-It-Yourself

Broadly speaking, the impetus of the 1975 crisis was away from collective activities—the welfare state, the large firm, and other durable institutions—and toward the individual. Do-it-yourself, which I interpret here as shorthand for what the philosopher Isabell Lorey calls "an individualized capacity for risk management," becomes an essential mandate. It's true, though, that the particular manifestation of do-it-yourself depends on whether you're a middle-class white man or an impoverished Puerto Rican woman.[12] Sustaining networks broke down at every level, but, as Lauren Berlant observes, "the lower you are on economic scales, and the less formal your relation to the economy, the more alone you are in the project of maintaining and reproducing life."[13] In my project, do-it-yourself encompasses a range of activities driven by often quite different impulses. But as I'll suggest, these activities have what Ludwig Wittgenstein might call "family resemblances." They intersect with each other, find inspiration in the same circumstances, and share a drive to make something out of what seemed like ruins.

Do-it-yourself is perhaps most famous for being an ethos of punk: record your own music, make your own labels, get in the van and go on tour. The artists and writers of *DIY on the Lower East Side* take up this ethos by starting literary journals out of their apartment, starting theory journals out of their offices, establishing poetry cafés, rebuilding abandoned schools as cultural institutions, and, perhaps most famously, opening galleries in deserted storefronts. Other forms of do-it-yourself became necessary after the wide cuts in city funding: do-it-yourself tenant advocacy, do-it-yourself after school programs, do-it-yourself banking. This is the kind of do-it-yourself celebrated in the January-February 1985 issue of *The Quality of Life in Loisaida*, titled fittingly, "Do-It-Yourself." Beginning publication shortly after the crisis, *The Quality of Life* showed readers how to make covers for their radiators to improve their efficiency, or how to save money by making your own Christmas gifts. For contemporary readers, DIY is best known in terms of home improvement, the kind of home renovation celebrated on *Home and Garden Television*. Own it yourself, get the drywall, run the electricity, drive to Home Depot, put up the tile. The writers Joel Rose and Catherine Texier literally undertook this process (without the Home Depot part), rehabilitating their apartment while working on their writing. So did Bimbo Rivas, the Nuyorican poet who helped convert another disused school building, P.S. 64, into El Bohío, a community arts center where Rivas would stage his plays. The other culture workers of my book undertook this process more metaphorically, using their art to improve their chances of survival. This spirit carried over into the creation of community gardens, homesteaded apartment buildings, and abandoned storefronts turned into galleries and places to sell handcrafted items. By the 1980s, the neighborhood had witnessed a range of innovative, DIY takeovers of space: from the Hawaiian burger place called Hawaii 5.0 to a gas station repurposed for a performance space, to the many galleries that opened in storefronts.

DIY was brought to bear, too, toward more political interventions. In 1980, the members of Colab illegally occupied a Delancey Street building owned by the city. After breaking the lock, they used the space to stage an exhibition that critiqued gentrification: they called it the *Real Estate Show*.[14] Police shut it down, but after the German artist Joseph Beuys publicly denounced the city, the city agreed to give Colab a nearby building for their use. That space became ABC No Rio, which became a center for community activism and art. Even before Fun Gallery, which kicked off the gallery explosion in the Lower East Side, DIY had been activated against the mandates of MAC and the Emergency Financial Control Board (EFCB).[15] This tradition would continue with other activist art groups, notably Group Material, who staged a range of shows calling attention to the neighborhood's art-driven redevelopment. As I'll argue in my afterword, these small-scale actions built the groundwork for ACT UP, a powerful, art-inflected movement that managed to intervene sharply in the national politics of AIDS.

The withdrawal of the welfare state and the demand for market-based solutions gave DIY a double edge. Cuts to state and city funding forced more and more people to do it themselves, whether that meant knitting radiator covers, rehabilitating buildings, starting their own literary journal, or dealing drugs. It's all fine and good for the state to enable experiments by tacitly approving the appropriation of city-owned space. It's another thing when the state, and the economy, demands that you manage yourself. After all, as the literary critic Jasper Bernes observes, "new forms of autonomy and self-management . . . are really regimes of self-harrying, self-intensification, and interworker competition disguised as attempts to humanize the workplace and allow for freedom and self-expression in work."[16] This self-management was a key facet of the version of capitalism that replaced Fordism, and it's not coincidental that the do-it-yourself aesthetic experiments of the Lower East Side happened at this moment.

DIY on the Lower East Side tracks all these versions of DIY, examining the multiple forms of do-it-yourself that became both appealing and necessary after 1975. Of course, going to New York in search of cheap rent and an artistic community is much different than starting a tenants' rights organization. When these writers and artists moved to New York, they were not necessarily interested in changing the lives of the impoverished around them, though each made impassioned cases for these lives' precarity. They sought mostly to make something out of the nothing of their own lives.

This something involved, for a time, developing ways of life that were outside of market-driven capitalism. That was the promise that post-crisis New York held for artists and writers: the possibility of focusing fully on aesthetic creation without the benefits of grants or the stability of creative writing programs. Because of the straitened circumstances of his background, Wojnarowicz had little choice. Acker, who came from money but broke with her parents in the late 1960s, made a more deliberate decision to work in the ruins. Both developed work that was open to the city around them. This was the old dream of bohemia that took shape in Baudelaire's Paris, whereby artists drew inspiration from desperation, borrowing autonomy from subjects denied access to the fullness of the economy.[17] It all ends, though, in gentrification, and while some argue that one can separate the neighborhood's creative lifestyles from its eventual high rents and middle-class residents, there's ample evidence to suggest that culture workers like Acker and Wojnarowicz cleared ground for copywriters and bond traders.[18]

And yet. Once a crisis has become part of history, its outcomes seem inevitable. As I note above, the 1975 crisis is, now, primarily understood as the moment that kicked off the austerity, inequality, and low-waged labor that characterize neoliberalism broadly. But there's plenty of room for thinking, too, that crises are moments of potential shift, where other forms of life might have emerged. "The idea of a new life is at once realistic and illusory," writes the geographer Henri Lefebvre, "and hence neither true nor false. . . . The space which contains the realized preconditions of another life is the same one as prohibits what those preconditions make possible."[19] The forms of life and work that took shape under Fordist capitalism seemed, for a time, inevitable, but as the Marxist historian Moishe Postone has demonstrated, over time these emerged as less an inevitable function of such capitalism, and more an ideological relationship between capital and labor. Waged work might seem to be an "ongoing process with no substantive end," but, at least for Postone, there is nothing inevitable about this state of affairs.[20] Thus while Fordism's decline, with its attendant wagelessness, indeed produces widespread precarity, it also presents a moment when the nature of work might be rethought.[21]

This is the utopian possibility at the moment of Fordism's destruction. What ultimately happened is that workers increasingly needed to go it on their own. But workers might have found a world where decreased labor time meant increased time to labor on their own creations: art, craft, the transformation of their living environments—away from what Postone calls "fragmented, empty work." DIY, then, may well be a way to insist, as

Kathi Weeks puts it, "that there are other ways to organize and distribute [productive activity]" and to "remind us that it is also possible to be creative outside the boundaries of work."[22] At its best, DIY is a lived form of critique, an insistence that labor be free from the organized structures of capitalism. While some of the culture workers of the Lower East Side ended up being financially successful, by and large, they moved to the neighborhood in order to experiment with ways of life outside of the regular-wage system. The destruction of value in New York cracked open a brick wall and offered a glimpse of a beautiful city behind that wall: the light-filled sky of a Martin Wong painting. This was the unproductive city, where labor time might be decreased and the nature of individual labor transformed. Writ large, the experiments of the Lower East Side were ones of opening up, even as they eventually became ones of shutting down.

Using a term drawn from the writer Ron Kolm, Siegle describes these experiments as a "suburban ambush": the writers, artists, and activists of the Lower East Side sought a world different from the Fordist world they'd fled, where workers owned their time and their labor.[23] While, by and large, DIY is absorbed into late capitalism itself, we can nevertheless see in DIY a *desire* for ways of living outside of the boundaries of work. "We loved Avenue A because we could be gay there," reflects the writer Sarah Schulman, "live cheaply, learn from our neighbors, make art—all with some level of freedom."[24] But as Schulman mourns, the suburban ambush could happen in reverse as well: the arc that begins in the 1975 crisis ends in widespread gentrification. Under gentrification, the lived critique of DIY folds into the self-management demanded by neoliberalism.

Books

These writers found literary forms that suited the ethos that Schulman describes—living cheaply, learning from one's neighbors, making art. Learning from their artist peers, they developed innovative work that appropriated the words of others; found new ways of publishing; incorporated their writing into visual art; and wrote reflexive narratives that reproduced the vibrant exchanges in their neighborhood. Some of what they wrote evolved into polished work published by major houses, but even this work tended toward the fragmentary and biographical. Because of its very informality—demanded by the conditions of its production, outside of the protective and nurturing structures of the creative writing classroom—DIY literature entails an immediate relationship to the historical circumstances in which it takes shape. As I will argue in the coming chapters, the forms taken up by the writers of my study are often ones of necessity: Wojnarowicz's highly portable sheets of paper, Acker's quickly composed journals, *Between C & D*'s publish-it-as-it-came-in ethos of the dot-matrix printer. Other works are slightly more formal and therefore slightly more self-conscious: the nuanced assessments that Lynne Tillman and Gary Indiana make as art critics and writers. These are writers who did not see value in or have the time to create highly polished works of literature: they valued, instead, the immediacy that came from informal modes of production. Their improvisational works mirrored the improvisation happening elsewhere in the neighborhood, especially the interventionist work of PAD/D, Group Material, and tenants' rights organizations.

All of these writers form part of an alternative literary canon from the 1970s and 1980s: a group of writers who achieved notice at the time, but who by and large had receded from public view by the 2000s. This invisibility happens in part because these writers embraced modes of production that were out of step with the dominant mode of the creative writing classroom. For McGurl, the Cold War university generates high-quality fiction in much the same manner as it generates patents in the labs across campus. Drawing on the ideas of Nicholas Luhman, McGurl demonstrates (to the ire of many a creative writer) how the university became a system characterized by many of the same features that Bauman locates with solid modernity.[25] But while it's true that writers like Acker and Rose did have some exposure to the writing classroom, they sought out shabby tenement apartments as their preferred scene of writing—though some of the writers I discuss, especially David Wojnarowicz and the Nuyorican poets, often had little choice about their living spaces.[26] Nearly all of the writers in my study would describe themselves in the terms Rose and Texier use in the introduction to *Between C & D: New Writing from the Lower East Side Fiction Magazine*: as "voices . . . not being heard in the usual gamut of conventional literary magazines."[27] None of the writers I recover would appear in the fifth volume of the *Norton Anthology of American Literature* or the *Heath Anthology of American Literature*. Being outside the systems of conventional literary recognition meant that they were here for a moment and then disappeared, potentially forever.

The prose writers of my study work, by and large, in a mode of narrative experimentation that parts ways with the more visible, flashier experimentation taking shape under the sign of postmodernism—though at the time, plenty of these writers were understood, and understood themselves, as postmodernists. Their work is reflexive and self-aware: concerned with how narrative and language create the self. Unlike postmodern writers like Thomas Pynchon or Don DeLillo, they are less likely to see the self as a product of large systems—capitalism, the surveillance state, the consumer economy—than they are to see the self as a product of its immediate environment. That's not to say that writers like Acker and Indiana are unconcerned with capitalism or consumerism, just that these concerns are often secondary to a concern with the immediate. They do not generally abstract away their world, in order to make grand statements about the Kennedy assassination, supermarkets, or even—to invoke their privileged object of rejection—the suburbs. Their unevenness, their refusal of closure, becomes here not a product of postmodernism *per se*, which, in some broad sense, deals with ontological or wide-historical breakdown. Instead, their unevenness results from the specific types of breakdown immanent to austerity, crisis, and the breakdown of waged employment. They are documents of survival and precarity, even as the lives of the writers themselves were not always precisely precarious.

In this sense, *DIY on the Lower East Side* joins a growing body of work on the experimental writing that occurred in the 1970s, 1980s, and 1990s. This work has coalesced around the term "New Narrative," a strain of writing primarily associated with Bay Area writers and characterized by awareness of its narrative frame, and self-conscious understanding of language.[28] Keystone articles by Rob Halpern and Kaplan Harris, the 2017 publication of *Writers Who Love Too Much*, a conference on New Narrative at UC Berkeley—have all served to shape New Narrative as an object of study. The frameworks that Halpern and Harris use for New Narrative are useful ones for thinking through the particular contributions of the DIY literature I take up here: reflexive, self-conscious, appropriating, informal. New Narrative dances with postmodern irony, but seeks instead a "textual performance that can recognize itself as a cultural construct."[29] Embracing instability, foregrounding the artifice of narrative, these techniques are well-suited to the post-crisis, DIY moment I describe here.[30] It's true that notions of a contingent or unstable self can, particularly in poststructuralist approaches to politics, turn away from questions of political economy. But the openness and self-awareness of the New Narrative mode makes it well-suited to absorbing and relaying the new demands on the individual self that emerged after the crisis.

By and large, these experimental writers have seldom been read as engaging their historical contexts in a mimetic way. This results from a now-fading, but somewhat dominant divide in the way that postwar literature has been received: properly postmodernist writers on one side, and realist, "identity" writers on the other side. Moreover, a larger divide—dating back to György Lukács—has marked experimental writing as non-mimetic and non-historical. For Lukács, it is realist writers who offer a "dynamic, complex, analytical rendering of social relationships." Experimental writers, on the other hand, tend almost inevitably toward "a loss of perspective and historicity."[31] My study understands this divide as having been complicated in two ways. First, recent criticism from critics such as Tyler Bradway, Anthony Reed, and Alex Houen holds that experimental writing engages with its historical context in rich ways.[32] Second, the particular forms of experimentation taken up by my writers lends itself to thinking through context. Incorporating, in the spirit of the New York School, the biographical "I," these writers often see their narrative settings and living circumstances as blurred.

The conditions that made their projects possible are the conditions that make their writing experimental. Just as, for McGurl, the products of the creative writing program reflect the space of the seminar room, the products of the Lower East Side reflect the changing built environment of the Lower East Side. The space produced by the crisis is the setting of these works. The value of these literary texts lies with the way that they always offer *more*: more people, more spaces, more messiness. If the eventual result of bohemian incursion into the Lower East Side is gentrification, these texts, at least, hope that their spaces of creation will remain open with crosscurrents. Searching for settings beyond their apartments, these registered the colliding forces at work in the aftermath of a crisis that shook the city's fundament.

Buildings

Not only do the writers who lived and worked in the Lower East Side in the wake of the 1975 fiscal crisis offer unique insights into emerging modes of living, working, and writing, they also invite us to continue to develop the methods by which we assess literature's relationship to built environments. In *The New Asian City: Three-Dimensional Fictions of Space and Urban Form* (2011), Jini Kim Watson shows how written and built form alike refract systemic changes. Commenting on a selection of realist short stories from 1970s Korea, Singapore, and Taiwan, Watson describes these works' "use of built form to signal and work through a range of historical processes and contradictions. In analyzing and comparing them, we can again conclude that urban transformations are a primary mediator of struggles over modernity, industrialization, and the place of the individual subject."[33] Although the New Asian cities she studies have different orientations to modernity and industrialization than late-twentieth-century New York, her analytical method, which moves between urban planning, geography, and literature, is one that *DIY on Lower East Side* will similarly take up.[34]

Watson's work builds on important earlier work by Carlo Rotella. Rotella's *October Cities* (1998) describes how literary writers "build textual places shaped by the minds of their readers"; these textual places draw inspiration from earlier literary texts while they also find their sources in "material places assembled from brick and steel and stone, inhabited by people of flesh and blood."[35] Also drawing on Rotella, Thomas Heise's *Urban Underworlds* (2012) considers how urban space creates collisions between impoverished and middle-class citizens. For Heise, such fiction "[encodes] for readers very abstract processes of capitalist development as dramatic stories of embattled communities that are struggling to redefine themselves."[36] For Watson, Rotella, and Heise, to write literature about the city is to reproduce, on some level, the city's built environment, to move through streets and into apartments and across parks, all of which are inhabited by a range of people from different social classes and ethnicities.

The texts the writers produced in these sites gave shape to forms of life that often seemed shapeless. Decayed buildings made the invisible problems of the welfare state's recession, the rising practices of self-management, and the ascendance of private markets sharply visible. This is clear from retrospective analyses like those of Christopher Mele, Kim Moody, and others; it is also clear from the symbolic ways that the Lower East Side sought to imagine itself as a war zone, with two bars named Beirut. In his history of the neighborhood's immigrant cultures published in 1995, the ethnographer Mario Maffi sets the scene for his book like this:

> After the first rather bohemian blocks, a kind of no-man's land opens up beyond Avenue A: the towering shells of empty tenements that stand as if bombed in some unheard-of war, the layers of debris scattered on the abandoned lots, the discarded furniture and household appliances cluttering the sidewalks, the hydrants turned open, feeding muddy puddles, and everywhere the hieroglyphs of signs, posters, graffiti. On the other hand, the city's skin seems to change, while a new territory is entered—a land of faces, words and scenarios radically different from the glossy images of so many slick magazines or Hollywood movies.[37]

Like many others, Maffi finds democratic possibility among the so-called ruins. For artists and writers, the built environment was at once means and theme. It offered a cheap place to work, but also inspired aesthetic imperatives about the nature of the crisis. Artists and writers found a wide range of ways to address this infrastructure, from cutting holes in it, to stenciling on it, to writing plays about it, to using it as setting, to making it into a living and working environment. They fulfilled what the philosopher Michel de Certeau wrote about in his famous chapter "Walking in the City": "People are put in motion by the remaining relics of meaning, and sometimes by their waste products, the inverted remainders of great ambitions."[38] Site of danger, site of decay, site of renewal, site of loss: in the Lower East Side, the meanings of abandoned space multiply.

These meanings are part of what Henri Lefebvre calls the production of space. Space, he argues, is neither a projection of the mind, nor dictated by power, nor merely a matter of everyday living. People do not bring themselves fully formed to space. Neither does space simply act on them. Instead, identities are a negotiation between the spaces an individual inhabits, their own ideas, and the ideas dictated by the state and other powers. Lefebvre maintains that "all 'subjects' are situated in a space in which they must either recognize themselves or lose themselves, a space which they may both enjoy and modify."[39] That is, people build their identities in an everyday life lived in an environment and make choices about their environment based on these identities. Indiana offers a quick example of what Lefebvre has in mind here. Out of a discomfiting environment, Indiana forges both a criticism and also an aesthetics. As I'll argue in chapter 4, Indiana's living environments inform both his mid-1980s art criticism for *The Village Voice* and his 1989 novel *Horse Crazy*. Good art, for Indiana, means art that speaks to the difficulty some people have in occupying space, and that reflects the many ways that power—what Lefebvre calls abstract space—seeks to control these people.

Lefebvre would classify Indiana's project as one instance of the production of space, and he would argue that every society—and, to a degree, every individual—produces its/their own space. Lefebvre's sense of production is linked to a Marxist sense of production, but it involves extra elements. Lefebvrian production necessarily entails "spatial practice[s]" that occur on the street. Consequently, Lefebvre's project, as McKenzie Wark has recently noted, celebrates "ebullient" possibilities as "groups acting within everyday life pursue their strategies as far as they will go" and "inventiveness is born from the everyday."[40] Therefore, although the phenomena Lefebvre observes often happen on a grand scale—monasteries, manors, and cathedrals in the case of medieval society, and banks, business centers, and airports for neocapitalism—these phenomena can and must produce space at the level of the local. The people who tried to rebuild the Lower East Side knew that they needed to produce local space in order to be visible on the grand scale. The activists around Charas, for example, seized the opportunities the fiscal crisis created to inscribe the neighborhood's space with their own perspectives and agendas in mind.

I don't think that every project happening in the Lower East Side had some kind of Lefebvrian magic associated with it. At least some of the projects—especially some of the galleries—seem to have acted in bad faith with the neighborhood, using it not as a basis to build a new future but as a way to repeat the successes of SoHo. Likewise, as both Mele and the geographer Neil Smith emphasize, many of the ideas circulating in the Lower East Side turned out to be congruent with the objectives of real estate investors and city planners—representations of space, not represented space. But lots of culture workers sought ways to rework the crumbling buildings of the everyday into inventive formations. Not quite the Paris of the Situationists that Wark lovingly describes, but not wholly unlike it either.

These literary works challenge notions that these buildings were somehow a space apart from the larger nation—a kind of "frontier" that needed resettling if it was to become useful.[41] As I note briefly above, these writers were hardly the only ones interested in the decaying buildings of the inner city. In the 1970s and 1980s, prominent sociological accounts framed the inner city as home to a population that had ostensibly found ways of living outside of waged work—but as welfare recipients and drug dealers. For critics of the welfare state, this was the "underclass," a group of subjects who, residing in a destroyed inner city, were adopting values that were at odds with those of the mainstream. The underclass narrative coupled the so-called "urban crisis"—characterized by "deep urban racial segregation, concentrated poverty, deindustrialization, physical decay, and near-bankruptcy"—with the ostensibly failed federal policies of urban renewal and the war on poverty.[42] Such policies came into particular focus around the 1975 crisis. Bankers, policy makers, and politicians pointed to the impoverished as the core problem of the city's overspending. The landscape of neighborhoods like the Lower East Side formed an essential precursor to contemporary conversations about poverty. Among others, Treasury Secretary William Simon's bestselling *A Time for Truth* presented the 1975 fiscal crisis as "America in Microcosm": evidence of the collapse of the post–New Deal liberal order.

As a sense of crisis began to mount in the 1970s, the underclass became an object of simultaneous fascination and revulsion. In 1977, for example, *Time* magazine ran a lurid cover story on the underclass that blended inner-city residents with their environments, warning that behind the "crumbling walls" of "pock-marked streets, gutted tenements and broken hopes" lived a "large group of people who are more intractable, more socially alien and more hostile than almost anyone had imagined." The underclass formation situated the city as alienated and estranged from the mainstream United States.[43] The worst of these accounts subsumed families receiving welfare, homeless alcoholics, street criminals, and the working poor into "one interchangeable unit identified not by income or dependence."[44] By situating the impoverished as unproductive and alien, the underclass formulation helped support the benefit-slashing narratives that emerged from the 1975 crisis and continued at a national level in the administration of Ronald Reagan.

And yet, perhaps because the term references class, "underclass" could be reclaimed for more structured analysis of poverty, as does the sociologist William Julius Wilson in *The Truly Disadvantaged*. Wilson did so in part to challenge the vicious narratives that had accumulated around the term. But he also found the term useful in outlining the shifts in work that had made the inner city a genuinely difficult place to live. For Wilson, the underclass is just that: a class formation that denotes a group left behind by working and middle classes alike. While the underclass narrative could be vicious, it dates from an era when notions of a "war on poverty" had not yet fully faded from the landscape. The inner city remained a problem to be solved, not a thing that could be dismissed fully from the public sphere. Today, when politicians talk about impoverished inner cities at all, they talk about them in terms of welfare that needs further cutting, or government waste, or criminality. The wide gentrification of the past thirty years is seen, from this perspective, as largely a good thing, a process that turns unproductive space into productive space. The debate about these spaces often seems settled; in the 1970s and 1980s, this debate remained lively. The term "underclass," then, both challenges notions of permanent poverty and reminds us of the ways in which poverty was discussed at the dawn of the current crisis. The underclass was both the beginning of a long discussion of abjection and a hinge term that connotes the structural position of poverty for the cultures I take up here.

I find the term "underclass" productive because of the way it hovers between criminal and impoverished, conveying the tensions of how disadvantaged populations were imagined by outsiders and culture workers alike.

The first part of the word conveys an underworld, a strange, expansive site of pleasures, aberrant behaviors, and fascinations.[45] This imaginary world circulated through the galleries, journals, and literature of my study, particularly in the way that graffiti was sometimes depicted as a "primitive" expression of impoverished African-Americans and Puerto Ricans. The second part of the word, by invoking class, invites the economic-based analysis that suggests, often at odds with the intentions of those who deploy the term, that poverty is less a problem of will and more a problem of economic structures. Though its architects framed the problem in cultural terms, the 1975 crisis signaled a broad shift in the economy, toward decreased benefits and increased wagelessness. "Underclass" conveys the complex way in which poverty was during the era in my study: a way to simultaneously signal fascination and structural problems.

At times, the writers I study here both telegraphed and benefited from a sense that the Lower East Side was an underworld. The writers who submitted work to *Between C & D* often framed their work in terms of, as one of the key terms listed on the front put it, "danger." Joel Rose's *Kill the Poor* can be lurid, as can some of the stories published in *Between C & D*. Just as often, though, these writers challenged this order. I'll argue in chapter 1, for example, that Wojnarowicz finds native intelligence and adaptiveness in the most down-and-out members of the underclass. Similarly, the Puerto Rican writers I take up in chapter 2 see richly bound networks around them, though networks that are under threat of fraying.

> O what a town . . .
> even your drug-invested pocket parks, playgrounds
> where our young bloods
> hang around
> waiting
> hoping that
> one day they too will
> get well and smile again
> Your love is all
> they need to come around
> Loisaida, I love you

wrote the poet Bimbo Rivas in 1974, in the poem that named Loisaida. Some ten years later, the playwright Reinaldo Povod writes a piece about a violent lover's quarrel that nevertheless reveals the block as a "temple" and the neighborhood as "SEPARATED into clicks but forming a WHOLE." These characterizations even carried over into the work of white writers like Catherine Texier. In *Love Me Tender*, Texier situates the Puerto Rican Mario as deeply tied to his community. And in Indiana's *Horse Crazy*, the unnamed protagonist recognizes that his love interest, Geoffrey, views the Lower East Side as a distasteful means of furthering his art.

Particularly from the present-day standpoint of a world where classes have been increasingly severed from one another, these writers' works retain something of what Samuel Delany, surveying his experiences in the Times Square of the 1970s and 1980s, praised as socially beneficial cross-class contact.[46] These writers worked, for a time, within what John Roberts calls art's "second economy," whereby the artist's poverty is not merely a "picturesque fantasy" but "the means out of which the artist produces a transformative or emancipatory relationship with the world" such that "[p]recarity and underemployment become the praxiological and symbolic material *of* artistic labour and conceptualization itself."[47] By the time they end their careers, writers like Indiana, Acker and Wojnarowicz have made it out of the second economy: their written works are published or their paintings hang in galleries. But in the beginning of their careers, which coincided with the 1975 crisis, they were alive to the precarity around them, in part because they lived such precarity. The relationship between these culture workers and the impoverished was characterized by lurid fascination and genuine sympathy, primitivism and nuanced analysis, opportunism and activism.

Art

In scrutinizing the transition from the 1975 crisis to post-Fordism, my study figures a changing art market as central to the formation of what would come to be called the "creative economy." If the decay and rubble were the most visible aspect of the post-1975 Lower East Side, the rapid influx of galleries into the neighborhood was the second most visible. In the 1980s, at a regional, national, and global level, the Lower East Side was known for the bright-burning, but temporary rise of a visual art scene, a scene whose best-known names—Jeff Koons, Keith Haring, Jean-Michel Basquiat—conjure a high-flying world of nightclubs, cocaine, and a booming art market.[48] But as commentators like Rosalind Deutsche note, this movement largely—though not wholly—swept in and out of the neighborhood without either changing it for the better or interacting with it.[49] Some one hundred galleries opened in the neighborhood between the late 1970s and 1985, when the movement more or less peaked.

Intertwined with the art scene in significant ways, the writers of my study scrutinized the new networks that these galleries enabled. While "creative economy" refers to a cluster of wide concerns, here I will take it to mean two related ideas: first, the ostensive autonomy of post-Fordist workers who take artists as models; second, in terms of redevelopment, the template these artists and gallery owners were in effect setting for what Florida and others would later encourage cities to plan. While there were tentative efforts to deploy art on the part of development—in chapter 4, I'll discuss the Edward Koch administration's proposed Artists' Homeownership Plan—these did not become full-fledged strategies for city planners until the 1990s. In tracing the ascendance of the creative economy, I extend conversations begun by Sarah Brouillette and Jasper Bernes. With different valences, both contend that literature and art entwine significantly with the forms of work that arose with Fordism's decline.[50] But while for Brouillette and Bernes, literature often fills a negative function, soothing the post-Fordist worker into thinking her work is meaningful, I'll sometimes depart from their conclusions in suggesting that literature can, at its best, also record the possibility for living and creating outside of the self-management demanded by post-Fordist work.

Writers, artists, and art critics worked closely together in post-crisis New York City. While its stories often castigated artists as superficial figures seeking cheap thrills, *Between C & D* included artwork from such artists in every issue. Wojnarowicz's monologues evidence tender sympathy for figures marginalized by poverty, but his visual work made him a central figure in the gallery scene, such that Mele uses Wojnarowicz as an emblem of the artists' misreading of their environment.[51] While Indiana used his *Village Voice* column to lambaste an art world in which "the most celebrated art is that which better fulfills the condition of the commodity fetish," his novel *Horse Crazy* depicts the strong appeal a young artist has for the Indiana-like narrator.[52] Tillman was a close friend of Craig Owens, the author of one of the most scathing critiques of the gallery scene, but as I note above, it would take her until 1998 to include a sustained account of gentrification in her fiction. And although Sylvère Lotringer's *Semiotext(e)* took up the powerful political projects of French Nietzscheans like Foucault, Deleuze, and Guattari, such projects competed with a sometimes uncritical embrace of downtown art. Lotringer would later struggle with his role in promoting the gallery scene, mostly as vectored through the legacy of Jean Baudrillard, a figure embraced by artists. Given a front-row view of the creative economy's emergence, the literary productions of the Lower East Side document the problems and possibilities of art's increasingly central role in post-Fordist economies.

The Lower East Side's writers considered the figures enabled by new art networks, like the risk-courting bohemian artist, as well as the figures such networks excluded, including working-class Puerto Ricans and the homeless. If the neighborhoods' art networks sometimes seemed stable, the writers recognized that they were repeatedly disrupted by everything from queer encounters between bohemians and the impoverished, to the plague of AIDS, to the tentative, but genuine efforts on behalf of writers and artists to call attention to conditions in the Lower East Side. Wojnarowicz's monologues make queer encounters especially visible; Indiana's work frequently conflated AIDS and gentrification as twin plagues; the community workshop Charas was at once a source of advocacy for the impoverished and a workspace for artists.

My study, therefore, covers a historical moment when the certainties of the creative economy were far from solidified. The texts I examine are filled with chance encounters, failed recognitions, and missed connections. Although they frequently depict gentrification as a steady force, they just as frequently imagine moments of community that posit alternate futures. This is most true of the Puerto Rican writers I discuss in chapter 2, who often conceived of their literary projects as explicit rejoinders to gentrification. It is also true, however, of writers like Indiana and Tillman, both of whom figure gentrification as a crisis for their fictional characters. Acker's work, too, looks different when viewed in this light; as I'll suggest in chapter 3, her narratives' celebrated contradictions reflect a world where she could be mistaken for a prostitute and where Fun Gallery could welcome celebrities a few blocks away from open-air drug markets. Such contradictions resulted from the proximity these writers had with their artist peers, a proximity that became more uncomfortable as the gallery scene came under more critique.

Ways of Reading the Lower East Side

As is hopefully clear by now, I see the 1975 crisis as both a moment of possibility for new forms of life and a moment when the neoliberal policies of the past forty years first took shape. My account of this tension has been shaped by recent debates in literary studies about literature's relationship to the political. In the past decade, the humanities have undergone a shift away from the poststructuralist-influenced methods that dominated the field from the mid-1970s until roughly 2008. This shift has taken a number of directions, but two major strands, sometimes understood as being in opposition, are crucial to my study. The first strand has focused on reading methods—a turn toward surface reading, formalism, actor network theory, and distant reading. For critics influenced by these schools, the project of unveiling what is hidden or repressed by a text—its less overt political content—is over. Instead, these critics urge that readers attend to what is on the surface of a text, or what it maps. Literary texts, these critics contend, offer ways to grasp a never-quite-intact social. By reading in this manner, these critics assert, they maintain literature's complex relationship to an ever-shifting social world.[53]

The other shift has been toward various Marxisms, which, in some sense, seek to make political critique *more* political by renewing a focus on political economy that was perceived to have been cast aside in the academy during the 1980s and 1990s.[54] Particularly in the wake of the 2008 fiscal crisis, these critics assert, it is crucial that critics understand how literature manifests strategies of economic development, new financial instruments, fiscal crises, and changing modes of work. These approaches have been seen as largely divergent from one another: one strand seems to engage in a kind of political quietism stepping back from the ostensibly political critique of poststructuralism, while the other, in some sense, asks readers to assess the ways that poststructuralism turned away from core economic problems.

In bringing the economic problems of the 1975 fiscal crisis to bear on a set of left-oriented literatures of the 1980s and 1990s, my study takes inspiration from the new Marxisms, tracing the omissions of the poststructuralist era at the moment they began to circulate widely. I make this point most clearly when I take up the odd confluence between *Semiotext(e)*'s "Schizo-Culture" conference and the 1975 crisis. At the very moment when a sustained critique of political economy was needed, I note, the academy began to embrace modes of thinking that turned away from the determinations of political economy and toward what Postone calls a "theoretical focus on agency and contingency."[55] I read *Semiotext(e)* as a site where poststructuralism entered the Lower East Side and shaped the aesthetics and sensibilities of my study's culture workers. This means, though, that the writers of my study were themselves well-versed in poststructuralist theory: they read theory, attended theory conferences, and often interwove theory into their writing. Part of my project, especially as I turn to *Semiotext(e)*, will be to show, as have Postone and others, how this theory missed the tectonic shifts in the economy that the 1975 crisis heralded.

And yet, for writers steeped in the theory of what has come to be called the "critique" era, adding a layer of critique to what were already critique-soaked discourses feels, in some sense, ahistorical. Here, thinking through literature's uses, and of what literature has to say on the surface, has been, for me, a vital framework for treating the literature of my study on its own terms. I want to resist, in other words, notions of unveiling what "was really happening," and instead allow the writers of my study to tell the stories that they found important in the post-1975 landscape. I have found, then, the insights of descriptive or surface reading—particularly the variant influenced by Bruno Latour—to be useful in accounting for the kinds of links produced by literature here. While this work has been rightly critiqued for its occlusion of larger-scale historical operations, it provides effective models for diagnosing what occurs between crisis and its resolution, the flight of capital and its return, abandonment and gentrification. I have found the open-endedness of Latourian-inspired methods to be useful in thinking through the moment of my study. I have found these methods useful even when, or especially when, as Margaret Ronda laments, they "[defer] causal claims in favor of open-ended descriptions of arrangements and networks."[56] In this period, culture workers, activists, and city planners alike thought that circumstances were up for grabs, and a variety of outcomes possible. Indeed, while Lefebvre is often understood as a Marxist critic, and thus at odds with surface reading, he himself frames such moments as ones of possibility, in which, at least potentially, the fundament of socially determining space might momentarily shift.

Latour notes that the tracing of such associations is especially crucial "in situations where innovations proliferate, where group boundaries are uncertain, when the range of entities to be taken into account fluctuates."[57] The Lower East Side was in exactly such a situation. The 1975 crisis, with its withdrawal of funding for the neighborhood, helped innovations proliferate and blurred the boundaries between groups. All of this left the human actors in the Lower East Side—working-class Puerto Ricans, gallery owners, artists, writers, activists, entrepreneurs—with a long list of new associations. Contact could occur in an emergency room, as it did for Acker. For Wojnarowicz, it occurred on a doorway or pier; for Indiana or Tillman, in the streets outside their apartments; for the writers and workers of Charas, in an abandoned school building. By accelerating capital withdrawal from the Lower East Side, the 1975 crisis provided a built environment that made new associations possible.

This study endeavors to trace these associations not only by attending to the networks that emerged between human actors, and between the human actors and their built environment, but also by attending to the material networks the literature itself engaged. Vibrating through the raw material of typewriter and drywall, pen and park, this literature moved along and mobilized networks of physical decay that characterized the post-crisis era. The writers living in the Lower East Side developed "beings of fiction," to use Latour's term, through a mix of observation and description, imaginative exposition, and reference to earlier bohemian traditions, especially those of the Beats and the Symbolic poets.[58] Formally complex, this literature articulated the intricate, evolving networks of a neighborhood in transition. In *Site Reading*, David Alworth scrutinizes supermarkets, dumps, roads, ruins, and asylums as they circulate through postwar literature and art, reading, for example, Don DeLillo's *White Noise* and Allen Ginsberg's "A Supermarket in California" alongside Andy Warhol's Brillo Boxes.[59] Giving sustained attention to one, local site, my study complicates Alworth's concerns by mapping associations around the broken buildings, vacant lots, and empty storefronts of the Lower East Side. I treat these as both intense sites of literary attention and prolific generators of aesthetic objects and subjects. The places that Alworth writes about—supermarket, dump, ruin—were not, in actuality, scenes of literary production (though William Burroughs's apartment was apparently quite a dump). In the Lower East Side, the writers lived in and alongside the falling-down buildings their works represent. And in documenting their neighborhood, these writers seldom lost sight of the terrible economic fallout from the 1975 crisis, recognizing that capital was a crucial force that shaped these spaces.[60]

DIY on the Lower East Side, then, takes up projects that assembled within multiple vectors: artworld institutional critique; the production shifts that characterized the 1975 fiscal crisis; the surge in activism that constituted the response to the crisis. At their best, these projects entail what Roberts calls a "heteronomous encounter with capital" whereby art provides a "space of encounter for praxis, critique, and truth."[61] I have, then, found Latour's flattened approach—beginning with what is here, and tracing networks from what exists—to be beneficial in mapping the contours of one neighborhood. But in taking up Latour, I retain a sense that larger-scale historical operations, including that of capital, racism, and settler colonialism—are at work in the historical shifts of my study. It is impossible to tell the story of the Lower East Side without acknowledging the heft of these forces. Thus, while I find Latour's *methods* beneficial, I often part company with his *conclusions*, and here I have found the work of Lefebvre, Neil Smith, David Harvey, and other critical geographers to provide a useful counter to some of Latour's more apolitical commitments. In a light sense, I present *DIY on the Lower East Side* as an interrogation of Latour's method, a sorting out of what might be useful from what seems reductive. I hope that in what follows, I can show how Latour's method can be deployed toward identifying projects that entail what Roberts calls "an open and reflective encounter between art and the totalizing critique of capitalism."[62] Yes, the totality of capital always wins, but it is worth returning to projects that resisted capital's imperatives in their moment, if only to recognize that artists, writers, and activists sought counter-examples to the financiers, administrators, and politicians who speak on capital's behalf.

Describing the wrangling that went on between the Beame administration over Roger Starr's infamous idea of "planned shrinkage" after the fiscal crisis, Kim Phillips-Fein observes that the powerful mandates to cut budgets "left little space for reimagining how the city might function."[63] Taking up an earlier New York, the literary critic Carlos Rotella describes writers as doing just this: "Like political operatives, developers, journalists, academics, and neighbors and strangers in conversation, literary writers are in the business of imagining cities."[64] City administrators like Felix Rohatyn and Roger Starr may not have been able to reimagine the city, but the writers living and working in the Lower East Side could do so. These writers were in this "business of imagining cities," too.[65] The dream-world of *Blood and Guts in High School*, which ends with Janeys "cover[ing] the earth," is just one of many manifestations of the alternate textual places created by the writers of the Lower East Side. Through the alternate-world-making afforded by literature, these writers imagined multiple futures. They understood, as Certeau puts it, that "stories 'go in a procession' ahead of social practices in order to open a field for them."[66]

Chapter Summaries

Chapter 1 addresses the immediate aftermath of the crisis and introduces the problem of the built environment that the rest of my study will examine. Wojnarowicz and Matta-Clark used the wild, open spaces of the post-crisis city to do their work; the cruising that provides material for Wojnarowicz and the cutting into structures that provides material for Matta-Clark necessitated ostensibly abandoned space. Matta-Clark, like many of his peers, took advantage of the post-crisis landscape to forge large-scale interventions into Fordist ways of living. Wojnarowicz searched the post-crisis landscape for small-scale narratives of the underclass. By setting the two against one another, I inquire into the possible futures that each artist's form projected from the abandoned city. Matta-Clark's work was successful in that the widely-praised High Line entails an apotheosis of his vision. Wojnarowicz's was less so in that post-Fordist New York turned increasingly away from the needs of the underclass *cum* precariat. Taken together, Wojnarowicz's and Matta-Clark's works offer a complex introduction to the problems and possibilities of the crisis.

Chapter 2 considers how Puerto Rican writers of the Lower East Side embraced a neighborhood culture of building in situ. From homesteading to community gardens, a range of activist projects sought to improve the neighborhood's built environment on its own terms. Its vacant lots and crumbling buildings became potent symbols of a broken social contract. If some artists and real estate developers would seek to rewrite this contract altogether, others sought to rebuild. I begin with Algarín and Piñero's 1975 anthology *Nuyorican Poetry*, examining how the tightly structured anthology assembles a world of disrepaired kitchens and absent landlords. Moving into the 1980s, I tell the story of El Bohío: the old P.S. 64 taken over by Charas. There, Bimbo Rivas and Tee Saralegui wrote and staged plays that interrogated the possibilities as well as the limitations of literatures produced in and by decayed space. These plays take up the concerns of *The Quality of Life on the Lower East Side*. Published out of El Bohío, this monthly journal mixed poetry and art with instructions on do-it-yourself radiator covers. I conclude with a discussion of Wong and Piñero's collaborations. The writers and artists I examine in this chapter introduce us to tenants in their dim kitchens, sitting on vibrant stoops, and forming strong community ties. Putting the bricks back in place, all of these productions imagine an open future for the Lower East Side, one neither limited to depictions of an abject underclass nor subsumed by images of the neighborhood as a bohemian "frontier."

In the same year as the fiscal crisis, Sylvère Lotringer hosted Gilles Deleuze, Félix Guattari, Michel Foucault, and Jean-François Lyotard at a landmark conference on "Schizo-Culture" at Columbia University, as part of his recently founded journal *Semiotext(e)*. Chapter 3 begins with this timely coincidence and expands in scale by mapping the relationships between literature, critical theory, and political advocacy that emerged in the period. I show how critical theory, in particular, shaped a range of writers' and artists' projects, and how that theory itself was often inspired by the decay and risk of 1970s New York. After recovering literature, art, and theory's shared histories in the Lower East Side, I consider *Semiotext(e)*'s legacy in terms of Acker's project. Drawing on Acker's unpublished journals—which describe her real, if momentary, encounter with poverty, one that left her struggling for medical care in the wake of widespread cuts to city hospitals—I map sites where she made contact with the city's "underclass." Returning to Acker's early work, I note the ways that she appropriated economic writing in accounting for the rapid changes she saw around her. Moving to *Blood and Guts in High School* (1978), I find Acker assembling her more fragmented early work into a sustained account of the post-crisis city.

Chapter 4 brings the work of Indiana and Tillman to bear on a running discussion about both urban development and the rise of the creative economy. Indiana wrote biting columns for *The Village Voice* where he sought out art that indexed changed in the city's built environment. Working with Owens and the artist Kiki Smith, Tillman wrote a series of highly innovative pieces for *Art in America* and other journals that she called "Madame Realism" stories. In these works, Tillman critiques the male-dominated, surrealistic art of David Salle, Julian Schnabel, and others by anchoring her speakers in the female body and built environment. In their fiction—Indiana's *Horse Crazy* (1989) and Tillman's *Haunted Houses* (1987) and *No Lease on Life* (1998)—both writers used the experimental tools of New Narrative to reflect on the tensions and problems of working in the rising creative economy.

Chapter 5 presents a case of DIY literary redevelopment: the journal *Between C & D*, printed in Joel Rose and Catherine Texier's rehabilitated tenement apartment at 255 East Seventh Street. Tracing the overlapping histories of the neighborhood's literary production, desktop publishing, and do-it-yourself renovation, this chapter figures Rose and Texier's work as anticipating the self-fashioning literary work increasingly necessary in the post-Fordist economy. Rose and Texier built a literary institution with very little means, carving living and writing space out of an apartment that had recently been used as a drug den. Their work enabled networks among all of the writers covered in earlier chapters. Like *Bomb*, *Benzene*, and *Redtape*, *Between C & D* was also interdisciplinary, incorporating artworks in every issue. *Between C & D*, I contend, archived the diverse literary responses to the post-crisis city, even as it pointed toward survival strategies for the post-Fordist world taking shape in its ruins.

My afterword returns to the vital work of Wojnarowicz to examine the long journey from the 1975 crisis to the struggle against the AIDS crisis in the late 1980s. Examining *Close to the Knives* (1991), I note how Wojnarowicz reused the fragmentary writing that I discuss in chapter 1 toward building a complex account of AIDS. Wojnarowicz worked with the activist group ACT UP, and *Close to the Knives* documents how an impulse to embrace precarity took new shape within the life-sustaining networks that had assembled in the Lower East Side after the crisis. The victories of ACT UP rejoin, but simultaneously make tragic, the widespread defeat entailed by gentrification.

The gentrification of the Lower East Side sets a terrible template for destroying the democratic possibilities of urban life; ACT UP created powerful shockwaves that yet reverberate through the activist Left. Both grew out of the ruins of the Lower East Side. Other positive legacies abound as well, in the wide proliferation of writing and art—small presses and journals, the many innovations of art's second economy. Even the tiny innovations of community gardens are, as the poet Jorie Graham once put it, guardian angels of little utopias. It would be shortsighted to pretend that the financiers who drove the 1975 crisis have the last word, though the world they created is undoubtedly powerful. As a culture, we should hope that they did not have the last word. That the ruins were, in many cases, quickly rebuilt, and that the self-managing dictates of DIY were sucked into managerial practices, is true. It's also true that desires to take care of oneself and one's neighbors, the desire to make art, the desire to craft a living space, the desire to write literature, are, in some sense, the desires that we as humanists often hold most dear.

Writing himself in the midst of the 1975 fiscal crisis, the eminent Marxist critic Marshall Berman looked back, as did many of the writers of my study, to Baudelaire. For Berman, the French poet struggled with Parisian modernity and sought "to find and create himself in the midst of the anguish and beauty of its moving chaos."[67] This is also the struggle of the writers I describe here, one documented in recent biographies of Acker and Wojnarowicz: a struggle that, more often than not, meant building alliances with those citizens left behind by the 1975 fiscal crisis and its attendant withdrawal of the welfare state. The Fordist city birthed both the Cross Bronx Expressway and the New York Municipal Hospital system, housing projects and rent control, neighborhood clearance and regulations about living environments. The crisis challenged all these things and more, creating "moving chaos." But the lived experience of that chaos is what enabled the literature here. The writers all exhibit what Berman dubs "a desire to live openly with the split and unreconciled character of our lives, and to draw energy from our inner struggles, wherever they may lead us in the end."[68] In what follows, I examine the results of their efforts.

Chapter 1

David Wojnarowicz, Gordon Matta-Clark, and the Fordist Crisis in 1970s New York

As the long networks of the Fordist economy broke down, the writer and artist David Wojnarowicz scoured the remaining landscape for evidence of new life among segments of the population that were quickly being labeled an unproductive underclass impeding its recovery. Other accounts, mostly those advocating for the city's redevelopment toward a post-Fordist economy of service work and finance, rendered the underclass as a problem to be solved, to be displaced from neighborhoods like Times Square, the Lower East Side, or the waterfront. Wojnarowicz, though, attends to the small, limited networks among these figures. To read Wojnarowicz's *The Waterfront Journals* (1996, written 1978–80) is to experience simultaneously the withdrawal of the welfare state, the impetus toward self-creation necessary for post-Fordist work, and the momentary falling away of Fordist discipline. These short works meditate on the possibilities of life in the ruined city, in the cracks and fissures left when capital withdraws its energies.[1] They represent the possibility of life persisting even when rent from the social fabric, with all the lassitude, terror, and fragility such life entails. My reading of them will establish some of the core problems of *DIY on Lower East Side*: how, in the wake of the fiscal crisis, culture workers like Wojnarowicz developed projects that refracted, scrutinized, and suggested alternatives to the official narratives of the city and the financiers advising it.

The broken buildings and rubbled lots on this ground were both inspiration for the crisis's dominant narrative—that the city's welfare state had failed—and a product of its constrained vision of the city's life. As landlords walked away from more and more buildings, New York began to seem a wild place where anything could happen. As I'll show, "anything" had quite different meanings for city planners, real estate developers, and culture workers. These groups' different approaches to the post-crisis landscape alternately merge and diverge. If what eventually emerges—gentrification driven by art—now seems inevitable, it was not so in the 1970s, and Wojnarowicz's work suggests alternate possibilities, a city that listened to and provided space for its most desperate citizens.

As I will for other authors in later chapters, I read Wojnarowicz's monologues as performing a kind of amateur ethnography. Wojnarowicz wrote the monologues as the city and the national economy were undergoing vast changes, which, for the purposes of this study, are best thought of as a shift from the Fordist regime of manufacturing and a relatively strong welfare state to a post-Fordist regime of temporary contracts and weaker state safety nets. Within both the specific context of New York and the wider context of post-Fordism, artists play important roles, variously documenting such shifts, taking advantage of abandoned space, and serving, as Luc Boltanski and Eve Chiapello observe, as the premier figures for post-Fordist work regimes.[2]

I'll set Wojnarowicz in a paradoxical relationship to Gordon Matta-Clark, the sculptor-architect who intervened within the city in larger-scale ways, often highlighting the degradation of the built environment from which the impoverished and working classes suffered disproportionately. Such degradation was accelerated by the crisis, prompting calls for redevelopment that would be answered by private developers. Matta-Clark was intensely interested in the possibilities for new modes of life afforded by the landscape, and he pursued these possibilities across a range of collaborative projects, including cutting into buildings, creating sculptures out of refuse, and founding a restaurant, FOOD, that served SoHo's rising arts colony. While Matta-Clark engaged the problems of the built environment more visibly, Wojnarowicz's monologues, with their documentary impulse, left a more lasting critique of the effect the crisis had on the city's abject populations.

In divergent ways, both Wojnarowicz and Matta-Clark theorize the relationship between humans and their built environment in 1970s New York. Their diverse paths to becoming artists and their varied works take shape within the changed cultural and economic circumstances signaled and furthered by the 1975 crisis. As Lefebvre emphasizes, such a relationship is by no means simple or direct. Like all space, urban space is "at once result and cause, product and producer."[3] Nor can the future effects of any such relationship be easily predicted. Lefebvre describes such as a "*stake*, the locus of projects and actions deployed as part of specific strategies, and hence also the object of *wagers* on the future—wagers which are articulated, if never completely."[4] Though both foreground a collision between human life and the built environment, I argue that Wojnarowicz asserts a more halting, more tentative, but ultimately more comprehensive account of humans surviving in the cracks and fissures that appeared after the collapse of Fordist modes of life.

The built environment was inextricable from the dynamics of the 1975 crisis. Business interests not only benefited from the welfare-state-cutting political agenda imposed in the wake of the crisis, they arguably precipitated the crisis by backing the city-supported office building boom of the late Lindsay administration, including the World Trade Center. Such projects helped raise the city's long-term debt by 48 percent between 1970 and 1975.[5] New York's problems were experienced by cities nationwide. But New York had a particularly high profile, as well as a deserved reputation as a city with an empowered working class, which had advocated strongly for its weakest citizens.[6] Across the postwar era, the city provided its residents a rich welfare state, including a robust public health system, strong schools, affordable housing, and direct benefits that helped many of its residents maintain a living wage. These characteristics put New York in the crosshairs of a rising turn against the welfare state among conservatives.

The crisis somewhat infamously resulted in Gerald Ford refusing federal aid to the city. On October 30, 1975, the *Daily News* headline read "Ford to City: Drop Dead." This headline has become infamous as an index of tension between New York and the federal government. Often less remembered are the ways that Ford's administration used the 1975 crisis to further a wide attack on the welfare state for which conservatives had been agitating since the New Deal. Ford himself had long voiced opposition to both the welfare state and the organized labor supporting it. And his opinions were mild in comparison to a powerful movement in the Republican party toward reduced taxes and smaller government.[7] While California's 1978 anti-tax Proposition 13 is sometimes remembered as the most important precursor to the Reagan revolution, all of the dynamics around Proposition 13 were already operating on a federal level, and New York's crisis was an excuse to force these dynamics. Anti-welfare-state conservatives saw New York's potential bankruptcy in positive terms, as an event that would tell local politicians, labor leaders, and welfare activists that, twenty years in advance of Bill Clinton's use of the phrase, the era of big government was over.[8]

Under pressure from these voices, the Municipal Assistance Corporation became a vehicle for a range of conservative (and, often, liberal) voices who asserted that the programs of the War on Poverty and Great Society had not only failed, but had in fact caused the crisis. In a 1977 *New York Times* editorial, for example, the board's head, Felix Rohatyn, flatly asserted that "Federal programs aimed at eliminating poverty do not work." He framed the "core-city population" as out of "society's mainstream," a realm from which they could only return through the alchemy of private enterprise: "Manufacturing facilities financed by the Development Corporation but operated by private corporations should be set up in industrial parks created for the purpose in cleared, now vacant ghetto areas."[9] Turning away from the long-term, structural causes of the fiscal crisis, Rohatyn and others blamed the welfare state and its beneficiaries.[10] Holding the inner-city impoverished (and city worker unions) responsible for the degraded environment in which they lived, accounts like Rohatyn's framed the underclass as irredeemable and abject and presented privatization as the only solution to their problems.

By all measures, Wojnarowicz himself started as one of the abject, someone who, but for willpower and luck, would have been counted among the underclass himself. As Cynthia Carr documents in her biography, Wojnarowicz emerged from a background of poverty and abuse.[11] After migrating to New York as a teenager, he struggled to survive in the late 1970s, first hustling and then working odd jobs, relying all the while on what Lucy Lippard calls "the tenderness he seems to have brought with him to even the most sordid encounters"[12] to make the allies that would eventually yield success. Wojnarowicz was a writer, artist, actor, and musician, perhaps most famous for his clashes with the Christian Right in the late 1980s. In the spirit of the downtown New York of the 1970s and 1980s, he was a polymath, producing visual art in a number of styles, even as he experimented with punk rock (3 Teens Kill 4), acting, photography, and film. Before he was any of these things, during the years when he toiled in obscurity, Wojnarowicz was a writer. Between 1978 and 1980, he produced a series of vignettes that he called "monologues." Cheap to produce, and highly portable, these monologues formed the initial core of Wojnarowicz's bid for artistic fame in the years when he lived hand-to-mouth, moving from one cheap apartment to another. Published in various forms over these years, they were collected after his 1992 death into *The Waterfront Journals*. Each of the forty-five vignettes catalogs a fragment of an underclass life. Wojnarowicz described these as "a collection of voices"[13] that he'd heard or overheard from "people once met and then left suddenly such as in car rides cross-country, early-morning rail encounters, overheard coffee shop conversations."[14] As you can likely hear, Wojnarowicz was influenced by Beat writers like Jack Kerouac and Herbert Huncke, but he applied the formal techniques of these writers to a more sociological purpose, a project that became urgent in the context of the fiscal crisis. As I'll explain below in my reading of the monologues, it is here that I see Wojnarowicz as working in a kind of Latourian mode, anticipating the work of sociologists like William Julius Wilson and Loïc Wacquant.

Queer theorists like José Muñoz and Jack Halberstam have usefully theorized the lives of men like Wojnarowicz in terms of their slant orientation to normative time and space.[15] Halberstam, for example, describes such lives as inhabiting "strange temporalities, imaginative life schedules, and eccentric economic practices," which contrast with the "long periods of stability" of so-called "productive citizens."[16] Muñoz similarly praises queerness's "ecstatic and horizontal temporality," which he views as a "path and a movement to a greater openness to the world."[17] Both critics figure queer life as opposed to "the practical and normalcy desiring homosexual" life of regular hours, heterosexual marriage, and child-rearing.[18] As Melinda Cooper has demonstrated, the middle-class white family was a regulating structure under Fordism, and continues to shape approaches to poverty in the post-Fordist era. Here, Wojnarowicz's work—with its focus on impoverished, nonnormative citizens—offers a productive site of connection between theorizations of queer life and theorizations of the underclass.

Much of the debates around the crisis concerned whether New York should be a city dedicated to normative time schedules and "productive" citizens, or whether it should instead welcome and support many different forms of life. As Wilson observed in his landmark *The Truly Disadvantaged*, by the late seventies, a mostly conservative narrative about the inner city—that its residents were fundamentally other to productive American life—had emerged in a wide swath of criticism. Works like James Q. Wilson's *Thinking about Crime* (1975), George Gilder's influential *Wealth and Poverty* (1981), and Charles Murray's *The Bell Curve* (1984) made similar arguments. The problems of the inner city stemmed from "different group values," and that no amount of government programs would alleviate the inner city's problems.[19]

Wilson's work specifically intervenes in a debate whose terms, by 1987, had become relatively fixed.[20] There is, then, a congruence between Halberstam's notion of queer space, as outside the "temporal frames of bourgeois reproduction and family, longevity, risk/safety, and inheritance," and the notion of a "culture of poverty" ostensibly opposed to such values.[21] The lives of poor African Americans and the lives of working-class homosexuals are, of course, sociologically much different, and yet they converge in Wojnarowicz's work. Wojnarowicz depicts a city that already harbors productive lives, even as these lives are unruly and disaccustomed to the normative time frames discussed by Halberstam. If the inner city, in the 1970s, became both a symbol of the welfare state's failure and a site of renewal for bored middle-class artists, Wojnarowicz's work complicates both dynamics in several important ways. Listening to the voices emanating from an ostensibly obliterated landscape, he catalogs the very desire for survival that Wilson so elegantly frames in his structural account of inner-city poverty. The voices in *The Waterfront Journals* want neither to give up nor to die; they actively seek something better for themselves, even if "something better" is unrecognizable from the standpoint of normative time.

My reading of *The Waterfront Journals* casts the account of queer life offered by Halberstam into histories of development, working backwards from Michael Warner and Lauren Berlant's "Sex in Public," which surveyed the New York landscape after the city had taken a post-Fordist turn and Times Square had undergone its near-total transformation into a site for middle-class heterosexual entertainment.[22] Warner and Berlant bemoan the heterosexualization of city space, a heterosexualization that drew on the legacy of urban theorist Jane Jacobs as much as it did Robert Moses in fostering neighborhoods that were "safe" for middle-class residents and tourists. In what follows, I inquire into the rough world that emerged after the Fordist city and before the post-Fordist city, and ask what shards of possible futures lay embedded in the disused spaces of manufacturing, futures not conscribed by the logic of renovation and redevelopment. Art historian Fiona Anderson has read Wojnarowicz's cruising in terms of its anthropological effects, arguing that his work "activated . . . past narratives of the waterfront." For Anderson, this means the symbolic imaginary of the port as a "ruin," as well as the history of the piers themselves, but her words apply equally well to the project of unearthing small histories of the underclass.[23] Blurring fact and fiction—and at times autobiography—*The Waterfront Journals* provides a narrative record of lives that appear in corners of the post-crisis city's disused landscape, only to disappear under the underclass-scapegoating logic of redevelopment.

Working with the resources he had available, Wojnarowicz scrutinized mediations between built environment and lived life. Sexual trysts might have formed one of his core motivations for engaging the city's broken corners, but such connections were not limited to sex alone. In this sense, Wojnarowicz's project anticipates that of Samuel Delany in *Times Square*

Red, Times Square Blue. In the face of Times Square's redevelopment, Delany insists on the community and cross-class, interethnic contact among porn theater audiences in the 1970s and 1980s. While Delany demonstrates how connective networks flourished in the intact theaters of Times Square, Wojnarowicz shows that they could also flourish in wilder spaces. Delany offers a useful framework for imagining Wojnarowicz's work as a "sociological" account of what was "beautiful along with much that was shoddy, much that was dilapidated with much that is pleasurable, much that is inefficient with much that is functional" about the neighborhood.[24] Despite the apparent dilapidation, Delany's Times Square swarms with forms of human productivity. Delany positions this productivity against the post-Fordist forms of what he calls "the more formal strategies of networking relations . . . want ads, resumes, recommendations, job applications, real estate listings, and social interest groups."[25] Wojnarowicz shows how Delany's project can be extended from the relatively stable, "productive" networks of theater regulars toward the barer, starker lives of what Delany calls the "fifteen-, sixteen-, and seventeen-year-old girls and boys who would go into a doorway and do *anything* with anyone for the four to eight dollars needed for the next bottle of crack."[26] Delany's work has justifiably become a touchstone for writers like Halberstam and Muñoz. Queer theorists can learn much from Wojnarowicz's project, since it offers an even more radical account of non-normative lives at a historical moment when such lives were an important locus of anti-welfare-state discourse.

Any account of these monologues must begin where Wojnarowicz himself began, with the need to self-create, to enunciate oneself as an artist without connections. Even as better-connected artists like Matta-Clark snapped up some of the last vestiges of state support to enact large-scale projects pointing to the unlivability of Fordist forms of life at the moment of their decline, Wojnarowicz scavenged the materials around him—a borrowed typewriter, the ability to live cheaply, free access to the ruined warehouses of the waterfront—to brand himself as a commodity worth supporting. With little resources, Wojnarowicz found means to thrive in a declining cultural economy, assembling his relationship to Fordist ruins with an insistent crawling that attended not to Matta-Clark's broad cuts but the dislodged bricks, unlocked doors, and negligent authority which allowed a set of small, temporary human connections to emerge in the post-crisis years.

I invoke Matta-Clark here not because he and Wojnarowicz worked together; by all accounts, they never met. Matta-Clark died of pancreatic cancer just as Wojnarowicz was beginning his career—he was one of many culture workers in this book that died too early. But Matta-Clark shared with Wojnarowicz an intense interest in the post-crisis New York landscape, in particular the warehouses along the waterfront. One of Matta-Clark's more well-known works, *Day's End*, involved using blowtorches and power saws to cut into a disused warehouse at Pier 52, near the end of Gansevoort Street. The result was a beautiful distribution of light, described by Matta-Clark as a "temple," something like the cathedrals he'd recently seen on a trip to Italy. Matta-Clark did what well-networked artists should do: he radically challenged the limits of art. His grand cuts took on nothing less than the history of Western architecture. His art, in the words of Anne Wagner, "set its sights at uselessness through what are processes of canceling or subtraction of basic architectural functions: what buildings aim to do and house—to shelter—from day to day."[27] For a range of observers, "abandonment" meant the failure of the old order. By cutting into the side of the Pier 57 warehouse, Matta-Clark asserted his own sense of how the old order might transform into the new—by admiring the old, and registering its contrast with the new. Working in spaces of abandonment, building on a pedigree that included a famous Surrealist father, a Cornell education, and a group of SoHo artist friends, Matta-Clark produced a range of innovative projects, and was supportive in a range of ways to the growing SoHo scene.

Matta-Clark's work fits into a wider pattern of post-Minimalist art that took the city itself as its raw material. These were projects that saw the decayed city as a source of what the artist Joseph Kosuth calls post-Minimalism's "radicalization of alternative materials."[28] While Minimalist artists like Donald Judd sought to foil the art world's focus on beauty and painting, the intervention of post-Minimal artists was more radical still. These artists saw COR-TEN steel, old cars, abandoned warehouses, and the like as "readymade" materials for sculpture and other aesthetic works. The sculptor Richard Serra embedded a 26-foot-diameter steel ring into a disused Bronx Street. The performance and video artist Joan Jonas staged a performance across a ten-block grid of SoHo, a massive "theater" whose walls were vacant lots and disused buildings.[29]

Post-minimalism reached an apex in the 1976 *Rooms* exhibit at P.S. 1 organized by Alanna Heiss. *Rooms* took place, at a moment of wide cuts to public schools, in a school building that had been abandoned in 1963 (it now houses MoMA PS1).[30] There, artists like Kosuth, Richard Serra, Carl Andre, and Lynn Hershman Leeson created projects that made use of the building itself. Andre, for example, filled the courtyard with small concrete blocks, intended to represent the children that once filled its space.

Marjorie Strider spilled urethane foam out of an upper story window and incorporated ladders to invoke "the interminable fire drills of my younger days in grade school."[31] Bill Beirne made recordings of a high school, which "document the kind of noise that children make when they are let out of class."[32] For the exhibition, Matta-Clark himself cut holes in the building's floors, an extension of the techniques he used at Pier 57. This exhibit is remarkable in the way that its projects, taken as a whole, trace the departed social life of the school as an institution. By playing recordings of school children, writing on blackboards, setting blocks in the courtyard as stand-ins for children, and cutting into the building itself, the artists of *Rooms* celebrated the built environment that the state deploys on behalf of children. In improvising their projects throughout the building, though, the artists gesture toward a coming world that will ask teachers to do it themselves. They created these objects at the very moment the city was withdrawing funding from its schools. Eventually, the city would restore such funding, but the fundamental moves toward austerity and market-based solutions were in place.

Matta-Clark sought a new city but one refactored from the old.[33] Throughout *The Death and Life of Great American Cities*, but particularly in the chapter "The Need for Aged Buildings," Jacobs stresses old infrastructure as a crucial part of the socioeconomically and developmentally diverse streets that form the core of her project. Rejecting the Modernist project of urban renewal, Matta-Clark similarly advanced a dissident fidelity to abandoned space, one that cast the improvisatory logic of reuse, long practiced by the impoverished and marginal, into the wide vistas of Earth and situated art. In writing about Matta-Clark, critics return repeatedly to language of the right to the city, and both his writing and his works, particularly those addressing housing projects, offer a warm, albeit sometimes naïve, regard for the city's impoverished residents. Matta-Clark often described his projects in terms of transforming the lives of those residents, as in a 1976 interview with Donald Hall describing his reaction to a group of radical Communist Milanese youth occupying a factory:

> My goal is to extend the Milan experience to the U.S., especially to neglected areas of New York such as the South Bronx where the city is just waiting for the social and physical condition to deteriorate to such a point that the borough can redevelop the whole area into the industrial park they really want. A specific project might be to work with an existing neighborhood youth

group and to involve them in converting the all too plentiful abandoned buildings into social space. In this way, the youth could get both practical information about how buildings are made, and more essentially some first-hand experience with one aspect of the very real possibility of transforming their space. In this way, I could adapt my work to still another level of the given situation. It would no longer be concerned with just personal or metaphoric treatment of the site, but finally responsive to the express will of its occupants.[34]

Here and elsewhere, Matta-Clark figured his projects in terms of altering not just the physical landscape of post-crisis New York, but the social fabric of communities like the South Bronx.[35] Many of his projects reflect these concerns: notably *Window Blow-Out*, which I'll discuss below, but also *Fake Estates*, for which he purchased small slivers of land from the city (colloquially known as "gutter space") as well as the amphitheater he constructed for La Plaza Cultural, a community garden built by the Puerto Rican activist group Charas in the Lower East Side.[36] Still, Matta-Clark has been largely received as an artist who aimed to address large-scale issues. Writing in the preface to the 2003 Phaidon retrospective of his work, Corinne Diserens summarizes: "Matta-Clark was fascinated by the multifaceted implications of occupancy in space, even if at times he had little control over that space as he tried to somehow negotiate its own nature and long-standing cycles and processes."[37] In the wake of the crisis, issues of "occupancy" and "control" became more and more urgent as city elites moved to refigure Manhattan from a working-class city whose economy centered on the needs of manufacturing to a (more) upper-middle-class city whose economy centered on finance, insurance, and real estate.[38] Whether such claims came from below or above—the growing neighborhood movements advocating, under Jacobs's influence, for more local control of occupied space, or the increasingly strident claims about unsustainable neighborhoods—notions of who could claim space and what they might do with it roiled unceasingly throughout the 1970s and 1980s.

Asked to contribute to a 1976 show at the Institute for Architecture and Urban Resources, Matta-Clark chose to exhibit broken windows from the Twin Parks housing project in the Bronx, one of the last public housing projects to be built in New York before the crisis. Matta-Clark displayed the windows as an insurrectionary act against the other architects of the show. One of them, Robert Meier, had helped to design Twin Parks. And displaying the windows wasn't enough for Matta-Clark to make his point. After a night of drinking, Matta-Clark borrowed an air rifle from Dennis Oppenheimer and shot out the windows of the Institute itself, after which its director, Peter Eisenman, had the windows replaced before the show opened. Reflecting on this episode, critic Thomas Crow figures this act as an intervention. "If this deterioration was intolerable to Eisenman and his colleagues," Crow finds Matta-Clark asking, "why was it tolerable day in day out in the South Bronx or Lower East Side?"[39] And Matta-Clark's work remained reclaimable in later decades, against the even more aggressive attempts by the Giuliani administration to render the underclass invisible. In the late 1990s, Rosalind Deutsche—an authority on art and gentrification—tied *Window Blow-Out* to the "broken window" theory invoked by Guliani, whereby small acts of vandalism are supposedly at the root of inner-city crime.[40] Deutsche notes that the main problem with the theory involves its seeming deliberate disengagement with the historical forces shaping impoverished neighborhoods, in particular absentee landlords and problematic urban renewal projects. For Deutsche, *Window Blow-Out* intervenes in this discussion by pointing out the hypocrisy of celebrating public housing design at a moment of broad cuts to neighborhoods like the South Bronx. Still, the very nature of Matta-Clark's project—cutting into buildings that he understood as "useless"—inevitably involves making decisions about what kinds of residents have a right to the city.

In this sense, the main impetus of Matta-Clark, as nearly all of his critics concur, was toward large-scale issues: the lived reality of abandonment in the Bronx cleaves from the what Matta-Clark called the "anarchitectural" possibilities of the spaces left by abandonment. Even as his diverse works could call attention to the deprivations produced by uneven industrialization, Matta-Clark was more interested in querying the ways that people writ large lived in the twentieth century—inside boxes—than in critiquing the structural causes of poverty. And even as he worked with destruction, his methods pointed toward renewal. As Crow observes, Matta-Clark first learned to cut through buildings by rehabilitating them. His construction skills were honed by carving lofts out of former factories, a practice that enjoyed more and more support from the New York City government throughout the 1970s.[41] And despite his critique of mainstream culture, Matta-Clark framed his work, at least at times, in terms of the same logic of development that would operate in Times Square. Defending his illegal work on *Day's End*, he stated to his lawyer: "The waterfront was probably never anything but tough and dangerous but now with this long slow transition period has become a veritable mugger's playground, both for people who go only to enjoy walking there and for a recently popularized sado-maschochistic fringe."[42] Matta-Clark here points to the very activity that would draw Wojnarowicz into the piers: the open sex that regularly occurred in these spaces. While an avowed leftist, Matta-Clark pointed the way toward private-public models of development that would assume more and more primacy in the aftermath of the financial crisis, and which reach, as I'll suggest, a kind of apotheosis in the High Line project completed in 2012.

Of course, both the emergence of the High Line (after decades of gentrification in Chelsea) and the relationship between *Day's End* and the cruising activity of the West End piers have complex histories. Such complications emerge with particular force in the series of photographs that artist Alvin Baltrop took of the piers during the 1970s in which apparent cruisers are visible outside, inside, and around the *Day's End* warehouse, *after* Matta-Clark did his cuts. If Matta-Clark's work foregrounded an arresting collision between human life and the built environment, the photographs point to a possible end-result of such a collision, albeit one that emphasizes the way that Matta-Clark's projects served as what Lefebvre calls a "wager" on the future. Looking back on the period from 2008, art critic Douglas Crimp, who saw both the art and cruising scenes up close, observes: "Perhaps more than Matta-Clark could have imagined, Baltrop's photographs portray the 'joyous situation' Matta-Clark said he wanted to achieve there; and they constitute rare and indispensable evidence of the proximity and simultaneity of artistic and sexual experimentation in the declining industrial spaces of Manhattan during the 1970s, a time of particularly creative ferment for both scenes."[43] Elsewhere, though, Crimp has noted the complications of the era in terms of the underclass, writing in his exhibit essay for *Mixed Use, Manhattan* that even as artists benefited from the city's crisis, "others lost their jobs and homes at the same moment that social services were slashed."[44] On the one hand, Matta-Clark's cuts made the waterfront permeable to a larger portion of society; on the other, they helped advance what would come to be called the creative economy by literally changing a site of industrial capitalism to a site of postmodern art.[45]

In contrast to Matta-Clark, Wojnarowicz's artistic projects focused on the small scale. He positioned such small-scale subjects against the broad vista of the "ONE TRIBE NATION," his term for a homogenous United States. He used such work to scale up, to become visible within the networks of the artistic community. As I'll suggest at the end of this chapter, this may have allowed him to grasp the sheer effort needed to become visible as a member of the underclass. Much of his visual art used collage with human figures rendered as small segments of a larger field. His *Rimbaud in New York* photograph series used a mask of the French poet juxtaposed against small sections of the city, including the inside of another warehouse. He also loved to photograph tiny things, such as this toad, from a work entitled "What is this little guy's job in the world?" In the text for the image (illegible as reproduced), Wojnarowicz meditates on problems of scale, asking "If this little guy dies does the world know? . . . Does an almost imperceptible link in the chain snap? Will civilization stumble?" In the monologues, Wojnarowicz pursued links in post-crisis New York's chains that he feared were imperceptible. Throughout his career, his answers to these questions was affirmative: the world should feel if a human huddled in a doorway cannot find a place to sleep, or is pursued by homophobic violence, or is, more basically, denied a right to exist.

Figure 1.1. What Is This Little Guy's Job in the World? Courtesy of the Estate of David Wojnarowicz and P•P•O•W, New York. The text in the upper right hand corner is illegible when reproduced at these dimensions. It reads: "What is this little guy's job in the world. If this little guy dies does the world know? Does the world feel this? Does something get displaced? If this little guy dies does the world get a little lighter? Does the planet rotate a little faster? If this little guy dies, without his body to shift the currents of air, does the air flow perceptibly faster? What shifts if this little guy dies? Do people speak language a little bit differently? If this little guy dies does some little kid somewhere wake up with a bad dream? Does an almost imperceptible link in the chain snap? Will civilization stumble?"

With the monologues, Wojnarowicz did what sociologists like Wilson and Loïc Wacquant began trying to do with increasing fervency as the Fordist city collapsed: show that even as the small niches of abandoned buildings and aimless streets were filled with poverty and crime, they were also filled with adaptive intelligence, generosity, and an insistent will to survive.[46] In the process of transforming his life into art, Wojnarowicz showed that parts of city written off not just by conservative politicians and developers but also by leftist artists like Matta-Clark had the potential to develop their own futures. But these futures would arrive with far less friction if the city had not been allowed to take shape with capital interests as its main organizing force.

Like Matta-Clark's work, Wojnarowicz's is a "wager" on the future, and elsewhere in his career, he likely helped accelerate the displacement of impoverished populations through his participation in the Lower East Side gallery scene of the 1980s. As I'll discuss in chapter 4, the visual art of the Lower East Side was undoubtedly important to the gentrification of the neighborhood. While not as bright a light as the celebrity-artists Keith Haring or Jean-Michel Basquiat, Wojnarowicz was, nevertheless, significant enough that one customer paid $10,000 in cash for a set of his paintings, after which the staff at Civilian Warfare spread the money on the gallery floor and rolled around in it.[47] And some of Wojnarowicz's visual art could be read as less sympathetic to impoverished populations. Surveying the art of the Lower East Side as part of an "underground scene" whereby "the symbols and images of abandoned buildings, empty lots, graffiti, and a thriving drug economy serves as the foundation of an urban aesthetic inclusive of music, art, fashion and literature," Christopher Mele concludes that this scene "provided to developers the images, symbols, and rhetoric to reinvent the neighborhood for middle-class consumers."[48] As Exhibit A, Mele singles out Wojnarowicz's *Junk Triptych*, "which portrays the social problems of drugs, money, and overdose that plagued the neighborhood," asserting that it "is arguably an uncritical representation that verges on the sensational."[49] The tension here, between Wojnarowicz the writer who expresses broad sympathy for the underclass and Wojnarowicz the painter who provides fuel for redevelopment, is one that I'll pursue throughout this book. Wojnarowicz, like all of his peers—including the wildly successful Basquiat and Haring—found himself in a vexed position. He was just trying to make it, but in doing it himself, he became part of a larger process whereby artists would, first, be valorized as a vanguard to reclaim neglected neighborhoods for a middle class returning to the city, and, second, be idealized as models for the emerging world of post-Fordist work. But that discussion is for a later moment, and a later chapter. In the monologues he wrote in the 1970s, Wojnarowicz tells the story of the underclass and their struggle to survive.

I'll set up my discussion of the monologues with an episode from Wojnarowicz's diaries. Flying on speed, Wojnarowicz recounts a tryst with a man with "a couple large feathers hanging from one shoulder by a piece of string, some decoration that perplexed yet gladdened me."[50] After they fuck, the two have the following exchange:

> Jesus, and I said, Yeah, whew. And he said, The fire really took this place apart, but man if these floorboards could talk.
> Yeah if these floorboards could talk, if those streets could talk, if the whole huge path this body has traveled—roads, motel rooms, hillsides, cliffs, subways, rivers, planes, trucks—if any of them could speak, what would they remember like me?[51]

In a destroyed building, no longer useful to the Jacobsian city, Wojnarowicz finds human connection and conceives of such in terms of buildings talking. Wojnarowicz devoted much of his writing to making the post-crisis New York landscape talk. Even as he drew inspiration (and syntax) from the mid-century observations of the Beats, Wojnarowicz continually returned his writer's eye to the landscape that he found most significant, the warehouses, piers, streets, and bars of the West side of Lower Manhattan. Throwing his lanky body into this landscape, watching, fucking, writing, Wojnarowicz gives flesh and meaning to the lives that development sweeps aside as one more impediment to growth, the "s&m crowd" of Matta-Clark's dismissive note.[52] If the writings of the Beats eventually found a home in the language of social unrest of the 60s—and, at least per Luc Boltanski and Eve Chiapello, served to invigorate the very corporate structures they sought to oppose[53]—their upcycling by Wojnarowicz serves instead to draw out the suspended time of the piers, in Wojnarowicz's words, "something outside the flow of regularity: streets, job routines."[54]

The figures in the monologues filter through cracks in the landscape. They don't make the cracks but rather adaptively make use of them. This can be seen in a long excerpt from Wojnarowicz's monologue, "Boy in Horn & Hadart's on Forty-Second Street," one of the earliest-written and most frequently reproduced monologues in Wojnarowicz's archive at the Fales Library at New York University. This monologue is one of six that Carr identifies as autobiographical; it narrates a tryst with a man who lives in the upper Eighties. As the two have sex, the police start breaking down the door. Fearing arrest, the speaker jumps out of the second-story window and runs into "a big courtyard" that spans "the whole length of the block." I'll quote the next part of the passage at length, as it highlights the relationship between body and space that I am identifying as the monologues' larger project:

> I kept trying basement doorways but they were all locked and I was afraid if I pounded on them someone would call the police so I ran almost the whole block and finally I went down this alleyway that came to a brick wall and there were some boards laying on the ground. I propped them against the wall and hid behind them. I left a little crack between them so I could see if the police came down the alley looking for me. After about twenty minutes I remembered my subway pass in my wallet so I got up and hid it under some other boards further away in the alley, then I crawled behind the boards again and sat there not moving until it got dark.I kept thinking the police would come any minute. When it got late I crawled out and started walking back through the courtyard trying doors on the opposite side. I finally found one building that had been burned out and I could walk through it to the front but there were iron bars over the window and an iron door that had a chain wrapped around the bars with a padlock on it.[55]

Far from desiring the "eyes on the street" that form the core of Jacobs's study and that became an important basis for the neighborhood-based movements of the 1970s and 1980s, the speaker maneuvers himself through unseen spaces, taking advantage of burned-out buildings. He both resists and makes use of the landscape, asserting his survival. His life takes shape in rattled cellar doors and the hope for unlocked doors.

He is like one of those figures in a Mel Rosenthal photo of the South Bronx, who stand in front of falling-down buildings with smiles on their faces, or perform flips over discarded beds, or skateboard exuberantly down the street. Of course, Rosenthal's subjects are often more innocent. He particularly loves smiling children. Rosenthal's photos offer a direct rejoinder to decades' rhetorical degradations of the underclass. The smiling children in the South Bronx deserve a future. Rosenthal sets the vast scale of the South Bronx's destruction against the smallness of his subjects' lives:

Figure 1.2. Mother and Daughter, Claremont Avenue in the South Bronx, ca. 1976–1983. Copyright The Image Works.

But by carefully selecting his subjects, Rosenthal implicitly argues that his viewers' sympathy be reserved only for smiling, productive citizens—not citizens who fuck, sell drugs, or otherwise mangle their lives. *The Waterfront Journals* articulate sympathy for a very different set of citizens, those to whom the abject "underclass" label would seem to apply more accurately.

Consequently, it's more appropriate to situate the monologues in the context of another infamous artwork from the era, the set of bronze casts that John Ahearn made for a Bronx police station in the mid-eighties. Aggressive, uneven, problematic, these casts came under quick controversy (and were promptly removed by Ahearn) because of the kind of citizen they represent. These were figures "in and out of jail," "in and out of jobs" and "in and out of junior high school."[56] Like the subjects of Ahearn's sculptures, the speakers in Wojnarowicz's monologues are unruly, stubborn, but insistent on survival. They describe often harrowing encounters: a young hustler who escapes death by jumping on a bus after a john pulls a knife on him,[57] a fourteen-year-old hitchhiker who jumps out of a moving car after being assaulted,[58] a man queer-bashed to unconsciousness.[59] In page after page,

Wojnarowicz frames these voices with an insistent will to live, if for no other reason than to tell their story. In doing so, he maps post-crisis New York in ways overlooked by city planners, indicating the empty doorways and risky spaces where such figures suffer, fight, and thrive. Wojnarowicz serves as implicit interlocutor, conduit, and representative of these lives.

Throughout the monologues, Wojnarowicz sets the struggle of small figures against the ruined landscape of New York. In the monologue entitled "The Waterfront. 2:00 AM. New York City," for example, Wojnarowicz depicts an abandoned, dangerous landscape that becomes the site of a sexual tryst:

> The entire façade of the place was covered in a dull gleaming ice, bricks having long ago tumbled down to the sidewalk and a slight smoke still rolling from the edges even now weeks after the fact. Far along the waterfront walkways were large ships with steel meshes of stacks and poles and lights burning effortlessly in the night. I could see stars through the upper stories of the hotel windows. A police car was idling nearby to ward off looters.[60]

Wojnarowicz depicts a scene familiar from accounts of New York in the 1970s: crumbling infrastructure, an ongoing fear of crime, even the specter of arson. "We descended into the shadows of a ramp leading down to an abandoned playground, trees catching headlights and casting skeletal lines like X rays against the brick wall of an outhouse that had long ago been chained shut. They had once found some guy down there naked and tied up with his own shirt and belt, his wallet and valuables gone."[61] Spatially rooted, tracking its speaker's movements from the waterfront up to the streets, and emphasizing his relationship to the streets—outside the door that opens for others—this passage neatly encompasses the multiple threads of Wojnarowicz's project in the monologues. Once a (presumably publicly funded) playground, this waterfront is now a site of crime. The only sense of government lies with the police.

The form Wojnarowicz used for such work was influenced by Beat writers, but also adopted out of sheer necessity. He wrote on single typewritten sheets that were readily portable as he moved, driven by poverty in the early years of his career from shared apartment to shared apartment. Such sheets provided an effective way to do what Latour calls "writ[ing] down everything" in the process of slowly assembling a social. Like Latour, Wojnarowicz documents what the actors in the landscape of post-crisis New York had to say about their lived environment. Indeed, Cynthia Carr describes Wojnarowicz's orientation toward such lives in terms of a sociological interest, writing that Wojnarowicz "wanted to understand how [the homeless] got to that shattered place."[62] As Carr observes, the monologue "Man in Casual Labor Office 6:30 AM" presents a bold example of such interest. That monologue begins with stark words: "I'm tired of being a tramp . . . my father was a tramp and he's dead . . . I'm a tramp and I don't want to be one . . . I stopped drinking . . . I wear only old-man clothes . . . I wash up every day . . . I work . . . and I'm still a tramp . . . Does anybody want to tell me the secret? How do I de-tramp myself? I read Machiavelli and he done me no good."[63] Stripped of the romanticism that Beat writers often attributed to such marginal figures, these sentences long for a social order that will support them. Far from bemoaning the failure of the welfare state, the man here presents a kind of suffering life that exists outside of the biopolitical measures of the welfare state. He is evidence, perhaps, for the continued necessity of such state aid in the long decline of the 1970s. And Wojnarowicz brings an ethnographic curiosity to the man. Listening to the man speak, Wojnarowicz notes in an early draft of the monologue: "What is the beginning of tramping? Digging through garbage? Smelly rooms with liquor store signs haunting the windows all night? What lines enclose or remove tramphood? Is it a figure of speech alien to one's condition, used to describe other than yourself? Is it a state of mind or body? Is it a style of walking? Does the idea of it hit you suddenly at a particular age: hold me close. . . . I just had a vision of myself after the tenth grade."[64]

Midway through *Reassembling the Social*, the sociologist Latour explains what he terms the "fifth source of uncertainty" in the social sciences, "writing down risky accounts." It is only by writing everything down, Latour asserts, that the social scientist might hope to "retrace the social."[65] Building on the entomological metaphor he uses throughout the book, he describes such an account in contrast to "methodological treatises [who] might dream of another world" as "written by ants for other ants, has no other aim than to help dig tiny galleries in this dusty and earthly one."[66] Moving through the dusty, earthly spaces of post-crisis New York, each monologue in Wojnarowicz's *The Waterfront Journals* digs a tiny gallery. The monologues are not, of course, assembled into a formal sociological study, and yet they perform work similar to Latour's social scientists, who, after all "should be inspired in being at least as disciplined, as enslaved by reality, as obsessed by textual quality, as good writers can be."[67] *The Waterfront Journals* points to the work fiction does in unearthing lost histories of the underclass, written by an amateur sociologist in situ.

In laying out the techniques of Actor Network Theory, Latour calls for a mode of writing that sticks as close to its subjects as possible; the notebooks he describes are designed to replicate the contours of the observer's situatedness as closely as possible. This, I argue, is the relationship between *The Waterfront Journals* and the post-crisis city. Taking shape within the uneven physical ruins of the city, but refusing, unlike Matta-Clark, to cut into these ruins, Wojnarowicz crafted a literary form that laid bare such cracks, peering into the dim spaces made visible by such cracks. In *Cruising Utopia*, queer theorist José Muñoz figures sites of public gay sex, which would include Wojnarowicz's piers, as moments of potential utopias that challenge the rationalistic system of heteronormativity and figure what Muñoz calls the "potentially utopian aesthetics of the cityscape" and imagine the "world-making properties of queerness."[68] Surveying a range of texts from postwar urban contexts, Muñoz argues that little utopias can be glimpsed nearly everywhere: in photographs of men's rooms, in abandoned Ohio shopping plazas, in Amiri Baraka's *The Toilet*. Each text, Muñoz contends, figures the possibility of alternate queer futures.

The places in *The Waterfront Journals* are places that do not exist or existed for only as long as Wojnarowicz focused his eye on them. They are not the site of large-scale transformation; they are not great monuments to a turn-of-the-century past; they are not the background to a sweeping narrative of the city. Their voices assert occupancy of the city even in situations where such occupancy seems utterly denied to them. The figure in "Woman in Coffee Shop on the Lower East Side" offers a vibrant example: "Sometimes when I'm walking through the streets I want my fingernails to grow long and hard so I can make scratches in the concrete or make grooves on the sidewalk or by concentrating real hard make all the windows shatter and rain down on the street."[69] This is a personal, small-scale apocalypse, a body occupying space in impossible ways. Likely, that's because when people watch this woman, they don't have good intentions: "[when] men hassle me on the street I wish I could raise my hand and suddenly dimes would be welded on their eyeballs so they couldn't see where they were going. And when guys on the street make kiss noises at me I wish I could make their dicks wither and drop off."[70] The woman has no future other than one where she disappears into those streets, a remnant of the post-Fordist city's reliance on basic human decency, rather than policy, as a foundation for community life. She articulates the invisible hierarchies that pervade Jacobs's streets and that Matta-Clark relies on to craft his vision. Her life is precarious and uncertain, a victim of what Lauren Berlant calls cruel optimism, where the less solid your ties to the formal economy, the more alone you are in making community.[71]

Wojnarowicz frames the woman's speech spatially, locating the monologue in a Lower East Side coffee shop. In doing so, he depicts the city as a menagerie of voices, filled with echoing sounds instead of abandoned and mute, as real estate developers, landlords, and artists would repeatedly frame the city during the 1970s. Both Neil Smith and Mele have argued that the notion of an "empty" city served useful functions for a range of economically motivated interests.[72] Smith argues that by framing the city as a "frontier," real estate developers were able to trade on suburb-dwellers' desire for authenticity, working within a long history of the frontier as a site of self-renewal for privileged classes grown decadent and soft. Such visions of emptiness, to be filled with the teeming neighborhoods of Jacobs's study, dominated accounts of abandoned New York.

Of course, the streets here are dangerous, as visible in one of the monologues that Carr identifies as about Wojnarowicz himself, "Boy in Coffee Shop on Third Avenue." This monologue, one of the collection's most chilling, depicts a figure who "used to hustle in [Times] Square" but doesn't anymore because "too many creeps wackos loonies."[73] The speaker recounts being picked up by a man who pays him twenty dollars. Because the john doesn't have money for a hotel room, the two walk to where city buses are parked on Forty-first and Tenth, where the man, after pretending to be a cop and threatening to arrest the boy, pulls a knife, rapes him, and starts walking him toward the river. Thinking quickly, the boy spots an empty city bus and gets the driver's attention by screaming, then runs, jumping between two parked cars to evade the man a second time.

The problem of such irreducible humanity was everywhere in New York policy. This episode brings to life a set of conditions familiar to city planners in the late seventies and early eighties: a Times Square filled with what historian Lyn Sagalyn depicts as "a motley cross-section of people—social misfits, sexual deviants, plain down-and-outers, alcoholics, druggies, teenage runaways, hustlers of all types, pimps, and buyers of sex."[74] As the Beame and Koch administrations sought to redevelop Times Square in the aftermath of the fiscal crisis, this aspect of Times Square—the dangers of an unruly underclass—posed a problem to be solved not through increased services, as critics like Columbia professor Herbert Gans advocated, but through what Sagalyn calls "imposing a high-caliber new economic order"[75] that would make it impossible for people like the boy and the john to conduct their business. The city's plan was predicated on the notion that city streets could become vibrant only if people like this boy were excluded from it. Disowned from a city increasingly focused on private ownership and from development logics focused on production, the figures in the monologues nevertheless assert ownership of their space, however temporary.

By recording the boy's—his own—story, Wojnarowicz makes his readers aware of the possibility for a more democratic city, even as he points to the crucial lacunas in government services. While readers don't learn anything about the boy's background, it is likely similar to that of Wojnarowicz himself—cast out of a lower-class family, with little means for survival aside from selling his body, but maintaining a desire to live, to "hang out together and do crazy stuff" with a friend he met in summer camp. Like Michel Foucault in the introduction to "Lives of Infamous Men," Wojnarowicz seeks to "snatch" this boy's life "from the darkness," for like the infamous men, boys like the boy "don't have and never will have any existence outside the precarious domicile of these words."[76] If not for his own stubborn, genial nature, Wojnarowicz himself might have vanished into such darkness, and the conditions of his existence would never come to the attention of other artists and critics. Laid plain, the boy's life—summer camp and all—bears witness to the bare life of a human actor striving to transform his circumstances, to return to the lost integration of whatever "summer camp" represents to him. Weeds growing in cracks, insects crawling over burned floorboards, these lives are, by and large, passed over because of their small scale. The monologue figures are, in the feminist philosopher Sara Ahmed's words, "willful," and here Ahmed's words on the spaces of willfulness apply nicely: "There can be joy in creating worlds out of the broken pieces of our dwelling spaces: we can not only share our willfulness stories, but pick up some of the pieces too. . . . We can say this, as we have been there, in that place, that shadowy place, willful subjects tend to find themselves; a place that can feel lonely can be how we reach others."[77] Speaking from the small-scale, shadowy places around the post-crisis city, the monologues stage scenes of willful subjects reaching other subjects.

Their words, though, manifest a desire to scale up (as did Wojnarowicz himself), as expressed in metaphors of perspective and mapping. The very first monologue in the collection describes a man in prison talking to a more experienced convict. As the two stand in the prison yard, they look out to the guard tower. The older man tells the younger man to "take your fingers and measure how big it is from here." The younger man does so, and the older man tells him "That's how high it really is."[78] Through language, the men rework their circumstances, shifting the relationship between the guard tower and themselves. This is the project of Wojnarowicz's monologues: to allow these underclass speakers to set their dimensions equal to the guard towers of city planners and developers. Another monologue describes a speaker pointing out places on a map, drawing a line from Austin, Texas, to Colorado, to Salt Lake City, to Vietnam, to Berkeley, saying "see here on this map, that's where I am."[79] To Wojnarowicz, maps operated on the wrong scale, missing the granularity of human lives found in the monologues. Maps, incidentally, were a recurring theme in Wojnarowicz's art; he would regularly impose garish drawings on maps, to demonstrate, it seems, the limitations of maps in recognizing human existences like his own.[80] In her biography, Carr argues that maps "remained forever mysterious to [Wojnarowicz] as an acceptable form of reality."[81] The earliest self-assembled version of the monologues at the Fales Library has a hand-drawn map on its cover. Wojnarowicz also incorporated maps into his art throughout his career, as in, for example, 1984's *Fuck You Faggot Fucker* (the title derives from a homophobic cartoon that Wojnarowicz found, reproduced in the lower middle of the work). The photos in the corners are too small to see at these dimensions, which is part of *Fuck You*'s argument. Those in the upper left, upper right, and lower right depict Wojnarowicz and his friend John Hall, both nude. They were taken in the theater of the abandoned Public School 164, which became the Charas/El Bohío building. (I discuss this building in the next chapter.) The one in the lower right depicts Brian Butterick—later a well-known drag performer—as Saint Sebastian. Wojnarowicz's point, here and elsewhere, is that people need better maps to see the kind of small figures that he depicts in the monologues.

Figure 1.3. *Fuck You Faggot Fucker*, 1984. Courtesy of the Estate of David Wojnarowicz and P•P•O•W, New York.

Creeping like an ant (or an Actor Network Theorist) across the devalued landscape of post-crisis New York, Wojnarowicz found lives of brave intensity and stubborn survival—the very opposite of the laziness and abstention increasingly attributed to the poor by politicians who used such depictions to justify what city commissioner Roger Starr announced as the "planned shrinkage" of city services from certain neighborhoods. Both Matta-Clark and Wojnarowicz saw their artistic roles as reimagining a derelict landscape. Working from radically different vantage points and with differing results, both men nevertheless sought to interrupt the slow domination of neoliberal capital, those forces that would make every bit of the landscape and its people reclaimable for profitable ends. Matta-Clark's vision—of making large-scale art out of abandoned infrastructure—would be the vision that eventually wins out.

Two projects, then, one that has become inscribed in art's firmament, and one that has lurked in the corners of aesthetic production, part of the lower-profile prose experiments that occurred throughout the Lower East Side of the 1970s and 1980s. One project made its mark, literally cutting holes into ruined buildings; the other existed for a long time in a transitive state. But for luck, coupled with boundless energy and an aptitude for making connections, Wojnarowicz might well have faded into the vast landscape of artists who never make it, what John Roberts calls the "second economy" of artists. Roberts defines the second economy as "that sphere of artistic and cultural activity that has little or no relationship to the primary economy of art: salerooms, auction houses, museums, and large public galleries," a "precarious realm of artistic production" that "operates in the same space as part-time waged labour, unwaged labour, and everyday social relations."[82] In the 1970s, Wojnarowicz occupied exactly this space; arguably, given his pedigree and connections, Matta-Clark was always a part of art's primary economy, even as his projects called this primary economy into question.

Matta-Clark's work falls into a broad tradition of non-sites, insurgent galleries, and other extra-institutional locations that helped develop art in what Rosalind Krauss calls "the expanded field." Wojnarowicz's work falls into a strain of narrative experimentation that broke company with both postmodern metafiction and the proliferating realisms of the 1980s. The arc of Wojnarowicz's work will play out in all of the literary experiments, from Nuyorican poetry to *Between C & D*, with which *DIY On the Lower East Side* is concerned. The arc of Matta-Clark's work will play out in the tenement buildings and storefronts which made such narrative experiments possible.

Fragmentary, concerned with marginal figures, capturing the risk and precarity of small-scale life, Wojnarowicz's monologues articulate a politics of the city that squarely recognizes the Lefebvrian production of space as controlled and monitored, while advancing concrete examples of de Certeauian tactics drawn from the lived life of survival. In this sense, Wojnarowicz's monologues anticipate later work that would reject the large-scale refashioning of the public sphere characteristic of the expanded field. Benjamin Buchloh presents Thomas Hirschhorn's "alters" as an example of work that rejects notions of sculpture as "autonomous objects and spaces exempt from the universally enforced banality of private property and the terror of controlled space."[83] The altars consist of collections of ordinary objects arranged in public spaces, designed to be both temporary and participatory. It is not simply that Hirschhorn makes use of detritus and locates his sculptures within the disused spaces of housing projects, and makes use of the fairly compensated labor of local residents; he sets them up so that they can be vandalized, stolen from, or added to. Instead of taking abandoned space as a precursor for conceptual work, Hirschhorn, like Wojnarowicz, attends to local relationships that repudiate abandonment.

If Matta-Clark saw in the Fordist crisis an apocalypse that would slouch toward a new Bethlehem, Wojnarowicz saw the survivors picking through the rubble, who used their own innovation to craft small utopias. The city's 2000s renovation of the disused High Line embraced a history of decay while proving a boon to developers who built condominium towers that start at $2500 a square foot—and which, ironically, often sit empty because they serve as investment vehicles. Indeed, the High Line begins blocks from the pier where *Day's End* stood in 1975. Deprived of the sustaining, albeit disciplinary, networks of the Fordist city, the subjects of Wojnarowicz's monologues would become the precariat, folding T-shirts and serving coffee as they watch more and more of the post-Fordist city cut off from their lives. In words appropriate to the stubbornness of these figures in insisting on occupying their space, Ahmed writes that "willfulness can be a trace left behind, a reopening of what might have been closed down, a modification of what seems reachable, and a *revitalization* of the question of what it is to be for."[84] Though the city's revitalization occurred under different terms, Wojnarowicz's monologues—like his life itself—stand as a trace, and a reopening, of the city closed down by the onset of post-Fordism.

My next chapter examines how the Puerto Rican poets and housing activists of the Lower East Side took up the challenge posed by Wojnarowicz in his monologues—that the city's ruins, seemingly empty, were filled with extant life. Wojnarowicz sought to record the voices emerging from these ruins. The poets and housing activists also recorded these voices, but sought to preserve the nature and type of lives narrated in the monologues. They created institutions and aesthetic objects that opposed the radical refactoring represented by Matta-Clark's project and post-crisis city planners. Instead of cutting holes in buildings, they sought to patch these holes up. In doing so, they, too, had to fend off notions that the Lower East Side was the site of an abject underclass. These crucial issues of the built environment will animate the work of critical theorists, writers, and artists that I'll discuss in later chapters.

Chapter 2

The Puerto Rican Working Class and the Literature of Rebuilding

On March 16, 1976, readers of *The New York Times*'s front page could read about a plan that the *Times* itself admitted was "unusual." The chair of the Municipal Assistance Corporation, Felix Rohatyn, suggested that the best solution to neighborhood blight might be to do away with the neighborhood altogether: "Take a 30-block area, clear it, blacktop it, and develop an industrial park with the whole package of tax, employment, and financing incentives already in place."[1] If these neighborhoods could no longer thrive, Rohatyn argued, it was better to pave them over. Rohatyn's plan points to a core logic that emerged from the 1975 fiscal crisis. Some New York neighborhoods, filled with unproductive citizens and falling-down buildings, might need to be written off completely, or at least reduced to a size more in keeping with the city's ability to serve them.[2] As historians of the crisis have contended, such reasoning drew on a wider push among conservatives to scale down what were perceived as the excessively generous provisions of New York's welfare state.[3] For these conservatives, abandoned buildings became potent symbols of the welfare state's failure. And for local business leaders, the land under these buildings could be put to better use, to position New York as a site for international investment. This is how the logic of what Neil Smith calls uneven development played out on the ground in New York. Landlords often deliberately abandoned buildings as a means to get rid of lower-income tenants, prompting a vicious cycle whereby the city cut aid to such tenants then used the resulting abandonment as a rationale for cutting more aid. City-level conversations dovetailed with accumulating accounts, at a national level, of an unproductive underclass that inhabited neighborhoods with abandoned buildings. In the context of housing, the most direct way to foster the market-based solutions beloved by the Emergency Financial Control Board was to encourage capital to withdraw from these neighborhoods so that their poor residents would move out and real estate developers could do their work. The writers I discuss in this chapter felt these realities, and fought back against them.

My first chapter addressed the immediate ruins wrought by the crisis and the possibilities of building new forms out of these ruins. I argued that while Gordon Matta-Clark focused on the large-scale possibilities for new kinds of life in these ruins, David Wojnarowicz found life already thriving within these ruins. Both projects, I contended, entailed what Henri Lefebvre calls a "wager" on the future of lived space. This chapter picks up where I left off with Wojnarowicz, examining the local, small-scale attempts to maintain and reclaim the Lower East Side—newly renamed "Loisaida"—for the working-class, largely Puerto Rican population still living in the Lower East Side. The term has a literary origin: it was originally used in a Don-Quixote-inspired-play put on by Bimbo Rivas and Chino Garcia. "Loisaida," Garcia maintained, originated as a solution to a linguistic problem: "the Latinos on the Lower East Side had a hard time always saying Lower East Side. So by saying Loisaida in Spanglish, it created a word for them to use."[4] Rivas later wrote a poem that used the term to celebrate the thriving life of the Lower East Side. Reprinted in an important community newsletter, *The Quality of Life in Loisaida*, the poem would be used as a raison d'etre for housing activists. Although my project as a whole scrutinizes the Lower East Side for literary and aesthetic responses to the 1975 fiscal crisis, much of what I argue here would apply equally well to parts of Brooklyn, Harlem, and the South Bronx. But the Lower East Side, because of its geographical location, was ahead of each of these places in both the struggle for housing and the art-driven gentrification that I will discuss in chapter 4.

As the networks of the Fordist compact fell away, residents of these neighborhoods sought to create new networks, and they often succeeded. I am using "networks" here to mean not technological networks but the type of networks that Bruno Latour has discussed throughout his project. In *An Inquiry Into Modes of Existence*, he describes networks as "the exploratory work that makes it possible to recruit or to constitute a discontinuous series of heterogeneous elements on the one hand and on the other something that circulates in a continuous fashion, once all the elements are in place, when maintenance is assured and there is no crisis."[5] Amidst the discontinuity resulting from the crisis, residents of the Lower East Side formed tenants' unions, rehabilitated buildings themselves and created community gardens that sparkled like jewels amidst the rubble of broken buildings. These organizations were grassroots attempts to build institutions that might sustain these neighborhoods after the funding cuts of the 1975 crisis.[6] Their work rejoined those voices who would summarize their communities as bereft of life, home to an underclass whose best future would be to move out of the city, making room for parking lots and condominiums. Both homesteading and community gardening seek to rework representations of space, challenging notions of the neighborhood as, variously, "waste," "debris," "to be razed," "vacant lots," "abandoned," and "to be developed."[7] If the neighborhood's residents could change the way others perceived the neighborhood, they hoped, then they might restore some of the lifeworld lost with the 1975 fiscal crisis. This was simultaneously a literary, activist, and artistic project. Writers, tenants' rights groups, and visual artists alike sought to rewrite the dominant narrative of the Lower East Side as home to an abject underclass.

Working alongside, and often within, these organizations, Nuyorican poets and playwrights sought to build a new world from the rubble. They viewed their neighborhood with the complexity and optimism of a Martin Wong painting. Emphasizing interactions between built environment and people, Wong's paintings captured the neighborhood's stark spaces, but always with a nuance and care that foregrounded the Lower East Side as a vibrant space. In *Portrait of Mickey Piñero at Ridge Street and Stanton*, for example, the poet Miguel Piñero stands erect, in shirt and red tie, reading his famous "A Lower East Side Poem," the words of which rim the painting's border.

That poem serves as something like an anthem for Nuyorican verse, articulating at once the possibilities and constrictions of lived life after the 1975 crisis. "There's no other town around that / brings you up or keeps you down," Piñero writes, describing a place with "no food" and "little heat" that nonetheless "make[s] my spirits fly."[8] Wong paints the sky with roiling red clouds. In the background are buildings with both bricked-in windows, dark, empty windows, and brightly lit windows. Above Piñero, an eight ball, a beer can, a screwdriver, and a razor float in outline. A gun labeled "UNDERCOVER 32" shoots a bullet against a heart made of bricks, but the bullet bounces back. The complex tableau here encompasses the contradictory possibilities of aesthetic expression in the Lower East Side after the crisis. Has Piñero's poetry cast a spell, whereby bullets never work? Is it he that has inspired the bright lights in the building behind him?

The vision in Wong's painting is that of a poet transforming his neighborhood. It's a utopian vision, the same that Miguel Algarín outlined throughout his work. For Algarín, the Nuyorican Poets Cafe, which he founded in 1973, on the eve of the fiscal crisis, was at once an intervention

Figure 2.1. *Portrait of Mickey Piñero at Ridge Street and Stanton*, 1985. Courtesy of the Estate of Martin Wong and P•P•O•W, New York.

into the disused built environment of the Lower East Side and an intervention into the dismissive public discourse around the underclass. For Algarín, through poetry, a street kid like Georgie Lopez might change his environment:

> What I found very valuable about what [Georgie] was writing was . . . a description of his world. The rats are both themselves and a symbol for the dope addicts that made Georgie's life really miserable. His mother can't hold on to a radio or a T.V., it just disappears. It worried me when this nine-year-old boy showed his inner world and his inner world was a vision of himself as DDT.[9]

In giving Georgie a home, in "helping him to understand volume, value, and the breath," Algarín hopes to rebuild his streets, and "his words come into the body and they change your chemistry right on the spot." As a result, listeners "will have understood and have experienced what happened right there. The registering will have been performed. The change will have been performed too."[10] Both Wong and Algarín imagine the poet who stands among ruins remaking these ruins, against long odds. The works I discuss in this chapter carry forward this sense of possibility, encoding what Latour has described as "the troubling and exhilarating feeling that *things could be different*." For Latour, no place conveys this feeling better a construction site, where the bricks, girders, and lumber have not yet been assembled into a building.[11] In the 1970s and 1980s, the Lower East Side was filled with building materials, mostly dissembled from existing buildings. Construction, gardening, painting, and the writing of literature all offered ways to rebuild, and in so doing to open up possibilities for living and creating. The outcomes of the 1975 fiscal crisis—increased inequality, broad gentrification—now seem set in place. But crises are, as the economic historian Alain Lipietz contends, moments of flux, in which arrangements of power might be rearranged.[12]

This is a tangled story, and this chapter will necessarily move toward a more utopian pole than chapter 1 or the following chapters. At the same time, I recognize that the actual history of the Lower East Side—to be played out in chapter 4's account of art-gentrification—is one of closing down possibilities for the subjects of this chapter, and of opening up possibilities for white bohemians. What looks like possibility folds back into necessity. But remnants of the struggle remain. At the intersection of Ninth Street and Avenue C, across from a boutique cocktail bar ($14 for a cocktail made with cumin syrup and tobacco essence), there's a community garden called La Plaza Cultural, the same one started by Charas in the late 1970s, to which Matta-Clark may or may not have contributed a sculpture. Walking past the chain-link fence, you might peer in and imagine a different world unfolding from the moment of this chapter, what Robin D. G. Kelley calls works that "enable us to imagine a new society."[13] In pursuing the projects of the culture workers covered here, which range from Algarín and Piñero's Nuyorican Poets Cafe to El Bohío to the handball court across the street from the painter Martin Wong's apartment, I'll trace the possible futures outlined in these projects, what Algarín called "a constitution for survival on top of tar and concrete."[14]

Building and Poetry

In his account of redevelopment on the Lower East Side, Christopher Mele argues that, in response to the crisis's capital divestment and cutting of services, the Puerto Rican community deployed "music, poetry, painting, and even gardening" alongside "traditional tactics, such as rent strikes and demonstrations."[15] In the Lower East Side of the 1970s and 1980s, homesteading, gardening, and poetry assembled the same sets of actors—symbols of Puerto Rican identity, crumbling buildings, hands, texts—in order to rework Loisaida as a habitable place. In Lefebvre's framework, city planners like Rohatyn sought to flatten the neighborhood, whereby lived experience "invariably gets crushed and vanquished by conceived *abstract space*."[16] Poets, builders, and gardeners resisted the imposition of abstract space by counterposing what Lefebvre calls "representational space," which summons "the history of a people as well as in the history of each individual belonging to the people."[17] Aesthetic symbols—starting with the neighborhood's new name, Loisaida—became a potent way to counter city planners' vision for the neighborhoods. Poems, occupied buildings, and gardens were infused with symbols of Puerto Rican history, asserting the rights of these residents to their city.

Through the work of poet and builder alike, the oppressive dictates of space momentarily fell away and new possibilities opened up. On the one hand, the Nuyorican poets I discuss here sought to alleviate feelings of spatial oppression. In "Gray Worlds," the poet Sandra Maria Esteves describes, "walls endlessly dead" which are "unconcerned for people who merely exist," for whom "to survive" is "no more than grayness."[18] On the other hand, poets and homesteaders alike sought to rebuild the environment such that grayness transformed into color. When the poet Pedro Pietri writes, "look at your hands / that is where the definition of magic / is located at," he could be talking about a builder, gardener, or a poet.[19] This magic flowed through hammer and pen, shovel and typewriter, building and paper. The crisis assembled new arrangements of people, ideas, buildings, and tools. In what follows, I'll suggest that the arrangements created by the Nuyorican poets mirror those created by builders and gardeners.

In the very midst of the crisis, Algarín and Piñero developed a do-it-yourself institution that forcefully articulated a local poetics of what they dubbed "Nuyorican" identity. Like "Loisaida," the term "Nuyorican" was itself revisionist, deriving from an insult thrown at the pair while they were visiting Puerto Rico.[20] Algarín founded the Nuyorican Poets Cafe in his apartment in 1973, later renting a bar on 505 East Sixth Street.[21] The Cafe was both an addition to the long list of literary institutions in the Lower East Side—with the St. Mark's Poetry Project being the most prominent— and an institution devoted to the local practices of neighborhood Puerto Ricans.[22] Indeed, Algarín has reflected that St. Mark's was out of reach for "neighborhood people from Avenue A and Sixth Street," thus necessitating the building of a new institution, the Cafe. Even as some poets—notably, Allen Ginsberg—read at both venues, the Nuyorican Poets Cafe developed its own, Puerto-Rican-centered identity. In starting the Cafe, Algarín and Piñero extended the legacy of street-level organizations like the Young Lords and Chino Garcia's Real Good Society. In the late sixties, these groups had fought the marginalization of working-class Puerto Ricans by demanding that the city recognize the real needs of impoverished communities like Loisaida and by creating their own, pragmatic institutions for the provision of housing, food, and other essential needs.[23] My work here focuses on the initial iteration of the Cafe; in the 1990s, the Cafe, opened in a new location, became famous as a locus for the "slam poetry" movement of that decade.

The anthology that Algarín published three years later, *Nuyorican Poetry*, would directly reference the crisis as a key force shaping the poets' work. Drawing on poets who had read at the Cafe, the anthology included work from Pietri and Esteves, as well as work by emerging writers like George Lopez and Martita Morales. In publishing the anthology, Algarín and Piñero capitalized on a wave of interest in Puerto Rican letters, inspired by everything from the highly visible activism of the Young Lords to the staging of Piñero's *Short Eyes* at Lincoln Center in 1973. Published by William Morrow, the anthology was designed to reach a wide audience, entailing what Urayoán Noel calls "an effort to legitimize New York Puerto Rican literature beyond the carefully regulated terrain of both mainstream and mainstream Puerto Rican literary traditions."[24] And yet, courting a wider audience by no means translated into quietism. Algarín included five poems from Pietri, whose "Puerto Rican Obituary" had appeared in the Young Lords' *Palante*; Esteves was similarly active in the Young Lords.[25] By containing such work in a well-constructed anthology, Algarín foregrounded and continued the community-building facets of the Lords' project, which had included, for example, day care programs and door-to-door testing for lead poisoning.

The anthology was an assertion of Puerto Rican life as it was lived in New York, replete with desperate settings within which speakers make strong claims for their right to live. Algarín recognized that the 1975 crisis was heavily bound up in assessing neighborhoods for their viability. As a result, Algarín knew that publishing such work entailed risks. Readers might be tempted to view the poems as missives from an abject world, where both landscape and humans are broken. The inner city, went a certain line of argument, was irredeemable, a "territory full of violence and despair" inhabited by "a group beyond mainstream politics and society" whose men posed a "menace" and whose women "avoided work, birthed illegitimate children, and lived on the charity of the welfare state."[26] Calls for austerity were driven by references to a so-called "culture of poverty" which held that "features that make the slum repellent to others actually please [the low-class individual]."[27] As I noted in chapter 1, neglected city neighborhoods provided for the welfare state's critics a prominent example of its failure. For such critics, the image of the decayed neighborhood occupied by irredeemable, unproductive figures offered evidence for how anti-poverty programs in particular had failed. Drawing on these narratives, the architects of the crisis argued that the city could no longer afford to provide services for "everyone," by which these administrators generally meant the impoverished.

Depictions of a "depraved" or "abandoned" site also threatened to provide real estate developers with rationales for why whites should move to the neighborhood: because it was a source of fascinating risks and invigorating danger. Literary critic Thomas Heise describes this view as imagining a "space that middle-class residents have sought to enter, not just run in fear from, a space in which to fantasize about other ways of living and being or to seek refuge from the stultifying domesticity that otherwise occupied their lives."[28] The middle classes flee the inner city with capital and return their gaze to the sites where capital has fled in order to renew and rethink their own situatedness in capital networks. In the 1980s, the favored term for this formulation was "frontier," as explained by the geographer Neil Smith in *The New Urban Frontier: Gentrification and the Revanchist City*.[29] The "frontier" term, with its settler-colonialist implications, has continued to haunt notions of "occupying" urban space, as Eve Tuck and K. Wayne Yang observe.[30] As both Heise and Smith argue, terms like "underworld" and "frontier" tend to obscure the lively world of neighborhoods like the Lower East Side, overlooking the many efforts to challenge the forces of urban policy and capital withdrawal.

Threading a path between the Scylla of the neighborhood's conditions and the Charybdis of the underclass narrative, Algarín needed to find ways to frame the poems' stark material as nevertheless part of a productive city. He needed both to refute the notion that Loisaida was a place apart *and* point to conditions that really were desperate. To do so, he introduces the anthology using housing rehabilitation as a metaphor, citing the work of street-based organizations who have organized to rebuild housing.[31] Describing a meeting between two such groups, the Renegades of Harlem and the Dynamite Brothers of the Lower East Side, Algarín observes that the two groups find common cause in moving from "street clubhouse rumbles to concrete decisions about rehabilitating buildings."[32] By taking over vacant lots and empty buildings, these organizations acknowledge the neighborhood's problems and show that the people who live in the neighborhood are productive, intelligent, and willing to address these problems. For Algarín, these efforts, especially when taken up by ex-gang members, offer a perfect analogy for the poems. These groups, after all, must communicate both with one another and with city institutions. In doing so, "two languages have met. The outlaw meets the institution."[33] The complicated interaction between street group, city institution, and community produces what the literary critic Mikhail Bakhtin calls a heteroglossic language, a mix whereby, in Algarín's words, "English nouns function as verbs," "Spanish verbs function as adjectives," and "raw verbs and raw nouns" express the "quality of experience."[34] In this way, Algarín describes the poets' project as attuned to community needs and committed to building something new. In order to avoid being shut down by city officials, after all, groups like the Dynamite Brothers and Renegades had to find ways of explaining their project to outsiders.

This was the larger mission of homesteading. Residents of Loisaida took the built environment into their hands and sought their own DIY solutions to the problems of the 1975 crisis. Homesteading began as an informal process, often called "squatting," but evolved into a practice supported and enabled by a network of organizations that provided money and expertise. Organizations such as the Lower East Side Catholic Area Conference, the Housing Development Institute, Nazareth Home, and Rehabilitation in Action to Improve neighborhoods led these efforts.[35] The city, haven taken ownership of a large number of landlord-abandoned buildings, responded by creating homesteading programs to assist these organizations, under the management of the Division of Alternative Management Programs. For example, the 1978 Tenant Interim Lease program let homesteaders manage, and eventually own, city-owned buildings.[36] While the number of buildings rehabilitated was small, both homesteading and squatting exerted a symbolic force that inspired a wider "community politics of resistance against disinvestment."[37] Homesteading became a vital way to reclaim housing stock that landlords had abandoned to the city, a rich source of neighborhood identity, and an assertion that the neighborhood's infrastructure was to be under the control of forces other than the free market. Such DIY building constituted a sustained response to the deprivations of the city both before and after the crisis. These DIY projects pointed, too, to an alternate future for the neighborhood than that promised by the Emergency Financial Control Board: homesteading became a means of resisting the demands for privatization that emerged around the crisis. Homesteading was particularly useful, for example, in rescuing city-owned buildings from real estate developers who would have surely evicted current residents. At the same time, homesteading, like so much of the other work I describe in this book, became itself a market-based solution to problems that were once solved by government funding.

Algarín imagined that poetry, like homesteading, might revive what he called "dead cities with no industry and no money to rehabilitate them."[38] Born in the Lower East Side, Algarín was immersed in the lived circumstances of demanufacturing, white flight, and capital withdrawal that both preceded and were accelerated by the 1975 crisis. As Juan Flores explains, the identity of Nuyoricans is inextricable from the material conditions in which Puerto Ricans came to occupy New York. "Prior to any cultural associations or orientations," Flores argues, "there are the abandoned buildings, the welfare lines, the run-down streets, the frigid winter nights with no heat . . . the conditions of hostility, disadvantage, and exclusion that confront the Puerto Rican in day-to-day reality."[39] As did many an observer in the 1970s and 1980s, Flores uses the abandoned building as a synecdoche for the set of material conditions against which the Puerto Rican poet struggles. These conditions include shabby apartments, bad schools, and difficult-to-find jobs. All of these threatened to dissolve Puerto Ricans into the landscape.

By and large, the anthology's poems assert themselves against dissolution, making sharp claims about the conditions in which their speakers struggle. The poems articulate a world that threatens to become formless. In "Twice a Month Is Mother's Day," Piñero describes a speaker whose "walls" are cloth; "Mama pushed back the walls of my room," and she has to "[remove] dead roaches from the coffee cup" as well as rats who will not die even though they consume "lead-paint-chippin' plaster."[40] Speakers pick roaches out of their cereal, compare themselves to "rat poison that will get into / the corner of the corner of the streets,"[41] and frame their surroundings in terms of "leadbase paint" and "rivers of garbage & filth."[42] In "A Poem for Joey's Mami's Struggle," Piñero traces a grim environment:

> On the top floor
> the fifth floor next door to god
> joe's little hermanito & big sister
> celebrate their years of pain
> their mother's years of strain receive
> an ode with miller high life beer
> flowin' freely from hand to mouth
> & back again.[43]

T. C. Garcia similarly hears "the futile sound of poverty / Divided 'n' afraid by stomach growls that envy / The shine of a car before the odor of baked bread."[44] Esteves describes "bedroom walls bare stagnant water / drenched colorless laugh" in which she dreams of "trees are where i wish to live / and play the dance of chinese wind chimes."[45] Throughout *Nuyorican Poetry*, speakers locate themselves in a landscape of deprivation as well as hope, reinforcing the strategy praised by Flores, whereby documenting lived conditions offers both a forceful articulation of identity and a critique of the forces that had wrought such conditions.[46]

However, it was still possible that a general reader might view the anthology as a missive from one of the "mysterious, menacing, pathogenic and isolated districts at the core of American cities" inhabited by a frightful underclass.[47] Such readers might, in other words, read the formlessness decried by the poets as an intractable feature of impoverished Puerto Ricans' lives. To counter such readings, the anthology contains its formlessness within a tight organization. The relatively short book is divided into three sections, each of which features an introduction by Algarín that carefully situates these poems for the reader. It is as if the roiling energies of the poems and the disorganized space out of which they emerge need to be contained by being explained. Poems might be "the story of people who are looking out at the system and trying to deal with it . . . [moving] out and [trying] to direct the bureaucracy."[48] Poems might also become what Algarín calls *dusmic*, "the process of transforming aggression being directed at you by another person (or, more generally, society) into your strength."[49] The book's structure provides an interface between the necessary formlessness expressed by the poems and the intact networks of the larger city.

In order to establish Loisaida as a place worth saving, housing activists and poets alike would need to challenge narratives of the underclass while simultaneously calling attention to the very real lived conditions of working-class Puerto Ricans. Their mission, as Algarín put it, was to "create a language that can absorb aggression without fantasy" and "insist on our right to make our words communicate our experience."[50] Here, Algarín alludes to a trope that has worried many a critic of Puerto Rican letters: the figure of the male "outlaw," who asserts a powerful identity that is bound to criminality and violence but risks being reduced to a "primitive" stereotype. This trope was a defining feature, for example, of Piri Thomas's 1969 *Down These Mean Streets*, and Piñero himself was often willing to deploy this trope as a means to attract interest and funding from white audiences. In the introduction to the "outlaw" section of the anthology, Algarín wrestles with a view of his neighborhood that he understands will shape the reception of *Nuyorican Poetry*.[51] He does so by reference to a 1975 Mel Gussow *New York Times* review of Cienfuegos's play *Conga Mania*. In this review, Gussow describes the play as the "barely filtered" material of a New York pocket park.[52] Algarín understands what is at stake in Gussow's review. He'd seen the reception of Piñero's *Short Eyes*, widely lauded as the authentic expression of prison life, and so Algarín knows that Gussow is "rap[ping] on the knuckles" of an artist perceived in terms of primitivism, who, critics imagine, "do not alter but merely copy life as semidocumentary theatrical experiences."[53] Algarín seeks to frame the work of the poets in terms of efforts to resist the real forces bearing on the neighborhood, forces that are elided when readers simply see *Short Eyes*, *Conga Mania*, or the anthology's poetry as "raw." In other words, Algarín risked reinforcing associations between poverty and Puerto Rican identity—what the writer Edgardo Vega Yunqué calls the "sorry ass ghetto story"—that threatened to subsume these writers' vibrant creativity under the curious gaze of white outsiders.[54]

Of course, renovation was as much of a problem as it was a solution, since plenty of real estate developers wanted to renovate the Lower East Side, too. We can see the contrast between different types of renovation in the work of Esteves. In "i look for peace great graveyard," "renovation" creates an unlivable landscape, producing what Noel calls "the physical and psychic debris that defined the Nuyorican street poet."[55] The speaker in Esteves's "i look for peace great graveyard" worries that she has "no face" or "bones to hold my walk." "Empty nude and sleepless," lacking "peace," she wonders "when will earth cease renovation."[56] The poem moves between formlessness and forms that the speaker rejects: a "metal flavor ribbon" tied to "kill the dream" and "tied around my hands."[57] She ends the poem by identifying a form that suits her: "trees are where I wish to live," where she might "play the dance of chinese wind chimes" and "hear the ancient pipe the breath / that touches my eye to see."⁵⁸ But a few years later, in her collection *Yerba Buena*, Esteves develops an alternate view of renovation. That collection ends with a poem, "a pile of wood," that directly relates the writing of poetry to work of the housing-rehabilitating Renegades, to whom the poem is dedicated. It begins by engaging the language of disintegration in "i look for peace": "dreams crumbling / waves breaking." But instead of remaining in this state, the plural speakers "take the hammers in our hands" and "build / a place called home." Building becomes an assertion of identity: "becoming who we want to be / taking hammers / we change / Y la gente saben que somos la tierra / con fuegos y manos junto cambiamos" ("And the people know that we are the land / with fire and hand together we change").⁵⁹ Reading the poem, the critic Eliana Ortega makes a similar claim to the one I'm trying to make. "The personal 'I' already liberated thus becomes the collective 'I,'" Ortega writes. She continues, "the 'we change' of a new generation that has become aware of their present reality and the need for a radical change right here and now."⁶⁰ That "radical change" occurs through rebuilding, assembling hammers, wood, and ground. "A pile of wood" imagines that simple tools can refashion ruins into an environment suitable for the speaker. Here and elsewhere, metaphors of rebuilding circulated as strategies to contest notions of Puerto Rican poets as *merely* describing their formless lives.

But rebuilding can also means limiting oneself to restoring what once was, and poets as well as activists wanted to create something new at the same time. Here, community gardening served as a critical metaphor for an as-yet-undefined future. In the "Social Space" chapter of *The Production of Space*, Lefebvre returns repeatedly to the image of a garden as a metaphor for how cities grow.⁶¹ Writing in the early 1970s, Lefebvre is looking back to cities like Venice and scrutinizing how the production of space involves multiple forces and actors, such that any given space, if it has not been too heavily managed by planners, grows organically. For Lefebvre, the organic often names spaces that are dynamic, that might offer futures other than those futures designated by planners. Of course, such spaces can just as easily become symbols, or be reserved for elites, or become empty, unusable spaces. A community garden, though, can be something altogether different: an attempt to reinstall a rhythm of the city in which all citizens can participate.

In the wake of the 1975 New York fiscal crisis and its attendant abandonment of property, the empty spaces of the Lower East Side were increasingly occupied by informal, innovative gardens. They were developed by a combination of countercultural activists, such as the Green Guerillas, and Puerto Rican Americans, who, as Miranda J. Martinez describes, fashioned their gardens in ways that mimicked similar gardens in Puerto Rico:

> [The] casita garden is designed to evoke traditional rural Puerto Rican life. The casita (or "little house") is an elevated wooden cabin whose design has been traced back to the indigenous Tainos. They are usually brightly painted to evoke dwellings on the island. They are conscious statements of pride in Puerto Rican folk culture, and they are practical by making the garden usable almost year round. Besides the casita, these gardens have some other common features that mark it as a familial, Puerto Rican identified space. There is commonly a shrine to the Virgin Mary and a Puerto Rican flag. Gardeners will decorate the garden as though it were a private home.[62]

Often, such gardens served as a literal extension of home; Puerto Rican American families would gather in them to enjoy a respite from overcrowded apartments. Community organizations like Charas supported the creation of such gardens, linking them to rising neighborhood activism around property ownership and city services.

The aesthetics of the gardens were cultivated as a reaction to, not a building upon, the post-crisis decay. As such, the gardens contrast a range of artistic projects that appeared in the 1970s and 1980s that fostered an image of urban ruin. By and large, the gardens, as both Sharon Zukin and Martinez have argued, were established in reaction to the political forces that sought to marginalize and defund neighborhoods like the Lower East Side. Even as they began to be supported by the city during the Beame administration, the gardens remained sites that stubbornly insisted on an alternate future than the one prescribed by the end of the welfare state and the market-based reforms posed by landowners. The gardens served wider aesthetic aims in the context of a neighborhood largely written off by city government. At the same time, the gardens' aesthetic force relied on a contrast with the decay around them, and some gardens—La Plaza Cultural, and to a lesser extent, Adam Purple's Garden of Eden—emphasized such contrast by incorporating reused materials from the broken city. But overall—from the homegrown *casitas* constructed by migrants from Puerto Rico in homage to their home country, to the countercultural impulse of the Liz Christy garden and the other works of the Green Guerillas—the gardens were intended to foster futures of neighborhood growth and self-sufficiency.

The anthology nods to the work of these gardeners through its many horticultural metaphors. "We have to grow," writes T. C. Garcia in "Under an Apple Tree," or "die on dirty poverty-stained corners" because "revolution is nothing other / than perpetual change."[63] In "The Book of Genesis According to Saint Miguelito," Piñero depicts a God who creates "ghettos and slums" with "leadbase paint," "garbage and filth," and "heroin & cocaine," which leave the people "lonely and hungry" and beget racism, exploitation, Wall Street, and foreign wars. The mood of the poem is defiant but bleak, aside from one short section:

> But before God got on that t.w.a.
> for the sunny beaches of Puerto Rico
> He noticed his main man satan
> planting the learning trees of consciousness
> around his ghetto edens

The only moment of optimism in the poem's bleak landscape, the trees of consciousness offer a minor but substantial oasis, the kind offered, in the context of the post-crisis 1970s of the Lower East Side, by the gardens that slowly spread throughout the neighborhood's vacant lots. Using a similar framework, in "Bruja," Jesús Papoleto Meléndez contrasts a plastic plant that "will not grow" with a *bruja* from Puerto Rico that "would have dug its hole / in through that concrete that is mand-made / & found itself a home / deep / where the earth is warm again," continuing "it would have raised its hand / to throw its brick / too."[64] In the poems of the anthology, natural imagery stands against the buildings and all they represent—green brujas, planted in a do-it-yourself garden.

In his conclusion to the anthology, Algarín writes, "A poem describes the neighborhood of the writer for the reader. There are poems, or rather, there are poets who describe conditions that are either in the past or in the future."[65] Algarín describes two temporalities here. The conditions of the past are all around him—the tenement buildings that badly need rehabilitating. The conditions of the future are planted around the corner, in the community gardens. Algarín rehearses a theme found across Nuyorican literature. Abandoned buildings and their rehabilitation are core to the Nuyorican literary project as it took shape in the 1970s and 1980s. Nuyorican writers as well as activists imagine their work as what Lefebvre calls a "spatial practice" that they hope will alter the space of the Lower East Side as it is represented to them. Bad landlords and abandoned buildings serve as synecdoches for lived life under "planned shrinkage," the widespread sense that these neighborhoods had been written off by the city. Their work serves as early documentation of how urban space is governed in the long crisis, with some built environments, home to an "unproductive" underclass, being abandoned altogether, and other built environments, home to a "productive" creative class, relying on aesthetics to attract capital. Housing activists and poets alike refuted notions that the Lower East Side was an abject, unproductive space—the kind of space that architects of the 1975 crisis had presented as evidence that the welfare state had failed. They entwined the problem of rehabilitating space with the problem of asserting that impoverished Puerto Ricans were adaptive, productive, responsible, and, indeed, entrepreneurial subjects. They refuted, in short, every characteristic attributed to impoverished Puerto Ricans by advocates of the underclass theory. Their efforts would be carried forward into the 1980s at a larger scale through an organization run by one of the anthology's poets, Bimbo Rivas, who worked with Chino Garcia, one of the housing rehabilitators that Algarín references in his introduction. Working with the organization Adopt-a-Building, the pair took over an entire abandoned school building and made it into, among other things, a theater.

El Bohío and Tenant Advocacy

On Tenth street, between Avenues C and D, the old P.S. 64 building had sat empty since 1975, a result, like so much else, of a combination of withdrawn city funding and neighborhood depopulation.[66] In the immediate wake of the crisis, public buildings such as schools, libraries, firehouses, and hospitals had become intense sites of resistance to government austerity.[67] Within the damaged, funds-starved environment of the Lower East Side, the empty school was a vector for action. Getting in was no problem. Someone had stolen the door. Someone had also stolen the wiring, parts of the plumbing, and the copper roof.[68] Seeing opportunity where others saw ruin, the members of Charas worked with Adopt-a-Building, took over the five-story building, and renovated it. Adopt-a-Building had recently received a federal Comprehensive Employment Training Act grant and had already begun training local residents as electricians, plumbers, and general contractors. They ramped up this training program for P.S. 64, repairing walls, rewiring electricity and phone service, pumping water out of the boiler room, and sealing off sections too dangerous to use.[69] They transformed the building into a center of neighborhood activism and aesthetic activity that would have a massive impact on the activist cultures of the Lower East Side; the aftereffects continue to reverberate.[70]

Applying the methods of homesteading on a larger scale, Charas did it themselves.[71] In the Charas archive at the Center for Puerto Rican Studies, there's a photo album that depicts groups of people moving in and out of the building, doing the work of rehabilitation. While, as von Hassel notes, the energies of homesteading were often directed at family dwellings, such homesteading occurred in a large, infrastructural sense in the rehabilitation of P.S. 64, which became the cultural and outreach center El Bohío after a long effort by community groups. Writing in the early 1990s, Maffi calls Charas "a true bulwark in Loisaida" that survived "gentrification, displacement, drugs, [and] decay."[72] Charas took over the building completely in 1981 and established the location as a cultural center. They hosted artists, dance performances, Teatro Charas, photography workshops, and a film series. From its origins with Garcia's Real Great Society in the 1960s, Charas continually built innovative programs that mixed artistic production with community outreach.

P.S. 64 was one of many buildings that were repurposed with the needs of residents in mind. A vital energy coursed through these efforts, driven by the powerful framework of do-it-yourself. Many of these efforts were documented by *The Quality of Life in Loisaida*, the monthly newsletter produced by Mary McCarthy and the Adopt-a-Building organization from March 1978 to December 1992. *The Quality of Life* presents a vital cross-section of endeavors to curtail, moderate, and fight landlord abandonment, the withdrawal of public services, and city-promoted gentrification. The January-February 1985 issue, entitled "Do-It-Yourself," reflects upon and sums up these efforts. The cover of the issue depicts a group of people, mixed in race, age, and gender. They are gathered in front of a visibly neglected building on Eighth Street between Avenues B and C. On either side of the building's doors, someone has painted black rectangles over a palimpsest of graffiti. The rectangles have two messages painted in white. On the left: "Don't Mourn, Organize Homes for the Poor." On the right: "Think of This As Low Cost Housing."[73] The people in the photo look ready to follow the murals' advice. They are gathered in small groups, standing erect, poised with purpose, and they appear to be prepared to enter the building and start a homestead. Inside, the issue offered examples of what the title meant. One article explained "Do-It-Yourself Banking": after the Manufacturers Hanover Trust on East Third Street closed, a community group opened the Lower

East Side People's Federal Credit Union.[74] An article called "Start Your Own Agency" similarly detailed the work of the Sixth Street Community Center in a formerly abandoned synagogue.[75] The center provided social services, job counseling, and education, and continues to survive today. Another page offered even more practical advice: instructions on how to make patchwork draperies out of fabric remnants. For the editors of *The Quality of Life in Loisaida*, do-it-yourself meant taking into your own hands what the government has stopped providing. The journal also included, notably, poetry, reviews of plays, and suggestions on how to make art. This use of the phrase outside of where we'd normally expect to find it—in the liner notes to a punk album, uttered from the stage at an underground music festival—speaks to the way the concept moved from group to group, building to building, assembling new sets of actors wherever it went. Well-meaning and complicit, activist and entrepreneurial, do-it-yourself became a widely shared ethos in the Lower East Side after the fiscal crisis.

Sharing and embodying all the social and political concerns of *The Quality of Life in Loisaida*, El Bohío was inspired by aesthetic concerns from the beginning. In short order, it opened a gallery, set up studio space—used by Keith Haring, among other artists, created a cinematheque, and organized programs to teach the arts.[76] For the purposes of my study, the most significant activity of El Bohío involved its theater, which, in the hands of Chino Garcia and Bimbo Rivas, served as a site for inspiration, a means of publicly narrating lived conditions, and a source of reflection on the promises and limitations of El Bohío itself. Long before the occupation of P.S. 64, Chino Garcia and Bimbo Rivas wrote and performed *Don Quixote de Loisaida*, which rewrote the story of Don Quixote into the Lower East Side. The pair performed segments of the play around the neighborhood as well as at theater festivals around the city. As Garcia recollects, performing the play brought the pair into contact with activist theater groups who had been working in the city since the 1960s, including The Living Theatre, Bread and Puppet Theater, and Teatro Campesino.[77] From the start, Garcia, like many an activist in the 1960s and 1970s, saw the seemingly impractical work of theater and the pragmatic work of housing activism as intertwined. One way to accomplish this was to sponsor theatrical projects that worked in a more or less direct mode, as had the poets of the Nuyorican anthology. Both Tee Saralegui's *How Would You Handle a Rent Strike?* and Emily Rubin and Luiz Guzman's *We Don't Want Cheese, We Want Apartments, Please* document the housing struggles and material problems of Loisaida. *How Would You Handle a Rent Strike?*, for example, describes a day in the life of Maria and Pedro Gonzales, a couple who live in the Lower East Side and suffer the negative effects of a neglectful landlord.[78] Performed in La Plaza Cultural, the community garden adjoining El Bohío, these plays are a direct extension of housing activism, using realism to document the community's problems.

But Rivas had been around long enough and been involved in enough struggles to understand the limits of this documentary approach. In his own plays, Rivas reflected on the possibilities, contradictions, and pragmatic problems of running El Bohío.[79] In plays like *Winos* and *Benito y Vasconpique*, Rivas drew out the issues that Algarín had worried over in the 1975 anthology. In particular, Rivas considered the tendency of outsiders to view Loisaida as an abject space of curiosity and its cultural productions as lively murals in a blighted landscape. He did so by developing texts that were highly reflexive about their literary work and reception.

In metatextual fashion, *Winos* features several actors who are trying to stage a play in Tompkins Square Park. They use the techniques of "method acting"—a trope that the play repeatedly has fun with, seemingly playing on the dissonance between the "degraded" site of the park and the "elevated" techniques made famous by the Actors' Studio in New York. Reviewing the 1981 production in the *New York Amsterdam News*, Yusef Salaam describes its central conceit: "the play concerns either winos in a park pretending to be method actors and/or method actors pretending to be winos . . . the play is a fantasy looking at reality and/or reality looking at fantasy."[80] The actor Jose has spent time living as a wino, though he drinks grape juice instead of wine ("so much that my urine is coming out black"). But as the play's creators, Eusebio and Cinderello, develop Jose into his part, the play's action is superseded by "real" drama in the Square, a lover's triangle involving the wayward Margo. The play continually blurs lines between the street life of the park and its own staging, suggesting the complicated ways in which Rivas saw his art relating to the community. To add further complexity, the play adds a white, middle-class character, a "lady" who walks her dog, Geraldo, through the park while her chauffer awaits. The other characters' interactions with Lady stage problems of class conflict.

> CINDERELLO: Hey lady not on the pantry. Take him somewhere else.
>
> LADY: Why? Tompkins Square park is for everybody. Including you Geraldo.

EUSEBIO: Is she for real? Hey lady! Our dinner is in there. Take that mutt away from here.

LADY: Come Geraldo. The people around here are not very friendly. Might as well be in Peoria.[81]

This comical interaction foregrounds different uses of the park (walking one's dog versus sleeping/eating/staging a play) as well as a gulf in understanding between different types of residents in the Lower East Side. As the play progresses, the Lady begins to see herself as a spectator with a "ring side seat" for the actions in the park.[82] But whether she is there to see the play with Jose as a wino character or the hijinks of Tivo and Augusto is never clear. *Winos*, then, not only scrutinizes the line between lived life in Loisaida but also asks how outsiders might confuse the two. Such problems seem to arise every time working-class Puerto Rican Americans interact with the increasing presence of whites in the Lower East Side.

Benito y Vasconpique is similarly reflexive. Set in "a poor village called Loisaida," and concerning a campus occupation, the play foregrounds the infighting after students take over a city campus. Reflecting at once on the 1960s struggles that expanded CUNY to all students as well as the problems of managing an organization once such a takeover occurs, the play emphasizes the difficulty of making a place like El Bohío work. Professors fight with student activists; student activists fight with the university board. As the play unfolds, Professora Vasconpique ("goes with irritation") gives a tour of the occupied university (she "resembles a tourist guide pointing out the different landmarks en route"[83]) to two would-be donors to the cause. Rivas presents the professor as compromised; she brags of "my students . . . my disciples" who "have brought glory to my cause!"[84] She is also sexually involved with the leader of the occupation. The occupiers have decorated the campus with "the various symbols of the revolution—Puerto Rican flag, movement flag (red, black, and green)" as well as "the names of the great revolutionaries, 'Che lives,' 'Malcolm X Library,' 'Pedro Albizu campus is alive,' peace symbol love flowers painted with spray cans."[85] The leaders of the occupation spend much of their time drinking and having sex with students. The university president, Bull Palaguerra, has decided he will give in to the occupiers' demands. He will set up a "cool aid water fountain" [sic] and add "chittlings and cuchifritos" to the cafeteria menu. He will also institute a new policy whereby "no student is to receive a failing mark."[86] When a television reporter shows up, the occupation leader and Professora

Vasconpique quickly stage a pretend class: "That T.V. crew expects anarchy and disruption. We're gonna give them the calmest coolest show they ever seen."[87] Overall, the occupiers are concerned with appearances, the professor with consolidating her own power, and the president with spending as little money as possible and maintaining his image. The mother of the occupiers' leader brings dinner to him.[88] Eventually, the police show up. Rather than confront them, the students "move the revolution to Loisaida" and make the professor ambassador to Brooklyn.

Set in an institution, performed in a former institution, *Benito y Vasconpique* scrutinizes the politics and possibilities of occupying P.S. 64. Like the students, the leaders of Charas had to secure permission from authorities who ultimately limit what can be accomplished, wrestle with infighting and distractedness among the occupiers, and, above all, consider how the occupation appears to outsiders. In writing the play, Rivas—a former student at P.S. 64, now part of an organization facing problems similar to the student occupiers—asks, in a playful, satirical manner, whether El Bohío is delivering on its promises. *Benito y Vasconpique* self-consciously examines not just the legacy of the revolutionary sixties but the possibilities involved with setting up one's own institution within existing frameworks. By exaggerating the occupiers' self-representation—Che Guevara, countercultural clothing, Puerto Rican flags—Rivas knowingly points to how others in the city perceive Charas, an organization that grew out of Chino Garcia's own experience in the 1960s.

Rivas's work marks a shift in the literature discussed in this chapter. Rivas's "A Job" and "A Poem for Loisaida" both worked in a more or less documentary mode. His plays, however, moved in an expansive direction, deploying an inventive self-reflexivity that later writers would point to as inspiration for a Puerto Rican literary project that superseded a mode of direct reporting. Rivas brought the literary sensibilities of the Nuyorican Poets to bear on the task of forging a new neighborhood. This task was one in which abandoned school buildings could become not centerpieces for a rising confluence between artistic innovation and post-Fordist celebrations of the autonomous worker but centers of identity and policy reform, and one in which vacant lots could become not symbols of a ragged frontier for middle-class artists but sites of community exchange. Unlike Algarín and Piñero, Rivas was an active participant in anti-gentrification struggles. He attended, for example, an infamous Board of Estimates hearing on the Artists Homeownership Plan, in concert with the Lower East Side Joint Planning Council.[89] Building on the insights that Algarín and Piñero had about the possibilities of grounding otherwise precarious lives in the concrete sites of poetic declamation, Rivas installed the lofty imaginaries of the Nuyorican Poets Cafe into the seemingly dead sites of P.S. 64 and its surrounding lots. Rivas pushed his literary vision into sites off the literary map. Rivas, I'd suggest, is the most visible hinge between the tedious, incremental work of helping poor people survive amidst capital's flight and the literary/artistic sensibility that would too often provide fodder for the real estate developers and gallery owners who sold the neighborhood as a fitting location for capital's return.[90]

Rivas's concerns would be carried forward by Edgardo Vega Yunqué (who also went by Ed Vega), a writer who played the lead in Rivas's *El Piraguero de Loisaida*.[91] Written in the early 2000s, Vega Yunqué's *The Lamentable Journey of Omaha Bigelow Into the Impenetrable Loisaida Jungle* takes the Lower East Side as it existed at the end of the 1990s and infuses it with a fantastical, magical realist vision. Puerto Ricans living in the projects plot to build their own navy in order to kick the US out of Vinques; brujas change from monkeys, to squirrels, to peacocks, and back again; the interior of a project leads characters directly to Puerto Rico. Nothing has really changed for Puerto Ricans—they're still scoffed at by white bohemians, and still suffering from wage depression and poor living conditions—but the arts, of both the dark and theatrical variety, allow Puerto Ricans to maintain an ironic dominance over the city. Vega Yunqué sets his novel against what he calls "some silly ass Puerto Rican ghetto story" that risks being "all we're known for."[92] In developing this intervention, Vega Yunqué looks back not to Nuyorican poetry—though he does reference the Cafe—but to the theater of Rivas. Rich in reflexive commentary about gentrification, Puerto Rican letters, and political struggle, Vega Yunqué's novel reconsiders the dynamics around El Bohío. It works as a fictional counterpart to Mele's nonfictional account of gentrification (a work it invokes directly). For my purposes, the novel features two interesting characters. First, one of its prominent characters is a playwright named Samuel Becket Salsipuedes; second, it presents a Lower East Side in which Puerto Ricans have redeveloped their living spaces as sites of fantastic, transnational power. Salsipuedes has composed an absurdist play that overlaps significantly with *Benito y Vasconpique*. It is set in "a model of an 1898 Neo-Gothic style public school building with the letters VSC in front of it," and the play concerns "a group attempting to wrest power away from the protagonist, El Gato."[93] Readers hear about the play from Salsipuedes's mother. She struggles to understand it but concludes that such is its virtue: "She couldn't figure it out. This made her very happy. What was the use of going to a play that was dealing with everyday reality?"[94] Flaquita reads the play in her apartment in the projects, which, readers learn, has a magical link to Puerto Rico. A character steps out of a bedroom and is soon "walking on a sandy beach with water that was blue and emerald rolling in on white foamy waves."[95] Vega Yunqué takes Rivas's project and imagines how it might extend into a broadly transformed Lower East Side, one where Puerto Ricans are no longer a marginal underclass but a community that wields irrepressible power. *The Lamentable Journey of Omaha Bigelow* makes the case that Rivas's literary production, though it quickly disappeared, left a long legacy for Puerto Rican letters in the Lower East Side.

At the end of his "Nuyorican Literature" essay, Algarín counseled his readers to "create spaces where people can express themselves and create that space expressly for that purpose, and you open it three to four times a week, and you wait, and your public will come, and they will bring their writing."[96] As Noel notes, this "reads like an advertisement for the Nuyorican Poets Café,"[97] and yet, at least in the 1980s, El Bohío fits Algarín's description even more precisely. Like the Nuyorican Poets Cafe, El Bohío served as both a literary and physical institution. As it moved into the 1980s, it was set against, while benefiting from, the art movement that helped gentrify the Lower East Side during that decade. In contrast to many of these art cultures (including some of the literary cultures attached to the gallery movement), El Bohío entwined the efforts of homesteading with literary production, carrying forward the efforts of Algarín and Piñero to set literature against the rapidly coalescing view of the Lower East Side as an empty "frontier" populated only by unproductive members of the underclass. Surveying these efforts, the painter Martin Wong brought them to bear on the visual arts scene that, in Mele's terms, would shift the neighborhood's image from "marginal and inferior to central and intriguing," eventually offering real estate developers the means to accelerate gentrification.[98] I'll have more to say about these artists in chapter 4, where I discuss the interventions into this scene accomplished by the writers Gary Indiana and Lynne Tillman. Among this visual art, Martin Wong stood apart, as a painter who took the neighborhood's broken bricks and, like the writers and homesteaders I discuss here, imagined how they might be reorganized to sustain existing life instead of blotting it out.

Martin Wong and Bricks

As I briefly mentioned earlier, Latour compares networks of reference—the complex accounts of how human and nonhuman actants interact—to a construction site. Such networks, Latour observes, are less like a straight road and more like "the everyday work of a Department of Roads and Bridges, with its corps of structural engineers and the back-and-forth movements of bulldozers on the construction site of a public works project."[99] This image is a favorite of Latour's. Construction sites make visible the contingencies, local connections, and immediate accounts that make up the social, in contrast to the overarching, purified, meta-statements about "capital" or "influence." The construction site provides Latour with a way of knowing about humans' relationship to nonhuman actants such as bricks, nails, hammers, drywall, and boards. The projects that I describe above, from the Nuyorican Poets Cafe, to Charas, to community gardens, all entail a gamble on the future. In concluding this chapter, I'll using the paintings of Martin Wong to theorize this gamble. Both Wong's specific project of featuring bricks in his paintings as well as the circumstances of his life—he lived in a run-down apartment on Ridge Street that he partly rehabilitated—made him an apt commentator on the themes I explore in this chapter. Loisaida was one of Wong's great subjects, and after he met Piñero at an ABC/No Rio show, Wong began incorporating Piñero's poems into his paintings.

Noting that Wong "stood apart" from artists like Haring, Sherrie Levine, Kiki Smith, and Philip Taaffe, John Yau praises Wong as "an artist of the local" who "lovingly painted crumbling tenement walls, one brick at a time, chain link fences, padlocks, and shuttered steel gates."[100] Moving to the Lower East Side in the mid-1970s, Wong first lived in a hotel so broken down that the ceiling of his room had collapsed. By all accounts, Wong shrugged, picked up a broom, and cleared out a living space. When the hotel was shut down, Wong walked around the neighborhood and asked people on the street if they knew of a place he might live. He found junkies on a stoop who pointed to the building behind him and said that the top floor was empty. The urine-smelling building would be Wong's home for the next decade, and it was from this site that Wong painted most of his brick work.[101] Among the artists working in the Lower East Side, Wong's work, built brick by brick and figure by figure, was highly attuned to the living circumstances of the Puerto Rican underclass who suffered disproportionately from the effects of the 1975 fiscal crisis. That crisis had helped make bricks—strewn across vacant lots, falling out of buildings—more visible than they had been before. Like the Nuyorican poets, Wong sought to disturb what the philosopher Jacques Rancière calls "the distribution of the sensible."[102] This is the way that subjects perceive "spaces, times and forms of activity" that allow them to understand the degree to which they share common goals, and inspires them to partake in governance.[103] Rohatyn and others dismissed the lifeworld of the Lower East Side as blight, and others saw the neighborhood as a source of primitivist fascination. In these distributions of the sensible, loose bricks were evidence of social breakdown. Like the bricks, the people in the Lower East Side were imagined as disconnected from "something common that is shared."[104] The Nuyorican poets, builders, activists, and gardeners challenged this sense of connection. Reflecting on these challenges, Wong shows all the ways that dislodged bricks, like people, are lively actants in the landscape of the post-crisis Lower East Side.

In several paintings, the strategy Wong adopts recalls the Harold Rosenberg photographs that I discuss in chapter 1. Like Rosenberg, Wong situates small figures, full of life, against a backdrop of crumbling bricks and bricked up tenements. In *It's Not What You Think, What Is it Then?*, for example, a large tenement building with bricked-in windows occupies most of the 60-by-48-inch canvas. In the foreground, Wong has painted scattered debris. The building is flanked by shadows; above it hovers a red sky. The overall look is bleak and apocalyptic.

Figure 2.2. *It's Not What You Think, What Is it Then?*, 1984. Courtesy of the Estate of Martin Wong and P•P•O•W, New York.

This is the ruined cityscape with no life, the kind contrasted, in the discourse of the 1975 crisis, with the livable world elsewhere in the city. If you were Roger Starr or Felix Rohatyn, this is one of the areas of the city that merits "planned shrinkage."[105] Who, after all, could survive here? But in the lower left corner of the canvas, two people are not only surviving, they are thriving. Sitting on a discarded couch, a couple hold hands tenderly, looking into one another's eyes. Wong has painted a gold glow around their heads. The painting's message is one that Esteves and Algarín could recognize. In "For South Bronx," Esteves described "hills of desolate buildings / rows of despair / crowded together / in a chain of lifeless shells." But though these buildings look lifeless, "at every moment / like magic the shells breathe / and take on the appearance of second cousins."[106] Here and elsewhere, Wong deployed his art to offset narratives of an unproductive underclass, or the landscape of the Lower East Side as bereft of life. At the same time, he calls attention to the lived conditions that challenge the couple's attempt at life.

In *No Es Lo Que Has Pensado*, bricks exist as the couple finds them: in a building they cannot use, and strewn about them in an undifferentiated mass. Here, Wong represents bricks as inert objects. They are part of the background against which the couple strains for life. In many of Wong's other works bricks pulse with energy. They arrange themselves into bulletproof hearts, or assemble into a frame-within-a-frame. Like homesteading or gardening, a Wong painting activates the seemingly dead material of the seemingly dead city. In *Attorney St. Handball Court*, for example, Wong uses bricks to frame a graffiti-covered concrete wall in the handball court of the painting's title, as well as a Piñero poem and hands that spell out a rap lyric in sign language. Inside the bricks, the painting overflows with disorder: not just the graffiti, but the violence of Piñero's words and the rap lyric. The frame's tightly organized bricks hold this disorder in, but do not cancel it out. The bricks have assembled on behalf of what's inside. Other paintings organize bricks into an erect phallus (*Mi Vida Loca*, 1991), hearts (*Lower East Side Valentine*, 1983), an altar screen (*Chinese Altar Screen*, 1989), and the Statue of Liberty (*The Flood*, 1984; *Untitled (Statue of Liberty)*, 1988). Elsewhere, too, Wong simply depicts buildings with meticulous, perfect bricks, which form the backdrop to tender scenes of family life. In *The Babysitter* (1998), a man plays with a child in the foreground, while a smiling woman looks on from a window in the building. The building's carefully painted bricks look brand new; they are sized perfectly, and frame a fire escape doorway with a meticulous arch. The contrasts here are especially sharp when Wong turns his attention to the falling-down hotel where he first lived. *My Secret World* (1978–81) reimagines the hotel as intact, with, again, well-organized bricks that frame a bright living space filled with Wong's own paintings, books, and a neatly made bed. These painted buildings rejoin notions of the neighborhood as a "war zone" or a thrilling frontier, conveying both permanence and wholeness. Keeping the neighborhood's voices intact, while providing them with support. Wong does the work of a housing rehabilitator.

Wong sought to rebuild the Lower East Side as a site that at once carefully embraced the lived life of the neighborhood's impoverished residents (*La Vida*, to use the title of one of his better-known paintings) and imagine a future for this site that challenges narratives of redevelopment in favor of an aesthetics of building. Roy Pérez has described Wong's orientation to "Nuyorico" in terms of "proximity," by which Pérez means a queer unsettling of ethnic categories.[107] For Pérez, Wong's work does more than document—it disrupts and unsettles the ways that others view Nuyorico.[108] Concerned with the promises of a boundary-disturbing queerness, Pérez implicitly locates such settled interpretations with identity movements—here, "latinidad." Extending Pérez's analysis, I'd suggest that Wong's project disrupts other settled interpretations of the neighborhood from the era: notably, those interpretations that emphasized terms like "frontier," "underclass," and "artist." These terms, which continue to operate in discourses of redevelopment, enact a distribution of the sensible whereby neighborhoods like the Lower East Side serve as locales for harvesting particular modes of life. In particular, graffiti sometimes serves in such a context as a mark of risk that can transfer to middle-class rejuvenation. Simultaneously fascinated with enjoying and offsetting such risk, Wong both participated in constructions of the Lower East Side as abject and resisted these constructions. This tension emerges in what critics like Pérez and Ramirez have observed as an aesthetic of "too much" or "obsession" in Wong's work. Pérez finds a generosity in Wong's project, describing the painter as "bring[ing] the fragments of racist capitalism—the dusty, the minor, the broken, the stolen, the abject, lo malo—into the foreground with erotic tenderness."[109] In his essay, Pérez sets this generosity against a perceived hardness of Nuyorican identity—the outlaw formation that I discussed earlier in the chapter. But as I hope I've shown with the examples of the anthology and El Bohío, Wong was extending a larger structure of generosity as much as he was doing the necessary work of countering an image of an outlaw frontier. Wong's generosity emerged out a structure of feeling and a searching for allies that maintained in many quarters of the Lower East Side after the 1975 fiscal crash.

Like Algarín, Wong lodged himself in "cracks in the city's infrastructure"; Wong depicts inhabitants "trying to eke out an existence" in these cracks.[110] Chronicling a moment of capital withdrawal, Wong registers the slow work of the homesteaders, but also the paradoxical role that art played in accelerating changes in the neighborhood. His work manifests what the queer theorist Jose Muñoz calls queerness's "insistence on potentiality or concrete possibility for another world."[111] If that world was not to come, if both artists and the impoverished were inevitably shunted into outer boroughs to make room for white-collar service workers, Wong's paintings and Piñero's poetry nevertheless offer aesthetic accounts of poverty at a crucial moment that refuse to caricature the underclass. Working brick by brick, Wong's paintings foreground the world of community gardens, tenants' organizations, and homesteaders, as well as the more stubborn, less domesticated lives that circulated outside of these organizations. Wong emphasizes the contingency of the Lower East Side. The future might be one in which "La Vida" persists, or it might be one in which all the storefronts close. Painted meticulously, his bricks show viewers a neighborhood continually being built. By interlacing Piñero's poetry with these bricks, Wong returns to the themes with which Algarín introduces his anthology, whereby building—bricklaying—and the poetic project are interwoven. His carefully detailed depictions of "people celebrating being alive" belied exterior views of the Lower East Side as abject, unproductive, or an exotic site of middle-class thrills.[112]

Conclusion

From the beginning, even anteceding the founding of the Nuyorican Poets Cafe, the literary production of Puerto Rican Americans in the Lower East Side was tightly tied to housing advocacy. The diverse examples of Algarín, Piñero, Esteves, Rivas, and Wong demonstrate both the paradoxes and possibilities of Puerto Rican literary art during this era. At times participating in characterizations of the neighborhood as an "outlaw" zone, at times taking up pen to fight the development that took advantage of such characterization, but almost always attending to the lived reality of the post-crisis built environment, the network of writers and artists discussed in this chapter bears witness to the cultural, political, and economic pressures exerted on working-class culture production during the ascendance of post-Fordism. Few of these culture workers made it out of the struggle alive; only Tato

Laviera, Algarín, and Pietri continued working into the twenty-first century, and all three fought poverty and disease for the rest of their lives. At once participating in a long history of ethnic literature in New York and pointing to sites where such literature faced long odds even in the better conditions of post-sixties literary production, the examples of these writers demonstrate the complicated impact of a shift from Fordist to post-Fordist modes of governance.

The Nuyorican poets developed institutions and projects that would support their literary assertions of identity and critique the living conditions of Puerto Rican New Yorkers. In doing so, they found in building rehabilitators a ready-made model for their work. In the poetry of the Nuyoricans, buildings tend to be sources of oppression—they are an important, and generally awful, interface between capital and disempowered subjects. In these poems, landlords charge too much rent, plumbing doesn't work, kitchens and bathrooms are sites of entrapment. In this respect, it makes sense that a significant portion of the Nuyorican project was devoted to idealizing the street, whether as figured as an outlaw zone or shared public space. To be inside was to be limited, and constantly reminded of one's disempowerment.

In several of Wong's important works, the sky seems ablaze. In *Sweet Oblivion,* for example, red-rimmed clouds form the backdrop to abandoned buildings and a vacant lot strewn with rubble. *The Flood* similarly features a red sky, as does *Stanton Near Forsyth.* Fires were and are an important way to represent the 1975 fiscal crisis: fires were set by landlords to collect insurance money and clear land for later development. In a national context, a phrase supposedly uttered by Howard Cosell while announcing the 1977 World Series, "the Bronx is burning," became shorthand for the city's troubles.[113] And in the summer of 1975, almost all of the fire stations threatened with closure saw protests.[114] Garth Hallberg's 2015 novel about the era is called *City on Fire.*[115] Apocalyptic, to be sure. And yet, the glowing skies in Wong's paintings, might also point to another reading, whereby the Lower East Side becomes apocalyptic, but in the sense of being open to multiple futures, as Julie Ault observes of Wong's paintings.[116] All of the culture workers I describe in this chapter looked around at the falling-down buildings produced by the crisis, and saw only ways to create spaces that might bear up such futures.

Chapter 3

Semiotext(e), Kathy Acker, and the Decline of the Welfare State

As I've been arguing in the past two chapters, the 1975 fiscal crisis wrought a revolution in both governance and aesthetics. Within this context, culture workers and critics alike sought new ways of describing the changed world of the 1970s. They found key terms that they could use in the writing of Michel Foucault, Gilles Deleuze, Félix Guattari, Jean Baudrillard, and others. This work circulated in the Lower East Side through a series of little black books published by Semiotext(e).[1] Those books grew out of a project that began in the same year as the fiscal crisis, when the critic and theorist Sylvère Lotringer held a conference at Columbia University entitled "Schizo-Culture."[2] Lotringer intended the conference to promote his new journal *Semiotext(e)* and introduce ideas that had been circulating in France but that had not yet found a foothold in the United States. Speakers at the conference included Deleuze, Guattari, Foucault, and Jean-François Lyotard. Of the four, only Foucault was well known in the United States; his *Madness and Civilization*, *The Order of Things*, and *The Archeology of Knowledge* had been published in the 1960s, and Foucault had already held positions at various American universities.[3] In the coming decades, all four men would go on to be household names in what came to be called "French theory." Their theory, though, was of a different sort than that which emerged at the famous 1966 "Languages of Criticism and the Sciences of Man" conference at Johns Hopkins. That conference, which prominently featured Jacques Derrida and Paul de Man, can be understood as the birth of deconstruction in the United States. The "Schizo-Culture" conference concerned, instead, "micropolitics," which traces the effects of power in seemingly surprising places: hospitals, schools, the psychiatrist's office. As a consequence of this institutional focus, micropolitical theory contents that we can learn about the political by focusing on those subjects repressed by these institutions, "explor[ing] the marginalized and excluded in order to challenge the pretenses of dominant epistemological and discursive systems."[4] As we've seen in the previous chapters, the "marginalized and excluded" were of intense interest to culture workers and policy makers alike in 1970s New York.

While micropolitics would be applied to all sorts of excluded populations at the "Schizo-Culture" conference, "marginalized and excluded" often meant, sometimes implicitly but often overtly, the underclass. On the one hand, this strand of theory was well-equipped to challenge a rising surveillance of the underclass whose habits and familial relations came under increasing scrutiny as the welfare state was dismantled.[5] On the other hand, this theory, broadly understood as a turn away from class politics and political economy, was ill suited to analyze the capital-driven austerity emerging from the crisis. The odd juxtaposition of this theory and the 1975 crisis would set a template for an ongoing incongruity between the theory circulating in humanities departments and the austerity constraining the futures of both the underclass and the universities housing these departments. Returning to the "Schizo-Culture" conference from the standpoint of the 2010s demonstrates that the oft-noticed tendency for such theory to abjure political economy was there from the start.

Like other institutions in my study, *Semiotext(e)* began as a do-it-yourself affair. It was founded in 1972 as one of a string of theory journals established across the United States. Unlike its peers, *Semiotext(e)* had little support from its host institution, Columbia University. Jeffrey Williams notes that these journals were widely sponsored by universities—which were in turn funded by the state. The quintessential story of the theory journal is that of *New Literary History* at the University of Virginia, where the president gave Roger Cohen $14,000 a year to begin a new journal.[6] As such, journals like *New Literary History* can be conceived of as "capacious beneficiar[ies] of the welfare state."[7] *Semiotext(e)* never received support from Columbia; there are letters in Semiotext(e)'s archive specifically disavowing this support.[8] These circumstances meant that *Semiotext(e)* "inhabit[ed] but [did] not [depend] upon the university."[9] Among the theory journals emerging in the 1970s, the self-funded and self-promoted *Semiotext(e)* was an outlier. It succeeded not because of institutional support, but because it drew on the lived circumstances of New York in the 1970s to propel itself forward. Like the artists that would eventually fill its pages, *Semiotext(e)* assembled within the contours of the decayed city. Lotringer sought to shake up the academy both by rejecting Columbia's support and foregrounding a wilder strand of theory than had emerged at the Hopkins conference. He'd later express misgivings about doing so, but by that time the die was cast.

Underfunding and this lack of institutional support shaped the trajectory of *Semiotext(e)* from the beginning. Lotringer maintains that the first few issues "were necessary to get the presses rolling: to assemble the production teams, acquire the contacts, and generate money and distribution lists."[10] These issues were created with volunteer labor, some of it contributed by undergraduates, which produced a messy process.[11] By resisting dependence on an institution, doing it themselves, the founders of *Semiotext(e)* charted a path out of the university's entwinement with the welfare state that seemed, at the time, as liberating as the theories that it promoted.

That said, Lotringer's version of do-it-yourself differed from the do-it-yourself of housing activists that I describe in chapter 2. While these activists sought to repair what was rent by the 1975 crisis, Lotringer's impulse was toward disruption. If he could run a theory journal at Columbia without the institution's support, that might be a way to critique the institution while retaining its protection. Lotringer viewed the work of assembling Semiotext(e) in the same way he viewed the theory at the 1975 conference: as a move toward breaking down repressive hierarchies. In this sense, Lotringer fell on the Matta-Clark side of the divide that I outlined in chapter 1: the intervention of Semiotext(e) was against the academy in the way that Matta-Clark's intervention was against the museum. As Jason Demers observes, this was part of a battle that Lotringer would wage throughout his career, against what Lotringer saw as the institutionalization of theory that should, for Lotringer, be a radical force for change.[12] The frameworks through which Lotringer viewed the do-it-yourself work of Semiotext(e) would be reflected in the conference's approach to the impoverished populations of Harlem. While some conference participants argued that the problems of Harlem lay with withdrawn benefits and decreased wages, on the whole, the conference tended to see Harlem as a positive example of how one might live outside of repressive institutions. Lotringer's embrace of DIY foregrounds the paradoxes of DIY at the moment of the crisis: some residents of the city were driven to DIY out of necessity, but others saw in DIY a countercultural liberation.

The "Schizo-Culture" conference was designed to get *Semiotext(e)* on the map. It was also meant to inaugurate the journal's move away from Saussurean semiotics and toward the theory that was really interesting to Lotringer: Deleuze, Guattari, and Foucault. According to Lotringer, the decayed state of crisis-era New York is what made the conference possible in the first place. The city was quickly becoming infamous as a site of crime and depravity, but this very disorganization had an overseas allure. Deleuze and Guattari, at least, agreed to show up partly for that reason. In Lotringer's recollection, New York City's conditions appealed to the Frenchmen *because* they seemed to confirm their theories. The New York of the 1970s was, in Lotringer's view, a place of "flamboyant psychosis" that would seem to confirm Deleuze and Guattari's paeans to Freudian psychosis in *Anti-Oedipus*.[13] Linked together, the conference and New York formed what Lotringer would later call the "rough and unruly city that was haunting the rest of the continent and that I was just beginning to fathom," concluding that the city "was the capital of French philosophy."[14] For Foucault, Deleuze, Guattari, and Lotringer, if what was needed was a wholesale dismembering of a repressive society, New York looked like it was the place to do it.

These impulses, though, sit uncomfortably with the wider discourses around the 1975 crisis. Others also had ideas about dismembering a repressive society, but they had in mind not constraints on intellectual thought, but on what they viewed as the fiscal constraints of a welfare state funded by taxes. In 1975, more than one conservative commentator viewed the physical decay of New York as evidence that the welfare state had run its course. For example, Alan Greenspan, then chair of Gerald Ford's Council of Economic Advisors, argued that New York's example indicated that Americans "needed to be taught the terms of a new moral politics."[15] By "new moral politics," Greenspan meant reductions in government spending: "There is no short cut to fiscal responsibility," he intoned to Donald Rumsfield, in what was rapidly becoming a Republican mantra.[16] As a whole, the Ford administration hoped that New York's "failure" might "question the ideological, economic, and political underpinnings of liberalism itself."[17] These commentators viewed the city's conditions as resulting from an overly generous welfare state that had, instead of ameliorating the problems of joblessness, caused these problems.[18] In the context of a larger conversation about urban decline, the conditions in New York provided conservatives with a ready-made example of how the welfare state had failed. In some sense, the French philosophers saw something of the same possibility in New York. They also saw the welfare state as overly managerial and repressive, producing robotic subjects who moved from school to corporation to psychologist's couch without ever experiencing freedom.

Lotringer's opening remarks offer a good summary of the conference's ideas. They also represent an important, early moment when certain ideas about disciplinarity and control were publicly aired in the United States. Particularly through Foucault's influence, these ideas would go on to shape discussions across the humanities. Lotringer spoke of a wide system of disciplinary power that affects all subjects more or less equally, "a tight fabric of constraints that lead gradually from the outwardly oppressive forms, such as the prison or the asylum, to the agencies that in appearance are the least suspect, the most positive, such as schools or the university."[19] He continued with a list of interlinked institutions that fostered such discipline. "Psychoanalysis has to do with politics, politics has to do with madness, madness has to do with creation, creation with drugs, drugs with prisons, prisons with asylums, asylums with the university, the university with Capital, and Capital with desire," he explains.[20] These are familiar themes of both Foucault's *Discipline and Punish* and Deleuze and Guattari's *Anti-Oedipus*. The former would be shortly be translated into English; the latter would be excerpted in future issues of *Semiotext(e)*. Writ large, these texts posit that discipline is undifferentiated—that poor Puerto Rican and affluent psychiatry patients fall under the same system manifesting in diverse, but ultimately even, ways.

In retrospect, such analysis can be understood as looking backward to the Fordist system of governance, which was being undone by the 1975 crisis. Emerging after the labor unrest of the late nineteenth and early twentieth century, the Fordist system sought, in large measure, to manage discontent between classes. To take one example, direct benefits under Fordism become, as Loïc Wacquant has argued, a way to prod lower class subjects in and out of the labor market. The state could extend relief when the economy couldn't provide enough jobs, and constrain benefits once the labor market tightened. In this way, the state offsets the potential for unrest that unemployment and precarity might otherwise provoke.[21] All that management was toward a specific purpose. Under Fordism, state governance sought to keep everyone in their place, even if, as Melinda Cooper has observed, such management used the Fordist family wage—earned by a white man—as its primary instrument of managing dissent.[22] The Fordist world was hierarchical but distributed benefits of all kinds more evenly than what came before or after it. But the 1970s crisis strongly undercut labor's power—some would argue that the crisis was deliberately accelerated for this purpose. That was certainly the case in New York. After the 1970s, the world would be divided between productive subjects—those who can be incorporated into free-market systems—and unproductive subjects—those members of the underclass who are beyond these systems, and must be contained or neutralized.

In the post-crisis world, much of what Lotringer identified as problems would, in coming decades, apply primarily to middle- and upper-class subjects who might well need to avoid the kind of psychic repression interlinked between university, psychiatry, and capital. Those problems were less applicable to those impoverished subjects who were being denied access to education, health care, and jobs in the midst of the city's fiscal crisis. The problem for these subjects was, instead, how to retain or extend these benefits. While these subjects might reject the overt surveillance of the police, they were often willing to accept the softer forms of surveillance entailed by the educational and health care systems in return for retaining such benefits. This is a complicated subject, of course. As I discuss below, it's true that while groups like the Young Lords advocated for retaining and extending, say, the New York Municipal Hospital system, they also, at times, accused this system of surveillance.

By and large, middle- and upper-class subjects might look admiringly on the figure of the criminal as a source of vital resistance to such repression; as Lotringer argued, "every crime" becomes "a violent way to challenge the functioning of a society which takes great pains to fit crime within the category of anomaly."[23] Lotringer's analysis here sharply diverges from the Nuyorican poets, who were busy challenging notions of the underclass as a site of fascination. Middle-class citizens might want to take up the challenge to "rid ourselves step-by-step of the very prohibitions by means of which the normative individuality is maintained."[24] But the underclass would rapidly face what Wacquant calls "punitive containment." Wacquant contends that the post-1970s strategy toward the impoverished was not surveillance, but, instead, mass imprisonment. And even the prisons resemble less the subtle exertion of power that Foucault describes in *Discipline and Punish* and more a matter of mass containment: what Wacquant calls the "swelling dungeons of the carceral castle."[25] This system was on the rise in New York 1975, visible in both rising anxieties about crime and the running discourses about the underclass that I discussed in chapter 2.

Speaking after Lotringer, his Columbia colleague John Rajchman made these themes even clearer. Rajchman described the conference's work as identifying a "politics of deviance" as well as an analysis of the "network of procedures, techniques, [and] strategies, through which modern man, the disciplined, surveyed, examined man, is produced."[26] Continuing in the same vein, Guattari offered an example of an institution furthering such techniques and procedures: "What school does," Guattari declared, "is not to transmit information, but to impose a semiotic modeling on the body."

For Guattari, school was a system that molded graduates for "factories and offices."[27] At the risk of hammering a point home too hard, it's worth noting that both public schools and CUNY were key targets for funding cuts after the crisis. The efforts of activists had helped secure free tuition at CUNY in the late 1960s; this free tuition became a frequent complaint among those advocating austerity after the crisis.[28]

Giving a lecture entitled "We Are Not Repressed," Foucault introduced the material that would become *The History of Sexuality Volume 1*. (He had given the same lecture at Berkeley earlier in 1975.[29]) While he doesn't use the term "micropower" in the lecture, he's clearly on the track that will lead to his elaboration of the term in *The History of Sexuality*. He concludes "We Are Not Repressed" by describing a "sexual technology" that causes "relations of power to function in the finest and most intricate elements of the body and its conduct."[30] In *The History of Sexuality*, he expands on this technology describing it as "infinitesimal surveillances, permanent controls, extremely meticulous orderings of space, indeterminate medical or psychological examinations, to an entire micro-power concerned with the body."[31] Foucault found evidence for such micro-power in the treatment of criminals and deviant children, but the micro-power itself was spread throughout the entire culture. Institutions, state or otherwise, work to both create the individual and discipline her. By examining these institutions carefully, Foucault, and the speakers at "Schizo-Culture" as a whole, sought to tease out forms of micro-power that threatened everyone.

These modes of inquiry sit uneasily alongside the rising accounts of the underclass shaping the response to the crisis. What the speakers at the "Schizo-Culture" conference critiqued—the assemblage of the disciplinary state targeted at the individual—was, at that very moment, evolving into a system that would forgo understanding the poor as individuals. That system would return to treating the poor as a mass—the undifferentiated group signaled by the term "underclass" at whom no reform could be aimed because they are presumed to be a species apart. A strand of European philosophy that would become indelibly important to literary studies in the coming decades emerged in New York at the very moment when, elsewhere in the city, forces were falling into place that would render its analytic frameworks outdated.

It was in this sense that the conference could describe Harlem as not a site of capital withdrawal and cut services but a wild "schizo city" where residents developed "cognitive life styles outside of the conformities idealized and mandated by and in the existing structures of urban order."[32] Elsewhere in the conference, there's evidence that the audience was made uneasy by this formulation. In *Schizo-Culture: The Event*, Lotringer and Morris include a transcription of a workshop on anti-psychiatry. The "Anti-Psychiatry Workshop" moves in a number of different directions, but the core discussion is between speakers who advocate on behalf of a radical psychiatry that might transform "social control as a model of performance" and speakers who contend that the real problem for their clients is "whether you're going to go on the subway, rather than eat, so you go on fasts at the end of the month before the welfare check," noting that such problems were experienced with acuity by "blacks in Harlem."[33] The latter speakers insist that "the project of radical politics and the project of psychotherapy are really quite different."[34] Roughly summarized, the debate is between those who see state services as a form of micro-power, and those who see state services as pragmatic tools for helping people "who can't make it from day to day."[35] The people in the latter camp are the same voices opposing the cuts made by the MAC board.

The clash between the reality of cut services and the ideal of fighting micro-power is most visible in a letter sent to Lotringer by attendee Betty Kronsky, which is in the Semiotext(e) archive:

> I think more has to be understood about the despair of living in the United States in 1975. We have given up on lucidity; our socioeconomic situation seems too murky to lend itself to analysis. We are too confused by the facts of our oppression—by the real facts, such as no jobs, a city about to default, news media reduced to the point where information becomes unavailable. Our French visitors came to us with an optimism which seemed to us glib and bizarre. Perhaps it would have helped if they had told us more clear stories about the revolution of 1968 (of which many of us are ignorant) and some of the changes in thought and behavior to which it led. We would have related well to concrete examples of semiological analysis of aspects of our world that could be illumed.[36]

By pointing to the city's financial crisis—the debt default that loomed on the horizon, and the subsequent evaporation of government assistance—Kronsky anticipates the crush that many living in neighborhoods like the Bronx would experience in the coming years as the state abandoned them. Although the theoretical apparatuses erected by the "Schizo-Culture" conference repeatedly turned to the plight of those living in the Bronx, few attendees shared Kronsky's sense of impending catastrophe.

This is the essential irony of the conference: it celebrated New York's impoverished residents as examples of outsiders at the very moment that the conservative architects of the crisis were themselves describing Harlem and like spaces pejoratively, as disorganized places where people lack desires to live normal lives, in particular to work or have families. Foucault, in fact, had already been telling people that the proletariat had adopted "good political conduct and the renunciation of open rebellion," and that the "underclass was now the site of theoretical and practical appeal."[37] For Foucault, the underclass held appeal as a group outside of traditional class politics, who harbored ways of resisting that exceeded such politics. But in New York, traditional class politics had established the city's robust welfare state. And at the moment of the "Schizo-Culture" conference, the forces of traditional class politics were fighting to maintain the benefits provided by that state. For example, when it became clear that First National City Bank had pushed for tremendous cuts in city services, DC 37 director Victor Gotbaum organized a protest of 10,000 workers at the bank's headquarters, followed in short order by protests that blocked the city's bridges, mass walkoffs, and sickouts.[38] None of these workers saw the city's welfare state as oppressive; they saw their efforts, instead, as speaking on behalf of "people in the streets—whose neighborhoods would be swept by fire and crime, whose subway trains would now run more slowly, whose children played in parks falling into disrepair and attended schools who that would lose teachers."[39] Even radical groups like the Young Lords saw these benefits as worth maintaining. They did not see the city's impoverished as outsiders offering alternatives to the dictates of micro-power. They saw the impoverished as people who needed the state's help, and were in danger of losing it.

The similarities between the theories that were proffered at the conference and the MAC board's rhetoric and policies become clear in an essay that Guattari wrote at the time. The essay, entitled "Gangs in New York," concerns what Guattari terms "South Bronx gang members." In a significant slippage, Guattari attributes actions to ordinary gang members that in reality were undertaken by the more organized—and more class-struggle-concerned—Young Lords. The Lords served as a militant wing of Puerto Rican civil rights movement as the Black Panthers had done for Black Power. Throughout the 1960s and 1970s, the Lords undertook a series of actions that called attention to the shortcomings of the Fordist welfare state as it concerned Puerto Ricans. Like the housing activists and poets I discuss in chapter 2, the Lords were both radical and pragmatic.

Guattari's essay concerns the Lincoln Detox clinic, an unorthodox addiction treatment clinic established in 1970 when the Young Lords occupied Lincoln Hospital in the South Bronx in order to protest the poor conditions there. In writing the essay, Guattari likely drew on a workshop about the clinic at the "Schizo-Culture" conference as well as Barrat's film. In the essay, Guattari applies ideas that he and Deleuze developed in the 1970s and which Guattari had presented in "Molecular Revolutions." In some form, the essay contains all the key concepts that scholars would later find useful in Deleuze and Guattari's *Anti-Oedipus* and *A Thousand Plateaus*, including notions of desire as a revolutionary force and minorities as a voice outside systems of capital.[40]

He begins by contrasting "marginal" with "minority." The former is destined to be recuperated—it's right there in the syntax, "a hidden dependence on society which claims to be normal."[41] But the latter "choose[s] to be definitively minoritarian."[42] As an example of minoritarian, Guattari offers "black and Puerto Rican gangs" who control "districts of the large cities." Such gangs have experienced "an acceleration of racial segregation" to the point where the "police only enter exceptionally into certain districts in New York."[43] Guattari invites his readers to look to these populations as a "blind social experiment on a large scale" because these minorities "explore the problems raised by the economy of desire in the urban field"; their exploration, he continues, "does not offer forms or models . . . and does not provide a remedy to something that would be pathological." Rather, their lifestyle "indicates the direction of new modalities of the organization of collective subjectivity."[44] Guattari contends here that African Americans and Puerto Ricans, in their very isolation, resist incorporation into the rigid, bureaucratic world of state solutions that he and Deleuze elsewhere decry. Guattari then offers the following evidence for these groups as having established "new modalities." First, gangs seem to be self-organized. Although these groups begin with a "rigid, very hierarchized, and even traditionalist organization," Guattari sees signs of change.[45] He pays particular attention to the women affiliated with the gangs, who, "unlike the males . . . do not feel the need for such a structure" and who seem to be forming "another type of organization" which might disengage from "the mythology tied to the phallic cult of the leader."[46] Not only have these gangs begun to organize in new ways, they have also begun to find solutions to their own problems, outside of state intervention. The example Guattari offers is the Lincoln Detox clinic. The clinic was set up as part of the Young Lords'

1970 occupation of Lincoln Hospital and remained in place until 1978, when it was shut down by the Koch administration.[47] Guattari claims that the clinic features a "staff made of old addicts," "doctors never have direct access," "the center has its own police," "the state of New York finally accepted to subsidize it," and that the clinic administers methadone "for years" such that it "constitutes a sort of artificial drug that definitively subjects ex-addicts to 'medical power.'"[48]

Guattari, then, assesses the Young Lords' actions as the work of "gangs" who control their own territory and resist state control. There are at least two points to be made here. First, the Young Lords were not precisely a "gang"; they were a political organization. And the gang members in the Barrat video are not Young Lords. Second, the initial Young Lords actions were made not on behalf of self-organization, but in protest against services that the state had cut. There were the seven demands listed at a 1970 protest rally at Lincoln Hospital:

> 1. No cutbacks in jobs or services in the emergency room or section K. 2. Immediate funds to complete the building of and fully staff the new Lincoln Hospital. 3. Door to door preventative care program emphasizing nutrition, child and senior citizen care. 4. We want a permanent 24 hour complaint table. 5. We want $140 a week minimum wage for all workers. 6. We want a day care center for the children of patients, workers, and visitors at Lincoln Hospital. 7. We want total self-determination of all health services through a community-worker board to operate Lincoln Hospital. This board must have shown its commitment to serve the people.[49]

These demands do not cohere well with what Guattari celebrates as "moving in space . . . singing, dancing, mimicry, caressing, contact, everything that concerns the body."[50] They are far more practical, and far more concerned with what the state is actually doing.

Guattari misrepresents the Young Lords as gang members because such an interpretation fits what he wants to believe about desire, molecular revolution, and repression at the individual level: "Desire is power." This assessment was out of step with what was actually happening on the ground in New York. That wouldn't matter if the theories at "Schizo-Culture" had simply disappeared or been taken up only by the art world. But they became the basis for a range of Left politics in the coming decades. Moreover, when Guattari lionizes the gang member as an outsider beyond the state, he misrecognizes the ways that the most radical politics in 1970s New York sought to build on the previous gains made by working-class New Yorkers. The Wages for Housework movement protested against welfare cuts and argued that welfare should be used to compensate women for housework. Writing from Brooklyn in 1975, Sylvia Federici observed, "In the very moment that she is deprived of the security provided by a husband's paycheck, the welfare mother gains a relative independence."[51] Both the Lords and the Wages for Housework movement joined a range of actions against austerity. In the academy, these struggles were largely forgotten. Federici's work has only recently been taken up, and the Lords are seldom written about outside of Puerto Rican studies. In comparison, the theories at the "Schizo-Culture" conference went on to influence a wide range of work, both in New York's art world and the academy.

While the conference itself quickly faded away, the schools of analysis it featured became the basis for a wholesale shift in the American academy in the 1970s, 1980s, and 1990s: an intense return to political concerns after the apolitical New Criticism of midcentury.[52] First Foucault's work, and then that of Deleuze and Guattari, energized a wide range of subfields: feminist theory, queer theory, postcolonial theory, and New Historicism. This theory was perceived as a "cyclonic force, throwing all the old assumptions into disarray," as the critic Joseph North puts it in *Literary Criticism: A Concise Political History*. As the intense theory debates have faded, this period in the academy has come under increasing reevaluation.[53] North's is one of many studies to argue that what began as a revolutionary movement ended up as a quietist state of affairs, offering, at best, a thin bulwark against the massive shifts toward privatization and market liberalization that dominated governance from the late 1970s onward. Foucault has been reread with particular intensity, both because of his centrality and his own late-career discussion of neoliberalism. The 2015 volume *Foucault and Neoliberalism*, edited by Daniel Zamora and Michael C. Behrent, situates Foucault within the exact shift inaugurated by the 1975 New York crisis, beginning with the observation that "Foucault did not content himself merely with questioning certain aspects of neoliberal thought; he seems, rather, to have been seduced by some of its key ideas."[54] Behrent's contribution contextualizes Foucault in terms of the post-1973 crisis in France, which, as it did in the United States, had the effect of reducing the state and supporting arguments for neoliberal models of governance. Eventually, as Behrent argues, "abandon[ing] the state as our model for understanding power" leads to the "argument that the state should cease to be the primary focus of engaging in politics."[55] Returning to the "Schizo-Culture" conference shows us that the problems identified by Zamora and Behrent in *Foucault and Neoliberalism* were firmly in place at the very moment when the work Foucault, Deleuze, and Guattari began to circulate in the American academy.

Focusing on marginal subjects, the discourses of the "Schizo-Culture" conference were largely uninterested in political economy, even as actions elsewhere in the city—strikes by public workers, protests against welfare cuts, the seizures of hospitals in impoverished neighborhoods—fought the MAC board's moves toward privatization and austerity. This turn away from political economy would shape the US academy and the Left more generally for decades. In their introduction to the recent *Contemporary Marxist Theory*, Andrew Pendakis and Imre Szeman make similar claims, observing that the "Marxist economic analysis of the kind practiced by (say) Joan Robinson, Harry Magdoff, or Ernst Mandel operated with disciplinary and conceptual coordinates so foreign to those of post-1968 French thought that the former could only be perceived by the latter as archaic, determinist, and plagued by untheorized metaphysical remainders."[56]

For Foucault, Guattari, and others, political struggle should occur at the site of the marginalized, not as part of class-based struggles.[57] The decline of the welfare state, which began in the 1970s and continued throughout the Reagan administration, now seems inevitable. But New York's residents clung to what they understood as a distributive system that worked for them. In some measure, the adoption of French theory in the academy has helped obscure this history. From the beginning, Lotringer intended to help French theory find a wider audience. His version of DIY involved a rejection of the academy. The "Schizo-Culture" conference was his first effort along these lines. A second, similar conference in 1977, organized around William Burroughs's work, would follow. The "Nova" convention was better publicized, in part because it featured names that were becoming more familiar: Patti Smith, Burroughs's collaborator Byron Gysin, Laurie Anderson.[58] The next step in Lotringer's efforts would be to publish small, cheap, books with the works of Deleuze, Guattari, Paul Virilio, and, most prominently and successfully, Jean Baudrillard. Those little black books would shape Semiotext(e)'s relationship to the writers of the Lower East Side, many of whom owned and read these books.

Kathy Acker's On-the-Ground Assessment of the 1975 Fiscal Crisis

In the novel *Horse Crazy* (1989), Gary Indiana describes a "boxed set of Calvino, probably unopened, piles of art magazines, [and] lots of current theoretical writings in paperback" that clutter an artist-character's apartment.[59] Given Indiana's propensity to reference Baudrillard or Walter Benjamin in his columns for *The Village Voice*, he likely didn't have to stretch his imagination here. The apartment's bookshelf is similar to his own and that of other writers in the Lower East Side. In the 1980s, those paperback copies of current theoretical writings were likely the small black books published in Semiotext(e)'s Foreign Agents series. These streamed out of St. Mark's Bookstore and became an influential part of the bohemian culture on the Lower East Side. As culture workers in the 1970s and 1980s, writers like Indiana often turned to French theory to explain their rapidly shifting culture. Wojnarowicz had all of the initial Semiotext(e) titles in his library, for example. And of course, Acker is probably the most famous writer who engaged directly with such theory; part of this chapter's task will be to trace the influence of Semiotext(e) on Acker's work in the context of post-crisis New York. As a press, Semiotext(e) would go on to publish a range of innovative writing, especially by women; Lynne Tillman's *Madame Realism* collection appeared under the Native Agents imprint edited by Chris Kraus (who would herself publish *I Love Dick* through Semiotext(e)).

Acker arrived in New York in the early 1970s. Even before the 1975 fiscal crisis hit, she knew what was at stake. Like Wojnarowicz, Acker lived close to the bone in the 1970s, adjacent to those segments of the population widely and rapidly being labeled an unproductive underclass responsible for the country's economic and moral woes. As Robert W. Snyder notes in *Crossing Broadway: Washington Heights and the Promise of New York City*, Washington Heights was holding on, but barely, in the early 1970s.[60] It was just across the river from the scene of the city's worst urban destitution, the South Bronx, and residents knew what was coming. By the 1980s, the neighborhood would be overrun with crime. These spaces of poverty animate Acker's literary project. One of the most prominent features of Washington Heights is the Columbia Presbyterian medical center. The center's presence became vitally important to Acker in 1971, when pelvic inflammatory disease drove her into its doors. In her unpublished journals, she recollects: "I walk into wooden hospital, emergency exit for Columbia Presbyterian hospital. Largest room wood walls puke yellow. Or rot yellow. . . . In front of folding chairs, wood booths. I sit in chair. I hurt."[61] The scene is shocking and ordinary, disturbing and workaday. It is one of thousands that occurred in New York alone in the 1970s, especially as the municipal hospital system began to fall apart in the wake of the crisis.

Since the mid-1980s, Acker has been a beloved—though sometimes reviled—writer. Her work appropriates passages from other, often male, writers; she foregrounds ties between political systems and private desires; she flaunts the taboos of a repressive society. All of these traits have made Acker a rich resource for critics. They find her critiquing "patriarchy," "capital-driven social values,"[62] a "postmodern society of control,"[63] "a culture of inescapably binding social inequity,"[64] "reason,"[65] and "the social, political, and cultural strictures that inhibit access to a nonlinguistic or bodily level of reality."[66] Generally, critics agree that Acker develops these critiques through her innovative narrative strategies. Alex Houen argues, for example, that Acker shows readers "how language and an aesthetics of existence are implicated in contemporary governmentality."[67] All of these analyses recognize and draw upon Acker's plagiarism, anti-narrative, exaggeration, and embrace of taboos. In opposition to conventional systems of control, critics have found in Acker "a model of reading and writing that opens multiple avenues for critical analysis and political action in the face of that inequity."[68] Although they are diverse in method, textual selection, and reading practices, these readings tend to take Acker's project on its own terms: free-floating patriarchy and postmodern control systems are both quite visible in Acker's project.

My analysis here moves a bit off the page and into Acker's living and working spaces. In the 1970s, these spaces formed Acker's immediate interface with the systems that she critiques. Post-crisis New York, with its austerity, blight, and artistic bohemia, serves as an important context for the problems that Acker takes up. This is true not just in the sense that the ugliness of the city becomes a basis for "eliminating the social, political and cultural strictures that inhibit access to a nonlinguistic or bodily level of reality," as Lee Konstantinou contends of Acker's "New York City in 1979."[69] It is also true in terms of the urgent social problems that Acker saw in her lived environment. Her project takes initial shape in the cramped, underfunded, and often desperate conditions of post-crisis New York. A close analysis of Acker's work from the 1970s, particularly *The Adult Life of Toulouse Lautrec*, reveals that Acker was just as concerned with the support systems that were falling away from the impoverished as she was with leveraging blight against the strictures of Fordism. The latter vision was certainly what dominated Acker's later work, and in this sense, all the critics I list above are correct about her project. It's also true, as Konstantinou suggests, that Acker's work would eventually become emblematic of the DIY ethos of post-Fordism.[70] I'll return to these issues in chapter 4, but I mention them here as a qualification for what follows.

Acker's work took shape for all the reasons her critics note. Like the Language poets she befriended and admired, she distrusted narrative, and sought to intervene within the controlling, master-discourse paradigm of narrative. Like Foucault, Guattari, and Lotringer, she sought to draw out problems of micropolitics, showing her readers how familial and governmental structures overlapped. Like the appropriation artists she worked alongside, she saw value in reshuffling the signs of consumer culture and art history. But her project was also shaped by the lived experience of post-crisis New York City. It couldn't help but be. The post-crisis circumstances are what allowed her to develop an independent life as a writer, particularly in the years before the success of *Great Expectations* (1980). During those years, Acker developed her literary vision as well as her political commitments within the landscape's ruptures and fissures.

Her relationship to the post-crisis city emerges as problems of both form and content. As with the Wojnarowicz monologues that I discuss in chapter 1, which were typewritten on a single page, Acker's journals were highly portable. Inside, they mixed plagiarized passages from other works with accounts of her day-to-day life. They were important enough to her for her to label them carefully. In some cases, she pasted in additional pages when she ran out of room or wanted to edit something. They record her development as a writer and her struggle to live. Reading them, it is difficult to tell where one impulse begins and another ends. If Acker's published works often read as coherent takedowns of capital and patriarchy (more than one critic has read *Blood and Guts and High School* as an "allegory"), they did not begin their lives as such. This is less true for the work after *Great Expectations*. By that point, Acker had developed a style, method, and reputation that she would retain in large measure through the end of her career. The ragged buildings, bad apartments, and underfunded clinics of 1970s New York leave their mark on her entire project. Even as Acker strips out the New York–related content, she retains a form that, as much as it was inspired by Burroughs and other avant-garde writers, bears the impression of the post-crisis city.

Acker's writing method—the one she describes in her journals of the time—involved overlaying personal experiences with writing exercises. In the journals, she not only records her immediate circumstances, but also theorizes how to incorporate these into her writing. "Three experiments," she assigns herself: "1) Diary. Copy sections about memory (N.Y. art scene vs. Spinoza). 2) Copy (to break copying, that time in me, for anarchy.) 3. Copy changing examples. Examples in philosophical investigations are usually uninteresting in themselves. Conceptual. If examples are taboo material, are intuitive. Therefore, change conceptual/conceptual to conceptual intuitive."[71] I take this to mean the following: Acker begins with her own memories, as recorded on the surrounding pages. She then copies from another work—in this case, Spinoza. She then overlays the copied passage onto her own work, which changes "conceptual/conceptual" to "conceptual/intuitive." Acker, in other words, did not start and end with the conceptual. Instead, she grafted the shabbiness and desperation of her lived environment into her conceptual art. Acker's journals show her moving back and forth between rewriting literary texts and rewriting her own biography.

Drawing on Acker's journals, Chris Kraus's *After Kathy Acker* provides a strong account of Acker's method. Kraus's essential statement about this method is as follows: "Acker worked and reworked her memories until, like the sex she described, they became conduits to something a-personal, until they became myths. This was the strength, and also the weakness, of her writing."[72] For Kraus, Acker takes a kernel of experience and assembles her work around this kernel. Mixed with fiction, this writing moved into her published texts more or less intact, and allowed her to compose rapidly. In the first page of the journal in which she composed *The Adult Life of Toulouse Lautrec*, Acker lays out a startling writing schedule: "1st section (4 weeks), 2nd section (3 weeks 3 days), 3rd section (2 weeks 6 days)," and so on.[73]

Acker's journals demonstrate that her aesthetic choices are often life choices. To take one glaring example, Acker's well-known turn to sex work was not, as she sometimes implied, a voluntary descent into *la boue* but a way to pay for the treatment of her PID. In the 1970s, Acker sought to live as cheaply as possible. She told the Language poet Ron Silliman that she lived on $15 a week. Kraus questions this number, but without a doubt, Acker was poor enough to apply for food stamps in 1975. She crafted her projects out of these circumstances, using what was at hand. In this sense, the crisis was a visible rupture with the past that made concrete all of the social and economic problems that critics find Acker critiquing. It was a massive rupture in the city's social fabric, legible, for everyone paying attention, as a turning away from collective and toward privatized life.

Like Lotringer starting *Semiotext(e)*, or Algarín and Piñero starting the Nuyorican Poets Cafe, Acker did it herself, as she was casting about for a method and self-presentation that would get her on the map. She lived in bad apartments and slept on people's couches when she could. She accepted whatever public support—a free clinic, food stamps—was available, at a time when the conditions of such support were rapidly changing.[74] These choices put her in close contact with the city's rising impoverished populations. Acker's mentions of poverty can seem didactic; there's a line in *Blood and Guts in High School* that reads, "This is how poor people get transformed into hamburger meat."[75] But she stood in line for food stamps alongside those poor people and went to clinics alongside them. They were her neighbors in the Lower East Side.

Written in the midst of the crisis, *The Adult Life of Toulouse Lautrec* works through the problems of withdrawn services raised by the MAC board. Acker began working on *The Adult Life of Toulouse Lautrec* in June of 1975.[76] It is the last book in what Acker calls her serial work. As she did with *The Childlike Life of the Black Tarantula*, she planned a chapter at a time, but she had also vowed to begin drawing her novels together with a stronger narrative organization, a step toward the more coherent work that Acker will produce in the 1980s. While writing *The Adult Life of Toulouse Lautrec*, Acker was surfing from couch to couch in downtown New York; by the end of 1975, she would move into her own apartment, after separating from Peter Gordon. She had met some success in New York—"here I'm some kind of star," she wrote to Silliman—but was still "sort of ek[ing] out a living."[77] Like everyone else in the city, she'd heard about the its impending crisis. She wrote to Silliman,

> 50,000 or something city workers 7% cops . . . just got laid off no relief the city's badly in debt it's gonna be a hot summer baby, no relief in sight, as I say this knowledge (knowledge is knowledge might at this point truth values are superfluous) of doom makes everyone act like he/she better grab do hold on to anything not only to survive but to enjoy he/she can . . . the Middle Ages . . . no, Rome at its decay as we sail into the Middle Ages on some tiny raft.[78]

Acker interprets the city's crisis in terms of "doom," and her reaction is to "hold on to anything not only to survive but to enjoy."

Written at the moment of the 1975 crisis, *The Adult Life of Toulouse Lautrec* works through what the crisis means for individual attachments, artists, and the poor. Acker threads part of her letter to Silliman into the novel, in a scene that describes waiting for food stamps:

> There's too many people. Thousands of people're sitting on rows of folding chairs in one tiny filthy room. . . . I'm one of those people. Nobody says a word. Nobody complains. More and more people enter the room. We go to another room and sit on identical folding chairs. One person says they're about to close off the cities cause our government can't handle the city problems any more and doesn't need the cities.[79]

The last line echoes her letter to Silliman almost exactly: "As I was waiting for food stamps some guy's telling me 'the government's gonna close off the cities within the next ten years cause they don't need the cities and they can't handle the incredible urban problems anymore.'"[80] The quotation eerily anticipates the plot of *Escape from New York*, one of many late seventies/early eighties films that narrated urban decline. It also speaks to the historical conditions of the crisis whereby voices on both Right and Left did not, indeed, want to address the problems of the city's impoverished. Contrasting the city's 1966 fiscal crisis—in which bankers saw lending to the city as a social good—with the 1975 crisis—in which bankers saw *refusing* lending as a social good—historian Michael Reagan contends that the crisis resulted from a shift in elite attitudes toward impoverished urban populations. By 1975, Reagan argues, bankers and other elites tended to see the impoverished as asking for too much and social programs as enabling a "culture of poverty." That is, instead of poverty being seen as a reason to provide social programs, social programs began to be seen as themselves causing poverty.[81] For Reagan, the 1975 crisis offered a "counterrevolutionary" opportunity for elites to stop spending on problems that many viewed as "insoluble." People living in the city suffered from, in conservative commentator Edward Banfield's terms, an "inability or unwillingness to take account of the future or control impulses."[82] So when the man talking to Acker in line for food stamps says that the city's leaders don't want to handle its problems, he's on to something (even if he seems a bit unhinged). Acker took the man's words quite seriously, and *The Adult Life of Toulouse Lautrec* can be read, in part, as a project that struggles with both the problems faced by impoverished populations and with the structural causes of those problems.

In suggesting that Acker responded to the poverty around her, I agree with Katherine Hume that Acker depicts "a world that is hostile to the focal figures and tries to dominate them."[83] For Hume, Acker "defines the very fabric of creation as disgusting and implies that pain is the nature of the universe" and "protests pain as unjust and unfair and assumes that we are somehow owed decent living conditions."[84] Acker's philosophical assessment of the world and her judgment of her immediate conditions contradict each other, according to Hume. Acker cannot quite reject the possibility that *something* might be done to alleviate the desperation of the poor. This contradiction makes sense, I'd contend, if we think of Acker as attacking the coalesced social formation of Fordism, but as recognizing, through her own experiences with New York's welfare state, that some aspects of this social formation were worth saving. As Melinda Cooper has argued, Acker wasn't the only one to feel this way. A range of actors in the 1960s and 1970s sought to "democratize the New Deal welfare state" by demanding that benefits be delinked from the "normative constraints of the Fordist family wage."[85] Such struggles were at the heart of the 1970s crisis, whereby elites use constrained fiscal conditions to forestall the democratization of benefits, and people struggle against the withdrawal of benefits.

The crisis brought a jarring set of contestations to light, and "[n]ormally opaque class relations became shockingly visible."[86] In its immediate wake, a range of groups—labor unions, parents of schoolchildren, neighborhood residents, the MAC board, conservative commentators—fought for their vision of the city.[87] *The Adult Life of Toulouse Lautrec* tracks this contraction from Acker's apartment on the Lower East Side. Using Montmartre as a stand-in for New York, Acker describes a world where streets are "filthy" and "[g]arbage cans and dogshit lie strewn over the sidewalks. Bums lie under the garbage for warmth. Cats run through the collapsing railings; the buildings landlords have burned down to collect insurance, their tenants can no longer pay the rent so why not burn down everything."[88] Later, a landlord "tried to burn down the building" because he "realized he couldn't keep collecting rent from people who had no money and were going through garbage cans, looking for food." Acker's frustrated narrator concludes "How're poor people supposed to live?"[89] Such poverty and decay form the matrix out of which Acker's narrative emerges. Poverty is the background and context for what happens to characters: "Marcia and Scott knew that if the cops ever noticed they were people and not pieces of garbage strewn on the street, the cops would beat them up and put them in jail. The cops would forcibly separate them. Being so happy that you forget everything. You don't know whether you love or don't love. Forget that you ever felt anything. Forget you can feel anything. You sleep because you have to sleep and you piss on the streets. You're learning to know everything a new way."[90] The crisis forced everyone in New York to learn everything in a new way, and in composing *Toulouse Lautrec*, Acker documents the affective and practical consequences of the crisis's shifts in governance.

Under the wrenching conditions of the crisis—Rome on a small raft headed to the Middle Ages—what can an artist do? She can research and write down what she finds. While critics have often read the sixth chapter of *The Adult Life of Toulouse Lautrec* as containing some of Acker's most direct statements about capitalism, close analysis shows that these statements are appropriated from other works: *Modern Capitalism*, by the Marxist economist Paul Sweezy; *The Worldly Philosophers: The Lives, Times, and Ideas of the Great Economic Thinkers*, by the economic historian Robert Heilbroner; and a 1974 article in *The New Yorker* on global capitalism by Richard Burnet and Ronald E. Muller. We can imagine Acker leaving her apartment to walk to the Strand bookstore on East Twelfth Street, searching for works that might help her figure out what was happening in the city. She goes home, reads them, and copies down passages word for word: a fast, efficient way to get these ideas into her text. "Appropriation," muses Acker's friend Robert Glück, "turns the writer into the reader."[91]

From Sweezy, she appropriates a wide history of capitalism, as practiced by "a handful of dominant exploiting countries" and "a much larger number of dominated and exploited countries."[92] From Heilbroner, she appropriates a passage on the Victorian economist and critic of imperialism John Hobson, which describes how inequality inevitably leads to imperialism because the wealthy have nowhere to put their money.[93] Burnet and Muller's article previews material from their 1976 bestseller *Global Reach: The Power of the Multinational Corporations*. In it, they inquire into the rising problem of globalized capitalism but in terms of how such a rise will affect American unions and workers—and the sense of common good at the heart of the Fordist compact. Acker reworks the following: "So now the nation's burden of debt is like a string drawn very taut: 2.5 trillion dollars in debt outstanding and more money needed to keep the economy growing, while the ability of borrowers to repay what they owe and to find more money is very much in question."[94] In these passages, Acker doesn't just use poverty as a location for her anti-hierarchical themes. She also laces through an attempt to theorize the crisis—not with Foucault or Deleuze but with relatively straightforward works of economic history.

But this approach also reminds readers of the inexpert position in which the artist finds herself in confronting economic theory. The sources of the crisis were difficult to sort out. Union activists suggested it was overspending on building; the MAC board suggested it was overspending on services; everyone thought it had something to do with the 1973 oil crisis. Acker suspected something more was afoot. By copying these texts directly into *The Adult Life of Toulouse Lautrec*, Acker reminds readers of how difficult it is to get a grasp of large shifts in the economy on the ground. The threads of Acker's later project are all there in *The Adult Life of Toulouse Lautrec*—and these threads were activated by the lived circumstances of the 1975 fiscal crisis. This early work, I'd contend, was written directly in response to the politics of austerity, abandonment of the underclass, and financial machinations that characterized the crisis.

Blood and Guts in High School and a New Map of the Lower East Side

In her next work, Acker begins to systematize the ideas of *Toulouse Lautrec* as a theory of the post-crisis city. The crisis leaves the Lower East Side with falling-down buildings, vacant lots, half-occupied abandoned buildings, and overcrowded buildings. Landlords encouraged this disruptive disorganized landscape, so that existing tenants—who were perceived as members of an unproductive underclass—would flee. The resulting drop in rents allowed a thriving art scene to flourish in which vast amounts of young people could live for little rent—alongside people who had never left, in part because they could not afford rent anywhere else. The social world of the Lower East Side, indeed its very physical form, was visibly disconnected. It was difficult for observes to trace anything like intact networks coursing through this landscape; the housing advocates that I discuss in chapter 2 made it their life's work to restore these networks. Beginning at least with György Lukács, critics have framed the novel as a way of imagining collective life. Collective life was difficult to envision in the Lower East Side of the 1970s and 1980s because so little of the built environment seemed intact. The Lower East Side was, in fact, held up as an exemplar of the opposite of collective life, as what happens when social energy withdraws from a neighborhood. This withdrawal was variously termed "white flight," "disinvestment," or "planned shrinkage," all metaphors that figure social life as moving elsewhere, even as another set of terms, "frontier" and "bohemia," portended its return. This is the world that allowed Acker, Wojnarowicz, Indiana, and others to develop their projects in the 1970s and 1980s. Drawing on the raw material of their own lives, these writers took up their environment as both content and form.

In *Site Reading*, David Alworth offers one way to conceive of works that take up their environment. In his own reading of the ruined Malta in Thomas Pynchon's *V.*, Alworth is mostly interested (like Pynchon) in the ways that social life continues despite—or even because of—a ruined environment. In other words, Alworth's reading of the ruins in Malta is optimistic. Like Pynchon and like the Nuyorican writers of chapter 2, Alworth looks for what continues to hold together the ruins. Even as Ħaġar Qim is being bombed, Malta "sustain[s] sociality, shoring up an entire society against its ruins."[95] But in New York, there were forces at work that wanted the Lower East Side to stay in ruins because a ruined landscape also meant a ruined welfare state. Acker's texts, famously far less organized than those of Pynchon, embrace the city's ruins.

Kraus suggests that *Blood and Guts* is itself a ruin, "a disjunctive but emotionally continuous work," which drew on Acker's dissolved relationship with Peter Gordon.[96] Kraus locates this relationship in the first thirty-one pages of the novel. Acker is Janey; Peter Gordon is Father. These scenes ostensibly take place in Merida, Mexico, but most of these pages take place inside Janey and Father's apartment, a social world of two; Acker represents this relationship through theatrical-style dialog, such that readers often imagine that only these two voices exist in the novel. Near the end of the passage, Father tells Janey, "Right now I just really like opening my door to this apartment and walking into my own space," signaling that the back-and-forth exchanges that have driven this section are over.[97] The first section describes Acker's living situation in the 1970s: relationships inside apartments.[98] At the time, Acker was living in a "dark railroad flat" at 341 East Fifth Street, between First and Second Avenues in the Lower East Side.[99]

The rest of *Blood and Guts in High School* operates at a large scale, expanding into big sociological accounts of the Lower East Side and exploring vast dream maps and fables. But the scale of these first thirty pages is as small as a dark railroad flat. Acker theorizes this scale shift in a passage that occurs midway through first thirty pages, one of the few in which Janey leaves the apartment.[100] Walking to the town marketplace, Janey encounters vendors selling "beetles about an inch to two inches" and "tiny cheap silver trinkets." Moving from this marketplace Janey encounters "monumental ruins." In the first set of these, "the stones are crumbling" and the "oldest buildings are so ruined you can hardly see them." As Janey walks on, she confronts other kind of buildings. Here, "the architecture is clean, the meaning is clear, that is, the function," which is "habitation." Janey concludes that the "scale is human." That's because she sees wells, but "no pictures or religious representations." The residents of these sections are, Janey decides, "[a] clean people who didn't mess around with their lives, who knew they were only alive once." The scale is human; Janey feels connected and at ease.

Not so in the next section which "contains the largest buildings, vast and fearsome," "heavily ornamented and constructed so beyond human scale they cause fear." One sentence later, Acker jars us further: "Why does Rockefeller need more money so badly he kills the life in the waters around Puerto Rico?" The last type of buildings are beyond human scale. They do not fit. Habitation on a human scale sits between ruin and overdevelopment—the very conditions of the Lower East Side after the 1975 fiscal crisis.

In the late 1970s, Janey might have made her observations walking from the Lower East Side to the downtown business district. The contrast between the Lower East Side's tenements and downtown was visually arresting. But in some sense, downtown's intact architecture contains capital that was redirected from neighborhoods like the Lower East Side. That's because the 1975 fiscal crisis was precipitated in part by the overbuilding of office space downtown. Between 1967 and 1973, the city added 66.7 million square feet of office space to Manhattan.[101] The Lindsay administration era push to build downtown meant three things at once: the city moved away from building housing; the city moved the focus of business from midtown to downtown; and the city overextended its credit. All three forces shaped the Lower East Side, and all three found their way into *Blood and Guts in High School*. In the "Rockefeller" passage, Acker directly refers to Dorado Beach, where Laurence Rockefeller built a resort in the early 1960s. But it's hard to imagine that Acker wasn't thinking at least a little bit about the hated World Trade Center, its twin towers nicknamed "David and Nelson" by downtown residents in the 1970s.[102]

Moving between scales, the first section of *Blood and Guts in High School* asks readers to think through how the apartment mediates Janey and Father's relationship, how some parts of the landscape offer habitation, and others fear. In Fredric Jameson's terms, this section performs a "cognitive mapping" of the city and the forces shaping it.[103] Habitation mediates between ruin and vast scales of fear, but habitation is entrapping; it binds Janey to the Father/boyfriend complex that she wishes to escape. Father is messing around with her life, and existing at the human scale is, unfortunately, unbearable. Habitation is impossible, and Janey cannot be one of the "clean people who didn't mess around with their lives, who knew they were only alive once."

In this passage, Janey can choose to scale the vast structure, where it is "easy to fall," or she can return to the ruins. Ruins it is. Leaving for New York City, she chooses a "New York City east-side slum" as her home. "She started to run from death. . . . She left high-school and lived in the East

Village."[104] The next section expands on this slum in detail. The small-scale life of the first thirty pages contrasts with the expanded, messy world of the next thirty pages. Janey leaves her apartment with Father to find liberation in the East Village slums. These sections contain a sociological account of the Lower East Side in the 1970s:

> *Slums of New York City.* A racially mixed group of people live in these slums. Welfare and lower-middle-class Puerto Ricans, mainly families, a few white students, a few white artists who, due to their professions, will never make it: poets and musicians, black and white musicians who're into all kinds of music, mainly jazz and punk rock. In the nicer parts of the slums: Ukrainian and Polish families. Down by the river that borders on the eastern edge of these slums: Chines and middle-middle class Puerto Rican families. Avenues of junkies, pimps, and hookers from the northern border; the southern border drifts off into even poorer sections, sections too burnt-out to be anything but war zones; and the western border is the Avenue of Bums.[105]

As *Blood and Guts in High School* proceeds, the closed world of Janey-Father opens to an expansive world but an unregulated one. The maps, fables, and plagiarism that characterize the middle part of the book take place literally and psychologically in a discontiguous landscape that Acker names the East Village. Janey embraces a wildly divergent life. "Anyone can do absolutely anything he or she wants," Janey observes, but "all you see day after day is a mat on the floor that belongs to the rats and four walls with tiny piles of plaster at the bottom."[106]

In the first section of *Blood and Guts in High School,* then, Acker taps into a vast shift in the city's priorities, from the immediate problems of the people around her to the concerns of people who work in downtown's vast buildings. Like Matta-Clark, Wojnarowicz, and the Nuyorican poets, she transforms a shift in governance into a shift in aesthetics. Those two realms are ostensibly separate in the 1970s.[107] Later, the creative economy brings governance and aesthetics together. At the time, Reaganomics aren't yet visible, much less "neoliberalism." Still, the signs are on the horizon, and Acker is smart enough to read them. Near the end of *Blood and Guts in High School,* a "Rich Do-Nothing" tells a Punk Rocker that "the rich are getting richer and the poor are getting poorer. The right wing is beginning to show its power in this country. Taxes are abolished and the schools are being shut down. Proposition 13 is going to take place all over this country. Everything economic and therefore everything is going to get worse."[108] Proposition 13 was the "tax revolt" referendum voted in by Californians in June of 1978, a keystone part of the rising neoliberal ideas that had been promoted by Milton Friedman and others since the 1940s. Daniel Steedman Jones describes tax revolt as an "alternative ideological infrastructure" that "was able to take advantage when economic and political events took a turn for the worse in the early 1970s."[109] A month after Proposition 13 passed, Manhattan Borough president Andrew Stein was in *The New York Times* editorializing on the link between Proposition 13 and the 1975 fiscal crisis. Ever since 1975, Stein claimed, the public had "recognize[d] that higher taxes only exacerbate the exodus of industry and increase public assistance rolls."[110]

As its members stated over and over again, the MAC board sought to sort out the proper distribution of people and resources. Their members argued that in the recent past, too many resources had gone toward sustaining the individual—to house, feed, and educate this individual. Moving forward, the city would shift its commitment to encouraging business instead. This meant, as the MAC board and landlords hoped, that money and effort would be distributed organically, without the heavy machinery of the Fordist state. The immediate result was a shift in the way the city's landscape looked: no longer whole, but broken. The MAC board changed the *form* of the city, too. Despite, or because of, its unevenness, *Blood and Guts in High School* narrates shifts in these boundaries as they occurred after the 1975 fiscal crisis. Bringing a complex assemblage of discourses together, Acker allows her readers to scrutinize the political, material, and social forms that collided after the crisis, at a moment when they had not yet been sorted. Building on the research that she undertook for *The Adult Life of Toulouse Lautrec*, Acker struggles to understand the relationship between the small-scale activity of moving into an apartment and becoming a writer and the larger-scale transformations of the city.

The Fordist order maintained buildings in an intact state. Buildings at once represented this order and were maintained by it: wages, public subsidies, regulation. The crisis and its runup produced an interrupted landscape. Amidst the intact buildings, there was rubble, disorganization, heaps, jumbles. You might walk down a street and see here, an intact building with the lights on; there, a building fallen into rubble; there, a building with a hole in it out of which drugs were dealt. Here, the Fordist order: people who live in buildings whose life binds to the city: "Right now I just really like opening my door to this apartment and walking into my own space."¹¹¹ There, the order broken down: people who are no longer bound to the city, the underclass that is elsewhere. These are the people that Martin Wong painted in his paintings and that Harold Rosenberg captured in his photographs. Broken bricks become undifferentiated. There is no narrative here. There, the beginnings of reuse: drug dealing, homesteading, squatting, redevelopment. Reuse might begin with a hole cut in the building if you were Gordon Matta-Clark or a drug dealer. You could call that reuse "appropriation." You could also cut a hole in *The Scarlet Letter* and make it part of your novel. "All of them even the hippies hated Hester Prynne because she was a freak and because she couldn't be anything else and because she wouldn't be quite and hide her freakishness like a bloody Kotex and because she was as wild and insane as they come."¹¹²

In Acker's body of work, *Blood and Guts in High School* is a hinge text between the experiments that Acker conducted in the 1970s and the more deliberate work of *Great Expectations, Don Quixote,* and *Empire of the Senseless.* Acker wrote it just before she became really successful and at the end of a long series of unstable living situations in which she, like Janey and the hideous monster, tried alternately to maintain the closed box of domesticity and to escape into ruins.¹¹³ By 1981, Acker had rented what Kraus calls "a large, newly renovated loft" owned by Jenny Holzer, and by 1983 Fred Jordan at Grove Books had bought her work, which resulted in a relationship that lasted until Acker's death in 1997.

All of this is to say that *Blood and Guts in High School*, like Wojnarowicz's *The Waterfront Journals* or Indiana's *I Can Give You Anything but Love*, documents an unstable period in Acker's life, and its form reflects the tensions of living circumstances of the post-crisis 1970s. That crisis was, through and through, a crisis about housing. And while Acker's work often seems to concern the small space of the patriarchal family more than the large space of the post-crisis city, it's also true that the larger crisis of the 1970s was entwined with traditional notions of the family. Cooper contends that the Fordist family wage anchored the Fordist order, whereby "the standard Fordist wage actively policed the boundaries between women and men's work and white and black men's labor, and in its social insurance dimensions, it was inseparable from the imperative of sexual normativity."¹¹⁴ Inasmuch as *Blood and Guts in High School* outlines the cultural imperatives of patriarchy, it also reflects the lived circumstances of transitioning from the stabilized world of the Fordist living space to the disrupted built environment of the post-crisis world. *Blood and Guts in High School* reflects tensions between a fading Fordist order of patriarchy and subsistence wages, to a rising post-Fordist order of temporary contracts, in which the patriarchy nevertheless reconstituted itself, albeit in more distributed ways. The shift from Fordism to post-Fordism was tied to the family's intimacy *and* to larger problems of government services and housing. Throughout her work in the late 1970s, Acker shows readers how the shifts of the post-crisis city moved between scales.

Autonomia: A Missed Opportunity

In the context of the 1975 fiscal crisis, the anti-welfare-state work at the "Schizo-Culture" conference was untimely. Five years later, though, Lotringer would publish work that directly addressed the problems of both the withdrawing welfare state and the changed modes of work that characterize post-Fordism. The Autonomia issue of *Semiotext(e)* documented the Italian Autonomia *Operaia* movement of 1977, "a movement born neither in the factory nor at university . . . a movement with service-workers, members of tertiary society and young precarious and casual workers as its vanguard."[115] Autonomia included work from, among others, Paolo Virno, Antonio Negri, and Franco "Bifo" Berardi. In recent years, Virno, Negri, and Berardi have become indispensable resources for scholars working on post-Fordist modes of life and labor.

The Autonomia issue is significant in two ways for understanding what it was like to live and create in the Lower East Side. First, what happened in Italy in 1977 is similar to what happened in New York at the moment of the fiscal crisis. Both moments involved a range of actors that extended well beyond the traditional working class: transit workers, welfare recipients, students, families, civil rights activists, feminists, and others organized to save firehouses, fight the raising of tuition at CUNY, protest wage cuts, and protest cuts in direct benefits. Activists blocked bridges, undertook wildcat strikes, occupied hospitals, and took to the streets *en masse*. Both movements saw the state shifting priorities away from ordinary people and toward capital and found radical ways to contest it. Second, theorists like Virno, Negri, and Berardi provide a crucial set of frameworks for understanding how post-Fordist capital harvests human creativity by, as Sarah Brouillette says, "treating all of social experience as a factory in which the universal human inclination toward creative play and invention becomes a laboratory from which new products emerge."[116] While these frameworks are not perfect—Brouillette contends that "their writings evince a clear wish to maintain a sublime mass that is at once outside property relations and the source of everything available for transposition into them"[117]—they nevertheless offer a way to think about the relationships between artist and capital that supersedes those relationships defined by gentrification or figured by the gallery-owner-entrepreneur.

In the United States, the Autonomia issue was ahead of its time—which may account for why, as Cussett argues, it entailed a turning point for *Semiotext(e)* the journal. Before that issue, Lotringer had published *Semiotext(e)* steadily, carving out a niche for the journal with both a freewheeling style and a dedication to Deleuze and Guattari. Arguably, Lotringer helped call the academy's attention to the pair, to the point where Fredric Jameson cites both in his important 1991 work *The Political Unconscious*. But the Autonomia issue resulted in no such impact, and after that issue, *Semiotext(e)* would appear only intermittently. None of the figures in the Autonomia issue found traction in US criticism until at least 1996, when the University of Minnesota Press would publish the collection *Radical Thought in Italy*.[118] Even then, it took the tectonic arrival of Michael Hardt and Antonio Negri's *Empire* in 2000 to really get their voices circulating.

With its attention to the actual political circumstances of the 1977 Italian revolt, the Autonomia issue made up for the faults of the "Schizo-Culture" conference. In many ways, it responded to the tension between the 1975 conference and 1975 crisis with which I began this chapter. In the introduction he wrote with Christian Marazzi—tellingly titled "The Return of Politics"—Lotringer references a core concept from *Anti-Oedipus*. Lotringer described "the body without organs of autonomy" as having "a history, and that history is Italian."[119] He goes on to frame the issue's contents as rooted in an urgent problem—the wide imprisonment of the leaders of Autonomia Operaia following the kidnapping and murder of former prime minister Aldo Moro by the Red Brigades—an organization with ties to, but not directed by, Autonomia Operaia. While the "Schizo-Culture" conference had largely avoided confronting political struggle directly, preferring to talk about psychiatry and prisons, the Autonomia issue was all about political struggle. And the politics it articulated were well suited to the problems of post-crisis New York. Inside the issue, both Bologna and Negri—to take two examples—directly addressed the crisis of the 1970s. Negri observes, for example, "The very *social-democratic project*, which since the time of Keynes has been at the center of capital's interests within the restructuring process, is now *subsumed to the indifference* of the possibilities of capital" with the result that it "is beginning to disintegrate."[120] For Negri, this disintegration means that class struggle must now widen to encompass a wide range of actors—not just the traditional working classes but the whole range of capital's dispossessed. All of this is to say that what became known as neoliberalism was well visible in the Autonomia issue, and that if scholars and activists had taken the issue's ideas seriously, the shift in the US left from anti-capital to cultural politics might have been invigorated by a sense of the shifts taking place in capitalist management—the very shifts that the 1975 fiscal crisis inaugurated in the US.

The Autonomia issue represents a might-have-been, the ghost of an alliance between the precarious, despised workers of the underclass and workers-as-artists. While these groups were ripped apart by the pressures of cut services, gentrification, and entrepreneurial capital, the Autonomia issue suggests that such an alliance could have played out differently than it did in the Lower East Side. It's also, as Cussett points out, the ghost of a critical theory that might have become genuinely oppositional instead of being absorbed into what Cussett calls "a strange breed of academic market rules, French (and more generally Continental) detachable concepts, campus-based identity politics, and trendy pop culture"[121] or, worse, a "jargon-filled, decontextualized approach" to criticism, a set of discourses that helped sell books and secure tenure-line positions.[122] It is in this sense that the Autonomia issue is a missed opportunity: a chance to weld the dissident energies around the 1975 fiscal crisis to the dissident energies of the 1977 movement in Italy.

Looking back on *Semiotext(e)*'s work from 2001, Lotringer writes, "the only French theories that were readily acknowledged, even avidly sought, in America were *not* those that could have helped people understand something about their own reality, but rather that offered something to hold on to, the crutches of structures (Lacan's 'symbolic'), the romance of meaning (Kristeva's 'semiotic' process), or the repeatable protocol of their endless undoing."[123] The sentiments that Lotringer expresses here about the American academy were ones he expressed throughout his career. He told Henry Schwartz and Anne Balsamo in 1996: "Structuralism is designed for the lazy. There's no research involved, you don't have to go to the library, no fieldwork (never mind Levi-Strauss), just plug your text into the machine and see what comes out. It was perfect for America. But that's not what I wanted to do."[124]

Acker, too, would come to lament the way her radical critique was nulled by the absorption of critical theory into the art world and academy. As Tyler Bradway summarizes, after Acker returned from London, she moved away from strategies of appropriation. She'd observed how the works of Sherri Levine, Richard Prince, and Jenny Holzer—artists "from whom I had learned much"—had become "simply stock in a certain stock market."[125] This leads her to reflect on Foucault, Deleuze, Guattari, and Baudrillard: "Suddenly and ironically, in this Anglo-Saxon climate, deconstructive, now known as postmodernist, techniques, became methods for applauding the society and social values composed by American postindustrialization."[126] In Bradway's terms, Acker began to fear "that an aesthetic practice, inspired by the 'simulacrum' and based in exchangeablity of text, cannot combat the values of postindustrial culture, let alone imagine a new field of social relations beyond it."[127] Acker, too, references the Autonomia movement as a productive site for theory: "When I had first read Foucault and Deleuze and Guattari and met Felix Guattari, I knew that these philosophes were working as they were working for cultural and *political* reasons and purposes. At that time, Deleuze and Guattari were deeply involved with Autonomia in Italy."[128] Acker doesn't say more, and insofar as I know, she doesn't discuss the Autonomia movement elsewhere (though she does reference it obliquely in *Great Expectations*). But the moment is tantalizing and in keeping with the strain of concern that I've identified in Acker's work from the 1970s—particularly her reference to Proposition 13 in *Blood and Guts in High School*. Her mention of Autonomia points to an alternative world in which the work of Acker, Deleuze, and Guattari might have been deployed not to critique the limits of the welfare state but to advocate for its radical extension.

Acker's concerns were directly rooted in her observations about art's cooptation by the financial markets and the gentrification that art helped produce in the Lower East Side. But she'd been in London while the actual art-wrought changes were occurring in New York. It was left to other writers, notably Gary Indiana and Lynne Tillman, to document these changes as they occurred. Embedded in the art world, Indiana and Tillman trace the way that art became implicated in postindustrialization. Their criticism and fiction lets us see how the changes that occurred in New York after the crisis were experienced by culture workers. Both critics struggle against the deployment of art by the city to further economic development, a state of affairs that would come to be known as the creative economy. My next chapter takes up these problems.

Chapter 4

The Rise of the Creative Economy

Art, Gentrification, and Narrative

After the 1975 crisis, the city took over a number of buildings that landlords had abandoned—a move that enabled much of the housing activism that I discuss in chapter 2 and shaped the landscape that I find Kathy Acker scrutinizing in chapter 3. Known as *in rem*, these properties were of high interest to real estate developers. By the 1980s, these buildings began to be transferred to developers in large numbers by the city's Department of Housing and Development—ironically, the very agency that was supposed to *prevent* landlord divestment from tearing apart low-income communities.[1]

But the situation in the Lower East Side, as a site of vibrant tenant advocacy, was delicate, and the city knew that housing polices would be better received if they could attract support from the middle-class citizens who had begun moving there. To do so, the administration of Edward Koch created the Artists' Homeownership Program. The program was designed to convert city-owned neighborhood tenements into middle-class housing under the pretext of helping artists find places to live. SoHo, after all, had been transformed with astonishing speed from an area "largely occupied by commercial slums" to a hip site for Wall Street traders and advertising executives to live.[2] Artists had played a key role in that transformation.[3] As SoHo became saturated, development interests turned toward the Lower East Side. At the same moment, art markets began to rise rapidly, with interest in new art crystallized by the sale of relative-unknown Julian Schnabel's *Notre Dame* for $93,000 in May of 1983 (it was the first work by Schnabel that was ever auctioned). In this context, the Artists' Homeownership

Program seemed perfect: a market-proven way to use the soft power of city policy to ease a housing shortage for middle-class workers. Hotly debated in neighborhood newspapers like *The Quality of Life in Loisaida* and *The East Village Eye*, the initiative was defeated after The Lower East Side Joint Planning Council organized efforts against it.[4] Nevertheless, it was an early and overt attempt to recruit art into the process of redevelopment—the nascence of what would later be called the creative economy—and as such, the program sets the terms under which this chapter proceeds.

While it failed, the Artists' Homeownership Program was an initiative among policymakers to formalize how culture workers fit into the post-crisis city. As gentrification began to coalesce into official housing policy, art became a crucial interface between systems of redevelopment and the on-the-ground life of the Lower East Side.[5] More generally, the lifestyles of artists, which, in their commitments to DIY, seem naturally entrepreneurial, came to be seen as models for the kind of self-directed work regimes that the crisis heralded.[6] Such entrepreneurialism was exactly what the Emergency Financial Control Board had, in the crisis's wake, sought to encourage in the city.

For the housing activists and writers I discuss in chapter 2, do-it-yourself meant creating grassroots institutions that helped fill the gap left by withdrawn city services. These groups saw the neighborhood as a space to be rebuilt so that extant life might continue. For artists and gallery owners, though, do-it-yourself meant entrepreneurial practices that were both made possible and inspired by the neighborhood's ruins. These groups saw the neighborhood as a space to create new modes of living that might break away from the calcified hierarchies of Fordist life, "present[ing] America in a new guise," as the writer Lynne Tillman reflects, "gay and straight, women and men, of all major religions . . . with conflicting values, both high and low, whose manifestations suggested varieties of obsession, disgust, beauty, pleasure and despair."[7] Tillman frames the Lower East Side as a utopian space of open identities, where values could conflict, where all subjects have a higher degree of autonomy. Artists like Tillman looked at the Fordist world and saw "disenchantment" and "inauthenticity," a dehumanized culture that foreclosed creativity.[8] In doing so, they worked within the terms of what Luc Boltanski and Eve Chiapello call the "artistic critique," a demand for more autonomy than that granted by the hierarchical world of Fordism, including the ability to pursue one's potential, manage one's time, and be creative. Boltankski and Chiapello trace this critique from the counterculture movements of the late 1960s to the management literature of the 1990s, observing that the former's demand for autonomy and authenticity eventually resulted in the latter praising the virtues of flexible hours, improving working conditions, and "making work more rewarding."[9] The middle period was a time of flux—when the hierarchical world of Fordism was in decline but the service-based, network world of post-Fordism was still assembling. This is the moment in which the Lower East Side began to fill with galleries and artists.

Boltanski and Chiapello's account gels with specific transformations in New York's economy, broadly conceived as a shift from manufacturing and manufacturing-related jobs to service work, a term that encompasses both white-collar jobs in finance, real estate, insurance, and advertising, and blue- or no-collar jobs in hospitality, retail, and healthcare. In order to trace the interface between such service work and the arts, this chapter scrutinizes the projects of two writers who worked as art critics. Both Indiana and Tillman used these jobs to scrutinize how art fit into the changes of the post-crisis city. Using the techniques of a rising literary movement called New Narrative, they interrogate the tensions that paid work exerts on one's identity as an artist. Broadly speaking, New Narrative emphasizes the constructedness of character and the struggle to use narrative to build community. In presenting characters who self-consciously interrogate their identities, Indiana and Tillman offer their readers a range of possible responses to the changes wrought by the galleries as well as to the forms of post-Fordist work that emerged from this era. Both brought the impulses of do-it-yourself to their jobs, bringing the dissident energies of artistic autonomy into confrontation with waged labor. At the same time, this chapter shows where do-it-yourself ran into limitations, as the ostensibly liberated zone of the Lower East Side began to seem constrained by the reconfigured economic circumstances that coalesced after the crisis. Gentrification was the primary way such constraints became visible, and both Indiana and Tillman scrutinize the way their jobs yoked them to the economic forces driving gentrification.

Art and Gentrification

Because of its high profile, and as a result of the influential work of critics like Neil Smith and Sharon Zukin, the Lower East Side's gentrification has become paradigmatic.[10] Before the crisis in the 1970s, gentrification was sporadic and limited—what Smith calls "first-wave" gentrification. The second-wave generation of the 1970s and 1980s set the terms for what would become powerful processes of displacement across the globe.[11] This gentrification stemmed from the combination of the inflated real estate market of the 1980s and the city's emergence as a global center of finance. The city welcomed artists as catalysts, who, taking over disused and abandoned properties, made neighborhood changes appear to be organic, while attracting investment from the liquidity sloshing through Wall Street as the bond market began to boom.[12] In these circumstances, ways of living and ways of working merged in linked processes of pursuing creative and fiscal autonomy. This is exactly what Jane Jacobs had predicted in *The Death and Life of Great American Cities,* a work that became something of a manifesto for the neighborhood movement of the 1970s. Jacobs links labor and redevelopment, predicting that such buildings offered opportunities to "pay for improvements in their living conditions . . . in labor and ingenuity."[13] The arts would not become a full-fledged *strategy* for changing neighborhoods until the 1990s, but what happens on the ground in the 1980s builds a base for these later efforts.[14]

New ways of working and gentrification come to be grouped under "the creative economy": the notion that the arts can and should foster economic development.[15] Initially conceived in terms of arts institutions—think of the Guggenheim Museum located in the industrial city of Bilbao—this value came to be seen in terms of art's ability to make changes in the built environment. Since the 1960s, artists and activists had been taking up disused urban spaces to make and display art, and eventually, city planners recognize these processes as being able to reclaim value from disused space. In this context, artists, gallery owners, and other culture workers serve as ideal workers and ideal landowners, because their very presence makes a neighborhood seem more livable, even within the still-rough edges of the 1980s Lower East Side.

As a result of these trends, the arts become seen as a way to fix broken work regimes and landscapes alike. For many culture workers in the 1970s and 1980s, the neighborhood's decrepitude energized work. "It was an abandoned space," the critic and artist Carlo McCormick recalls, "where, due to the larger woes of the city, whatever transgressions a bunch of artist-types might be up to in its neglected nether-zones were granted unprecedented free rein."[16] Anything could happen, as Tillman puts it: "the city grew fields of the unfamiliar and unexpected, which trumped the humdrum," and when the shows and parties were over "you never had to stay; you could usually walk home."[17] But even at the time, others were cynical. Reviewing a show at Artists' Space in the January 1982 issue of the *East Village Eye*, Richard Armijo noted the irony of white artists using African

American and Puerto Rican faces as subjects; he grumbled, "when artists decide to set up residence in a Puerto Rican neighborhood, obviously the usual hands-off policy towards the underclass has been breached. But who benefits?"[18] Armijo's comments were relayed by critics like Craig Owens and Hal Foster. Both observed the terrible irony of white "graffiti artists" helping to displace the very underclass on whose art they drew. Foster, for example, scoffed that the gallery scene might call itself an "avant-garde," but its "artists and dealers largely replicate the art world, expand its market; they have also served as reluctant accomplices in the gentrification of this neighborhood—in the displacement of its subcultural, racial, and ethnic groups."[19] The gallery scene, uptaken into national media cultures, provided developers with a symbolic vocabulary to promote the Lower East Side as not just a place where rents were cheap, but one that might provide the invigorating acid bath of risk and the found poetry of diversity. Artists, in other words, made the neighborhood cool, helping less bohemian residents to refactor the Lower East Side from an abject space of abandonment to an inspiring site of entertainment.

Working in the neighborhood's broken landscape, the artists and writers of the Lower East Side offered early examples of a mode of living for the workers of this new economy that might satisfy their demands for new work regimes, with less rigid schedules and more autonomy.[20] Artists appeared to be self-sufficient, setting their own schedules and developing their own work spaces. They also seemed to have exactly the kind of creativity that management would come to find desirable. The Fordist world, for all its safeguards, seemed to some observers rigid and calcified, a producer of not just mass-manufactured goods but what Herbert Marcuse famously called "one-dimensional men." Artists seemed to offer multidimensional lives, countering the limited choices of the forty-hour work week and its attendant repetition. This was, as contemporary commentators pointed out, a revamping of Modernist notions of bohemia, though integrated into capitalist development in more widespread and intense ways than in earlier decades.

But outside pressures placed on the neighborhood meant that this wide-open field of improvisation could solidify into singular narratives. Culture workers walked a thin line between embracing the open possibilities of the neighborhood and watching their work be transformed into fixed narratives: the savant graffiti artist who misrepresents impoverished residents, the gallery catering to rich professionals, the art that decorates a distasteful night club. The finance-driven art market could quickly transform a friend into an affluent celebrity; the opening of an art gallery might increase rents, shoving longtime residents out.[21] Media attention to the artist or gallery might cause the neighborhood to become a simplified symbol of bohemia, rendering one's living space unrecognizable.[22] This attention threatened, too, to change the very conditions of one's environment as rents rose to unaffordable levels. In this manner, the open space of the Lower East Side became embroiled in questions of who has a right to the city.[23] In their criticism and fiction, Indiana and Tillman set these questions in motion, allowing their readers to recognize, examine, and find alternatives to the dominant narratives offered by, on the one hand, city planners, and, on the other, the critics and activists that opposed these plans.

Indiana's Search for the Art of the Imminent at *The Village Voice*

Gary Indiana—the name was self-adopted—moved to the city from California in 1979. After dropping out of U.C. Berkeley, he'd lived an itinerant life, working here and there as an actor, finding whatever jobs he could to support a creative lifestyle. Settling in the Lower East Side, he did more of the same, staging his own wild plays at the newly opened Mudd Club. He also began writing fiction, which he published in some of the new literary magazines emerging in downtown: *Bomb, Benzene, Between C & D*. But Indiana needed regular work, and when *The Village Voice* offered him a job as their art critic, he took it—but resented the way it yoked him to the city's art establishment, which he viewed as increasingly entwined with capital. Taken as a whole, Indiana's work for the *Voice* exhibited tension between the idealized life of the bohemian—one he thought he'd found in the cheap rents of the Lower East Side—and the demands of being a professional critic.

His own compromises led him to denounce compromises elsewhere. He was particularly suspicious of art that claims autonomy for itself—since in his experience, such autonomy had been nigh impossible to achieve. Indiana sought to live as an artist, and the cheap rents of the Lower East Side, coupled with the neighborhood's vibrant artistic community, would seem to allow such a lifestyle. His *means of living*, though, pointed him, in uncomfortable ways, toward a mode of life that took on this lifestyle in form only—the Wall Street trader who collects art or the advertising executive who imagines her work as artistic in part because she lives in a bohemian neighborhood. Granted, writing for *The Village Voice* isn't quite like working for Ogilvy—but it's not living independently as an artist, either. Indiana's columns became a way for him to voice his discontent with this situation. His novel *Horse Crazy*, which he wrote during his time at the *Voice* and which features a protagonist who works as an art critic, provides a way to reflect on the systems that produce his discontent.

Indiana started his column in 1984, and he left the *Voice* in 1987. His tenure corresponds almost exactly to the rise and fall of the East Village arts scene, which, while it began in the late 1970s, began to attract money and national attention around 1984, and receded after the 1987 stock market crash.[24] Respected critics like Owens and Foster could write all the high-minded critiques of art's mercantilism they wanted. Indiana was going to offer his analysis at street level. Indiana leveraged "the place I was at the time"—a rent-controlled apartment at a gentrifying Second Avenue and Eleventh Street—to scrutinize the problems and possibilities of the art he saw around him. He filtered his criticism through the long history of living in uncomfortable, marginal spaces that he depicts in his 2015 memoir, *I Can Give You Anything But Love*: "a claustrophobic child-sized room on the third floor" in the Haight-Ashbury section of San Francisco" or the "seedy desuetude" of the Bryson Apartments in Los Angeles.[25] Indiana's lived circumstances are what Pierre Bourdieu describes as bohemian in the sense of "near to the 'people,' with whom it often shares misery" but "separated from them by the art of living that defines it socially."[26] As Bourdieu demonstrates, though, the bohemian life is rife with tensions, most of which concern making a living. Indiana played out such tensions in his repeated attacks on the confluence of art and commerce.

At the time, what seemed most notable about Indiana's columns was what recent critics would call their "affect." He often approached art through what Sianne Ngai describes as unconventional aesthetic categories. In *Our Aesthetic Categories*, Ngai scrutinizes the "cute," "zany," and "interesting," which, she contends, call forth "specific powers of feeling, knowing, and acting," which in turn "play to and help complete the formation of a historically specific kind of aesthetic subject."[27] Ngai celebrates what she calls the "weak attraction" of these categories, their ability to appeal to a range of feelings but in so doing, to catalog the states of mind that characterize post-Fordism. Like Ngai, Indiana deploys unconventional aesthetic categories as "reminders of the general fact of social difference and conflict underlying the entire system of judgment and taste."[28] Though Indiana was capable of drawing on conventional aesthetic categories, he just as frequently worked in the modes celebrated by Ngai. Writing of a flower show, he locates the category of "cute" with "pseudotopiary, such as ivy grown over the form of a stuffed bear holding a tambourine" and "real nature-objects dipped in 24K gold, summer in the morning and winter in the afternoon."[29] While Indiana deploys "cute" in a more damning way than does Ngai, his column here points to the way that he responded to the city's art in unconventional ways that were rooted in his own feelings, which were, more often than not, hate and disgust. In Indiana's columns, all art—flower show and art exhibit alike—"require[s] and call[s] up an idea of human beings being with or among other human beings in a very specific way," as residents of a city that was once democratic and is now ruled by markets.[30] For Indiana, an affective approach to art lets him challenge the calcifying standards set even by the best-intentioned critics, such as the left-leaning critics of *October*. Hate and disgust were the trashy remainders of the neat symmetries of the nascent creative economy.

Indiana kicked up particular disgust by contrasting artworks with the lived circumstances of the city. Reviewing an art gallery installed at Chase's SoHo branch, he observed how his own Lower East Side branch seemed to discourage lower-income bankers by understaffing its tellers.[31] "In an effort to persuade low-income and erratic types to take their unproductive money elsewhere," he began, "the larger Manhattan banks have introduced a revolutionary new idea: the hour-long bank line." After an extended riff on banks' attempts to "humanize" themselves through farcical videos with "Valium-like voiceovers," he proceeds—in only the last third of the review—to discuss, first, the art at Chemical Bank's headquarters, which he describes as "a space shaped and lighted to suggest a mausoleum-turned-boutique at the bottom," and which, displaying African American art, contradicts Chase's support of the Apartheid government and exploitation of "thousands of entry-level black employees." He then examines the SoHo branch of Chase bank, where "at last, there is a bank that is also an art gallery." Indiana concludes by suggesting that Chase sell art as well as hang it, in order to "bring art, the buyer, and the spiritual bond that currently unites them together in their proper home." For Indiana, the story of art in the city never ended at galleries or museums. Art was part of the city itself, immanent to the changes in commerce, real estate, and culture that roiled the city after the 1975 fiscal crisis.

As the city climbed out of its fiscal-crisis-shaped hole, sharp contradictions emerged between a finance-driven art market and the social circumstances of the city's impoverished. For Indiana, such contradictions manifested as a "baldly mercantile direction" in the art world,[32] the result of which was a "time in which the historical sense is generally anathema."[33] While Indiana grouped a range of art under this damning category, two categories emerge as repeated sources of scorn: the neo-Expressionist art of Schnabel, David Salle, and others, and the graffiti-influenced art that filled Lower East Side galleries. Indiana was hardly alone in this assessment. Accounts of these artists as mercantile became dominant features of art criticism in the 1980s and 1990s, accounts that were canonized as Owens, Foster, and others became keystone figures in both art history and wider accounts of postmodernism.[34] But here, as elsewhere, Indiana puts his own spin on these now-familiar debates. He didn't like the aesthetics of such art, but he especially hated the stink of money about it. As exhibit one, Indiana presented the Saatchis, the art collectors and advertisers who had helped elect Margaret Thatcher and who used their privilege to promote art that lined their own pockets—by buying up Schnabels on the cheap and then sponsoring exhibits on Schnabel at London's Tate Museum.[35] To Indiana, the Saatchis represented everything terrible about the art market in the 1980s: the willingness of both artists and dealers to collaborate with power as well as the privileging of profit over aesthetics.

Indiana also hated what he perceived as these artists' focus on the self, whereby "the desire to be seen presumes an a priori understanding between the artist and the cosmos, exempt from social reality" or "the art of 'self-expression'—organic, explosive, repetitious, obsessive—rather than art that exhibits a perspective on its own materials, containing a certain calm, a certain measure, a focused address."[36] Part of what made Schnabel, Salle, and their ilk irritating was their self-promotion. In one column, Indiana recounts Schnabel suggesting that Indiana fly to England to see Schnabel's show at the Tate. In another, he observes of "artists who have been good and get better" that "not all of them have time or inclination to sit, stand, or recline for publicity photos."[37] The publicity-seeking artists weren't stupid, of course. They knew that a quickly accelerating art market meant that self-promotion could pay big dividends. By proclaiming their autonomy loudly, such artists hoped to become sources of financial value as well as cultural value. In doing so, these artists exemplify what would become a familiar paradigm of post-Fordism: the notion that, in Richard Florida's words, such capitalism "[takes] people who would have once been viewed as bizarre mavericks operating at the bohemian fringe and [places] them at the very heart of the process of innovation and economic growth."[38]

The art objects that Indiana liked—those that provoked less disgust—foregrounded their material and social origins. Broadly speaking, this was the art of institutional critique. Such objects might, like Haacke's sculptures, point to "the social, economic, and ideological forces that permeate [art]"[39] and create "cracks in the wall of necessity, suggesting truths to people who might otherwise not hear them."[40] In a wider sense, they could, like Nancy Chunn's prison-themed paintings, "ask [viewers] to be conscious that art and life are inextricably connected—that we all live in the same world, which is not a happy place in most places."[41] They might also produce an "art of reflection rather than intervention" by helping viewers think through art and its environment, as he characterized the work of Vera Lehndorff and Holger Trülzsch.[42] They also might index material conditions by exaggerating their representation, as Indiana claimed Hunt Slonem's fabrics of animals did. Indiana praised their "very ebullience and baroque elaboration [which] deliberately refract our gaze from felicitous Eden *to the inorganic world*, where Slonem's souvenirs of vanquished flora and fauna can exist only as nostalgic decoration."[43] John Wilkins's watercolor blowups of cereal packaging "set off sensory desires and manipulate them toward an imaginary completing. As pictures 'on their own,' replete with the tissuelike naturalness of watercolor veiling, they stimulate a highly *modern fear of the inorganic assuming autonomy.*"[44]

Indiana particularly admired art that interrogated its own environment, as was the case with conceptual artist Joseph Kosuth's "Zero or Not." In that work, Kosuth covered Leo Castelli's gallery with a paragraph from Freud's *The Psychopathy of Everyday Life*, such that "the parts of the space that define volume (including air conditioning grilled, alcove side walls, the elevator, light sockets, windows, and so on) break the text in numerous places."[45] Indiana assert that by calling attention to the gallery as a material space, Kosuth "revealed the lineaments of aesthetic desire without refusing to gratify it altogether; his work *detoxifies* desire." Indiana continually sought out art that disrupted the viewer's sense of hermeticism and instead reminded viewers of art's challenging, sticky relationship to the material world. But it's also true that if Indiana enjoyed seeing Kosuth deconstruct the gallery, that's partly because Indiana never felt fully comfortable in galleries themselves. He wrote as someone who has "seen many chaotic interiors, and lived in plenty of them, too."[46] In the Lower East Side of the 1980s, these weird corners were built of decayed bricks and populated by the homeless. Indiana poked holes in the insular art world inhabited so naturally by critics like Owens and Foster to let in the dirty air of a post-crisis city.

These problems emerged with particular clarity in Indiana's response to a famous moment in art history—the installation in downtown's Federal

Plaza of Richard Serra's *Tilted Arc*. Like other city art critics, Indiana was asked by the law offices of Gustave Harrow to provide a statement defending *Tilted Arc*. Given Indiana's commitments, one would assume that he and Serra would be allied. After all, Serra set the intransigence of *Tilted Arc* against what he called in another context the "corporate baubles" of public art through which "IBM signif[ies] its cultural awareness."[47] And Douglas Crimp summarizes Serra's work as "practices [that attempt to] reveal the material conditions of the work of art, its mode of production and reception, the institutional aspects of its circulation, the power relations represented by these institutions—in short, everything that is disguised by traditional aesthetic discourse."[48] Serra wanted work that resists the art-finance that Indiana decries, even as his expensive materials meant that he inevitably had to tangle with such forces in order to produce his work.

Indiana refused Harrow's request, and used his April 16, 1985, column to savage Serra as a "debutante."[49] Indiana suggests that a more apt subject for the plaza, given Reagan-era cuts to the welfare state, might have been the "genre of public sculpture known as the Homeless."[50] In drawing this connection, Indiana, intentionally or not, joined a range of affective responses to *Tilted Arc*. Installed at a moment of both cuts in government funding—directly affecting the workers in the Javits building—and larger Reagan-era anti-government anger, Serra's sculpture was interpreted on the one hand as an affront to already frustrated federal workers[51] and on the other as an example of misused public money.[52] Some critics also tied it to the material conditions of post-crisis New York, as in a CBS news segment that visually compared *Tilted Arc*'s rust to rusting cars along the Hudson.[53] Moreover, the work became a target for both public urinators and amateur graffiti artists. Looking back on the controversy, Harriet F. Senie suggests that as such, *Tilted Arc* "made visible worsening conditions of the urban environment that were usually ignored" and "brought the effects of current real estate redevelopment policies directly in the middle of an official federal space."[54]

Indiana wasn't claiming, as did some of Serra's detractors, that the work *attracted* the homeless. Instead, he was suggesting a more structural connection: the corporate and government forces to blame for the homeless problem were also responsible for *Tilted Arc*. Indiana was hardly the only person to invoke the homeless as a visible symptom of the economic fallout from the Fordist crisis. In the 1980s, the homeless provided a sharp contrast to a suffering working class easier to bracket out geographically. In his history of the poor in the United States, Michael Katz observes that the homeless emerged, at least for a brief moment in the 1980s, as an exception to the cold logic of the underclass. In New York, the underclass could be shunted to outer boroughs, rendering their plight invisible in the public spaces of Manhattan.[55] But the homeless remained as a visual reminder of the problems of the crisis, and homelessness became a way to talk about poverty without acknowledging the structural issues of the housing crisis, demanufacturing, and slashed public benefits. The homeless, visible in both affluent and gentrifying neighborhoods, represented human misery that was less easy to ignore than that occurring in the South Bronx or the Lower East Side.

Indiana's affective response to Serra's work differed sharply from the art-critical defenses of it. Serra had been a rising presence in the art world throughout the 1970s, and *October* was a particular admirer. *October*'s critics lined up to testify on Serra's behalf. Invoking the Nazi war on subversive art, Benjamin Buchloh strongly rejected affective accounts of *Tilted Arc*: "the art of the avant-garde—reemerges now as the threat of crime and terrorism hiding behind Serra's rusty wall, as well as the mounds of garbage and packs of rats it supposedly attracts."[56] Rosalind Krauss presented a more formal defense, arguing that *Tilted Arc* "is constantly mapping a kind of projectile of the gaze that starts at one end of Federal Plaza and, like the embodiment of the concept of visual perspective, maps the path across the plaza that the spectator will take. . . . Like vision, its sweep exists simultaneously here and there—here where I am sited and there where I already imagine myself to be."[57] Reading Chief Judge Edward Re's words suspiciously, Crimp pointed to the sculpture's deconstruction of city surveillance: "I urge that we keep this wall in place and that we construct our social experience in relation to it, that is, out of the sights of those who would conceive of social life as something to be feared, despised, and destroyed."[58] All three critics make cases for interpreting *Tilted Arc* as autonomous art insulated from the post-crisis city that had indeed left a good deal of rusting infrastructure around, as well as a good deal of homeless people.

But for Indiana, living on the Lower East Side and keenly aware of the social problems of poverty and homelessness, Serra's plight was at best meaningless and at worst a symptom, not a critique, of the bonds among corporate wealth, governance, and art. He snarled that Serra was "assuming noblesse oblige over large numbers of citizens who—hypothetically, anyway—own the space that the work occupies," depicting Serra as an extension of the "corporate and governmental hegemony" that created the rest of the plaza. Indiana's view of Serra's sculpture could never be Crimp's view because Indiana couldn't stop seeing it from a rent-controlled apartment on Eleventh Avenue, where he struggled to make his own writing become art. It's illuminating to compare Indiana with Crimp in this regard—both queer men, roughly the same age, who became well-known art critics in New York during the 1980s. In *Before Pictures*, Crimp describes his living environments as gateways to his next opportunity. Unlike Indiana, Crimp was rapidly absorbed into exclusive art circles after college, befriending Johan Bultman, the son of Abstract Expressionist painter Fritz Bultman, whose New York home was full of Cornells, Klines, Pollocks, and Stouts.[59] Crimp also worked at the Guggenheim from 1968 to 1971 as the curatorial assistant to Diane Waldman.[60] Crimp, then, was almost immediately established in a world largely alien to Indiana, who tended to make friends of the seedier sort.

For Indiana, living environments always seemed to pin him in place, and this experience made him sympathetic to others who seemed similarly trapped. In his analysis, Indiana yokes *Tilted Arc* to the vibrant debates around gentrification in the Lower East Side, suggesting that *Tilted Arc* bears something in common with art that commodifies poverty by fetishizing impoverished people that "[dress] with a certain flair and [have] an engaging rap programmed into its circuitry."[61] As Indiana notes, the Javits building also processes immigration applications; thus some of the very residents of the Lower East Side and elsewhere that were displaced by artists, produced graffiti, and were most at risk of being homeless, might encounter Serra's sculpture as a hindrance, not a benefit. For Indiana, however much *Tilted Arc* interrogated its environment, it remained cut off from the problems of the fiscal crisis. Buchloh and the other *October* critics wanted to extend Serra's critique of the gallery system into a critique of New York's inequality; Indiana felt too keenly the deprivations of such inequality, and wasn't buying this line of argument at all.

Madame Realism's Rejection of Spectatorship

Indiana pushed the external contradictions around the art world of the 1980s, drawing the city into his criticism. Scrutinizing the charged world of the gallery scene, Lynne Tillman pushed their internal ones, pointing to the moment of aesthetic spectatorship as tyrannical. She recognized the crucial ways in which the gallery visitor's gaze adhered to the gaze of real estate developer and policy planner, as well as how quickly that gaze might be resituated into a wealthy bond trader's loft. Tillman's idiosyncratic Madame Realism pieces, which she began writing in 1984 and continued writing into the 2000s, ask her readers to rethink what it means to look at a painting or sculpture in a gallery by refusing to pretend that art criticism can be transparent. She wrote the bulk of the early Madame Realism pieces for *Art in America,* a journal that, under Craig Owens's editorship, had published both a crucial article celebrating the East Village scene—Walter Robinson and Carlo McCormick's "Slouching Toward Avenue D"—and, in the same issue, Owens's own scathing account of the scene, "The Problem With Puerilism." Both pieces would shape discussions of the gallery scene for decades. Working in a quieter mode, the Madame Realism pieces record and refuse the pressures placed on spectatorship by rising art markets.

The experience of spectatorship had seen wide challenges in the 1960s and 1970s. First minimalist and then conceptual artists sought to call attention to the ways that galleries and museums alike structured the spectator's experience. For these artists, good art needed to call attention to the physical and institutional circumstances of its setting. But by the 1980s, the art of institutional critique had been displaced by the flashy return of painting, though, as Indiana's columns show, artists like Haacke continued to produce work in this vein. Building on the legacy of conceptual art, Tillman found opportunities to emancipate herself from spectatorship. At a time when any moment of spectatorship might morph into a problem of art's mercantilism, or cooperation with gentrification, Tillman helped her readers query and challenge the spectator's position. This means, as Robert Siegle observes, that Tillman's pieces foreground the "economic and ethnic divisions in the city" excluded by "an unreflective elitism that can pervade the world of high culture."[62]

These ethnic and economic divisions were sharp during the period when Tillman was writing. By 1986, the beginning of Edward Koch's third term as mayor, a new city had emerged in strikingly visible ways, symbolized by the many high-rise condominiums that had been built starting in the late 1970s. (One of the more prominent was Trump Tower, completed in 1983.) The fastest-growing industries in the city were those that catered to international capital, with the securities industry, for example, adding 67,000 jobs between 1977 and 1989.[63] From here on, the city would be focused on finance, insurance, and real estate, what the business press called a FIRE economy. In the art world, the effects were what Rosalind Deutsche calls "massive economic privatization"; by this, she means "the art-market explosion, attacks on public funding," and "growing corporate influence on exhibition policies."[64] These trends were amplified by a new style of art that emerged from the Lower East Side, the Simulationist art of Peter Halley, Jeff Koons, and others. At the time, these artists were perceived as "shrewd manipulators of the art market" which "represented the worst cynicism and commercialism."[65]

Critics like Owens, as well as Lower East Side artist collectives like Political Art Documentation/Distribution (PAD/D) and Group Material, sought to disrupt the galley system that they saw as entwining art, governance, and gentrification. The first and most high-profile of these interventions was Colab's Real Estate Show, in which members broke into a disused, city-owned building on Delancey Street and launched an exhibit designed to foreground what they called "the system of waste and disuse that characterizes the profit system in real estate." After the artist Joseph Beuys joined a press conference on the event, the city granted the group a building across the street, which became ABC No Rio. Other artist groups followed Colab's example. Perhaps the most well-known of these collectives is Group Material, who staged a "Peoples Choice" exhibit featuring family objects from the residents of the Lower East Side. Similarly, PAD/D staged the "Art of the Evicted" at El Bohío in 1982, and a street-based effort called "Out of Place" highlighted the social problems attendant with the opening of galleries in the neighborhood.[66] Sholette admits that PAD/D's efforts, though, resulted in only in "a prudent form of 'political art' becom[ing] briefly fashionable in the art world," the limitations of which became the reason for the group's disbanding.[67] Among these groups, there was plenty of impetus to disrupt the galleries' experience of spectatorship that had come to dominate how outsiders and insiders alike viewed the Lower East Side of the 1980s. In her art criticism, Tillman followed the examples of Owens and art-activists in foregrounding the circumstances under which the gallery revolution took place.

Like Indiana, Tillman worked with one foot in the art world. Not only did she collaborate with the artist Kiki Smith, one of her best friends was Owens, who edited *Art in America* beginning in 1981. Tillman began publishing art criticism slightly later than Indiana. While her first Madame Realism piece appeared in 1984, the bulk of them were published in 1986 or after. Tillman began writing the Madame Realism pieces at a time, then, when the wealth-oriented policies of the Koch administration and the market-facing art of the Lower East Side seemed to have merged into a conflux of art-finance. The entrepreneurial spirit of the Lower East Side's galleries now dominated the city's art world as a whole, bringing the acceleration of finance capital into the art world. Tillman, living in a Lower East Side environment that seemed faster and faster, opted for slowness.

Her first move was to develop a persona which might disrupt the reader's identification with either artist or critic. The name Madame Realism is an ironic riff, as Tillman explains, on "Sir"realism [sic] (surrealism), born out of reflection on the Surrealist artist Méret Oppenheim, whom Tillman interviewed in the 1960s.[68] While "graffiti art" was and is a useful term to describe the work of Keith Haring, Futura 2000, Fred Braithwaite, and others, at the time, critics often used a more encompassing term, "neo-Surrealism." Writing in the mid-1980s, Stephen Westfall, for example, used the term to describe Kenny Scharf, Keith Haring, Rodney Alan Greenblat, Braithwaite, and Futura 2000. Notably, Westfall does not differentiate between graffiti and non-graffiti artists here: neither Scharf nor Greenblat was, strictly speaking, part of the graffiti scene, but Haring, Braithwaite, and Futura 2000 were.[69] More widely, Westfall asserted, the "lyrical, outsider's taste" that characterizes Surrealism could "be read everywhere" from the conceptual work of Halley, Ashley Bickerton, and Philip Taffe to Jeff Koons's aquariums with floating basketballs.[70] By adopting this name, Tillman rejoined the fast-moving, glitzy world of the East Village gallery scene. She did so on her own terms, and Tillman's particular choices in developing this character were designed to help readers gain distance from the scene. Madame Realism at once looked back on a longer tradition of female situatedness in art history and responded directly to particular circumstances of the East Village art scene.

In challenging the strong, male personalities of Scharf and Koons, as well as the urgent polemics of Owens and Foster, Tillman crafts a persona that recedes and drifts, refusing the imperatives of the art-spaces she occupies. Reflecting later, Tillman observes that Madame Realism thinks in "ways that were not part of what art criticism or art history would be doing."[71] Rancière would recognize Madame Realism: she is the museum-goer who refuses the museum's imperatives, counting herself able to walk away, to eavesdrop on other visitors, to have other thoughts—to do anything, actually, other than subject herself to the tyranny of the art on the walls. In *The Emancipated Spectator*, Rancière writes:

> The spectator also acts, like the pupil or the scholar. She observes, selects, compares, interprets. She links what she sees to a host of other things that she has seen on other stages, in other kinds of place. She composes her own poem with the elements of the poem before her. She participates in the performance by refash-

ioning it in her own way—by drawing back, for example, from the vital energy that it is supposed to transmit in order to make it a pure image and associate this image with a story which she has read or dreamt, experienced or invented.[72]

These words could have been written for Madame Realism. In each piece, Madame Realism approaches art objects—usually in museums, but sometimes at galleries—and does everything except what a critic is supposed to do. She eavesdrops on fellow visitors; she draws seemingly absurd connections between what she sees and what she has thought; she frequently thinks of leaving. Nearly every piece ends with Madame Realism safely at home, lying in bed or staring out the window, untransformed by what she has witnessed.

Rancière helps poke holes in what often seems like the unbalanced relationship between artist and ordinary observer. Art, for Rancière, should "allow us to be absorbed in our thoughts, to distance ourselves, to have a moment of rest."[73] Working decades before Rancière's work became well known in Anglo-American circles, Tillman developed a critical practice that refused to take the art seriously amidst the all-too-serious debates of the 1980s art world. She worked to find places outside the closed circle of artist-entrepreneur-critic that coalesced in the 1980s and carried forward toward the world of the post-Fordist worker and the creative economy. She did so by practicing asides:

> Madame Realism read that Paul Eluard had written: No one had divined the dramatic origin of teeth. She pictured her dentist, a serious man who insisted gravely that he alone had saved her mouth.[74]

Or by going home to bed:

> Madame Realism put the paper down and the day's words and phrases bounced in front of her eyes. She turned out the light, got comfortable, and fell into a deep natural sleep, undisturbed even by the screams in the street.[75]

The essays meander, muse, digress, and contemplate. There is no urgency. Everything can wait. You can walk away. Indiana gets this feeling, but only fleetingly, and he often has to leave the city to do it. Tillman cultivates this sense of calm in the Lower East Side, among the screams in the street and the homeless, in museum crowds and on the bus.[76] In effect, Tillman refuses to do her job as an art critic. If such work is supposed to tell readers why they should or should not visit a particular museum or gallery—acting as an extension of the art economy—Tillman urges readers, in Kathi Weeks's terms, to "pursue opportunities for pleasure and creativity that are outside the economic realm of production."[77] Describing her apartment, Madame Realism tells readers, "She liked the bars. She had designed them. Madame Realism sometimes liked things of her own design."[78]

Tillman anticipates Rancière by continually admitting failure. For example, in "Madame Realism: A Fairy Tale," Tillman writes: "Perhaps I am looking for something else, she theorized, and by misplacing things I am actually displacing things, displacing what I think I know, the familiar. The way art does. She wrote invisibly in her margin: If art has a purpose, is it to point to the absence of invention?"[79] Madame Realism emphasizes contingency and alternate interpretations but seldom with an eye toward direct critique. In "Madame Realism's Imitation of Life," for example, Tillman writes, "After Madame Realism left the room, one woman said, 'I think that is Madame Realism, but do you think a fictional statement can ever be true?'"[80] Madame Realism shows her readers how going to a museum inspires all sorts of contradictory feelings and actions: she pisses in the toilet that's supposed to be part of the art, she eavesdrops on museum-goers who compare their own bodies to those in Renoir's paintings. She shows readers how to walk away. Tillman almost never talks about art history, or art criticism: she seldom takes what she sees in front of her seriously. She announces this project midway through "On the Road with Madame Realism," writing, "Those indignant people who wrote to *Art in America* are right. I'm not a professional museum-goer. I do go to museums and galleries, but I'm especially drawn to out-of-the-way places, like houses of famous dead people, where society preserves what it deems instructive and valuable."[81] Living in the middle of a neighborhood transformed by art, already concerned about gentrification and its effects, Tillman looks for answers outside of the charged environment of the Lower East Side.

Just before she leaves the gallery in "Madame Realism and the Imitation of Life," Madame Realism muses, "Nothing ever worked the way it was supposed to, everything having unintended effects, and all you could do was get used to it. Like getting used to living in a world of knock-offs, she mused, and said goodbye to her friend, leaving the opening without ever having looked at what was on the walls."[82] You could start a gallery, and feature a poor graffiti artist, and perhaps it would turn into a world of fruitful exchange between artists and the underclass. The hope for graffiti as a resistant form was everywhere, even among critics like Foster, who imagined that graffiti artists could circulate their "sign against the code, [marking] a territory through alien property."[83] But for Foster, Owens, and Indiana, the only possible response to the tragedy of underclass art becoming commodified and exploited was to decry the tragedy with polemics. Instead, Tillman invited her readers to exit the zero-sum game of art's increasing entwinement with industry. Moving through a range of art-spaces, Tillman disrupts the cultural economy at the moment of its ascendance.

None of it mattered too much: some things will get remembered, others will be thrown away. These are the lived circumstances of the gentrifying Lower East Side that Tillman will mourn in 1998's *No Lease on Life*. As Madame Realism says of Coney Island, "Buildings in various stages of dilapidation are festooned with faded signs announcing good times and cheap thrills which one can no longer have. At least not here, she thought. Coney Island was not salvaged and collected. Looking around, Madame Realism didn't conjure notions of pleasure but ones of death and loss, of what gets remembered and what gets thrown away."[84] If the Lower East Side risked becoming a carnival ride for middle-class observers, that might not last forever in Madame Realism's world. As a persona, Madame Realism stood outside everything that the East Village scene *and* its critics stood for, counseling her readers to walk away and head back to their rooms, where they might dream ways to exit all of it. Refusing the work of the critic, Tillman interrupts the continuities between living and working that were assembling in the Lower East Side. In her novels of the era, she draws out this critique, showing readers in particular the ways that the creative economy failed for women.

The Post-Fordist Worker and the Art Novel

In their criticism, both Indiana and Tillman responded to the critiques lodged by Owens, Foster, and others against the "puerile," mercantilist, art emerging from the Lower East Side. For these critics, these problems were both symbolized and amplified by the role that artists played in gentrifying the Lower East Side. At the time, it was clear to most commentators that art had taken a bad turn. For Foster, the art of the East Village entailed "an acceptance of the cultural division of labor (of the marginal role of the artist as romantic, entertainer, purveyor of prestige goods) and a legitimation of social subjection and authoritarian tendencies in the present."[85] The Modernist critiques lodged by Minimalism and Conceptualism were over, and artists, instead of offering an outside to capitalism, had become at best peripheral to critique and at worst absorbed into capitalism.

But what was not precisely visible to these critics, and has become clear since, was the role that artists might play in providing a model for a new kind of worker. In a range of ways—from the management literature studied by Boltanski and Chiapello in *The New Spirit of Capitalism* to the government initiatives studied by critics of the creative economy—the landscape in which the artist was located was shifting. In this context, narrative literature plays, as Sarah Brouillette has demonstrated, a complex and shifting role. On the one hand, Brouillette contends, such literature traces and evaluates the cultivation of the worker as an autonomous, creative subject, drawing on the affordances of narrative form to show readers the uneasy, frustrated position of the worker in post-Fordist times. On the other hand, literature helps to explain and justify these new social arrangements, encouraging readers, for example, to develop an "authentic expressive self" that they can bring to their post-Fordist job, or to develop a "faith in one's distance from market imperatives" that might make one "better able to engage in work that would prove both economically and socially productive."[86] In other words, literature may help readers recognize the limitations of the type of work demanded by the creative economy, while at the same time, potentially reinforce for readers the ideal of the artist's lifestyle at the core of the creative economy.

Both *Horse Crazy* (1989) and *Haunted Houses* (1987) feature artist characters who desire, but fail to find, artistic autonomy. Their criticism helped readers identify strategies to navigate the cathected formations of art-gentrification. Their fiction, though, shows readers the painful compromises required to adopt these critical positions. For Indiana, it means admitting that privately he loved the artists he despised. For Tillman, it means recognizing that the shift to post-Fordist modes of life offered liberating possibilities for women, even as these possibilities were cut off by lived reality.

The self-scrutinizing potential of *Haunted Houses* and *Horse Crazy* derives from these works' thematic and formal choices, which share elements with the New Narrative movement that emerged out of San Francisco in the 1970s and 1980s. (Tillman and Indiana were both included in the recent anthology of New Narrative writing edited by Dodie Bellamy and Kevin Killian, *Writers Who Love Too Much*; the pair describe Tillman as "the mother of us all."[87]) Influenced by rising poststructuralist theories of language and writing, New Narrative is characterized by a reflexive awareness of how language creates meaning, and, by extension, how all writing is artifice.[88] Throughout New Narrative works, characters scrutinize how their selves are constructed out of the social material around them. As I note in my introduction, while "properly" postmodern writers like Don DeLillo and Thomas Pynchon present characters as functions of larger, often national systems, New Narrative writers focus on local manifestations of the social.[89] Tillman told Siegle, in very New Narrative terms, "If you're not reflecting on the fact that you're writing with sign systems, if you write as what you're writing is totally transparent, a given, than I think you're in a lot of trouble."[90] Writ large, New Narrative adopted the rising poststructuralist focus on the linguistic construction of reality toward helping readers understand how narrative worked.

Critics writing on New Narrative often locate it within the movement literature of the 1960s and 1970s, whereby self-conscious narration creates communities and motivates activism. But the New Narrative mode, with its constant self-interrogation and questioning of the possibility of relating to others, also lends itself well to thinking through post-Fordist demands on the worker. For critics like Paulo Virno, Mauricio Lazzarato, and Isabell Lorey, the post-Fordist worker, cut off from the hierarchies and securities of the Fordist wage and its attendant separation between workplace and home, finds her whole self—her personality, her identity, her intellect—harvested by the workplace and deployed to find the next gig. According to Lorey, post-Fordist modes of production "challenge the whole personality, its intellect, its thinking, its capacity for speaking, its affects."[91] That's because the instability of post-Fordist labor makes workers dependent on the goodwill of others to secure their next gig. In the late 1960s, workers demanded greater autonomy in the workplace. The eventual result, even for manual workers, is a situation where "one *has to* express oneself, one *has to* speak, communicate, cooperate, and so forth . . . the subjects of that production must be capable of communication—they must be active participants within a work team."[92] Both *Haunted Houses* and *Horse Crazy* foreground characters consciously aware of how self-making and self-fashioning collide with and become necessary to making a living. As such, they are well-suited to making visible the "complex interplay of economy and personality that defines contemporary work."[93] Tillman's female characters fail to support themselves as artists, and endlessly ask themselves why. Indiana's queer characters find ways to support themselves, but find their authenticity compromised by the effort.

Haunted Houses, the Fordist Wage, and Making It in the Lower East Side

The Lower East Side of the 1970s and 1980s made a lot of promises to the artists and would-be artists that moved there. Like SoHo, the neighborhood might offer new ways of living that would allow artist and worker alike more control of their time, more opportunities for creativity, more autonomy—the terms of what Boltanski and Chiapello call the artistic critique. A city in crisis is a city open to new possibilities: you might produce works that "breathed freely and remained connected significantly to the everyday"[94] or find a "fertile artistic environment and a new frontier for change in the social order."[95] More politically, you might resist "postwar suburban political consensus that sets the city and its lives aside, and to the breaking up, repressing, and reordering of urban populations according to the needs of the new economy."[96] Emerging from the collapse of the Fordist order represented by the 1975 fiscal crisis, the art of the Lower East Side was supposed to entail a new way of living and to critique the ways of living that still held on from midcentury. This tendency is so pronounced that when Robert Siegle wrote a book about the literary scene in the 1980s, he called it *Suburban Ambush*—a war waged against the deadness of the suburbs, and the development of forms of life with starkly different goals and values. In hindsight, we can read "suburban ambush" as a variation on the artistic critique—a rejection of the calcified Fordist order represented by the suburbs.

Haunted Houses has two characteristics that are essential for sorting out how writers in the Lower East Side moved between thinking of themselves as artists and thinking of themselves as post-Fordist workers. First, Tillman marks its characters explicitly as products of Fordist childhoods—they move from hierarchized, well-organized spaces based on a stable Fordist wage to flattened, disorganized spaces of precarity. These are the spaces celebrated in accounts of the Lower East Side as a haven for artists. Second, Tillman makes her characters relentlessly question the ways in which their selves are constructed, and how these constructions relate them to other people. Artistic lifestyles should provide new ways to construct these selves, but the demands of both lingering Fordist patriarchy and the deflated welfare state mean that these attempts fail.

On one level, *Haunted Houses* is a work thoroughly indebted to second-wave feminism, joining work by Acker, Margaret Atwood, Toni Morrison, and others that made the 1980s a decade in which women's concerns were at the forefront of literary production. But in the art world, things were slightly different. By and large, this world was experiencing a shift from the women-friendly pluralism that had energized the art world in the late seventies and early eighties, to a Neo-Expressionism that would dominate art markets and sideline the significant contributions of female artists.[97] *Haunted Houses* is concerned, we might surmise, with the situation that Tillman found herself in in the 1970s and 1980s, a world where the possibilities for feminist art never seemed greater, but one in which these possibilities were constantly shrinking. More widely, as Melinda Cooper argues, this is a world in which the solidities of the Fordist regime have fallen away, but one in which the certainties of the Fordist wage have also fallen away, and in which the work of social reproduction continues to fall on women. Fighting to make it in the city, Tillman's characters encounter rich men who rape them, boyfriends who sideline their creativity, and dead-end jobs that foreclose their aspirations.[98] These are characters who believe, as one character quotes Merleau-Ponty, that "[c]onsciousness always exists in a situation," and that situation is one of enclosure, not liberation.[99]

At the same time that *Haunted Houses* looks on the gender hierarchies of the Fordist era, it charts the uncertain paths that its protagonists take out of this era. In the New York of the 1970s, there was already wide recognition of what Cooper has argued: that the Fordist order had depended on a family wage. For civil rights and feminist activists, it would only be by cracking open this wage—expanding it to unwaged work and ensuring that it applied to nonnormative subjects—that the promises of the Fordist compact could be genuinely fulfilled. The family was at the core of the set of anti-welfare-state reforms that lay at the heart of the 1975 crisis. Reading a series of reports issued by First National Bank in the early 1970s, the historian Michael Reagan describes how bankers viewed "women headed households" as particularly problematic, because these households tend to be those receiving welfare.[100]

The bankers' concerns were not idle. Activists associated with the Wages for Housework movement, then building a stronghold in Brooklyn, recognized that welfare's direct benefits might be, in fact, a way to extend the breadwinner wage of Fordism to single women, including single women of color. The women of this collective saw the crisis for what it was: a resistance to the demand that the wageless labor of women be compensated. This is the knife's-edge moment described by Cooper, when "public assistance benefits, however menial, were functioning like a social wage for unmarried women" at the very moment "employment opportunities and access to higher education for both white and nonwhite women were expanding as never before," a "profoundly liberating development."[101]

Using the techniques of New Narrative, *Haunted Houses* takes up the problem of culture workers moving to New York and struggling to write their stories. It charts a pattern that was emerging in the 1970s and 1980s, whereby middle-class workers began to move out of the suburbs and into what had previously been marginal neighborhoods—the foundation of second-wave gentrification.[102] It tells the stories of three women: Jane, Emily, and Grace, women who have moved out of their suburban homes and who seek to find, in the seemingly more open world of the New York art scene, more egalitarian forms of life. Each aspires to be some kind of artist; each encounters men who make this process difficult; each flees a past in which their identities were tightly controlled.

The "haunting" motif binds all three characters to the Fordist era. They begin their narrative arcs in their childhood homes; these are the houses in the novel's title. The first chapters map the contours of these homes. These homes are both patriarchal and located in suburban areas. These are the stable spaces of Fordism, and all three women's character arcs take them from these spaces to the city. These women are products of the circumstances that Cooper describes in *Family Values*, wherein the gender arrangements of the Fordist compact persist well after its decline, and are activated by the revolt that Boltanski and Chiapello describe. None of them go anywhere. They struggle for a while, find role models of women who live outside these systems (Edith, sustained on her dead husband's money; Sinuway, a transplant from another culture), but they find no after to Fordism: "The older woman said many things that the younger one listened to but would not hear until years later, and then like an echo."[103] The men around them find opportunity after opportunity: Jimmy with antique store and theater, Felix with painting, Mark with his play. Their position is Jane's position: "Their arguments were often about the ineffable and she found herself speechless in the face of Felix's libertarian awfulness and Jimmy's veiled masculine strivings."[104] The women in *Haunted Houses* cannot be artists—or Emily can, but she has to move away from New York to do so.

In a New Narrative mode, the three protagonists continually interrogate their selves as constructed. For example, Grace imagines herself as "a kind of box of odds and ends. The nothingness overwhelmed her, thoughts of death slipping into her mind like poison-pen letters." Similarly, Emily, reflecting on her relationship with her friend Christine, asks "Are we lesbians and we don't know it?" as she "walk[s] fast to speed up her thoughts." Jane writes in her diary: "Something rendered is invisible. What did I think about BEFORE when I was young? I'm part of what I was thinking about then but it's not there anymore. The sum of my parts is invisible. Jane liked that line, 'sum of my parts,' a person could be added to or subtracted from, or a person could add up to anything."[105] All three characters emphasize that their selves are constructed. Their sense of their constructed selves both stems from and reveals these characters' precarious existence; they are searching for a form of life that will stabilize them, and continual self-interrogation seems both a natural means to identify such a form, and shows readers the struggle to do so.

In his reading of *Haunted Houses*, Siegle describes its style in ways that the New Narrative critics would recognize: "startlingly direct and 'unliterary,'" "unmannered and undercoded," and "resisting any totalizing illusions that would weave an organic whole out of disparate and contending elements."[106] That's in part a way of saying that the novel doesn't readily cohere: its three protagonists never meet, and their individual narrative arcs move in spirals rather than lines: each ends slightly less dissatisfied than they began, having made a decision to move, take a new job, or take a new lover. Siegle has to work hard to develop a reading of *Haunted Houses* that fits his own argument that a "fiction of insurgency" had taken root downtown, one that sought to "corrode rather than conform to the commodity formulae toward which latter-day modernist fiction trends."[107] There's little corrosion in *Haunted Houses*; it works in a quieter, more resigned mode. But its contradictions make it a rich document for scrutinizing the complicated position in which a culture worker like Tillman found herself in the late 1970s and 1980s, particularly as a woman.

From the perspective of the present, it seems clear that these artists flee into what Boltanski and Chiapello call the "projective city," a place of more autonomy, but less security.[108] What seemed like a wholesale change in living becomes, in the long view, a shift between modes of capitalism. In *Haunted Houses*, Tillman is skeptical of this flight. Developed through a feminist lens, *Haunted Houses* critiques the idealism of "frontier" space, a largely masculine realm in which subjects rework both self and environment. Instead, *Haunted Houses* points to the rising stasis of capital's return by focusing on the continuities between suburb and city.

Tillman plays out the contradictions of *Haunted Houses* in a work that functions as a kind of sequel to it, 1998's *No Lease on Life*. As the critic Diarmuid Hester demonstrates, *No Lease on Life* is a post-gentrification novel, one that takes up, from the perspective of 1994, the accelerating displacements that took place in the Lower East Side.[109] That novel's protagonist, Elizabeth, a few years older than Jane, Emily, or Grace, has found stability in the Lower East Side. She reads as a more grown-up, settled version of the characters in *Haunted Houses*. Unlike the three protagonists in *Haunted Houses*, Elizabeth does not have endless plans of *becoming*. She has arrived, but she has arrived at a point of stasis. She works in a kind of cell—a proof room full of "white, college graduates, middle-class misfits who accepted inferior jobs and were not ambitious" at a financial magazine. She has taken the job "with reluctance."[110] Tillman herself worked a similar job in the 1980s while she completed *Haunted Houses*. In *No Lease on Life*, Elizabeth has reached a point of stasis, but appreciates the benefits such stasis brings: health care and a pension plan. Ironically, Elizabeth has achieved what the families of Jane, Grace, and Emily achieved under Fordism. But that also means that she has encountered the stasis and hierarchy that form the targets of the artistic critique.

In turn, this stability has altered her perspective on the neighborhood. For Elizabeth, the Lower East Side is not a place of interesting thrills and new encounters: it is, instead, a place where she faces the same problems day after day: struggles with her landlord, struggles with the homeless youth outside her apartment, an attempt to help a young prostitute, a continual sense of the neighborhood's filth. What might have seemed romantic in past years—fucking on dirty clothes in a young artist's apartment—has become a site of disgust: "Elizabeth couldn't remember if she found this scene romantic when she was twenty. Fucking on dirty clothes. She was too old to be young, couldn't revive her adolescence like a comeback career."[111] In attending to people on the street, *No Lease on Life* conveys the unevenness of gentrification. The homeless and prostitutes, far from energizing the protagonist's self, dislodge and depress this self. *No Lease on Life* serves, in some sense, as a cautionary tale about the possibilities of a neighborhood where "anything could happen," and presents the limits of the vision offered by the Artist Homeownership Program. Instead of autonomy, Elizabeth gets drudgery. Her colleagues "worked in fear. They feared the reduction of their hours, they feared learning that they were no longer needed, maybe only one or two of them, they feared becoming redundant."[112] In Hester's compelling terms, *No Lease on Life* serves a "riposte" to the art-driven changes I describe in this chapter, serving as an anti-gentrification novel.[113] It reveals gentrification as a failure, providing its subjects with nothing more than deadness.

Haunted Houses traces the emergence of a form of life. The New York of the 1970s and 1980s seemed to offer liberation from the hierarchies of the Fordist era. For a while, artists and writers could live on very little, and this afforded them opportunities to build new kinds of affiliation, which are partly realized in artist collectives and the flourishing of nonnormative identities. The transformed welfare state, accompanied by the cheap rents afforded by withdrawn capital, made it possible to imagine new vistas. These conditions allowed for a momentary redistribution of the sensible, in which, for example, the New Narrative writer Bruce Boone might imagine "a community of the future that exists only in dreams."[114] These conditions made the possibilities of a new world seem more and more visible.

But in *Haunted Houses*, women show up to take advantage of these conditions only to find themselves hemmed in at every turn. Their world ends up being a world not of fallen limitations but of new ones imposed, both in terms of gender models carried over from the Fordist era and in terms of limited possibilities for work as they moved further into the 1980s. If Tillman's peers envisioned an amazing future once the Fordist state was blown away, Tillman is less optimistic. She doesn't quite buy the notion that there's a suburban ambush to be had here. What's to be had instead is a continual renegotiation, in the very terms that Cooper points to, of the welfare state's categories.

Tillman's characters want to do it themselves: they go to the right places, they seek the right way of living, they cultivate models of other people who did it themselves. They seek to tell their own stories, even as they recognize that these stories are built from the fragments of others' stories. But they end up showing readers that do-it-yourself depends heavily on what you mean by "yourself," or, at least, that there are few possibilities other than "coupling up," as Brouillette puts it in a review of Cooper's *Family Values*.[115] Tillman's novel, more pessimistic and low-key than its downtown peers, expresses a truth about bohemian life not quite visible at its moment. In contemporaneous works by Tama Janowitz and Mary Gaitskill, women are disappointed by men; in *Haunted Houses*, they're disappointed by themselves. *Haunted Houses* depicts these women's lives as unresolvable, but unlike Acker's *Blood and Guts in High School*, where the violence of being a woman explodes everywhere, *Haunted Houses* works to keep things locked down. There's no rage, no exit: just a turn inward. Tillman writes, "Home was a room that smelled too empty. The chair was uncomfortable" and "Sometimes I feel like there's no difference between my body and this chair I'm sitting in. In a funny way I think I don't exist."[116] You could move from one set of boxes in the suburbs to another set in the city, and it might be that things were supposed to change, but they do not change.

Horse Crazy and the Problem of Loving the Artist

In his columns, Indiana assessed a wide range of the city's cultural productions, always with an eye toward how art might express its own material conditions. But at the same time, Indiana often used his columns to complain about writing them. In a June 1985 column, he notes, "The reader has had to hear my ideas and opinions every week for over a year, and I have had to come up with them every week, often with a deep sense of embarrassment over having quite so much to say about things that my not, in many cases, finally be worth entertaining an opinion about." As an aside, he adds, "A writer who never tires of hearing his own voice must be singularly blessed or cursed. Not I, not I."[117] In another column, mourning the death of his friend Carlos Claren, he takes the lament further: "You know, the way we live now, especially here, you don't get an hour to sit quietly in a room and simply think about someone: *I'm late with my column*."[118] As if to prove his reluctance to produce content week after week, two columns, "The Physiology of Taste" (January 7, 1986) and "The Wages of Angst" (July 15, 1985), consist entirely of quotations from other authors.[119] Like Elizabeth from Tillman's *No Lease on Life*, Indiana was ambivalent about regular work, and his columns exhibit a tension between his role as a critic and the identity he seeks to maintain outside of this role.

In turning from his columns to fiction, Indiana scrutinizes and carries forward such tension. He does so in part by reversing the terms of his columns. If his columns praised art that pointed outside itself to its material conditions, *Horse Crazy* presents a narrator literally embracing autonomous art—symbolized by an artist comically insulated from the world around him—to avoid such experience. His failure to avoid the problems associated with this artist provides much of the novel's tension. Published in 1989 but set in 1985 and written throughout the late 1980s, *Horse Crazy* describes a nameless, Indiana-like narrator's hopeless, unconsummated relationship with a younger artist named Gregory.[120] It is alternately funny, lyrical, and confessional, composed in a largely realist mode interspersed with long asides—characteristic of New Narrative.

The novel's focus in the main is on the 1980s New York art world: the narrator writes reviews for a weekly "magazine" that sounds much like *The Village Voice*; Gregory creates photo-collage art that sounds like the mid-eighties work of David Wojnarowicz mixed with Richard Prince's appropriation (Indiana had a relationship with the former and praised the latter in a 1985 column). In interviews, Indiana has positioned Gregory as a kind of naïve East Village artist "like most young men in Manhattan at the time" as the narrator scoffs.[121] *Horse Crazy* presents a narrator whose public tastes may run to the kind of non-gentrifying, non-mercantile art praised by Indiana the columnist, but whose private tastes draw him to the very kind of artist that Indiana the columnist hates. While it's true that Gregory works in photo-collage, some of his work also sounds like Indiana's account of David Salle in *The Village Voice*, as an artist "for whom just about anything visual can work as material: slap it on over slide-projected beaver or some fabric samples and you've got the whole history of art jumping out in all directions."[122]

By 1989, Indiana's portrait of Gregory had become something of a trope, used by Lower East Side writers to untangle the complicated experience of living in a gentrifying neighborhood that their work itself was helping to gentrify. Work by Mary Gaitskill, Catherine Texier, Tillman, Patrick McGrath and others take up and mock the privileged bohemian artist who is so self-involved that he (and it's always a "he") can't see his own pretension and ineptitude. But why engage Gregory, then? Is *Horse Crazy* on the one hand a typical Lower East Side novel and on the other a tale of Indiana's own failed relationship? Bearing in mind Indiana's struggle against *Tilted Arc*, I'd suggest that the answer is more complicated: that Indiana views Gregory as an index of shifting, art-driven changes in the city's governance and finance, though one in which he is implicated himself. After all, the narrator compares Gregory to something that sounds very much like *Tilted Arc:*

> There is a wall I run up against, again and again (a dream). At times what is needed is this blank, horrendous wall. You rise up flush against its solid, gritty surface and can't move any further. Even if you thwack your skull repeatedly against this wall, becoming bloody and insensible, the wall doesn't know you, doesn't yield, doesn't pity. A pitiless wall, a pity. That's how it is. Let's say you think of leaping over it. Well, perhaps you can. But you don't think you can, which is the same as not being able to. It's too high, just looking at it brings on a spasm of fear. You think: I'll smoke a cigarette, have a drink, come back to it. And your absence adds an inch or so to the wall. You return: my God, that's a big wall. You seek advice about methods of jumping, phone people up. They tell you not to think about it, just jump. Jump blind. Or they might say, Don't force yourself,

take it easy. Jump in little stages. Or: Maybe you're up against the wrong wall. Or: trying walking around the wall. Slinking around it. Pretend the wall isn't there. Walk through the wall.[123]

But since the narrator is talking about his love interest here, the relationship between wall and person is more complicated. Indiana can't dismiss this version of *Tilted Arc* as the product of a debutante, as he had Serra, for he loves the debutante. But like *Tilted Arc*, this wall indexes a range of social experiences: while at first, this wall seems to be Gregory himself, as the novel proceeds, it becomes clear that the wall is instead more like the crisis that the narrator finds himself in, both as a gay man (thus far) undiagnosed with AIDS and as a would-be artist immobilized by the networks around him. The wall's stasis is the narrator's stasis, and its physicality is the physicality of the infected body and the materially real history of the neighborhood. *Horse Crazy* repeatedly returns to two problems, that of a neighborhood infected by gentrification and a body infected with AIDS. The narrator may decry Yuppie tastes—in one of the novel's finer passages, he ruminates on the way people who seem "refreshingly sympathetic, strong-minded, subtle, well-informed" will nevertheless prattle on about their "passion for inanimate objects"—but as he readily admits, Gregory is just such an inanimate object, one who emerges, at the novel's end, as nothing but a stain on the wall seen poorly from across a crowded bar.[124]

Moreover, objects like *Tilted Arc* cannot be readily dismissed in *Horse Crazy* because they invade the narrator's living space. The narrator describes his apartment as filled with objects he hates: an oversized metal chair, an unwieldy desk that is "the bane of my kitchen, as the built-in shelving is the bane of my study, the flimsy fiberboard closet and yellow foam chair the banes of the living room/bedroom area." He continues, "I know I could easily, easily become paralyzed, if I think too long about the blue desk in the kitchen, but about all the related, unsatisfactory things which make me less than perfect, the things Gregory will instantly notice. The childish objects I save and leave out in the open, for lack of more precious objects. The general look of disorientation, the visible evidence of mental asymmetry."[125] These objects interfere with courting Gregory: comically, the narrator begs a friend to help him clean his apartment, only to be shamed when he learns that Gregory has heard about his desperation.

One reason for objects being so unwieldy is that they contrast with the fragility of bodies infected with AIDS: "you watch as your body entertains your enemies at dinner, its loyalties divided between you and them, and after a while you become hypnotized by the disappearance of yourself."[126] Watching an old lover die in a hospital room, the narrator reflects, "suddenly a chair takes on an incredible solidity." The narrator observes of a dying friend, "If he knocked on wood he'd probably break his hand."[127] And the narrator associates the disorienting conditions of his apartment with the terrible truth of the death that surrounds him, a past of the living but socially dead that appear at the edges of consciousness the moment he turns away from the insistent present that Gregory represents. For the apartment also "carries the faint musty smell" of "[a]n era of pickups and bizarre micro-affairs with boys whose point of reference belonged to another planet altogether, the underbelly of Young America. Disturbed youths and borderline schizos harvested off Second Avenue in the doldrums beyond midnight, lean bodies and adorable faces that evaporated in daylight or loitered for days in a carnal stupor."[128] Friends dying of AIDS, desks that won't move; the narrator's fugue seeks to avoid all such past things.

Horse Crazy foregrounds, in ways that Indiana's columns do not, the situatedness of Indiana's critique in queer space. While the bulk of Jose Muñoz's work on queer space concerns space of positive potentiality—sites of what he calls "queer utopia"—he also acknowledges, drawing on Virno, that the power of "bad sentiments [that] can signal the capacity to transcend hopelessness . . . sentiments associated with despondence contain the potential for new modes of collectivity, belonging in difference and dissent."[129] It follows that such sentiments form part of what Muñoz calls "another way of being in both the world and time, a desire that resists mandates to accept that which is not enough."[130] In her work on willfulness, Sara Ahmed similarly articulates a productively uncomfortable form of queer space, a willfulness that develops out of "a bodily experience of not being accommodated by a space: how a space is organized can become what 'gets in the way' of a forward progression."[131] And for Ahmed, such discomfort is productive, resulting in, "a practical craft that is acquired through involvement in political struggle, whether that struggle is a struggle to exist or to transform an existence."[132] It's not quite the case to say that Indiana articulates queer aesthetics; after all, some of the art he targets in his columns are icons of queer aesthetics, as with Keith Haring. Instead, he brings a queer discomfort to his objects of critique.

Indiana the novelist recognizes a complexity about the creative economy that Indiana the critic does not. The shiny objects of this economy, while ephemeral and damaging to the social life of the city, are nevertheless appealing. Gregory both makes shiny objects and, by living in a still-impoverished section of the Lower East Side, serves as an agent of gentrification. But to the narrator, Gregory offers a respite from the troubling problem of social history. He continually runs to Gregory in order to turn away from both the compromised realities of his job and the awful specter of the narrator's friends dying from AIDS. The narrator thus experiences tension between damning the mercantilism of the art world—as Indiana did in his columns—and embracing the distraction provided by Gregory.

This tension is never clearer than when the narrator reflects on his own working circumstances. Ostensibly, these are better than those of Gregory: the narrator has "made it." But as it turns out, to make it is to have one's creative freedom absorbed into one's work:

> Therefore, I considered, the so-called freedom I enjoy, in contrast to Gregory's servitude in his menial job, his status as a wage slave, only makes me more aware of the impossibility of any freedom, since everything I do contributes to everything that oppresses me and everything that oppresses him. . . . If I write and publish my writing, I end up selling out my inner life in order to remain alive, everything that lives within me becomes something for sale, therefore the more I write the less existence I have, consequently the more I produce and expands if I write less, the less I write the freer I become, but in order to remain free it's necessary to sell my writing, and so, the less free I am, the freer I appear to be.[133]

These are the problems visible in darker ruminations of theorists like Virno: artistic autonomy always requires a compromise with post-Fordist capital.

The novel's own form performs this problem: ever the art critic, the narrator relentlessly aestheticizes everything he sees, as in this account of their first dinner together: "A waiter, who seemed about three feet high, set down enormous menus and two water glasses. The menus, bound in brownish vinyl, felt clammy. The amber water glasses had a malarial cast," or "I can imagine Gregory ten years ago, even more beautiful than he is now, like a smooth doll unmarked by experience."[134] Of course, part of this is Indiana's critical voice seeping into his novel, but it's also true that *Horse Crazy* is the story of a man driven crazy because he can't stop being a critic. This means that he has difficulty engaging with the lived history taking shape around him.

The novel shifts tone, however, when it addresses AIDS. For such passages, which describe ex-lovers and friends dying in hospitals or dying alone in their apartments watching television, the novel slows down and stops aestheticizing. In interviews, Indiana describes *Horse Crazy* as overtly designed to resist aestheticizing AIDS, against what he calls "so-called realist books that followed a politically correct line. They had all these absurd myths—that illness ennobles people; that it makes them into better people; that kind of thing."[135] The novel would seem to emphasize as much by contrasting a non-aestheticized AIDS with an aestheticized everything else. In *Horse Crazy*'s aesthetic economy, AIDS presents what Rancière calls a "suprasensible experience" that the novel's aestheticized passages resist. AIDS intrudes whenever the narrator stops being an art critic—something he cannot do elsewhere in the novel. *Tilted Arc* may, for Indiana, obliterate all sorts of lived reality with its arrogant material project, but in *Horse Crazy*, Indiana recognizes the complications involved with engaging such lived reality: the tension that Rancière describes between "a politics of art" and "an art of politics."[136]

One of Indiana's more moving columns concerns Meg Webster's *Hollow*, installed on the grounds of the Nassau County Museum. Responding to Webster's work, Indiana restages the problem of discomfort he associated with *Tilted Arc*: "in *Hollow*, everything has been arranged to sidestep a received experience of normality within nature. Yet the piece is restorative, tonic, contemplative . . . at peace with its own contents. As if someone, in the night, had moved the refrigerator into the bathroom, and you woke and got something out of it with no geographical uncertainty."[137] This kind of art-enabled ease with the environment—what Indiana saw Serra attacking, and what *Horse Crazy*'s narrator cannot resolve—leads Indiana to observe: "*Hollow* makes you feel that living and dying are important processes to pay attention to, and that everyone is always doing both. You could die even if you belonged to the country club, and you could live even if you don't."[138] Linking social conflict with the material reality of death, Indiana's reading of Webster's work serves as a summation of art's ambivalent possibilities in post-crisis New York. In doing so, he conveys what Ahmed calls "joy in creating worlds out of the broken pieces of our dwelling spaces . . . We can say this, as we have been there, in that place, that shadowy place, willful subjects tend to find themselves; a place that can feel lonely can be how we reach others."[139] Throughout columns and novel, Indiana brought his broken dwelling places to bear on the rising tensions of a post-crisis city that increasingly deployed art to mediate its own uncomfortable transition. At a moment of clarity, when the narrator is out of the lulling influence of Gregory, he notes, in reference to AIDS "We used to say: How can we live like this? And now the question really is: How can we die like this?"[140] Questions of how to live and how to die underpin *Horse Crazy*, establishing the terrible stakes of the tensions produced by a city shifting towards finance and an art world happy to enable such.

Conclusion

After the 1975 fiscal crisis, city planners had several goals. Slashing public funding for housing and direct benefits, they sought to encourage gentrification as a means to counter the "blight" of impoverished neighborhoods. With manufacturing in decline, they sought to shift the city's economy toward a service model. The first shift found a ready precedent in the conversion of SoHo from manufacturing district, first to artists' colony, then to hip location for lofts. The second shift encouraged wider shifts in work, from the industrial, hierarchical mode of Fordism to the service-oriented, networked mode of post-Fordism. The art boom of the Lower East Side played a crucial role in both cases. By returning to the 1980s work of Gary Indiana and Lynne Tillman, we can trace the ways that writers both resisted and refracted these trends. Across their criticism and novels, Indiana and Tillman offer readers ways to orient themselves to the highly charged artworld of the 1980s. The idiosyncratic critical projects of both interrupt the calcified conclusions that art critics produced in the 1980s, anticipating Rancière's emphasis on the knowledgeable spectator. Their fiction helps readers see how culture workers struggled to orient themselves to new forms of art-inflected work.

The creative economy promises much: that instead of the dull, grinding work of the nine-to-five office or the factory shift, the worker finds work that rewards her, and in which she is free from the hierarchical management that characterized earlier moments of capitalism. The broken buildings and vacant lots of the Lower East Side offered a site for the creative economy to flourish, in ways that were both resisted by and reinforced by its artists. But the promises of the creative economy were already falling short in the 1980s. Scrutinizing the art world from the perspective of the Lower East Side, Tillman and Indiana's work foregrounds these limitations.

Chapter 5

Between Fordism and Post-Fordism
The DIY Literature of Between C & D

When Joel Rose and Catherine Texier started producing a literary journal on their dot-matrix printer in 1983, they called it *Between C & D*. The name was literal: the pair lived at 255 East Seventh Street, about halfway between Avenue C and Avenue D. "Between C and D" was the address they'd give to cab drivers who were reluctant to drive them down the Lower East Side's most forbidding blocks. But *Between C & D* named something more, as Robert Siegle notes in his chapter on the journal: "bohemian culture colliding with the mayhem of gang life" and "the economic warfare of food and water, housing and heat."[1] The politics of austerity imposed after the 1975 New York fiscal crisis amplified, and often created, the mayhem and the warfare.[2] In *Between C & D*, Rose and Texier printed the experience of living at this address—the sounds of breaking glass, the shouting echoing through vacant lots, the people moving through the tenement building—but also the networks that assembled between bohemians and gang members, bodegas and tenements, boilers and fire hydrants. Chattering out of the printer, the pages of *Between C & D* reproduced the post-fiscal-crisis Lower East Side in all its complexity.

During the years *Between C & D* ran, the editors of a literary journal were not the only people to take an active interest in the Lower East Side's built environment. So did politicians, real estate developers, entrepreneurs, and activists. Landlord abandonment had left Alphabet City especially bereft after the 1975 fiscal crisis.[3] But in the 1980s, real estate developers slowly began to move back into the neighborhood, aided by a number of city policies. The combination of abandoned buildings and real estate opportunities created predictable strife. As I discussed in chapter 4, the Artists' Homeownership Program, hotly opposed by neighborhood activists, became a nexus for questions of who had a right to housing. Alphabet City's transitioning real estate market meant that East Seventh street in particular, where Rose and Texier set up shop, accommodated a range of rents. For example, a nineteen-unit building in the mid-1980s could have rents ranging from $256 to $835, which meant that a single walkup might contain "generations of Puerto Rican families paying modest rents, squatters, college students . . . drug addicts, blue-collar workers . . . fashion designers, musicians, and management trainees."[4] Living in and rehabilitating one of those walkups, Rose and Texier solicited literary works that evinced a complex, even contradictory, environment at the level of both content and form.

Returning to *Between C & D* reveals not only a crucial hinge between modes of production, literary and otherwise, but also new insights into how literary projects record as well as respond to the built environments of gentrification. *Between C & D* documents the Lower East Side as a space produced by a wide range of different groups: Puerto Rican housing activists, gallery owners, working-class Poles, entrepreneurs, and makers of community gardens. Henri Lefebvre observes that "groups, classes, or fractions of classes cannot constitute themselves, or recognize one another, as 'subjects' unless they generate (or produce) a space." And how do they produce such a space? For Lefebvre, they must "mak[e] their mark on space." Otherwise, they "will lose all pith and become mere signs, resolve themselves into abstract descriptions, or mutate into fantasies."[5] In the post-crisis years, groups, classes, and fractions of classes marked space in the Lower East Side in a number of ways: by reclaiming vacant lots as community gardens, by making art out of refuse, by reusing old buildings. These groups often had to resist fantasies imposed on the neighborhood, particularly notions of the Lower East Side as some kind of wild "frontier." Produced in a rehabilitated apartment building, *Between C & D* is at once an example of such marking and a record of others' markings.

During the 1980s, outside pressures, particularly real estate developers and national media, threatened to make the Lower East Side a mere system of signs: a set of fantasies about danger and risk, often subsumed, as Neil Smith has observed, under the master term "frontier."[6] Acknowledging and incorporating this problem, *Between C & D* tracked a complex Lower East Side, the kind of world that Rose describes in his 1988 novel *Kill the Poor:* "hard boys on the corners, teenage girls with their babies hanging outside buildings, brickwork coming down, junkies lined up, old men hanging out windows listening to the sounds of salsa, the big box, the ghetto attaché, the pothole traffic, the Kool Man ice cream truck, the Chihuahua dog."[7] Though it includes junkies and hard boys—components of the risky frontier fantasy—this list encompasses a broad cross-section of the social world of the Lower East Side. Readers glimpse a neighborhood brimming with activity. This was the world that *Between C & D* recorded on a dot matrix printer set in front of Rose and Texier's open window on East Seventh street.

A range of elements assembled to make *Between C & D* possible: among these, the redeveloped apartment itself, an open editorial policy, and a dot-matrix printer were crucial. These let *Between C & D* engage the themes that I've examined in previous chapters: the decline of the welfare state, rising art markets, a clash between working-class and bohemian residents, the influence of French theory, the legacy of 1960s identity movements, and the steady forces of feminism and queer rights. To be a writer in the Lower East Side of the 1980s was to experience all of this at once. *Between C & D*, therefore, engaged multiple senses of "between": between the 1975 fiscal crisis and the post-Fordist recovery, between mimeographed zine and Web-based journal, between art and literature, between working-class Puerto Rican and middle-class gentrifier. It could do all this because the apartment building itself was between ruin and redevelopment.

This quality of being "in between" has meant that *Between C & D* has itself often slipped out of critical sight. Siegle's *Suburban Ambush* (1989) remains the only major monograph to devote an entire chapter to the journal, though Elizabeth Young and Graham Caveney's *Shopping in Space* (1993) as well as Catalina Neculai's *Urban Space and Late Twentieth Century New York Literature* (2014) cover *Between C & D* briefly. Texier and Rose promoted writing that eschewed the dominant literary paradigms of its era as outlined by Mark McGurl in *The Program Era*. Only some of the work that *Between C & D* published falls under what McGurl calls "technomodernism" (literature that "emphasizes the all-important engagement of postmodern literature with information technology"), or "high cultural pluralism" (literature that "joins the high literary values of modernism with a fascination with the experience of cultural difference and the authenticity of the ethnic voice").[8] Much of what Rose and Texier printed were works that simply didn't fit into any paradigm.[9] At the time, the journal was praised for such. Writing to Rose, the postmodern author Mark Leyner found *Between C & D* to be a "bracing effervescent antidote to those countless collections of anemic, inevitably academic, neo-junk that we've all come to know and loathe."[10] In fact, some of what Rose and Texier printed had trouble finding an audience elsewhere. Many contributors found themselves in a position like the unnamed protagonist in *Oriental Girls Desire Romance*, a novel that Catherine Liu would go on to publish after one of her stories appeared in *Between C & D*: "Someone told me I was writing a coming-of-age novel, and I thought, is that like a bildungsroman? I said, oh no, no, it's a novel of ideas, but that didn't sound right either. In any case, not being able to call it by some name . . . made it impossible for certain editors, certain cognoscenti on whom the future of this book depended, to really believe that the book was anything at all."[11] Dennis Cooper similarly worried that his experiments in genre had alienated readerships, lamenting in a letter to Rose that his novel *Closer*—excerpted in *Between C & D*—had been "rejected all over the place."[12] *Between C & D* courted work that might shake up the literary firmament, and it wasn't particular about either the credentials of its writers or the possibility of its writing finding a mainstream market.

This outsider literary sensibility allowed *Between C & D* to highlight networks of objects and actors at work under the shifting conditions of the post-crisis years. Rose and Texier's local, political interests extended, in other words, into their aesthetic commitments, and those interests as well as commitments included foregrounding the journal's modes of production. Each folded page of *Between C & D*—pulled out of its plastic baggy, tractor strips still attached—revealed a different corner of the neighborhood to its readers, while the stories themselves foregrounded the block-by-block connections between different groups living in the Lower East Side. In short, Rose and Texier sought to encompass everything that came through their window. That's not to say they didn't exert editorial authority, just that their editorial ethos reflected the variations of their environment. Texier recalls how their apartment building included tenants identifying with a wide variety of classes, ethnicities, and sexualities who also engaged in different types of occupational labor. *Between C & D* documented it all, aiming to capture what Texier calls "the cross-pollination of viewpoints and talents" of the time.[13] In what follows, I tell a new story about *Between C & D*, one that recreates the spaces as well as the technologies that afforded its aesthetics and its politics.

The History of *Between C & D*

The story of *Between C & D* begins in 1981, when Rose and Texier purchased a dilapidated tenement apartment at 255 East Seventh Street. Having bought the apartment as part of a co-op with a group of other residents, they proceeded to renovate it in a manner suited to post-fiscal-crisis DIY. They hauled in drywall, rewired electricity, and fixed the building's boiler—with the help of existing building residents, including a skilled interior house painter from Switzerland.[14] The nearby Bowery Lumber delivered drywall, which had to be hand-carried up the stairs. Little work was done according to code, but the city inspector passed it anyway. Like many artists that moved to the Lower East Side in the 1970s and 1980s, Rose and Texier came looking for a cheap place to live.[15] As did other "homesteaders," they pooled their money with a group of others and bought the building, securing for themselves a cheap place to live in Manhattan. In some sense, what they did was wholly rational. In another sense, what they did was brave and foolish, "all outlaw" in Rose's words, because the dilapidated building had become a place outside the law, a structure cut off from networks of private as well as public development.[16]

Similar buildings, abandoned by their landlords, blighted the Lower East Side of the late 1970s and early 1980s. When historians like Christopher Mele, Kim Phillips-Fein, or Kim Moody describe the devastation to the built environment wrought by the 1975 fiscal crisis, they invoke these buildings as both evidence and symbol. Mele, for example, begins his chapter on the crisis by explaining that "in the early 1970s, many of those who owned property in Loisaida began to walk away from their buildings, leaving uninhabitable and often burned-out shells that soon transformed the landscape into a haunting and urban war zone."[17] Phillips-Fein gives similarly prominent placement to such a building, quoting a letter that South Bronx resident Lyn Smith wrote to senator Jacob Javits, in which Smith describes a child's death resulting from playing in such a building. For Phillips-Fein, Smith's letter is evidence that "many in New York . . . felt they were abandoned" by the federal government in the wake of the crisis.[18] And as Mele demonstrates, both landlords and city agencies deployed such imagery in support of "free market appeals" that were supposed to redress abandonment, but that in the end helped make abandonment a tactical investment strategy.[19] The imagery of the "burned out" Lower East Side became a self-fulfilling prophecy, working in local, state, and national registers to as potent symbols of social and economic decline.[20]

Before Rose and Texier ever purchased it, the building at 255 East Seventh Street itself expressed the constrained economic, social, and political circumstances of the post-crisis years. In her own reading of *Between C & D*, Neculai is correct to interpret the pair's work in terms of the struggles for housing that roiled the Lower East Side in the 1980s and culminated in the 1988 Tompkins Square Riot. For Neculai, because housing involves so many different actors—"individual and institutional, private and public actors, material and social logistic, legislative provisions, ideological and representational practices"—it inevitably incorporates the neighborhood as a whole.[21] But redeveloping the building wasn't just about housing: it was also about situating oneself at a nexus of collective social life. For Rose and Texier, the apartment became form, a container for the bursting energies of the neighborhood. In this sense, redevelopment—the stripping of walls, the reworking of electrical, the painting, the installation of new building materials—was the beginning of their literary project. By redeveloping the apartment, they created a space to write and publish others' work. Their work made the building a safe and stable point from which to view the street; the low cost of living allowed them time to write. They made something meaningful out of the building, and this initial act of making allowed more meanings to proliferate.

None of this should be surprising. As we now know, buildings matter to literary production. McGurl, after all, puts the physical space of the seminar room, or at least the university, at the core of *The Program Era*.[22] More specifically, a range of critics working in media as well as infrastructural studies have described how literary production emerges from a conflux of built environment, technological changes, and the imaginary function of literature itself.[23] In *Corridor: Media Architectures in American Fiction*, for example, Kate Marshall scrutinizes how literary and architectural form interact with one another. "Architecture itself," she writes, "functions in the environment of the literary system, and vice versa, and the surfacing of the architectural form in twentieth century literary accounts of architecture forms a flashpoint in the mutual irritation of both systems."[24] The humble hallway, by moving people through buildings, carrying sound, and connecting rooms, functions like narrative itself, but the emergence of the hallway as an important architectural feature of living environments in the twentieth century also transforms narrative. The corridor is at once a "real technolog[y] of circulation" and an "idealized [image] of social relations."[25]

In the case of *Between C & D*, the most salient architectural feature proved to be the open window: a necessary part of living without air conditioners. "I heard that book more than I wrote it," Rose told Siegle, speaking of *Kill the Poor*. Rose wrote this novel during the early years of *Between C & D*, and the first issue of the journal included an excerpt from it.[26] The noisy sounds of a city floating in through the window circulate in a lot of stories published in *Between C & D*, not just Rose's. On the very first page of the very first issue, Texier describes the sounds that float in through an open window in her story "The Red High Heels": "Three o'clock in the morning in a Lower East Side tenement apartment with Puerto Rican voices yelling mothafucka followed by a cascade of broken glass, and vanishing women's laughter mixed with the lingering smell of a long-dead barbecue fire."[27] For Texier, the open window functions as more than just a convenient detail of setting; it actively mediates the interactions between her characters and between her characters and their environment. Its broken glass, casement, wall, and frame remind Texier's characters of the ethnic and class lines that separate them. This window—as it controls in varying degrees the flow of information from the street to the room—also offers a way of thinking about *Between C & D* itself. Rose and Texier seldom pretend that they are immersed in the street; instead, they listen through the window.

I don't want to suggest, though, that Texier and Rose were voyeurs, who saw the streets as mere fodder for entertainment or inspiration. Instead, they struggled not only to hear but also to document those voices that float in through their window, voices that would otherwise be ephemeral. New technologies of print promised to represent those voices with a previously unrealized immediacy and authenticity. Recent scholarship in media studies, particularly that influenced by Friedrich Kittler, has shown readers that devices like phonographs, typewriters, and cameras shape the modes of thought and expression that move through them.[28] In this sense, Rose and Texier's dot-matrix printer—at once a high-tech typewriter and the leading edge of digital production—serves as a mediator between the lived conditions of the Lower East Side and the increasingly computer-driven world taking shape around it. Their printer was a metaphor for *Between C & D*'s editorial policies as well as a material means by which the relationships between individuals and the built environment of the Lower East side were experienced, represented, and imagined.

Shortly after moving in to 255 East Seventh Street, Rose bought his first computer: an Epson QX-10. In doing so, Rose joined a growing group of writers and computer enthusiasts who were switching from typewriters to computers as word processors. As Matthew Kirschenbaum reports in his history of literary word processing, this upgrade was made possible by the advent of integrated systems, which included CPU, monitor, and storage in one box, requiring less technical know-how than earlier systems.[29] Having worked on *The Seneca Review* in college, Rose almost immediately imagined that a computer-printer combo could constitute a "press."[30] The idea that

Rose and Texier eventually developed was innovative: word process the issues and then print them, 500 at a time, on the Epson printer. If Rose and Texier left the journal unbound, with tractor strips intact, they could distribute it as soon as it came out of the printer. The pair did need to find a way to keep the pages together, a problem they solved by using a gallon Ziploc bag, the same as that used by neighborhood dealers to store decks of heroin. Through the transparent baggy, readers could view cover art produced by artists such as Kiki Smith, Barbara Kruger, and Art Spiegelman, that Texier, Rose, and whoever else was around to help pasted onto each issue by hand.[31] This is one of many indications that Rose and Texier knew what they were doing: those bags would help them find an audience looking for literary dope cut with the dust of abandoned buildings.[32]

Each issue of *Between C & D* featured a new, edgy tagline, like "Sex Drugs Violence Danger Computers." Printed in the lower right side of the cover, stacked typically one word per line, these promised that the format, like drugs and violence, was as cutting-edge as the journal's content. To some extent, they were right—their process was cutting-edge. This fact has often, however, been overlooked because dot-matrix printers, like the one Rose and Texier used, have never been fetishized in the way computers have been. A recent AMC series about the rise of the personal computer, *Halt Catch Fire*, illustrates this point. In two episodes, one from the first and one from the third season, that series features hapless entrepreneurs trying to sell their dot-matrix printers to a Comdex audience, with damning results. First, they are conned out of their booth by the show's protagonists; in a later episode, their dot-matrix printer catches on fire. The show's writers here recognize a historical reality: dot-matrix printers were efficient, but such efficiency tarnished their output, seemingly as bland and boxy as the printer that churned it out. And the output, too, was often difficult to read. As Kirschenbaum notes, the submissions guidelines for many a journal in the early 1980s would prohibit submissions printed on dot-matrix printers.[33] In a November 1982 *PC Magazine* article, the literary agent Dominick Abel scoffed that reading a dot-matrix printout always gave him the "subliminal suspicion that [he was reading] the product of a factory rather than an individual."[34] (As it turns out, Abel was Rose's agent at the time.) Dot matrix printers, in short, have seldom been sexy, a state of affairs reinforced by recent studies of media, which have, by and large, neglected dot-matrix printers in favor of studying other, seemingly more creative, hardware.[35]

Energy and money being in short supply on the Lower East Side, the dot-matrix printer offered the most efficient possible means of moving Miguel

Piñero's or David Wojnarowicz's words from street to print. Dot-matrix printers have a small built-in computer and memory buffer; the computer acts as both input processor and output processor. The memory buffer lets the printer print lines backwards, and also stores nonprinting characters, such as instructions for carriage returns.[36] The dot-matrix printer straddles a line between the typewriter, which relies on only human memory and input, and the computer itself, which translates all alphanumeric characters into ones and zeroes. Notably, early dot-matrix printers could be used directly with keyboards; the Internet now features several tutorials on how to "make a typewriter" out of old keyboards and dot-matrix printers. Like the scroll that Jack Kerouac used to write *On the Road*, dot-matrix papers take continual feeds of fanfold paper. They can print continuously for hours.

But that's only after the text has been stored in a computer. Because of the limited interoperability between computer formats in the 1980s, Rose or Texier had to key each manuscript in by hand.[37] Even as late as 1989, David Foster Wallace noted in a letter to Rose that there were "a lot" of errors in the original copy of "Crash of '69" (published in the Fall/Winter issue of that year) and that "75% of them" were typos.[38] These examples demonstrate that Texier and Rose retained a very human connection to their content. Even as *Between C & D* gestured toward the rapid modes of production that characterize contemporary online magazines, it retained the slowness of typing manuscripts in by hand. In these ways, *Between C & D* combined a human attention to nuance with the uniform inhumanity of the dot-matrix printer's writing machine. Rose and Texier's work with *Between C & D* was the very essence of the do-it-yourself process that I have described throughout this book. It both embodied the entrepreneurialism that post-crisis polices sought to encourage and documented the fallout from the crisis itself.

As a DIY literary institution, *Between C & D* was like the small buffer on its Epson printer. It took the neighborhood's often-messy stories as input, held them for a short while, and then moved them out into the literary world, dirt and all.[39] Print runs were inherently limited by the printer itself. For every issue, Rose and Texier had to run the printer 24 hours a day. To save costs, Rose hacked up a mechanism to feed ink to the printer's ribbon. Printing the journal by themselves, in a minimal dot-matrix print produced on hacked hardware, was a decision born of necessity. Dot-matrix printers were relatively cheap, and the font that Rose used consumed the least ink. It was also, though, an aesthetic decision; Rose liked the "high tech" but low-resolution look of the font. The dot-matrix form meant, too, that every issue pointed to its origins, in that readers were always aware of where *Between C & D* had been made. Part of the lore around the journal included the fact that it was printed in Rose and Texier's tenement, information passed along with the sale of each issue, and circulated through English departments, bookstores, and readers as *Between C & D* extended its reach out of New York and into the nation.

Between C & D and the Aesthetics of Downtown

Every issue of *Between C & D* contained instructions for use below the table of contents: "Instead of flipping the pages right to left, do it bottom to top." To flip through these pages is to experience a continuous flow of text, uninterrupted by images or variations in font or typography. This is in direct contrast to the stories' content, which varies sharply. In my first chapter, I discussed David Wojnarowicz's monologues. These short works, often composed on a single page of single-spaced typewritten paper, recorded conversations held in doorways, on street corners, on empty piers, abandoned playgrounds, and other small spaces of post-crisis New York. I argued that these monologues represented a group of people quickly being labeled the underclass, a precariat that would soon be left behind by rising post-Fordist models of governance. As lively and interesting as these works are, though, they threaten to represent only one thread of the rich fabric of New York's downtown.

Between C & D scales the work of the monologues up from the doorway, where two people can have a conversation, to the apartment building, where many people live alongside one another. Lots of different kinds of people show up to tell their stories in *Between C & D*: working-class Puerto Rican writers Reinaldo Povod and Piñero; experimental African American performance artists like Darius James; innovative women writers like Lynne Tillman and Kathy Acker; the Chinese-American graduate student Liu; the queer art critics Cooper and Gary Indiana. And the stories written by these writers often share an interest in cataloging the Lower East Side as a site of juxtapositions.

Their mode of publishing meant that from the beginning, *Between C & D* had an immediacy about it that distinguished it from many of its peer journals downtown: *Bomb* in 1980, *Benzene* also in 1980, *Redtape* in 1982, *Cover* in 1986, all of which were similar in appearance both to one another and to art magazines like *Artforum* and *Art in America*.[40] With its simple, DIY aesthetic, *Between C & D* is closer in spirit to the mimeographed journals that circulated earlier in the 1960s Lower East Side: Ed Sanders's *Fuck You/a magazine of the arts*, Amiri Baraka and Diane Prima's *The Floating Bear*, or the house journals of Les Deux Magots and Le Metro.[41] By adopting this DIY aesthetic, *Between C & D* was able to represent the neighborhood, from its perch in the furthest reaches of Alphabet City, in ways that avoided some of the problems that writers like Mele and Smith have ascribed to the downtown arts scene of the 1980s. At their worst, the aesthetic productions of this scene, from the promotional flyers of galleries to the art itself, reinforced images of the Lower East Side as abject, dangerous, and thus a site for middle-class thrills. Through their editorial curation and choice to embrace the flat look of the dot-matrix printer, Rose and Texier qualified and challenged these fantasies.

By embracing the printer's machine-writing aesthetic, Rose and Texier captured the neighborhood's collective life as varied and contradictory, replete with class, ethnic, and professional differences. It's difficult to market a lifestyle when formatting is abjured altogether. Through their editorial and aesthetic choices, Rose and Texier resisted allowing *Between C & D* to contribute to the marketing of the Lower East Side as home to an edgy, arty lifestyle. By 1984, the year the first issue of *Between C & D* appeared, the problem of such marketing was already clear. As I detail in chapter 4, in 1984 the art world itself was actively questioning art's role in gentrifying the neighborhood; prominent articles in both *Art in America* and *October* openly pointed to the gallery scene's intertwinement with the real estate industry.[42] Rose and Texier were wary about the uses to which their work might be put, and they let the printer do some of that work instead. *Between C & D* was a notebook, not a brochure.

Comparing *Between C & D* to a project like *Redtape*—which included some of the same authors—draws out the literary manifestations of this divide. In its most famous issue, "Cracked Mirror," *Redtape* depicted the Lower East Side as grim, dangerous, and edgy, replete with the pleasures and fears of Alphabet City as a Burroughsian Zone: a site of junkies, prostitutes, and broken landscapes.[43] But this was editor Michael Carter's curatorial eye at work, and this eye often obscured as much as it revealed. Carter, notably, included several images from Philip Pocock's 1981 *The Obvious Illusion: Murals from the Lower East Side* in order to drive home the idea that the Lower East Side was a wild, ruined frontier.[44] In *The Obvious Illusion* Pocock's work, reproduced in color, often included people and other living things, but the images Carter chose were reproduced in black and white and absent of humans. These murals, bereft of life, appeared alongside other dark, expressionist, artworks littered with skeletons, grainy shots of street traffic, and distorted glimpses through chain-link fences.[45] This was, in Kurt Hollander's terms, a depiction of "low life" instead of "low rent." In the introduction to *The Portable Lower East Side,* a journal with goals similar to *Between C & D,* Hollander explains "low life" as a kind of made-up category—a romanticized version of life in the neighborhood. Low rent, in contrast, is what Hollander calls a "common social context."[46] The Lower East Side of the 1980s crackled with these contested meanings, and accounts of the neighborhood tended to oscillate between romanticizing low life and documenting low rent.

By emphasizing "low life," *Redtape* foregrounded some assemblages— among junkies, prostitutes, graffiti, vacant lots, and artists—over others— working-class Puerto Ricans, activists, writers, and redeveloped buildings. In turn, the works it published meant different things than those in *Between C & D,* even when both journals published the same authors. Patrick McGrath was a major contributor to *Between C & D,* and served, for a time, helped Texier and Rose edit the journal. But as published in *Redtape*'s "Cracked Mirror" issue, McGrath's Gothic narrative "Gazebo" reads as a celebration of low life.[47] McGrath's story is a macabre depiction of decay and drug abuse against the backdrop of a grim landscape: "a small, pale, slender, dark thing against the great gray wall of the building, and beneath her the terraces falling away into the deep gloom of the park."[48] Holly Anderson's poem in the issue, "Lower East Side Mesostics 81–82," is similar. Spelling out "Loisaida," the name the Nuyorican poet and activist Bimbo Rivas had given the neighborhood in 1977 to encourage community pride, Anderson writes: "It's gristLe / and bOnes here; / the lIfe: can comfort come from / needleS / or night trAin?" From here, the poem proceeds to describe a woman who was "elegant a year ago" with "pearls" and a "wool suit" who now sleeps on the street.[49] By the time readers get to Kathy Acker's excerpt from *Don Quixote,* Acker's description of Arab leaders as "liars" read as more indications of humanity gone feral, instead of the experiments in sense-making that serve as part of Acker's larger project.[50] Similarly, Wojnarowicz's "man in a lower east side tenement room," whose facing page features an obscene Stephen Lack work of graffiti in an abandoned building, comes across as evidence of the characters' desperation instead of their will to live (as I argue more widely of the monologues in chapter 1).[51] Controlled and curatorial, "The Cracked Mirror" reads like a pamphlet selling the Lower East Side as a place for someone who longs to live on the "edge" where they might meet "daily danger on the streets." Smith recognizes that real estate investors in particular found this narrative about the neighborhood unexpectedly valuable.[52] "The rawness of the neighborhood," he notes, citing the work of 1980s art critics, was "part of the appeal."[53] By and large, *Redtape* traded on this rawness, reinforcing the worst stereotypes of the neighborhood.

For Rose and Texier, the dot-matrix aesthetic could intervene in this formation. The printer's minimalist typography and lack of images meant that readers needed to draw their own conclusions about what connects these stories. Instead of taking the neighborhood's sociality for granted, *Between C & D* reminded readers that the connections between Puerto Ricans and white bohemians, blue collar and white collar workers, buildings and people, were assembled block by block and brick by brick. The simple inclusion of tractor holes reminded every reader of *Between C & D* that the journal was printed in the apartment named by the title. Referencing the printer's machinery, the tractor holes refer to the printer as a mediator. In fact, they look like a window frame on the issue itself. Rose and Texier chose the Ziploc bag to reference the heroin and cocaine dealt down the street. But the bag, combined with the ironic taglines—"subway crime," "danger," "violence," "murder"—also mocked its readers for pretending that a bag of literature, or heroin, made them edgier or more autonomous. This was especially true when one of the stories in the bag has a character actually buying a bag of heroin and speeding off in a luxury car, as was the case with Anthony Bourdain's "FAO" from volume 2, issue 1.[54]

The journal's style emerged to become that of the dot-matrix printer, a style both capable of recognizing the proliferating difference of the Lower East Side and of recognizing that such difference comes down to ones and zeroes. Rendered in dot-matrix print, Darius James's *Negrophobia* encounters none of the problems of authenticity-based marketing that it would later encounter when printed with a cover. Deploying dot-matrix's undifferentiating form, *Between C & D* fulfilled a radical version of postmodernism that avoided some of the pitfalls of "authenticity marketing" that accompany the period's more popular identity writing.[55] In McGurl's argument, much postwar creative writing is the product of a vast machine for producing excellence. *Between C & D* hacked its hardware and didn't much care if its writing or its form looked perfect.[56] Striving to meet the streets as closely as possible, the printing head of *Between C & D* also scanned the random access memory of the Lower East Side, accessing the neighborhood's randomness in ways that its peer publications did not.[57]

No literary journal published in New York in the 1980s (and few elsewhere) was as eclectic as *Between C & D* and therefore as invested in resisting the expected, stereotypical narratives that were being told about the city after the 1975 crisis. In volume 2, issue 2, for example, one might begin by reading an excerpt from the Canadian writer Yolande Villemaire, then read a piece from the Puerto Rican playwright Reinaldo Povod, then one by translator of the *Egyptian Book of the Dead* Normandi Ellis, then one by the radical African American novelist Darius James, then a feminist piece from Texier, then a typically queer piece from Gary Indiana, then a postmodern performance piece from Peter Cherches, then a poem from Eileen Myles, ending with a piece from the punk Serbian poet Nina Zivancevic.[58] Rose and Texier selected writers who both described the Lower East Side on their own terms and sought to imagine a new world. While Mario Maffi may go too far in claiming that for Rose, Texier, and the other writers in *Between C & D*, the neighborhood "ceased to be just another exotic, romantic, or decadent ingredient, and became again a community carrying on a century-old experience," it seems absolutely true that Rose and Texier worked hard to engage the neighborhood as a site of existing residents and buildings with real life in them rather than as an abandoned frontier.[59]

From *Between C & D's* very first issue, Rose and Texier understood Lower East Side writers to be documenting downtown instead of curating it. In their introduction to the 1988 anthology of *Between C & D*, Rose and Texier describe the writers they published as "closer to urban archeologists than to landscape artists or campus sociologists, and regardless of their backgrounds, they choose to explore the underside of life—the frontier where the urban fabric is wearing thin and splitting open."[60] In this phrasing, one can see just how much Rose and Texier wrestled with the problem of representing the Lower East Side. They use the charged term "frontier," but instead of describing the writers as cowboys, Rose and Texier use the term "archeologists," who document what they find. And by saying that the urban fabric is wearing thin, they acknowledge the ways in which post-1975 policies drove the neighborhood to a breaking point. Whatever these writers found, Rose and Texier published, and the uniform dots of the printer made it all look even: there was no need, as *Redtape* did, to be sure the story on page 42 matched the image on page 43. The dot-matrix form helped everything that came in through the window to seem part of one long story, but this story broke into chapters that were often quite different.

The low overhead afforded by the printer, coupled with a willingness to publish whatever came in the window, meant that Rose and Texier could publish work from writers who evaded multiple categories and who had difficulty, as a result, finding a place for their work. Rose and Texier were especially good, for example, at publishing the work of innovative queer writers. In publishing early work by Cooper, Wojnarowicz, and Indiana, *Between C & D* foregrounded the vibrancy, insecurity, and danger of gay male life. Volume 1, issue 4, featured a stunning poster that Marion Scemama and Wojnarowicz made for the journal.[61] The background is black. The left panel depicts him slumped against a wall, his mouth bloodied. The photo is barely exposed. The flash of the camera hits his forehead, the brightest part of the picture. He wears what looks like a leather bomber jacket and a T-shirt that looks dirty but may just be darkened. His eyes stare vacantly into the distance. In the text that accompanies the image, Wojnarowicz contrasts a newspaper account of a lower court upholding a Georgia sodomy law with a description of his near-murder by a john. The same issue featured "Wrong," a Dennis Cooper story that details the violent death of three homosexual men.[62] Almost immediately, *Between C & D* was recognized for its attention to the increasingly dangerous lives of homosexual men. After reading the issue, Tom Ho, then the arts editor of *New York Native,* wrote to Rose, "The poster followed by Dennis Cooper's lead story was like being assaulted and battered by the reality and unreality of the violence of and directed at homosexuals and our lifestyle."[63] Ho's praise isn't idle; one of the few gay newspapers at the time, the *New York Native* had covered the AIDS crisis since its early days, publishing in particular Larry Kramer's "1,112 and Counting" in the March 1983 issue. To Ho, both poster and Cooper story conveyed the reality of a world where the city's hospitals were running out of space for AIDS patients, even as mayor Koch refused to acknowledge these conditions.[64]

Queer writing was just one example of *Between C & D*'s wide reach. The lead pieces from James's *Negrophobia* (1992) were vividly experimental, combining racial stereotypes and exaggerated violence, in a landscape only loosely recognizable as New York.[65] In this sense, James's work shares aesthetic affinities with writers like Acker (whom James befriended in the mid-1980s). In other ways, though, James's intense engagement with African American history makes his work wholly different from anything else with which it shared space in the Ziploc bag. As scholarship on *Negrophobia* has shown, James engages a tradition of radical African American writing, in particular Ishmael Reed and James's contemporary Paul Beatty.[66]

In Ronald A. T. Judy's account, the Carol Publishing Group initially sought to market *Negrophobia* as "a Burroughsesque pop-schlock phantasmagoria," but that strategy shifted toward foregrounding controversy over the book's cover, which features imagery derived from Sambo.[67] After both a Brooklyn bookstore owner and a black employee of Carol itself objected to the cover's "racist" imagery, Carol's publicity director, Fern Edison, sent a memo to a reviewer at *The New York Times,* in which she points to "complaints from people both within and outside the company, about what some view as the 'racist' nature of the cover design."[68] Edison's claims made it into the review, in which reviewer Esther Fein notes, "The cover . . . has made some black employees and associates of the publishing house cry racism."[69] Judy reads the memo as Edison's attempt to position the book for the cultural studies market, for whom questions of "What is the proper way to represent blacks?" were, at the time, the subject of many a cultural studies article (James subsequently lectured at colleges to promote the book).[70] While *Negrophobia* would go on to sell reasonably well, Judy's point is that, in his words, "*Negrophobia* does not fit any of the recognized categories of literature."[71] This description, I'd contend, also fit much of the writing at *Between C & D*. In publishing James, *Between C & D* brought the jarring disjunctions of James's live performances to the page, performances that entailed the cross-class, cross-race encounters occurring everywhere in the Lower East Side.[72] James's example manifests the boundary-pushing possible with a DIY journal; *Between C & D* provided James a home for work that was otherwise hard to place.

Catherine Liu, too, produced work that evaded categories, neither "institutionalized modernist realism" nor "Chinese-American melodramatic fiction," as Liu puts it in the preface to the 2012 edition of *Oriental Girls Desire Romance.*[73] That novel, a series of loosely connected episodes written in stream-of-consciousness mode, began as excerpts in *Between C & D*.[74] The first, appearing in volume 3, issue 2, is "Monday in the Park with Brian," a freewheeling, stream-of-consciousness story that leads the protagonist from Tompkins Square Park to SoHo and back to the Lower East Side.[75] The second is "Fat Man," which describes the protagonist's father, who "loves China. Weeps great alligator tears for his country" and takes his children to political meetings for expatriate Chinese in SoHo.[76] Now a well-published academic critic who teaches at the University of California, Irvine, Liu was attending graduate school at CUNY and living in the Lower East Side when her work appeared in *Between C & D*. Like *Negrophobia*, Liu's novel scrutinizes the racial and class collisions of the Lower East Side, in Liu's case along vectors of Asian American identity. By ranging between China, the Lower East Side, and the protagonist's Ivy League education, the novel interrogates ideas of Asianness as they are imposed on the protagonist, even as it scrutinizes, like James, the possibilities and problems posed by an environment of cheap apartments and living "from hand to mouth, from job to job."[77] Like Indiana and Acker, Liu attacks consumer culture, but from the viewpoint of a recently emigrated Chinese mother: "[My mother] was overwhelmed by the task of maintaining a home in a foreign country. She often didn't know which household products to buy. She didn't know the secrets of American housewives, who were always supposed to be on the lookout for new cleaners, scrubbers, brushes, and soaps. She had to make everything up as she went along."[78] Living in the Lower East Side, out in a world "teeming with stylish young things, all in pursuit of fame and fortune and glamour and fun,"[79] befriending Acker, reading theory from Semiotext(e), Liu breaks her ethnic identity into ones and zeroes.

The Process of *Between C & D*

As novels written during the early days of *Between C & D*, both *Kill the Poor* and *Love Me Tender* reflect on the journal's production process. Rose does so by cataloging the marks made by humans on an apartment building very much like 255 East Seventh Street. Texier does so by tracing a network of humans and nonhumans in and around the building. As novels made up of short chapters, some of which first saw life in the journal, both also reflect *Between C & D* in their form. Taken together, *Kill the Poor* and *Love Me Tender* take stock of the possibilities and problems of assembling stories in the post-crisis Lower East Side. Neither felt compelled to bind these stories together tightly: the loose contracts of the rented apartment on the one hand and the temporary affair on the other work in a manner akin to the dot-matrix printer.[80] (Though it would be inaccurate to characterize their divergence wholly in terms of gender, it's nevertheless true that *Kill the Poor* is about building and *Love Me Tender* is about relationships.) Both novels include artist characters, but these characters form only part of their rich narrative fabrics. Like *Between C & D* itself, they challenge accounts of the Lower East Side as a primarily bohemian space full of the "creative class."

Kill the Poor relates the story of a housing cooperative that has taken over two landlord-abandoned buildings on "Avenue E." Readers hear from the building's diverse residents, who include several Puerto Ricans, an artist, a gay man, a graduate student in social work, and a pottery maker. With residents who pay a range of rents and who have different backgrounds, the building represents a typical tenement in the transitioning 1980s. It's modeled on 255 East Seventh Street, which was, as both Rose and Texier recall, occupied by similarly diverse characters. But the fictional building also works like *Between C & D*, and the novel's narrative links residents' stories together in the same loose way that the printer does for *Between C & D*'s stories. The novel's main plot concerns the narrator's struggle to keep the building both intact and functional. This means fighting off a rent strike, working to renovate, and helping residents figure their way into the building's origin narrative. *Kill the Poor* repeats this narrative, a version of "how a group of homesteaders took the building over from the landlord," at several points.[81] If, as Smith, Mele, and others argue, redevelopment frequently relied on narrative, in *Kill the Poor*, narrative relies on redevelopment.

To return to the terms from Lefebvre with which I began this chapter, everyone in *Kill the Poor* does something to "make their mark" on the physical space of the building. This often literally translates into building practices. For example, Ike and Beneficia have quite different ideas about exposed brick: for Beneficia, whose tastes seem to run toward industrial chic, it was important that "all the old plaster is knocked off the walls" resulting in a look where "nothing" is "knocked out or busted."[82] When he views the wall, Jo Jo can read its message clearly: lacking "graffiti" or "filth," the exposed bricks differentiate Beneficia from the surrounding neighborhood, a message she reinforces when she tells Jo Jo, "what you see is the sweat of collective labor . . . the sweat of our collective brow, all the brows who live here."[83] For Ike, though, the exposed brick is impractical, and he recovers it with lath, plaster, dirt, and Sheetrock. Another character, Mewie, "tear[s] down all the walls" to "open up his entire space, even put the bathroom right out there in the open" only to find that he has taken down a load-bearing wall, which results in the death of three of his cats when the ceiling falls.[84] If we remember that for Rose, rehabilitating the apartment and creating *Between C & D* were part of the same impulse, we can see that different modes of rehabilitating a building are also different narrative modes. As *Kill the Poor* progresses, the process of managing the building and the process of managing the narrative merge.

The most important character to make his mark on the building is Carlos DeJesus. For middle-class readers, DeJesus is at first troubling. His belligerence, difficulty, and general problem-causing seem to reinforce the worst stereotypes of the "underclass," as an abject Other outside of the post-Fordist economy. I should say, too, that Rose has indicated that the real DeJesus was apparently terrifying, flashing a gun at Rose several times. The novel, though, maintains a grudging respect for DeJesus; he is, in fact, the novel's most important character after Jo Jo. And he figures into the building's backstory in a complicated way: he's not the one who abandoned the building, and Jo Jo seems to believe him when he says he chased off junkies with a baseball bat. That, we can say, is the first mark that DeJesus makes on the building. Like Jo Jo, he clears space for himself and his family.[85] But this original act works with the homesteaders' narrative in ways that produce problems: "He hadn't paid rent in eight years. He hadn't seen the landlord in five years. All he saw were junkies and thieves. Now these people come, calling themselves homesteaders, and say they bought the building and they don't pay him no respect, they're not even civil. Certainly they don't ask him to join them in their homestead. Assholes come to play landlord with him. Let them try to make money."[86] Essentially, *Kill the Poor* sets DeJesus's story against the larger story of the building.

The mark that DeJesus eventually makes on the building is more permanent: he pours gasoline into his own apartment and lights it on fire. He does so to disrupt the homesteading that he sees as pushing people like himself out of the neighborhood. In having DeJesus set the fire, Rose reworks the meaning of the buildings that burned down with frequency after the 1975 crisis. By setting the fire himself, DeJesus sets in motion a chain of events that result in JoJo being jailed, thus using the fire to *resist* gentrification. In contrast, burned-down buildings in the historical Lower East Side often provided an impetus for gentrification, by making other buildings cheaper, offering empty plots for developers, and increasing the aura of risk that brought artists to the neighborhood.

Rose further complicates DeJesus's character by linking him to Miguel Piñero in the novel itself. When Steven Spielberg arrives in the neighborhood to shoot *Batteries Not Included*, he wants to hire "Miguel Piñero, the playwright and actor" to play the movie's "heavy."[87] When Piñero turns out to look too skinny, DeJesus steps in to play the part. Rose was close friends with Piñero, and published him in *Between C & D*. Particularly in its first volumes, *Between C & D* published material from Puerto Rican writers regularly. In its depiction of DeJesus, I'd argue, *Kill the Poor* articulates the social, economic, and cultural complications of this crossover.

Love Me Tender, too, has plenty to say about these complications. With a form similar to *Kill the Poor*—short, episodic chapters, flashbacks, abrupt transitions—*Love Me Tender* assembles a cast of characters that looks very much like an issue of *Between C & D*: older and younger artists, filmmakers, Puerto Rican drug dealers, exotic dancers, uptown heiresses. *Love Me Tender* develops its loose plot around the love affairs of Lulu, who occupies a sublet apartment on Avenue A near Tompkins Square Park.[88] She dates Julian (a poet-musician turned junkie), Henry (a David-Salle-like older artist), and Raphael (a filmmaker), all while screening phone calls from a mysterious man named Mario (who turns out to be the Puerto Rican son of a local drug dealer). Lulu works for a cabaret in Tribeca; there, she befriends Mystique, an older woman who has been in the city for years, and goes to work for Salvine, an Upper West Side housewife also from France.

If *Kill the Poor* registers the marks that different humans make on a rehabilitated tenement building, *Love Me Tender* follows the networks in which the apartment is situated. On the surface, these are the bohemian networks that should provide a foundation for the creative economy, a world where interpersonal networks lead the creative worker to the next project.[89] *Love Me Tender* examines the effort needed to maintain networks among these characters in a city where everyone is otherwise disconnected:

> Everybody Lulu knows in New York lives in a transient apartment. Two, three, four rooms without a hallway, lofts with the paint peeling off the walls, shelves of books and a few useless objects scavenged from previous lives in other apartments or lofts on the other side of the country, on the other side of the Atlantic, shared with former lovers or groups of friends, alienated from parents, siblings, their own culture, their country, the rest of the world.[90]

While Texier the author sees the Lower East Side in terms of rich networks, her narrator sees the city as a set of uncertainly linked apartments, filled with useless objects, alienated from the stronger networks of kin. If *Love Me Tender* depicts a rising creative economy, it critiques the terms of this economy by noting its characters' states of disconnection. Mystique returns to Dayton, Ohio, only for her mother's death. The links between these characters develop haphazardly: an ad answered in *The Village Voice*, an accidental job hiring (Lulu applies as a bartender at the Blue Note but is hired as a dancer), and, most consistently, a misplaced telephone call. The novel repeatedly returns to images of people cut off from the neighborhood's networks: the character Mystique's "red fear," which "wrings the guts of young women at night alone in strange apartments," the character Salvine imagining her lover Julian.[91] But the figure to which Texier repeatedly returns is the homeless woman Tillie, who may have been Salvine's former friend Laura Morris.[92]

As does *Kill the Poor*, Texier's novel does particularly intense work with its Puerto Rican characters. In *Kill the Poor*, these characters form a willful opposition to gentrification. In contrast to the lonely apartments, for example, Puerto Rican families "sit around narrow apartments just like hers, except theirs are for real, with a handful of squeaking kids, popping half-Buds, listening to *salsa* blaring out of extra-large boxes sitting atop the kitchen table. Eating spicy roasts bursting with golden fat."[93] Unlike the novel's other characters, who have only their memories to link them to kin, these connections to kin are rich and developed. But in order for Lulu to cross into this network, much work needs to be done. The diversity that supposedly drives the creative class proves here difficult to encounter even on a surface level.[94] When Lulu first encounters Mario in the flesh, she berates herself for thinking in stereotypes: "You're racist, she thinks. You're fucking racist! Just because he's got a dark skin and white Pumas. Just because he smells of the street, you see him as a drug dealer, robber, rapist," but later, when she walks out with him, "another world opens up, a world she barely stares at like a stage when she walks around the neighborhood by herself."[95]

At the beginning of the second chapter, Texier uses a neon sign with a letter missing as part of a list of an apartment's disorienting elements: "Smell of cat piss. Red neon sign blinking CUCHIF ITOs reflected from across the street on the kitchen wall. Bustle of cockroaches scrambling for cracks."[96] Every time Mario appears in the narrative, the alien voices in the street and their accompanying "CUCHIF ITOS" signs become less alien. As Rose will do with the character DeJesus, Texier refuses to delimit Mario's presence. The fluctuations around Mario's character become especially visible in a moment that will sound familiar to anyone who has ever entered a store that primarily caters to the needs of another ethnic group: a scene where Lulu purchases religious candles, "two green ones for money, two orange ones for success, four red ones for passion." Mario mocks her for it: "Theresa, he says to the owner behind the counter. This *gringa* believes in your fucking candles!" Texier includes this sort of thing throughout her text: "Lulu thinks his skin is spicy, that his sweat tastes like hot curry and he laughs saying she just stereotypes him, you know, big cock, strong smell, virile man."[97] And acknowledging the stereotypes that interrupt the pair's contact allows Texier to include material that might otherwise seem exoticizing:

> Mario tells her his grandmother died on New Year's Eve, they all stayed with her day and night taking turns. Him and mami

and papi and his little brother and the priest held her hand the whole night until there was not a breath left in her. She let go just when dawn broke. There was this pink light piercing the darkness and the candles stretched long flames just for an instant, I swear to God, Lulu, those flames grew real long, it was as if they were celebrating her spirit breaking loose. She died with the first light of the first day of the year. Isn't that beautiful?[98]

Framed by the bodega, in which Mario belongs but in which Lulu is an outsider, this passage conveys Mario's world as one of long family networks, belying both stereotypes of the underclass as disconnected and abject and stereotypes of the urban primitive who spontaneously produces graffiti for the admiration of white art critics.

But more than this—it is Lulu's relationship with Mario that offers a blueprint for a new world. Not because this relationship merely crosses racial and class lines, but because Mario's vibrant family networks repudiates both the urban underclass narrative and the rising creative economy narrative. Two stories told about the postindustrial city by two different groups, these stories combine to create a city that is "for" artist-professionals like Lulu and "denied" to working-class families like Mario's. By both incorporating Mario's story into a novel that otherwise describes the ascendance of the creative industries, and by acknowledging the work necessary for Lulu to cross into Mario's world (the overcoming of stereotypes, the real fear, and so on), *Love Me Tender* points to an alternate future for the Lower East Side, one that fulfills the promises of the neighborhood as a "multi-ethnic laboratory."

In depicting DeJesus, Rose attributes a vibrant urge for life to the Lower East Side, but one inassimilable to conventional ideologies of the underclass. Rose depicts a Lower East Side buckling with willful subjects, those who "[get] in the way of what is on the way."[99] From David Wojnarowicz to Gary Indiana, from Rose to Miguel Piñero, *Between C & D* was filled with "willfully unpolished, subversively intelligent authors."[100] By depicting a neighborhood with tentatively maintained networks, Texier points to the limitations of the creative industry as a model for development, instead pointing to the extant networks of kin, culture, and things that belong to Puerto Rican families as a site of real possibility. Both novels dwell on the possibilities latent in the neighborhood traced by *Between C & D*, in which writers like James, Liu, Cooper, and Wojnarowicz could relay their voices without making compromises with the creative writing industry of the Program Era. But what's subversive in one era often becomes hegemonic in the next, and the final section of this chapter will consider *Between C & D*'s do-it-yourself publishing in terms of the post-Fordist modes of work that were ascendant in the 1980s, but are now dominant. These modes of work are more than happy to incorporate willful subjects who do it themselves.

Conclusion

In addition to the art on the front cover, almost every issue of *Between C & D* had something cool thrown into that Ziploc bag: the Wojnarowicz poster, hand-printed coasters, a John Fekner audio disk. When Rose and Texier ran out of things to include, they photocopied something interesting and imprinted it with the words "Between C & D." For volume 4, issue 1 (released in Winter 1988), they included a photocopy from the November 3, 1985, issue of the *New York Times Magazine*. The photocopy encompasses part of an article by Samuel G. Freedman about immigration in the city, with a pull-out quotation that optimistically opines, "the revitalization of New York, the city behind the golden door, is nothing if not the sum of a million stories. And each of them, like all immigrant stories, is a kind of epic."[101] Adjoining the excerpt is an ad for Leona Helmsley's Harley Hotel. By winter 1988, when *Between C & D* volume 4, issue 1, was published, Helmsley was second only to Donald Trump as the city's most famous real estate developer, known for ads that insisted on the personal stamp she put on her hotel's luxuries.

This found art, I'd contend, juxtaposes the "revitalization of New York" as "the sum of a million stories" with a queen of development (already being indicted for tax fraud). In some sense, of course, this found art is just a cheeky contradiction with the stories inside the journal. But given the changes occurring around 255 East Seventh Street, particularly those involving immigrant populations, this inclusion also indicates that Rose and Texier knew what they were doing—that their literary journal, situated within a rapidly gentrifying Lower East Side, was part of a process by which the larger city was moving from welfare state to real estate, and from manufacturing to service jobs.[102]

With writers like Povod, Cooper, James, and Liu, *Between C & D* accepted the raw feed of literary projects that veered from a day-in-the-life-of-struggling-writer to reworked second-generation immigrant story. A trope from Liu's "Monday in the Park with Brian" helps frame the problem as well as the possibility I'm trying to get at here. Midway through the story, Liu writes: "Deny me once I said, deny me twice I will rise up from the ruins like a great deranged bird and fly over the tops of the bare-limbed trees of Tompkins Square Park to a place where finally, I will be able to rest."[103] Other writers of *Between C & D* deploy similar imagery: the ghost in Dennis Cooper's "Wrong" (volume 1, issue 4) or the artist who wants to swim to New Jersey in Patrick McGrath's "Lush Triumphant" (volume 3, issue 3).[104] It's not a stretch to say, then, that in allowing Liu to do it herself, *Between C & D* let Liu find her wings. To rise up from the ruins: such was the aim of not only every writer in *Between C & D*, but also the post-crisis policy goal for New York itself, and the program set by real estate developers in the Lower East Side. Here is the complicated form of do-it-yourself that took shape after the 1975 crisis.

The time of post-Fordism is the time of doing it yourself. For the writers of this study, this truth became clearer and clearer the further one moved away from the 1975 fiscal crisis. Fittingly, this period has recently become itself the subject of fiction. Novels such as Rachel Kushner's *The Flamethrowers* (2013) restage the problems and possibilities of the Lower East Side for contemporary readers.[105] Reflecting on the crisis and its aftermath, Kushner has commented that at the very moment the factory disappeared from New York, forms of art arose wherein one could be an artist "almost through attitude alone, which has some shadowy logical connection, perhaps, to the rise of the service economy."[106] Kushner points to a conflux between the rise of the post-Fordist service economy, which remade New York City completely after the 1975 crisis, and the kind of art that proliferated after Minimalism, which was dominated, from SoHo onward, by a DIY spirit. In this sense, *Between C & D* follows in the tradition of FOOD, the restaurant that Gordon Matta-Clark, Carol Gooden, and Tina Girouard founded in SoHo in 1971, or any number of Lower East Side galleries—Fun, Gracie Mansion, Nature Morte—which did it themselves.

One way to theorize the "shadowy logical connection" in Kushner's statement would be to point to what Saskia Sassen describes as the rise of an informal economy, whereby the large-scale production of factories moved to small-scale service industries often located in the home. Sassen summarizes these industries as focusing on "customized production, small runs, specialty items, and fine food dishes," all of which "are generally produced through labor-intensive methods and sold through small, full-service outlets. Part of this production can be subcontracted to low-cost operations, sweatshops, or households. Besides reducing labor costs, this enables production to take place in cheap space, a considerable advantage in a time of strong demand for centrally located land."[107] Customized production and small runs: Sassen's words apply almost uncannily to *Between C & D*. Sassen is mostly talking about low-income workers making apparel, footwear. In 1991, it was not yet a common observation that precariatization had spread to the middle classes.[108]

Another way to theorize Kushner's idea would be to draw on the ways that artists have come to be seen, under post-Fordism, as the ideal workers: people who love their job, value creativity, and who don't mind working unpaid overtime. Such models "privilege autonomy," even as they promote "an aesthetic practice driven not by the solo author's self-definition and self-validation but rather by a constant unraveling of the ideal of her self's priority and sufficiency."[109] In flight from the rigid institutions of corporations and university, writers like Rose and Texier found, like many others in the Lower East Side of the 1980s, self-definition and self-fulfillment. "The density of that life," Texier writes, looking back on the era, "the particular color and taste of it, its thickness, its furious liveliness, I wouldn't know how to find words to describe it."[110] The running spirit of *Between C & D*—its rejection of hierarchies and institutions, its foregrounding of malleable identities—also fits well with rising notions of an economy that relies on aesthetic autonomy. This doesn't mean, of course, that either literature or art translates directly into modes of living for web designers, but it may mean that "artists and writers [provide] a conceptual grammar and vocabulary" for thinking through the possibilities and problems of the shift to post-Fordism.[111]

To be sure, in *Love Me Tender*, Texier had recognized this problem, describing living in New York as

> the feeling of being permanently onstage and having to perform well at all times. Even nonactors feel compelled to compete as freely as if a Broadway career was at stake. You have to know how to play with signs. A lot of it has to do with your looks: fifties nihilistic crossed with early sixties nerd, a touch of punk, a sea of black. A strident haircut. A drop-dead expression on a living face. Everybody priding themselves on not being normal, but, coming from Europe, you have no idea what American normal can possibly mean. . . . New York is no different than Paris, or Montreal, or Amsterdam, or L.A., but instead of offering well-established codes, New York demands that you be ahead of constantly changing ones.[112]

Texier describes here a self who has no "authentic" core. Instead, the self is a precarious one who must keep up with constantly changing codes. And "playing with signs," after all, is what post-Fordist workers do and do best. As Boltanski and Chiapello observe in *The New Spirit of Capitalism*, in the post-Fordist economy, workers' "main source of value is the ability to take advantage of the most diverse kinds of knowledge, to interpret and combine them, to make or circulate innovations, and, more generally, to 'manipulate symbols,' as [the management theorist Robert] Reich puts it."[113] If one squints, one can read the project of *Between C & D* in these lines: gathering diverse kinds of knowledge, combining them in an innovative ways, and playing with the symbols churned out of a dot-matrix printer.

Between C & D, though neither born-digital nor persisting as digital, represents the leading edge of the self-production that now characterizes the lives of all creative workers. Self-printed, self-distributed, self-created, *Between C & D* anticipates a moment when opportunities to work for free are plentiful, but real jobs are scarce. Working for free as writers, using computers, hoping for a break, Rose and Texier create value within a rising network economy by imagining these networks before they were translated into information technology. These literary works show that the neighborhood itself provides a model for thinking networks by brokering connections within apartments and across blocks.

Rose and Texier's mode of production and their inventive response to the straightened resources of post-Fordist governance meant that *Between C & D*, like *Semiotext(e)*, Piñero's work, and the other DIY projects I've described here, heralded a world in which self-funding and self-invention were norms of post-Fordist work. In other words, *Between C & D* mapped a world that was disappearing even as it pointed to the mechanism—literally, in the Epson products used to make it—that would hasten its disappearance. From the perspective of 2020, where every subject harvests her own life to get by, it's clear that Rose and Texier anticipated the life practices of bloggers with MacBook Airs, makers with Etsy shops, YouTube stars with iMovie, and the host of post-Fordist workers who never leave their jobs as long as their cell phones are with them. DIY begins voluntarily but becomes mandatory. Putting printout after printout into Ziploc bags, Rose and Texier did it themselves, and helped a lot of other people do it themselves along the way. They showed that literature could thrive outside the Fordist machines of the Program Era, just as the characters in its stories thrived in a New York with a withdrawn welfare state.

Like Wojnarowicz, Acker, and Rivas, and the other culture workers of my study, Rose and Texier threw themselves into the Lower East Side: their family histories, their writerly ambition, their education, their cynicism, their openness. Together, Rose, Texier, apartment, computer, and printer constitute a writing machine, an assemblage out of which coalesced narratives that manifest the neighborhood in direct ways. For Rose and Texier, the Lower East Side is a matrix, and the dot-matrix printer an ideal apparatus for making its particular textures visible. However, doing so—generating data about space—became part of the imperatives of post-Fordism, and their project can be seen, too, like many of the works discussed in *DIY on the Lower East Side*, reclaimable for capitalist projects. *Between C & D*, in other words, is Janus-faced. It looks back to 1975 and forward to the 1990s and 2000s, when the practices that Rose and Texier pioneered became dominant and inescapable.

Afterword

ACT UP and the Divergent Possibilities of DIY

> Piece by piece the landscape is eroding and in its place I am building a monument made of fragments of love and hate, sadness and feelings of murder. . . . At the base of this shrine I place the various elements that define each person who has died or is dying.[1]
>
> —David Wojnarowicz, *Close to the Knives*

In the above passage from his late writing, Wojnarowicz draws together all of the themes of *DIY on the Lower East Side*: dissolution and building, the rush of violent feelings and the tender connections of community, the possibilities of art and the terrible precarity of living. At their best, the culture workers of the Lower East Side sought to build things that reflected the tension between a broken landscape and the reproduction of life. The fictional shrine Wojnarowicz describes recalls his own visual art, which often used collage to juxtapose contrasting elements. But the shrine also recalls the aesthetic of the community gardens that I describe in chapter 2, pieces of folk art made by ordinary people, who sought ways to make their environment just a little better as the city withdrew funding and attention from the neighborhood. "Fragments of love and hate, sadness and feelings of murder" is also not a bad way to describe *Between C & D*. Made quickly at a moment of crisis, the shrine Wojnarowicz describes catalogs the lives of people destroyed by the crisis. It is a work of imagination; readers sense that it will hold for only a little while.

A few pages later, after giving examples of people he knew that have died of AIDS—one guy that he thought was an asshole until he learned he was dying, one man he'd seen only on the street and is now visibly sick—Wojnarowicz continues, "I have always viewed my friends as checkpoints in a series of motions of resistance to the flood of hyenas in state or religious drag."[2] In the mid-1970s, the "flood of hyenas" had come to take away the nurturing networks of state support; by the late 1980s, they were restricting the distribution of AZT and allowing AIDS patients to die in poorly staffed city shelters or, worse, on a bench in Tompkins Square Park. In 1975, the architects of the city's financial crisis had chosen which form of life the city would support: entrepreneurial, moneyed, implicitly white, straight, and male. After 1975, everyone else would have to go it on their own.

But as I've argued throughout this book, the architects of the crisis could not fully dictate what happened after the crisis, and by the end of the 1980s, the vibrant communities that had assembled in the crisis's wake had grown strong enough to mount a fierce resistance against the hyenas' agenda. There was, in other words, an imagination that had not yet been gentrified, even as gentrification would draw on the products of this imagination. In *The Gentrification of the Mind*, Sarah Schulman draws on her own experiences living on Ninth Street in the Lower East Side to set the complacency of gentrification against the vibrancy of ACT UP. The "most recent American social movement to succeed," she contends, did so because "AIDS activist culture is the opposite of gentrification."[3] While she never states it directly, it's clear that Schulman believes that the pre-gentrification cultures of the Lower East Side had much to do with establishing the groundwork for ACT UP's successes. Enmeshed with art, drawing on the legacy of Lower East Side–based groups like Colab and Group Material, ACT UP changed the conversation about AIDS patients on first a local and then a national level. In this afterword, I'll briefly take up the ways that ACT UP carried forward the best impulses of the post-crisis Lower East Side, using Wojnarowicz's *Close to the Knives* (1991) as a literary bridge between these moments. While not a central member, Wojnarowicz was involved with ACT UP from the late 1980s until his death. In *Close to the Knives*, Wojnarowicz reused the material that I discuss in chapter 1, the fragmentary monologues that documented the possibilities of precarious life after the crisis. Wojnarowicz's late work offers a useful record of how the problems of the 1975 crisis were translated into the AIDS crisis.

Close to the Knives consists of seven loosely linked essays. There's some logic to calling the book a memoir: the bulk of it consists of biographical accounts of Wojnarowicz's childhood, his relationship with Hujar, and his experiences in the Lower East Side. These alternate with angry denunciations of the figures that Wojnarowicz blames for the AIDS crisis. *Close to the Knives* includes, for example, the incendiary essay that Wojnarowicz wrote for the 1989 exhibition *Witnesses: Against Our Vanishing* in which Wojnarowicz calls Cardinal O'Connor a "fat cannibal" because O'Connor helped restrict the distribution of AIDS information in New York. In alternating fury with biography, *Close to the Knives* situates ACT UP's anger within the precarious circumstances of men like Wojnarowicz. Importantly, though, Wojnarowicz repeatedly reminds readers that he no longer lives in the transient circumstances with which his career began: he notes that, sometimes to his chagrin, the walls around him are much more solid than they were in the late 1970s. Like Acker and others, Wojnarowicz has found success and stability in post-crisis circumstances. This place of relative solidity is what allows him to develop the complex assessments of *Close to the Knives*. Despite its subtitle, "a memoir of disintegration," *Close to the Knives* is often concerned with the ways that intact spaces give one the courage to speak.

As I noted in chapter 1, the monologues were free-floating works that Wojnarowicz published in various forms between the early 1980s and his death. In the fourth essay from *Close to the Knives*, entitled "Being Queer in America: A Journal of Disintegration," Wojnarowicz reuses two of the monologues: "Man on Second Avenue 2:00 A.M." and "A Kid on the Piers Near the West Side Highway." Here, though, instead of serving as representative voices from a void, they appear in a relatively structured essay with numbered sections. The title of the essay asks readers to understand them as an argument. The essay moves between the unstructured, free-floating narrative of the monologues and the more composed, focused accounts of Hujar's death: "There he is propped up in the white sheets with all the inventions of his day leading in and out of his body.... I am amazed at the color of his face and how as he slips closer to death his body looks more healthy."[4] "Being Queer" takes the raw material of the monologues and encloses them within a structure, giving readers context for understanding the monologues' significance: they document the terrible neglect of people that the state ignores, or, worse, targets for active discrimination.

Within these numbered sections, Wojnarowicz also includes another piece of text that he'd used earlier: that from the poster that was included in *Between C & D*'s second issue. "In my dreams," Wojnarowicz writes, "I crawl across freshly clipped front lawns" in order to "wake you up and tell you a story" about a violent queer-bashing. This notion of breaking through was at the core of ACT UP's agenda, and Wojnarowicz meditates on these tactics later in *Close to the Knives*: "To turn our private grief for the loss of friends, family, lovers and strangers into something public would serve as another powerful dismantling tool. It would dispel the notion that the virus has a sexual orientation or a moral code. It would nullify the belief that the government and medical community has done very much to ease the spread or advancement of this disease." Wojnarowicz proceeds to make a very specific suggestion for how one might turn "private grief" into "something public": "I imagine what it would be like if, each time a lover, friend or stranger died of this disease, their friends, lovers or neighbors would take the dead body and drive with it in a car a hundred miles an hour to washington d.c. and come to a screeching halt before the entrance and dump their lifeless form on the front steps."[5] These are the tactics of ACT UP, whose members staged die-ins, carried gravestones, and otherwise used art as a powerful dismantling tool. At one protest, Wojnarowicz wore a jacket that read "If I die, dump my body on the stairs of the FDA." These confrontations required both a willingness to take up the awful instability of street life and a stable space from which to speak.

In chapter 1, I argued that Wojnarowicz deployed the terrible circumstances of his upbringing in order to represent the precarity of those most threatened by the 1975 crisis: the impoverished, the housing-insecure, those living on the streets. Taking up the same tools—and, often, the same passages—in addressing AIDS, Wojnarowicz captured in writing the essential anger that drove ACT UP. In the monologues, Wojnarowicz depicted lives that were fragile and tentative, present for only a moment on a street corner or in a coffee shop. These lives fit into the cracks and open doorways produced by the crisis. Writing about AIDS, Wojnarowicz returned to these lives, but used everything he'd learned in the intervening years to build a powerful edifice around them. *Close to the Knives* shuttles between street scenes, Hujar's hospital room, and Wojnarowicz's loft. The later essays construct continuous lines from these lives up to Gracie Mansion and Washington. Despite the stability he'd achieved, Wojnarowicz maintained an angry insistence on his right to live. He grounds his critiques of Edward Koch, Jesse Helms, and Ronald Reagan in the violent disarray of queer-bashing, meditating on the impossible paradox of neatly clipped suburbs and the momentary utopias of the Lower East Side coexisting in the same country. In taking up AIDS, Wojnarowicz shows his readers the power of both the fragmentary and the continuous, the sprawling experiments of narrative and the formal structure of the polemic. He'd climbed himself from the streets into the relatively safe space of Peter Hujar's loft, and he would not let go of this space easily. The power of *The Waterfront Journals* derives from its rawness; *Close to the Knives* encloses such rawness within recognizable structures. ACT UP mixed rawness and structure; it would not have been possible without either the wild imaginaries of the Lower East Side or the relative stability that evolved alongside such wildness.

Of course, ACT UP was a movement that was much larger than the Lower East Side and drew on a range of tactics, states of feeling, and motivations for its efforts. As the sociologist and activist Deborah Gould notes, ACT UP arose out of a long period of AIDS activism, and the anger and urgency of ACT UP were motivated by the Hardwick case that Wojnarowicz cites in his poster. But the emotional register that Gould traces in her book correspond almost directly to the emotional register of *Close to the Knives*. Attending to Wojnarowicz's writing as it took shape from 1978 to the late 1980s shows readers much about how the 1975 crisis set both the terms and situational possibilities for one strand of ACT UP's work. And as Gould demonstrates, ACT UP left a long legacy, both as "the site from which a new, queer sensibility emerged and took hold, a sensibility that was embraced by lesbians, gay men, and other sexual and gender outlaws across the country" and the site from which later anti-globalization activism took inspiration.[6] Indeed, Leslie J. Wood and Kelly Moore describe ACT UP as "the single most important organization" in galvanizing the protest actions of the 1990s that culminated in the Seattle protests of 1999.[7] *Close to the Knives* traces the roots of ACT UP's sensibility back to the precarity produced by the 1975 fiscal crisis.

In voicing his anger, Wojnarowicz drew on the same capacity for network-building that allowed Texier and Rose to publish *Between C & D*, for art-activist groups to resist gentrification, for the Nuyorican poets to build the Poets Cafe, for Acker, Tillman, and Indiana to find success as writers. By repackaging his own writing from the post-crisis era, *Close to the Knives* foregrounds both the fragility and the possibility produced by the welfare state's withdrawal. The kinds of actions that Wojnarowicz urges, the kinds of actions practiced by ACT UP, simply would have not been possible without the network-building in the Lower East Side. At their best, the culture workers and activists of the Lower East Side drew energy and power from dissolution, but needed, too, the capacity to build, even if building took only the form of a small shrine.

But this building required Wojnarowicz to encounter all of the paradoxes of art-driven gentrification: the way making neighborhoods stable means leaving behind the very encounters with precarity that had originally driven his art. By the time he wrote the material in *Close to the Knives*, Wojnarowicz was living in Hujar's loft at 189 Second Avenue. He'd moved there in 1988, just after Hujar's death, and just after learning that he himself was HIV positive. After a long period of precarious living, Wojnarowicz had a stable place to live. He depicts the tensions of such stable living in a passage from *Close to the Knives* that I'll quote at length:

> I walk this hallway twenty-seven times and all I can see are the cool white walls. A hand rubbing slowly across a face, but my hands are empty. Walking back and forth from room to room trailing bluish shadows I feel weak: something emotional and wild forming a crazy knot in the deep part of my stomach. On the next trip from the front of the apartment to the back, I end up in the kitchen, turn once again and suddenly sink down to the floor in a crouching position against the wall and side of the stove in a blaze of wintery sunlight. . . . How the world is so much like dream sleep with my glasses hidden somewhere along the windowsill above the bed; there's a slow stir of measured breath from next to me and through the 6:00 a.m. windowpanes I see what appears to be a dim forest of trees in the distance, leafless and shivering, but it's just some old summer plants in a window box gone to sleep for the season. I think of these trees and how they look like the winter forests of my childhood and how they were always places of refuge: endless hours spent among them creating small myths of myself or living in hollowed-out trees or sleeping in nests twenty times larger than crows' nests made of sticks instead of twigs. . . . So here I am heading out into the cold winds of the canyon streets, walking down and across avenue c toward my home with the smell and taste of him wrapped around my neck and jaw like a scarf.[8]

As he'd done elsewhere, in this passage Wojnarowicz reminds readers of why he loved the broken spaces of the post-crisis landscape: they reminded him of the forest in which, as a child, he took refuge from his father's violent abuse. But he writes it from the viewpoint of a solid, familiar apartment—one that Wojnarowicz was fighting to keep in the wake of Hujar's death.[9]

Throughout this book, I have emphasized the dual nature of culture workers moving to the Lower East Side. On the one hand, there is no doubt that artists and writers helped make the neighborhood desirable for the more affluent residents that would follow them, just as they had done in SoHo. On the other hand, in the intervening years, the neighborhood was the site of inventive ways of living and creating. At their best, these ways of living and creating posed a challenge to city administrators' efforts to produce a New York landscape tailored to the interests of financiers and elite workers. This is what Schulman means when she sets the imagination in opposition to gentrification. For Schulman, the lifestyles made possible by the Lower East Side's cheap rents were, in crucial ways, sites of utopia. "Urbanity," Schulman argues, "is what makes cities great, because the daily affirmation that people from other experiences are real makes innovative solutions and experiments possible."[10] The homosexuals, artists, writers, performers, activists, and entrepreneurs who moved to the Lower East Side in the 1970s and 1980s often did so not because they saw the neighborhood as a good investment, but because they were fleeing forms of life that they found restrictive, and often dangerous. Arriving in a neighborhood still home to a vibrant working class, they often found ways of finding common cause with these residents.

In highlighting the oppositional qualities of the Lower East Side, Schulman describes creativity in ways that John Roberts and Gregory Sholette might find familiar. Using different terminology, both Roberts and Sholette locate political dissidence with all of the artists who never achieve success. Roberts calls this group the "second economy" of art, while Sholette's term is "dark matter."[11] These are the low- or un-waged culture workers who form the matrix out of which successful artists (and writers) emerge. One one level, these culture workers are badly exploited: in attending gallery openings, going to readings, buying books and art supplies, they further their own precarity in order to prop up the successes of others. But on another level, because of their living circumstances, low- or un-waged culture workers bear witness to the exploitation of others. Second-economy culture workers do not precisely represent a class formation, and yet may be, as Sholette contends, sources for ways of living other than those dictated by capital, a "shadow or surplus archive" that preserves oppositional ways of living for future generations.[12] But sometimes, too, such opposition takes shape in the present, and inasmuch as the lifestyles of the artistic Lower East Side mostly provided templates for gentrification and the creative economy, strands of these cultures were capable of assembling into sites of angry opposition. For Schulman, this is exactly what happened with ACT UP. Drawing on the improvisation and oppositionality of DIY, ACT UP erupted into public consciousness during this moment. With ACT UP, all of the narrative and aesthetic techniques of acknowledging alterity that I have traced here—Wojnarowicz's monologues, Kathy Acker's narrative experiments, the Nuyorican poets' improvisation, Tillman and Indiana's critiques of the art establishment—came to fruition.

As I note in my introduction, *DIY on the Lower East Side* would not have been possible without its important predecessor, Robert Siegle's 1989 *Suburban Ambush*. For Siegle, the most important facet of the artistic cultures of the Lower East Side was the way that they resisted and attacked the sedate ignorance of the suburbs, from which many of them had fled. In *Close to the Knives*, Wojnarowicz, too, decries the suburbs, what he calls alternately the world of the "ONE-TRIBE NATION" or "the Universe of Neatly Clipped Lawns."[13] For Wojnarowicz, the suburbs were the place that had oppressed him as a child, and that continued to oppress him in the present by being the site of homophobia. The paradox, though, is that Wojnarowicz himself eventually found a version of security in the built environment of the city. The decay and dissolution of the post-crisis Lower East Side eventually give way to the solidities of gentrification. Schulman describes this process as the suburbs coming to the city: the suburban ambush in reverse. And while Schulman, like others, takes pains to distinguish the writers and artists she loves from the gentrifiers she hates, the very fervency of her insistence points to a broadly accepted fact: the innovations in living and creating that characterize the Lower East Side play a central role in the neighborhood's gentrification. By all accounts, the suburban ambush fails, because gentrification transfers the problems of the suburbs to the city.

But the important question here is "What's left after the ambush?" If we think of the writing experiments of the Lower East Side not as simply an opening-up of freedom, but as foregrounding the process of self- and neighborhood-construction, what do those experiments tell us about the encroaching pressures to "do it yourself" in the 1990s forward? I began *DIY on the Lower East Side* with the premise that contemporary scholars have much to learn from the literature produced in downtown New York in the aftermath of the 1975 fiscal crisis. I have argued that the crisis left an indelible mark on these writers' projects, shaping the ways they thought about modes of living, working, and making art. At times, these writers engaged in direct activism. More often, they documented what they saw around them. The networks that they describe held for a while; the very fact that these works were produced at all testifies to the utopian possibilities of a neighborhood that allowed writers affordable rents, time to learn their craft, and contact with people from a range of backgrounds.

In doing so, these writers often reached across a gap that the artworld was unable to bridge: between the bohemian, free-floating world of the intellectual refugee and the more fixed world of the underclass. Their ways of writing and living took shape in the terms of the artistic critique. This left them recruitable for the creative economy and post-Fordism writ large. But the self-fashioning is accompanied by, and often matched to, accounts of these writers' neighborhood and neighbors. Their writing leaves behind a trace of the struggle for another world. Their descriptiveness pulls them toward other facets of the artworld, who themselves struggled to document the shifting landscape around them, and whose struggles were often unrealized: the efforts of PAD/D, Group Material, and Colab. These groups both interrogate art-driven gentrification and forge links between artists and the populations they were displacing. In setting up shop in the shifting space of the Lower East Side, these writers documented the shifting possibilities for life in the neighborhood.

I write at a moment when one of the most direct beneficiaries of post-crisis New York sits in the White House. Donald Trump's business boomed as a result of tax polices favoring real estate development in New York; his presidency has amplified the worst impulses of the crisis in blaming the impoverished, immigrants, and minorities for problems that were caused by the irresponsible capitalists of the 2000s. His administration's detainment of immigrants, support for war crimes, continued cutting of benefits, and wide ignoring of climate change have been cause for deep despair among wide swaths of Americans.

Looking back at the moment in New York that created Trump, I have come to avoid notions that everything after the 1975 fiscal crisis was determined from the beginning. The writers in my study did not believe this: they decried the forcing-out of the working class, resisted new work regimes, criticized cuts in benefits, and believed that new ways of living were possible. Like the activists and artists taken up by Robin D. G. Kelley in *Freedom Dreams: The Black Radical Imagination*, these writers imagined "cognitive maps of the future, of the world not yet born" that drew from "struggle and lived experience."[14] I find these writers particularly energizing because they worked, by and large, outside of the great machines of creative writing programs. In this sense, their work provides a foundation for the messy avant-garde of the second economy. I join the sometimes-baffling hopefulness of Roberts's *Revolutionary Time and the Avant-Garde* in sensing that DIY could have been more than a mode of consumption or work. And if the artists of my study often seemed complicit in the economic shifts wrenching the city out of its working-class New York past, they, too, were capable of fierce resistance, particularly as AIDS became a more and more dominant feature of the cultural landscape.

At a moment when history's arc seems impossibly fixed, I find these culture workers' joy in self-creation liberating, even as I acknowledge that self-creation quickly becomes a tyrannical mode of working and living under neoliberal capitalism. I see this self-creation as this literature's specific contribution to the often-bleak circumstances of the post-crisis moment. Working in uneven bursts, culling together materials at hand, being generous to their neighbors, these writers sought a new world. In some broad sense, they failed, but I refuse to accept that failure was the only possible outcome. The example of ACT UP and its vital legacy suggests that DIY is more than the self-management of the neoliberal worker; it is, too, a way of asserting that even the most precarious are capable of self-organization and defense of the reproduction of their fragile lives. At its best, the literature of the 1970s and 1980s Lower East Side traces the possibilities of such self-organization. These writers offer a vital map of the possible within even the bleakest circumstances. Their legacy reminds us of the ongoing role that literature and the arts play in documenting and defining such possibility.

Notes

Introduction

1. For accounts of the crisis, see Kim Phillips-Fein, *Fear City: New York's Fiscal Crisis and the Rise of Austerity Politics* (New York: Metropolitan Books, 2017); Michael Reagan, "Capital City: New York in Fiscal Crisis, 1966–1978" (PhD diss., University of Washington, 2017); Kim Moody, *From Welfare State to Real Estate: Regime Change in New York City, 1974 to the Present* (New York: New Press, 2007); William Sites, *Remaking New York: Primitive Globalization and the Politics of Urban Community* (Minneapolis: University of Minnesota Press, 2003); William K. Tabb, *The Long Default: New York City and the Urban Fiscal Crisis* (New York: Monthly Review Press, 1982).

2. Quoted in Tabb, *The Long Default*, 39.

3. This is the case made by, among others, David Harvey, *A Brief History of Neoliberalism* (New York: Oxford University Press, 2005); Phillips-Fein, *Fear City*; and Reagan, "Capital City." Reagan, for example, describes the crisis as "a dramatic restructuring of city governance, an experiment in rolling back the social programs of the Keynesian state won through decades of social movement organizing, for both labor and black liberation" (12).

4. "Betty Kronsky to Organizers of the Schizo-Culture Conference," November 18, 1975, Lotringer and Semiotext(e) Archive Series 2A, box 9, folder 32, Fales Library and Special Collections, New York University.

5. Kathy Acker, *Blood and Guts in High School* (New York: Grove Press, 1984), 56–57.

6. Using similar language, Michael Reagan describes the Emergency Financial Control Board as a "radical use of state intervention to undo the networks of civil society that had grown up around and buttressed the Keynesian state." "Capital City," 16.

7. Zygmunt Bauman, *Liquid Modernity* (Cambridge, UK: Polity Press, 2000).

8. Robert Siegle, *Suburban Ambush: Downtown Writing and the Fiction of Insurgency* (Baltimore: Johns Hopkins University Press, 1989).

9. Siegle, *Suburban Ambush*, 9–10.

10. In *The New Urban Crisis*, a work that, in part, recants his own conclusions in *The Rise of the Creative Class*, Florida laments that the accumulation of wealth in "superstar cities"—the very places that served as models for creative cities in his earlier book—has generated income divides that mean "blight, poverty, crime, addiction, racial tensions, violence, structural unemployment—all the things that people of my parents' generation thought of as strictly urban problems—have taken up residence in the suburbs, too." *The New Urban Crisis: How Our Cities Are Increasing Inequality, Deepening Segregation, and Failing the Middle Class—and What We Can Do about It* (New York: Basic Books, 2017), 153.

11. At Sixth Street, Bowery merges into Third Avenue, which continues north. Canal and Bowery intersect at the southwestern corner of the area I'm defining here. To the east, Canal Street ends at East Broadway, which angles northeast until it ends at Grand Street, which ends at FDR drive adjoining the East River.

12. Isabell Lorey, *State of Insecurity: Government of the Precarious* (London: Verso, 2015), 89.

13. Lauren Gail Berlant, *Cruel Optimism* (Durham, NC: Duke University Press, 2011), 167.

14. Gregory Sholette, *Dark Matter: Art and Politics in the Age of Enterprise Culture* (London: Pluto Press, 2010), 67. See also Alan Moore and Marc H. Miller, eds., *ABC No Rio Dinero: The Story of a Lower East Side Art Gallery* (New York: ABC No Rio, 1985); Alan Moore and Jim Cornwell, "Local History," in *Alternative Art, New York, 1965–1985: A Cultural Politics Book for the Social Text Collective*, ed. Julie Ault. (Minneapolis: University of Minnesota Press; New York: The Drawing Center, 2002), 321–65.

15. On Fun Gallery, see Christopher Mele, *Selling the Lower East Side: Culture, Real Estate, and Resistance in New York City* (Minneapolis: University of Minnesota Press, 2000), 229; Grace Glueck, "A Gallery Scene That Pioneers In New Territories," *New York Times*, June 26, 1983; Rene Ricard, "The Pledge of Allegiance," *Artforum* 21, no. 3 (1982): 42–49.

16. Jasper Bernes, *The Work of Art in the Age of Deindustrialization* (Stanford, CA: Stanford University Press, 2017), 10.

17. See Pierre Bourdieu, *The Rules of Art: Genesis and Structure of the Literary Field*, trans. Susan Emanuel (Stanford, CA: Stanford University Press, 1996), 54–68.

18. For two accounts protesting the notion that the culture workers of the Lower East Side enabled gentrification, see Sarah Schulman, *The Gentrification of the Mind: Witness to a Lost Imagination* (Berkeley, CA: University of California Press, 2012), and Moore and Cornwell, "Local History." For two canonical accounts of the Lower East Side's art-driven gentrification, see Mele, *Selling the Lower East Side*, and Neil Smith, *The New Urban Frontier: Gentrification and the Revanchist City* (New York: Routledge, 1996).

19. Henri Lefebvre, *The Production of Space*, trans. Donald Nicholson-Smith (Oxford: Blackwell, 1991), 189–90.

20. Moishe Postone, *Time, Labor, and Social Domination: A Reinterpretation of Marx's Critical Theory* (New York: Cambridge University Press, 1993), 354.

21. For an account of art and wagelessness that converges partly with the account I'll offer here, see Leigh Claire La Berge, *Wages Against Artwork: Decommodified Labor and the Claims of Socially Engaged Art* (Durham, NC: Duke University Press, 2019).

22. Kathi Weeks, *The Problem with Work: Feminism, Marxism, Antiwork Politics, and Postwork Imaginaries* (Durham, NC: Duke University Press, 2011), 12.

23. Siegle, *Suburban Ambush*, xi.

24. Schulman, *The Gentrification of the Mind*, 32.

25. Mark McGurl, *The Program Era: Postwar Fiction and the Rise of Creative Writing* (Cambridge, MA: Harvard University Press, 2009), 365–71.

26. Siegle writes, "[M]ost of them avoided writing programs or loathed their repressive, or formulaic, or actively reactionary teachers." *Suburban Ambush*, 3.

27. Joel Rose and Catherine Texier, "Introduction," in *Between C & D: New Writing from the Lower East Side Fiction Magazine*, ed. Joel Rose and Catherine Texier (New York: Penguin Books, 1988), ix.

28. Rob Halpern, "Realism and Utopia: Sex, Writing, and Activism in New Narrative," *Journal of Narrative Theory* 41, no. 1 (2011): 89.

29. K. P. Harris, "New Narrative and the Making of Language Poetry," *American Literature* 81, no. 4 (2009): 806.

30. Halpern, "Realism and Utopia," 83.

31. György Lukács, *Realism in Our Time: Literature and the Class Struggle* (New York: Harper & Row, 1964), 82.

32. Anthony Reed, *Freedom Time: The Poetics and Politics of Black Experimental Writing* (Baltimore: Johns Hopkins University Press, 2014); Tyler Bradway, *Queer Experimental Literature: The Affective Politics of Bad Reading* (New York: Palgrave Macmillan, 2017); Alex Houen, *Powers of Possibility: Experimental American Writing Since the 1960s* (Oxford, UK: Oxford University Press, 2012).

33. Jini Kim Watson, *The New Asian City: Three-Dimensional Fictions of Space and Urban Form* (Minneapolis: University of Minnesota Press, 2011), 131.

34. Admittedly, the two regions share characteristics in their relation both to displaced colonial subjects and to international finance.

35. Carlo Rotella, *October Cities: The Redevelopment of Urban Literature* (Berkeley, CA: University of California Press, 1998), 3.

36. Thomas Heise, *Urban Underworlds: A Geography of Twentieth-Century American Literature and Culture* (New Brunswick, NJ: Rutgers University Press, 2011), 10.

37. Mario Maffi, *Gateway to the Promised Land: Ethnic Cultures on New York's Lower East Side* (New York: New York University Press, 1995), 15.

38. Michel de Certeau, *The Practice of Everyday Life* (Berkeley, CA: University of California Press, 1988), 105.

39. Lefebvre, *The Production of Space*, 35.

40. McKenzie Wark, *The Beach Beneath the Street: The Everyday Life and Glorious Times of the Situationist International* (New York: Verso, 2011), 101.

41. See Smith, *The New Urban Frontier*.

42. Michael B. Katz, *The Undeserving Poor: America's Enduring Confrontation with Poverty*, second edition (Oxford, UK: Oxford University Press, 2013), 163. Phillips-Fein notes that these discourses intensified after the 1977 blackout. For writers like Pat Buchanan and Midge Decter, the looting during the blackout was evidence that "[t]he social order of New York had collapsed as thoroughly as its fiscal politics, and a strict new discipline seemed the only solution" (*Fear City*, 276–77).

43. Loïc J. D. Wacquant, *Urban Outcasts: A Comparative Sociology of Advanced Marginality* (Cambridge, MA: Polity, 2008), 48.

44. Katz, *The Undeserving Poor*, 209.

45. For a literary-critical account of the underworld, see Heise, *Urban Underworlds*.

46. Samuel R. Delany, *Times Square Red, Times Square Blue* (New York: New York University Press, 1999), 111. Delany writes, "[G]iven the mode of capitalism under which we live, life is at its most rewarding, productive, and pleasant when large numbers of people understand, appreciate, and seek out interclass contact and communication conducted in a mode of good will."

47. John Roberts, *Revolutionary Time and the Avant-Garde* (New York: Verso, 2015), 31.

48. For important contemporaneous celebrations of this scene, see Ricard, "The Pledge of Allegiance"; Ricard, "The Radiant Child," *Artforum* 20, no. 4 (1981): 35–43; Walter Robinson and Carlo McCormick, "Slouching Toward Avenue D," *Art in America* 72, no. 6 (1984): 134–61. For contemporaneous critical accounts, see Craig Owens, "The Problem with Puerilism," *Art in America* 72, no. 6 (1984): 162–63; Rosalyn Deutsche and Cara Gendel Ryan, "The Fine Art of Gentrification," *October* 31 (1984): 91–111. For an overview of these cultures that challenges received accounts of Basquiat, Haring, Koons, and others, see Alison Pearlman, *Unpackaging Art of the 1980s* (Chicago: University of Chicago Press, 2003).

49. Deutsche and Gendel Ryan, "The Fine Art of Gentrification."

50. Sarah Brouillette, *Literature and the Creative Economy* (Stanford, CA: Stanford University Press, 2014); Bernes, *The Work of Art in the Age of Deindustrialization*.

51. Mele, *Selling the Lower East Side*, 234–35.

52. Gary Indiana, "Imitation and Its Double," *The Village Voice*, February 24, 1987.

53. For keystone examples of such work, see Stephen Best and Sharon Marcus, "Surface Reading: An Introduction," *Representations* 108, no. 1 (2009): 1–21; Caroline Levine, *Forms: Whole, Rhythm, Hierarchy, Network* (Princeton, NJ: Princeton

University Press, 2015); David J. Alworth, *Site Reading: Fiction, Art, Social Form* (Princeton, NJ: Princeton University Press, 2016); Rita Felski, *The Limits of Critique* (Chicago: University of Chicago Press, 2015).

54. For important examples of this work see Leigh Claire La Berge, *Scandals and Abstraction: Financial Fiction of the Long 1980s* (Oxford, UK: Oxford University Press, 2015); Brouillette, *Literature and the Creative Economy*; Bernes, *The Work of Art in the Age of Deindustrialization*; Annie McClanahan, *Dead Pledges: Debt, Crisis, and Twenty-First-Century Culture* (Stanford, CA: Stanford University Press, 2017). Luc Boltanski and Eve Chiapello's *The New Spirit of Capitalism* (New York: Verso, 2007) has been an important influence on many of these works.

55. Moishe Postone, "The Current Crisis and the Anachronism of Value: A Marxian Reading," *Continental Thought & Theory* 1, no. 4 (2017): 41.

56. Margaret Ronda, "The Social Forms of Speculative Poetics," *Post45*, April 26, 2019, http://post45.research.yale.edu/2019/04/the-social-forms-of-speculative-poetics/.

57. Bruno Latour, *Reassembling the Social: An Introduction to Actor-Network-Theory* (Oxford, UK: Oxford University Press, 2005), 11.

58. Bruno Latour, *An Inquiry into Modes of Existence: An Anthropology of the Moderns* (Cambridge, MA: Harvard University Press, 2013), 233–56.

59. Alworth, *Site Reading*, 20.

60. Drawing on Lefebvre, Smith, and other urban theorists, Myka Tucker-Abramson critiques Alworth for abstracting literature away from the totality of capital. See "Make Literary Criticism Great Again (Review of David Alworth's Site Reading: Fiction, Art, Social Form)," *boundary 2*, September 26, 2018, https://www.boundary2.org/2018/09/myka-tucker-abramson-make-literary-criticism-great-again-review-of-david-alworths-site-reading-fiction-art-social-form/.

61. Roberts, *Revolutionary Time and the Avant-Garde*, 35.

62. Ibid.

63. Phillips-Fein, *Fear City*, 208.

64. Rotella, *October Cities*, 3.

65. Ibid.

66. Certeau, *The Practice of Everyday Life*, 125.

67. Marshall Berman, *All That Is Solid Melts into Air: The Experience of Modernity* (New York: Simon and Schuster, 1982), 170.

68. Ibid., 171.

Chapter 1

1. Katz, *The Undeserving Poor*.

2. Many such projects, including Matta-Clark and Wojnarowicz's *Rimbaud in the City* series, are collected in the exhibit catalog for *Mixed Use, Manhattan*, a 2010

exhibition at the Museo Nacional Centro de Arte Reina Sofía. See Lynne Cooke and Douglas Crimp, eds., *Mixed Use, Manhattan* (Cambridge, MA: MIT Press, 2010).

3. Lefebvre, *The Production of Space*, 142.

4. Ibid., 143.

5. Moody, *From Welfare State to Real Estate*, 54.

6. See Joshua Benjamin Freeman, *Working-Class New York: Life and Labor since World War II* (New York: New Press, 2000).

7. Phillips-Fein, *Fear City*, 93, 95. For an extended discussion of the response of the Ford administration, including Treasury Secretary William Simon, chair of Council of Economic Advisors Alan Greenspan, Arthur Laffer, and Donald Rumsfield, see 92–108.

8. Ibid., 96.

9. Felix G. Rohatyn, "Indeed, 'the Moral Equivalent of War,'" *New York Times*, August 21, 1977.

10. Katz, *The Undeserving Poor*, 164. See also Tabb, *The Long Default*.

11. Cynthia Carr, *Fire in the Belly: The Life and Times of David Wojnarowicz* (New York: Bloomsbury, 2012), 213.

12. Lucy Lippard, "Passenger on the Shadows," in *David Wojnarowicz: Brush Fires in the Social Landscape*, ed. Lucy Lippard. 2nd ed. (New York, N.Y: Aperture, 2015).

13. David Wojnarowicz, *Memories That Smell like Gasoline* (San Francisco: Artspace Books, 1992), 36.

14. Ibid., 45.

15. Judith Halberstam, *In a Queer Time and Place: Transgender Bodies, Subcultural Lives* (New York: New York University Press, 2005); José Esteban Muñoz, *Cruising Utopia: The Then and There of Queer Futurity* (New York: New York University Press, 2009).

16. Halberstam critiques David Harvey for the latter's dismissal of queer lives as "lifestyle choices" and yet if one looks at both critics from the viewpoint of a Lefebvrian "right to the city," some slippages occur between their views. Even as Halberstam seems primarily interested in working-class queer life, she reads Harvey as dismissing such life, even as Harvey's own account seems squarely targeted at *middle- or upper-class* homosexuals.

17. Muñoz, *Cruising Utopia*, 25.

18. Ibid., 27.

19. William J. Wilson, *The Truly Disadvantaged: The Inner City, the Underclass, and Public Policy*, 2nd ed. (Chicago: University of Chicago Press, 2012).

20. Wilson himself argues that the inner city did, indeed, have specific problems, but that such problems stemmed from the isolation of a largely unskilled labor pool of African Americans in neighborhoods like Harlem and the Lower East Side (61). Such isolation stemmed from both the exodus of middle-class African Americans from such neighborhoods in the fifties and sixties, as well as the final

death of manufacturing in Northern cities. Wilson writes: "substantial job losses have occurred in the very industries in which urban minorities have the greatest access, and substantial employment gains have occurred in the higher-education-requisite industries that are beyond the reach of most minority workers" (102).

21. Halberstam, *In a Queer Time and Place*, 6.

22. Michael Warner and Lauren Berlant, "Sex in Public," in *Publics and Counterpublics* (New York: Zone Books, 2002), 187–208.

23. Fiona Anderson, "Cruising the Queer Ruins of New York's Abandoned Waterfront," *Performance Research* 20, no. 3 (2015): 135–44. Along with Carr, Anderson provides one of the most thoughtful accounts of Wojnarowicz's cruising in relation to the abandoned landscape of the piers. She continues later in the essay: "Cruising at the queer space of the piers, as Wojnarowicz's work demonstrates most readily, was a cross-temporal collaboration with its former inhabitants made possible by the cumulative architectural memory of the piers and warehouses" (143). My work here builds on Anderson's project, emphasizing the connection between Wojnarowicz's work and contemporaneous accounts of a degraded underclass.

24. Delany, *Times Square Red, Times Square Blue*, xviii.

25. Ibid., 174.

26. Ibid., 159.

27. Anne M. Wagner, "Splitting and Doubling: Gordon Matta-Clark and the Body of Sculpture," *Grey Room* 14 (Winter 2004): 29.

28. "No Exit." *Artforum* 26, no. 7 (1988): 112–15.

29. Douglas Crimp, *Before Pictures* (New York: Dancing Foxes Press; Chicago: University of Chicago Press, 2016), 176.

30. See Institute for Art and Urban Resources et al., eds., *Rooms, P. S. 1: [Exhibition] June 9–26, 1976* (New York: The Institute, 1977). See also Rosalind Krauss's essay on the exhibit: "Notes on the Index: Seventies Art in America. Part 2," October 4 (1977): 58–67.

31. Institute for Art and Urban Resources et al., *Rooms, P. S. 1*, 125.

32. John Russell, "Gallery View: An Unwanted School in Queens Becomes an Ideal Art Center," *New York Times*, June 20, 1976.

33. Jacobs's relationship to the underclass—what she calls "slum-dwellers"—is complicated. On the one hand, she emphasizes that so-called slums can be sites of vitality similar to Greenwich Village; on the other, she is quick to frame some city residents as abject, particularly in her (admittedly timebound) use of the term "pervert." Delany forgives her for this, explaining it as a problem of her generation.

34. Quoted in Corinne Diserens, ed., *Gordon Matta-Clark* (New York: Phaidon Press, 2006), 186. The youths Matta-Clark met were part of the wider Autonomist movement of 1970s Italy. I'll return to this movement at the end of chapter 3, when I discuss an issue of *Semiotext(e)* devoted to it.

35. There's little evidence that he ever involved "neighborhood youth" in his work directly.

36. Documentation of this is hard to come by. The website for La Plaza Cultural makes this claim, but few if any Matta-Clark scholars mention it. I'll discus Charas in more detail in chapter 2.

37. Diserens, *Gordon Matta-Clark*, 6.

38. Freeman makes this case most clearly in *Working-Class New York*. See also Moody, *From Welfare State to Real Estate*, and Tabb, *The Long Default*, as well as Robert Fitch, *The Assassination of New York* (New York: Verso, 1996).

39. Diserens, *Gordon Matta-Clark*, 105.

40. Rosalind Deutsche, "The Threshold of Democracy," in *Urban Mythologies: The Bronx Represented since the 1960s*, ed. John Alan Farmer (New York: Bronx Museum of the Arts, 1999), 94–101. Introduced in a 1982 article in *The Atlantic Monthly*, this concept maintains that small problems—a panhandler, a broken window—are at the root of the social decay found in neighborhoods like the South Bronx and the Lower East Side. The idea went on to become a keystone of mayor Rudy Giuliani's campaign against crime.

41. Diserens, *Gordon Matta-Clark*, 31. On city support for lofts, see Sharon Zukin, *Loft Living: Culture and Capital in Urban Change*, 25th anniversary ed. (New Brunswick, NJ: Rutgers University Press, 2014).

42. Emphasis mine. Quoted in Diserens, *Gordon Matta-Clark*, 12.

43. Baltrop's work also features in the catalog for *Mixed Use, Manhattan*, Cooke and Crimp, eds. Anderson ties Wojnarowicz to Baltrop in "Cruising the Queer Ruins of New York's Abandoned Waterfront." Douglas Crimp, "Alvin Baltrop: Pier Photographs, 1975–1986," *Artforum International* 46, no. 6 (2008): 262–73.

44. Cooke and Crimp, *Mixed Use, Manhattan*, 89.

45. Brouillette, *Literature and the Creative Economy*.

46. Wacquant, *Urban Outcasts*; Wilson, *The Truly Disadvantaged*.

47. Quoted in Elizabeth Seton Kirwin, "It's All True: Imagining New York's East Village Art Scene of the 1980s" (PhD diss., University of Maryland, 1999), 14. Marisa Cardinale, who worked at Civilian Warfare: "The whole climate was about incredible economic growth, and there was a feeling like this was the pot of gold and it was going to go on forever." Quoted in Kirwin, 286.

48. Mele, *Selling the Lower East Side*, 221.

49. Ibid., 235.

50. David Wojnarowicz, *In the Shadow of the American Dream: The Diaries of David Wojnarowicz*, ed. Amy Scholder (New York: Grove Press, 1999), 146.

51. Ibid., 147.

52. Lynne B. Sagalyn, *Times Square Roulette: Remaking the City Icon* (Cambridge, MA: MIT Press, 2001), 81.

53. *The New Spirit of Capitalism* makes this point more generally about the counterculture of the 1960s, on which the influence of the Beats was strong.

54. Wojnarowicz, *Memories that Smell Like Gasoline*, 146.

55. David Wojnarowicz, *The Waterfront Journals*, ed. Amy Scholder (New York: Grove Press, 1996), 70.

56. Jane Kramer, "Whose Art Is It?," *New Yorker*, December 21, 1992, 81. As Kramer details, Ahearn's sculptures provoked complaints among "angry and respectable neighbors who complained about negative images—ghetto images—and convinced [Ahearn] that he should take them down," 82. He did. These found an initial home at P.S. 1, and now reside at the Socrates Sculpture Park in Queens.

57. Wojnarowicz, *The Waterfront Journals*, 36.

58. Ibid., 20.

59. Ibid. 104–5.

60. Ibid., 109.

61. Ibid., 111.

62. Carr, *Fire in the Belly*.

63. Wojnarowicz, *The Waterfront Journals*, 85.

64. Quoted in Carr, *Fire in the Belly*, 100.

65. Latour, *Reassembling the Social*, 128.

66. Ibid., 124.

67. Ibid., 126.

68. Muñoz, *Cruising Utopia*, 45, 48. Muñoz takes queer theorists like Lee Edelmen and Leo Bersani to task both for refusing a politics of the future—which both Edelman and Bersani identify with heteronormativity—and for eliding cross-class and cross-racial identifications in favor of what Muñoz calls "reproduc[ing] a crypto universal white gay subject that is weirdly atemporal" (94). Even as Muñoz concurs with, for example, Edelman's analysis of the child as the culture's primary repository of the future, Munoz challenges the brackets that both critics draw around a narrow version of queer abjection.

69. Wojnarowicz, *The Waterfront Journals*, 32.

70. Ibid. 32.

71. Berlant, *Cruel Optimism*, 167.

72. Mele, *Selling the Lower East Side*; Smith, *The New Urban Frontier*.

73. Wojnarowicz, *The Waterfront Journals*, 35.

74. Sagalyn, *Times Square Roulette*, 6.

75. Ibid., 81.

76. Michel Foucault, "Lives of Infamous Men," in *Essential Works of Foucault, 1954–1988: Power*, ed. Paul Rabinow, vol. 3 (New York: New Press, 1997), 161–62.

77. Sara Ahmed, *Willful Subjects* (Durham, NC: Duke University Press, 2014), 169–70.

78. Wojnarowicz, *The Waterfront Journals*, 3.

79. Ibid., 7.

80. Of Wojnarowicz's visual art, Lucy Lippard notes, "Wojnarowicz used maps as a metaphor for government, and tore them up to destroy boundaries—national

and moral" (27). I am contrasting the micro-maps drawn by the monologues with the macro-maps that Wojnarowicz resisted.

81. Carr, *Fire in the Belly*, 256.

82. Roberts, *Revolutionary Time and the Avant-Garde*, 22, 24, 25.

83. Benjamin H. D. Buchloh, "Detritus and Decrepitude: The Sculpture of Thomas Hirschhorn," *Oxford Art Journal* 24, no. 2 (2001): 49.

84. Ahmed, *Willful Subjects*, 140.

Chapter 2

1. Francis X. Clines, "Blighted Areas' Use Is Urged by Rohatyn: Rohatyn Urges a City Plan for Industry," *New York Times*, March 16, 1976.

2. Rohatyn's pronouncement followed fast on the heels of Roger Starr's more infamous proposal for "planned shrinkage" of the city's neighborhoods. Starr's words quickly produced an uproar, while Rohatyn's went largely unnoticed.

3. For a summary of the MAC board's sentiments along these lines, see Phillips-Fein, *Fear City*, especially 276–81.

4. Carlos Garcia, "Saving Preservation Stories: Diversity and the Outer Boroughs: The Reminiscences of Carlos 'Chino' Garcia," interview by Layla Vural, New York Preservation Archive Project, November 3, 2017, http://www.nypap.org/wp-content/uploads/2017/12/Garcia_Chino_20171113.pdf. For a more expanded account of the term's origins and use, see Liz Ševčenko, "Making Loisaida: Placing Puertorriqueñidad in Lower Manhattan," in *Mambo Montage: The Latinization of New York City* (New York: Columbia University Press, 2001), 293–318.

5. Latour, *An Inquiry into Modes of Existence*, 36. My use of the term is also influenced by Caroline Levine's account of networks as "patterns of interconnection and exchange that organize social and aesthetic experience." Levine, *Forms*, 113.

6. See Malve von Hassell, *Homesteading in New York City, 1978–1993: The Divided Heart of Loisaida* (Westport, CT: Bergin & Garvey, 1996); Miranda J. Martinez, *Power at the Roots: Gentrification, Community Gardens, and the Puerto Ricans of the Lower East Side* (Lanham, MD: Lexington Books, 2010).

7. Malve von Hassell, "Names of Hate, Names of Love: Contested Space and the Formation of Identity on Manhattan's Lower East Side," *Dialectical Anthropology* 23, no. 4 (1998): 376. See also Amy Starecheski, *Ours to Lose: When Squatters Became Homeowners in New York City* (Chicago: The University of Chicago Press, 2016), 53. For an account of housing activism in the Lower East Side in the context of financialized rental housing, see Desiree Fields, "Contesting the Financialization of Urban Space: Community Organizations and the Struggle to Preserve Affordable Rental Housing in New York City," *Journal of Urban Affairs* 37, no. 2 (2015): 144–65.

8. Miguel Piñero, *Outlaw: The Collected Works of Miguel Piñero* (Houston: Arte Publico Press, 2010), 4.

9. Miguel Algarín, "Volume and Value of the Breath in Poetry," in *Talking Poetics from Naropa Institute: Annals of the Jack Kerouac School of Disembodied Poetics*, ed. Anne Waldman and Marilyn Webb (Boulder, CO: Shambhala Publications, Inc, 1978), 334.

10. Ibid., 334–35.

11. Latour, *Reassembling the Social*, 89.

12. Alain Lipietz, *Towards a New Economic Order: Postfordism, Ecology, and Democracy* (New York: Oxford University Press, 1992), xi.

13. Robin D. G. Kelley, *Freedom Dreams: The Black Radical Imagination* (Boston: Beacon Press, 2003), 9.

14. Miguel Algarín, "Nuyorican Literature," *MELUS* 8, no. 2 (1981): 91.

15. Mele, *Selling the Lower East Side*, 200.

16. Andy Merrifield, *Henri Lefebvre: A Critical Introduction* (New York: Routledge, 2006), 111.

17. Lefebvre, *The Production of Space*, 41.

18. Sandra Maria Esteves, "Manhattan," in *Yerba Buena: Dibujos y Poemas* (New York: Greenfield Review, 1980), 13.

19. Miguel Algarín and Miguel Piñero, eds., *Nuyorican Poetry: An Anthology of Puerto Rican Words and Feelings* (New York: Morrow, 1975), 151.

20. For a fuller discussion of this term, see Urayoán Noel, *In Visible Movement: Nuyorican Poetry from the Sixties to Slam* (Iowa City: University of Iowa Press, 2014), 45.

21. Miguel Algarín and Bob Holman, eds., *Aloud: Voices from the Nuyorican Poets Cafe* (New York: H. Holt, 1994), xi.

22. For accounts of these other institutions, see a pair of books by Daniel Kane: *All Poets Welcome: The Lower East Side Poetry Scene in the 1960s* (Berkeley, CA: University of California Press, 2003) and *"Do You Have a Band?": Poetry and Punk Rock in New York City* (New York: Columbia University Press, 2017).

23. Noel, *In Visible Movement*, 43. Noel observes, "Poetry, and performed poetry in particular, was central to the Puerto Rican Movement of the 1960s and 1970s, from the Young Lords to the Nuyorican Poets Cafe and beyond" (xix). In addition to Noel, see Juan Flores, *Divided Borders: Essays on Puerto Rican Identity* (Houston: Arte Público Press, 1993). For an account of Nuyorican literary production in the context of Puerto Rican activism in the twentieth century, see Lorrin Thomas, *Puerto Rican Citizen: History and Political Identity in Twentieth-Century New York City* (Chicago: University of Chicago Press, 2010), 245–48.

24. Noel, *In Visible Movement*, 46.

25. Young Lords Party and Michael Abramson, eds., *Palante: Young Lords Party* (New York: McGraw-Hill, 1971), 16–22.

26. Katz, *The Undeserving Poor*, 205.

27. Edward C. Banfield, *The Unheavenly City Revisited* (Boston: Little, Brown, 1974), 62–63. Quoted in Michael Reagan, "Capital City," 88. For an account of

how the "culture of poverty" idea shaped discourse around the crisis, see Reagan, 56–102. For an overview of the underclass narrative, see Katz, 203–64.

28. Heise, *Urban Underworlds*, 15.
29. Smith, *The New Urban Frontier*.
30. Eve Tuck and K. Wayne Yang, "Decolonization Is Not a Metaphor," *Decolonization: Indigeneity, Education & Society* 1, no. 1 (2012): 28.
31. Algarín and Piñero, *Nuyorican Poetry*, 13.
32. Ibid., 14.
33. Ibid., 18.
34. Ibid., 19.
35. von Hassell, *Homesteading*, 3.
36. Mele, *Selling the Lower East Side*, 206.
37. Ibid., 207.
38. Algarín, "Nuyorican Literature," 89–92.
39. Flores, *Divided Borders*, 186.
40. Algarín and Piñero, *Nuyorican Poetry*, 123–24.
41. Jorge Lopez, "About the Rats," in Algarín and Piñero, *Nuyorican Poetry*, 42. Translated by Miguel Piñero.
42. Miguel Piñero, "The Book of Genesis According to Saint Miguelito," in Algarín and Piñero, *Nuyorican Poetry*, 62.
43. Algarín and Piñero, *Nuyorican Poetry*, 70.
44. T. C. Garcia, "Message of My People," Algarín and Piñero, *Nuyorican Poetry*, 76.
45. Sandra Maria Esteves, "I look for peace great graveyard," Algarín and Piñero, *Nuyorican Poetry*, 136.
46. Noel, *In Visible Movement*, xxii.
47. Katz, *The Undeserving Poor*, 206.
48. "do not let," Algarín and Piñero, *Nuyorican Poetry*, 89.
49. Algarín and Piñero, *Nuyorican Poetry*, 129.
50. Ibid., 24.
51. A review in *Library Journal*, for example, asserts that in the anthology "the rawness of inner-city life is not disguised." Dayle Manges, "Nuyorican Poetry (Book Review)," *LJ: Library Journal* 101, no. 6 (1976): 819.
52. "Stage: 'Conga Mania': Play in Nuyorican Fete Is Set in Pocket Park," *New York Times*, February 19, 1975.
53. Algarín and Piñero, *Nuyorican Poetry*, 23. Describing *Short Eyes* in *The New York Times,* for example, the critic Clive Barnes used a monetary metaphor to describe the value of the play for a wider audience: "Just as you don't need to be a silversmith to know when a coin has an honest ring to it, you need not have been in prison to know instinctively that in a very large part Mr. Piñero is documenting its degradation, customs, and hopes." "Theater: 'Short Eyes,' Prison Drama," *New York Times*, March 14, 1974. Algarín and Piñero, *Nuyorican Poetry*, 23.

54. Edgardo Vega Yunqué, *The Lamentable Journey of Omaha Bigelow into the Impenetrable Loisaida Jungle* (Woodstock, NY: Overlook Press, 2004), 99. In an interview, Vega told Carmen Dolores Hernández, "I am not drawn in by ghetto literature. That is the manner in which the United States . . . but also the literary institutions—creates a myth, the myth of the ghetto, in order to keep the Puerto Rican, the Afro-American, whoever, separated from society's material benefits. . . . In movies, as in literature, our stereotype is that of the killer, the shantytown, the prostitute." Carmen Dolores Hernández, ed., *Puerto Rican Voices in English: Interviews with Writers* (Westport, CT: Praeger, 1997), 206.

55. Noel, *In Visible Movement*, 76.

56. Algarín and Piñero, *Nuyorican Poetry*, 136.

57. Ibid., 136.

58. Ibid.

59. Esteves, *Yerba Buena*, 90. My translation.

60. Eliana Ortega, "Sandra María Esteves' Poetic Work: Demythicizing Puerto Rican Poetry in the U.S.," in *The Commuter Nation: Perspectives on Puerto Rican Migration*, ed. Carlos Antonio Torre and William Burgos (Río Piedras, PR: Editorial de la Universidad de Puerto Rico, 1994), 341.

61. Lefebvre, *The Production of Space*, 68–168. Lefebvre writes, for example, "Could it be that the space of the finest cities came into being after the fashion of plants and flowers in a garden—after the fashion, in other words, of works of nature, just as unique as they, albeit fashioned by highly civilized people?" (82).

62. Martinez, *Power at the Roots*, 47.

63. "Under an Apple Tree," Algarín and Piñero, *Nuyorican Poetry*, 117–18.

64. Algarín and Piñero, *Nuyorican Poetry*, 173.

65. Ibid., 181.

66. In *Direct Action: An Ethnography* (Oakland, CA: AK Press, 2009), David Graeber attributes the city's decision on P.S. 64 to a "gentleman's agreement" that involved squatters withdrawing from the Christadora hotel in exchange for activists getting the use of P.S. 64. Graeber does not cite sources directly, but here is his account: "El Bohío in turn came into being when, in 1979, some of them, working with some former Panthers, squatted the Christadora, a beautiful but then abandoned settlement house located directly east of Tompkins Square Park, and towering over the surrounding neighborhood. This eventually led to a stand-off with the city government, who were ultimately willing to resolve the matter by offering the squatters the abandoned schoolhouse down the street, the former P.S. 64" (267).

67. On the widescale protests and occupation of city buildings, see Phillips-Fein, *Fear City*, 222–55.

68. Garcia, "Saving Preservation Stories," 19.

69. See "P.S. 64/El Bohio (Former)," Places That Matter, accessed September 14, 2018, https://www.placematters.net/node/1432; Garcia, "Saving Preservation Stories."

70. The building was sold by the city in 1998, and since then has remained undeveloped.

71. Graeber, *Direct Action*, 267. Tracing community action in the 1970s and 1980s, Graeber describes the building as "the effective political center of the network of squats and community gardens in the area surrounding Tompkins Square."

72. Maffi, *Gateway to the Promised Land*, 31.

73. "Cover," *The Quality of Life in the Lower East Side* 8, no. 1 (February 1985): 1.

74. Father Jack Washington, "Do-It-Yourself-Banking," *The Quality of Life in the Lower East Side* 8, no. 1 (February 1985): 7.

75. "Start Your Own Agency," *The Quality of Life in the Lower East Side* 8, no. 1 (February 1985): 11.

76. See Maffi, *Gateway to the Promised Land*, 31. Maffi's first chapter offers an excellent overview of the diverse social and cultural programs happening across the Lower East Side in the 1970s and 1980s.

77. Garcia, "Saving Preservation Stories," 11.

78. Tee Saralegui, "How Would You Handle a Rent Strike?" (1978), The Records of CHARAS, Inc., Center for Puerto Rican Studies Library and Archives, box 6.

79. In his survey of Lower East Side cultures of the 1980s, Mario Maffi lists four plays from Rivas: *The Winos, Coco Baile, El Piraguero de Loisaida,* and *Benito y Vasconpique*. (Vega played the lead in *El Piraguero de Loisaida*.)

80. Yusef A. Salaam, "Winos: Dramatic Tale of Drunks, Drugs, and Dreams," *New York Amsterdam News*, December 5, 1981.

81. Bittman (Bimbo) Rivas, "Winos" (n.d.), The Records of CHARAS, Inc., box 6, Center for Puerto Rican Studies Library and Archives.

82. Rivas, "Winos," 19.

83. Bittman (Bimbo) Rivas, "Benito Y Vas Con Pique" (1987), The Records of CHARAS, Inc., box 6, Center for Puerto Rican Studies Library and Archives.

84. Ibid., 8.

85. Ibid., 15.

86. Ibid., 35, 27.

87. Ibid., 33.

88. Ibid., 39.

89. "You Can Do It: Artist Housing Issue Defeated," *The Quality of Life in the Lower East Side* 6, no. 12 (April 1983): 5. The ever-colorful Rivas testified "The commandment 'Thou Shalt Not Steal' does not apply to muggers only." The Artists Homeownership Program was to convert abandoned (in rem) properties to "cooperative housing for artists of moderate incomes ($40,000–$50,000 per year" (Mele, *Selling the Lower East Side*, 238). The city had targeted a property on East Eighth Street between B and C.

90. See Mele, *Selling the Lower East Side*, 236–432.

91. "I played the lead in Bimbo Rivas' El Pirägüero de Loisaida, 50 performances in the storefront theater on 6th Street between 1st Avenue and Avenue A, and then about 100 more in the Orpheum." Edgardo Vega Yunqué, "City Lit: Yanqui Doodle," City Limits, September 1, 1998, https://citylimits.org/1998/09/01/city-lit-yanqui-doodle/.

92. Vega Yunqué, *The Lamentable Journey of Omaha Bigelow*, 99.

93. Vega Yunqué, *The Lamentable Journey of Omaha Bigelow*, 60, 80.

94. Ibid., 113.

95. Ibid.

96. Algarín, "Nuyorican Literature," 92.

97. Noel, *In Visible Movement*, 48.

98. Mele, *Selling the Lower East Side*, 220.

99. Latour, *An Inquiry into Modes of Existence*, 126–27.

100. John Yau, "All the World's a Stage: The Art of Martin Wong," in *Martin Wong: Human Instamatic*, ed. Antonio Sergio Bessa (London: Black Dog Publishing, 2015), 43.

101. Wong told Yasmin Ramirez, "I decided one night I was gonna find an apartment, and that I would just ask people in the street if they knew of any apartments for rent. Then I came here. I got to this corner and there were some kids down there—I didn't realize they were drug dealers. So I asked them about apartments and they said the top floor's been vacant for a long time." Martin Wong, "Chino-Latino: The Loisaida Interview," interview by Yasmin Ramirez, in *Martin Wong: Human Instamatic*, ed. Antonio Sergio Bessa (London: Black Dog Publishing, 2015), 111.

102. Jacques Rancière, *The Politics of Aesthetics: The Distribution of the Sensible*, trans. Gabriel Rockhill, Bloomsbury Revelations (London: Bloomsbury Academic, 2013), 12.

103. Ibid.

104. Ibid.

105. Joseph P. Fried, "City's Housing Administrator Proposes 'Planned Shrinkage' of Some Slums," *New York Times*, February 3, 1976. This policy would "hasten the population decline" in neighborhoods like the South Bronx by cutting city services, which, in turn, would enable the city to cut even more services to such neighborhoods. This policy was controversial and retracted almost immediately by the Beame administration.

106. Esteves, "For South Bronx," *Yerba Buena*, 84.

107. Roy Pérez, "The Glory That Was Wrong: El 'Chino Malo' Approximates Nuyorico," *Women & Performance: A Journal of Feminist Theory* 25, no. 3 (2015): 277–97.

108. Ibid., 280.

109. Ibid., 285.

110. Dan Cameron, "Outside Looking In: Martin Wong and New York in the 1980s," in *Martin Wong: Human Instamatic*, ed. Antonio Sergio Bessa (London: Black Dog Publishing, 2015), 103.

111. Muñoz, *Cruising Utopia*, 1.

112. Yasmin Ramirez, "La Vida: The Life and Writings of Miguel Piñero in the Art of Martin Wong," in *Sweet Oblivion: The Urban Landscape of Martin Wong*, ed. Amy Scholder, New Museum Books (New York: Rizzoli, 1998), 33.

113. For a brief gloss on this history, see Joe Flood, "Why the Bronx Burned," *New York Post* (blog), May 16, 2010, https://nypost.com/2010/05/16/why-the-bronx-burned/.

114. Ibid., 230.

115. In *Fear City*, Phillips-Fein observes that "for many New Yorkers, the city's willingness to cut back on fire protection was the most shocking aspect of the fiscal crisis." *Fear City*, 228. One homesteader describes this history: "Those were the years of fire on the Lower East Side. I saw building after building burned and abandoned. . . . I had been born in one of those burning buildings. I knew the names of family and people who had lived in those burned-out shells. I had walked through those now-empty spaces to deliver groceries, to visit. I had slept there. Even though they now lay abandoned, I could look at the windows of those ruins and name the people who had inhabited each apartment." Sergio Mendez, "Lower East Side Memories," *The Quality of Life in the Lower East Side* 10, no. 2 (1987): 16, 21.

116. Ault, Julie, "Martin Wong Was Here," in *Martin Wong: Human Instamatic*, ed. Antonio Sergio Bessa (London: Black Dog Publishing, 2015), 83–96.

Chapter 3

1. A note on formatting: Semiotext(e) is both a collective and a journal. I refer to the former without italics and the latter with italics.

2. The conference is extensively documented as part of New York University's Downtown Collection at the Fales Library, and drawing on the Semiotext(e) archive, Lotringer and David Morris recently organized the proceedings into a volume called *Schizo-Culture: The Event*, published by Semiotext(e) in 2013. Jason Demers covers the conference in *The American Politics of French Theory: Derrida, Deleuze, Guattari, and Foucault in Translation* (Toronto: University of Toronto Press, 2019), 149–58. While his conclusions differ from mine in adopting a generally laudatory approach to the conference, Demers does valuable work throughout his book in establishing context for the conference by noting the crosscurrents of interest and influence between the American counterculture and Deleuze and Guattari.

3. Sylvère Lotringer, "Introduction to Schizo-Culture," in *Schizo-Culture: The Event*, ed. Sylvère Lotringer and David Morris (Semiotext(e), 2013), 16.

4. Daniel Zamora and Michael C. Behrent, eds., *Foucault and Neoliberalism* (Malden, MA: Polity Press, 2016), 54. Micropolitics is a complex concept, and I necessarily oversimplify it here. See Karen Houle's contribution to *Gilles Deleuze: Key Concepts*, in which she explains how micropolitics entails a turn away from "classic political ontologies," whereby "the political does not begin with, or come to a full stop at the edge of the human world, but weaves the entire register (social, mental, natural/material) into the political." "Micropolitics," in *Gilles Deleuze: Key Concepts*, ed. Charles J. Stivale, 2nd ed. (Montreal: McGill-Queen's University Press, 2011), 107.

5. For a specific account of how this scrutiny emerged around the fiscal crisis, see Reagan, "Capital City." For a broader account of how the family came under increasing pressure under post-Fordism, see Melinda Cooper, *Family Values: Between Neoliberalism and the New Social Conservatism* (MIT Press, 2017). Cooper observes, for example, that what seems a disproportionate focus on direct benefits—welfare—was actually core to the mode of governance that emerged from the 1970s crisis.

6. Jeffrey J. Williams, "The Little Magazine and the Theory Journal: A Response to Evan Kindley's 'Big Criticism,'" *Critical Inquiry* 39, no. 2 (2013): 404.

7. Jeffrey J. Williams, "The Rise of the Theory Journal," *New Literary History* 40, no. 4 (2009): 697. Williams figures the theory journal as an amalgam of postwar "little magazines" like *Partisan Review* and the *Kenyon Review* and the scholarly journals that had proliferated since the early part of the century. For broader accounts of the Keynesian state and English departments, see Greg Barnhisel, *Cold War Modernists: Art, Literature, and American Cultural Diplomacy, 1946–1959* (New York: Columbia University Press, 2015); Evan Kindley, *Poet-Critics and the Administration of Culture* (Cambridge, MA: Harvard University Press, 2017).

8. Henry Schwarz and Anne Balsamo, "Under the Sign of Semiotext(e): The Story According to Sylvère Lotringer and Chris Kraus," *Critique: Studies in Contemporary Fiction* 37, no. 3 (1996): 209.

9. Ibid.

10. Quoted in Schwarz and Balsamo, "Under the Sign of Semiotext(e)," 209.

11. This messiness is still evident in *Semiotext(e)*'s archive at New York University's Fales Library. One letter from an early editor complains about the first issue's typesetting, which suffered from "a lack of time, people, typists, typewriters, and organization." Moreover, the journal was beset by intrapersonal conflicts: a letter from one participant complains "the last straw for me—so to speak—was to learn that the journal had been secretly confiscated and removed to someone's home so that myself and the other people who worked on it could not have access to it. I find this ridiculous and incomprehensible. Why was the journal confiscated and by what and whose right? This is a prime example of the atmosphere of paranoia under which the group operates."

12. Demers, *The American Politics of French Theory*, 145.

13. Lotringer, "Introduction to Schizo-Culture," 15. Writing of the artist who is "demonstrating for our benefit an eminently psychotic and revolutionary

means of escape," Deleuze and Guattari frame these artists as "speaking from the depths of psychosis." Gilles Deleuze and Félix Guattari, *Anti-Oedipus: Capitalism and Schizophrenia* (Minneapolis: University of Minnesota Press, 1983), 134.

14. Ibid., 16.
15. Phillips-Fein, *Fear City*, 164, 163.
16. Quoted in Phillips-Fein, 164.
17. Phillips-Fein, 96.
18. Thomas J. Sugrue, *The Origins of the Urban Crisis: Race and Inequality in Postwar Detroit—Updated Edition* (Princeton, NJ: Princeton University Press, 2014), 4.
19. Sylvère Lotringer, "Introduction: The French Connection," in Lotringer and Morris, *Schizo-Culture*, 44.
20. Ibid., 45.
21. Loïc J. D. Wacquant, *Punishing the Poor: The Neoliberal Government of Social Insecurity* (Durham, NC: Duke University Press, 2009), 290.
22. Melinda Cooper, *Family Values*, 8. The Fordist wage resulted in "normalization of gender and sexual relationships" and defined "African American men by their exclusion from the male breadwinner wage and African American women by their relegation to agricultural and domestic labor in the service of white households" (8).
23. Lotringer, "Introduction: The French Connection," 46.
24. Ibid., 47.
25. Wacquant, *Punishing the Poor*, 295.
26. Lotringer and Morris, *Schizo-Culture*, 51, 52.
27. Ibid., 194.
28. Freeman, *Working-Class New York*, 259:
29. Stuart Elden, *Foucault's Last Decade* (Malden, MA: Polity Press, 2016), 46.
30. Michel Foucault, "We Are Not Repressed," in Lotringer and Morris, *Schizo-Culture*, 159.
31. Michel Foucault, *The History of Sexuality* (New York: Pantheon Books, 1978), 145.
32. "Schizo-City," description of workshop, reproduced in Lotringer and Morris, *Schizo-Culture*, 98.
33. "Anti-Psychiatry Workshop," reproduced in Lotringer and Morris, *Schizo-Culture*, 101, 100.
34. Ibid., 103.
35. Ibid., 102.
36. Kronsky, "Betty Kronsky to Organizers of the Schizo-Culture Conference."
37. Michel Foucault, "Le Grand Enfermement," in *Dits et Écrits, Vol. I, 1954–1975* (Paris: Gallimard, 2001), 1170–71. Quoted and translated in Zamora and Behrent, *Foucault and Neoliberalism*, 81.
38. Phillips-Fein, *Fear City*, 124–35. First National's Jac Friedgut was an early and forceful advocate for cuts. In memos such as "The City's Budget Mess" and in presentations to the New York Congressional Delegation, Friedgut argued that the

city's municipal wages were too high, welfare had increased sixfold, and the city was offering too many "free or discount services, such as higher education, mass transit and hospitals." Subcommittee on Economic Stabilization of the Committee on Banking, Finance and Urban Affairs, H. of Rep., 95th Cong., 1st S., "Securities and Exchange Commission Staff Report on Transactions in Securities of the City of New York," August 1977, 194, https://www.sec.gov/info/municipal/staffreport0877.pdf. For accounts of Friedgut's memos, see *Fear City*, 84–85; Reagan, "Capital City," 62–79.

39. Phillips-Fein, *Fear City*, 124–25.

40. In *Anti-Oedipus*, for example, the two praise Jack Kerouac as one of the "men who know how to leave, to scramble the codes, to cause flows to circulate, to traverse the desert of the body without organs. They overcome a limit, they shatter a wall, the capitalist barrier." *Anti-Oedipus*, 132–33.

41. Félix Guattari, "Gangs of New York," in *Chaosophy: Text and Interviews 1972–1977*, ed. Sylvère Lotringer, trans. Taylor Adkins (New York: Semiotext(e), 2009), 291.

42. Ibid.

43. Ibid., 292.

44. Ibid.

45. Ibid.

46. Ibid., 293.

47. By 1978, the program was accused of financial malfeasance. Charles Schumer, then a state assemblyman, lead the charge toward shutting the program down. Ronald Sullivan, "Bronx Drug Program Called a 'Ripoff': Political Controversies Reported Auditors Uncover Abuses Strong Action Opposed," *New York Times*, November 28, 1978.

48. Guattari, "Gangs of New York," 293–94.

49. From sign held in photo in Young Lords Party and Abramson, *Palante*, 103.

50. Félix Guattari, "Molecular Revolutions and Q&A," in Lotringer and Morries, *Schizo-Culture*, 187.

51. Silvia Federici and Arlen Austin, eds., "Women and Welfare," in *The New York Wages for Housework Committee 1972–1977: History, Theory and Documents* (New York: Autonomedia, 2017), 102.

52. David Morris traces the conference's disappearance in his afterword to *Schizo-Culture*, noting that "only a handful of academic publications give [the conference] any mention, none published before 2003." Lotringer and Morris, *Schizo-Culture*, 204–5.

53. Joseph North, *Literary Criticism: A Concise Political History* (Cambridge, MA: Harvard University Press, 2017). In addition to North, see François Cusset, *French Theory: How Foucault, Derrida, Deleuze, & Co. Transformed the Intellectual Life of the United States* (Minneapolis: University of Minnesota Press, 2008); Nicholas Birns, *Theory after Theory: An Intellectual History of Literary Theory from 1950 to*

the Early Twenty-First Century (Buffalo, NY: Broadview Press, 2010). More broadly, the shift away from theory-influenced accounts has been called "post critique." For an overview of this idea by one of its strongest articulators, see Felski, *The Limits of Critique*.

54. Zamora and Behrent, *Foucault and Neoliberalism*, 2.

55. Ibid., 30.

56. Andrew Pendakis, ed., *Contemporary Marxist Theory: A Reader* (New York: Bloomsbury Academic, 2014), 3. Particularly after the 2008 crisis, a range of criticism has emerged to fill this lacuna. See, for example, La Berge, *Scandals and Abstraction*. The dissymmetry between the circumstances of the fiscal crisis and the ideas of "Schizo-Culture" has been observed more widely of the theory era. North observes that the period of literary-theory-influenced criticism, while a "progressive turn, and perhaps . . . a turn to the more radical left," occurred at the same time that "neoliberalism established itself as an unquestioned global hegemony, leaving the left in disarray in every sector." North, *Literary Criticism*, 9. Read retrospectively, the divide between "Schizo-Culture" and the 1975 crisis becomes a divide in the academy that maintains at least until 2008. Moishe Postone notes: "The current global crisis, however, has dramatically revealed the fundamental limitations of such newer approaches—including those associated with thinkers as disparate as Habermas, Foucault, and Derrida—as attempts to grasp the contemporary world. It also has exposed the one-sidedness of what had been termed the 'cultural turn' in the humanities and the social sciences." Postone, "The Current Crisis," 37.

57. For an account of these struggles across the twentieth century, see Freeman, *Working-Class New York*. For accounts of the union-based resistance to the cuts of the fiscal crisis, see Phillips-Fein, *Fear City*, 205–67.

58. See Ted Morgan, *Literary Outlaw: The Life and Times of William S. Burroughs* (New York: W. W. Norton & Company, 2012), 581–85.

59. Gary Indiana, *Horse Crazy* (New York: Grove Press, 1989), 68.

60. Robert W. Snyder, *Crossing Broadway: Washington Heights and the Promise of New York City* (Ithaca, NY: Cornell University Press, 2015).

61. Kathy Acker, "Memory Experiments II" (May 1974), 30, Kathy Acker Notebooks 1968–1974, box 3, folder 9, Fales Library and Special Collections, New York University.

62. Susan E. Hawkins, "All in the Family: Kathy Acker's Blood and Guts in High School," *Contemporary Literature* 45, no. 4 (2004): 656.

63. Michael W. Clune, *American Literature and the Free Market, 1945–2000* (Cambridge, UK: Cambridge University Press, 2010), 104.

64. Katie R. Muth, "Postmodern Fiction as Poststructuralist Theory: Kathy Acker's Blood and Guts in High School," *Narrative* 19, no. 1 (2011): 90.

65. Kathryn Hume, "Voice in Kathy Acker's Fiction," *Contemporary Literature* 42, no. 3 (2001): 503; Lee Konstantinou, *Cool Characters: Irony and American Fiction* (Cambridge, MA: Harvard University Press, 2016), 140.

66. Konstantinou, *Cool Characters*, 142.

67. Alex Houen, *Powers of Possibility: Experimental American Writing Since the 1960s* (Oxford, UK: Oxford University Press, 2012), 149.

68. Muth, "Postmodern Fiction as Poststructuralist Theory," 90.

69. Konstantinou, *Cool Characters*, 140.

70. Ibid., 154.

71. Kathy Acker (1974), 21, Kathy Acker Notebooks, ales Library and Special Collections, New York University Libraries.

72. Chris Kraus, *After Kathy Acker: A Literary Biography* (South Pasadena, CA: Semiotext(e), 2017), 58.

73. Looking back on this period from 1989, Acker told Sylvère Lotringer, "I wrote so many pages a day and that was that. I set up guidelines for each piece, such as you'll use autobiographical and fake autobiographical material, or you're not allowed to rewrite. I really didn't want any creativity. It was task work, and that's how I thought of it." Kathy Acker and Sylvère Lotringer, "Devoured by Myths," in *Hannibal Lecter, My Father* (New York: Semiotext(e), 1991), 8.

74. Kraus claims that such was true of writers and artists more generally: "Throughout the 1970s, welfare, unemployment insurance, and disability SSI were the de facto grants that funded most of New York's off-the-grid artistic enterprises." Kraus, *After Kathy Acker*, 123.

75. Acker, *Blood and Guts*, 56.

76. Kraus, *After Kathy Acker*, 117.

77. Kathy Acker to Ron Silliman, 1975, Ron Silliman Papers, Special Collections & Archives, UC San Diego Library. Kraus dates this letter as early June 1975. Kraus, *After Kathy Acker*, 120.

78. Ibid.

79. Kathy Acker, *The Adult Life of Toulouse Lautrec*, in *Portrait of an Eye: Three Novels* (New York: Grove Press, 1998), 211.

80. Acker to Silliman, 1975.

81. Reagan, "Capital City," 62–125. Freeman's *Working-Class New York* offers a similar view: "In the recession and budget crisis, financial leaders saw an opportunity to undo the past, to restructure New York along lines more to their linking than those drawn by decades of liberalism and labor action. They wanted less and less costly government, fiscal probity, and the desocialization of services and protections for the working class and the poor" (258).

82. Edward C. Banfield, *The Unheavenly City: The Nature and Future of our Urban Crisis*, quoted in Reagan, "Capital City: New York in Fiscal Crisis, 1966–1978," 86. Views on the left are collected in Daniel P. Moynihan and American Academy of Arts and Sciences, eds., *On Understanding Poverty: Perspectives from the Social Sciences*, Perspectives on Poverty 1 (New York: Basic Books, 1969). For an overview of attitudes toward the "undeserving poor," of which the "culture of poverty" is a subset, see Katz, *The Undeserving Poor*. For the legacy of the "culture

of poverty" idea, see Susan D. Greenbaum, *Blaming the Poor: The Long Shadow of the Moynihan Report on Cruel Images about Poverty* (New Brunswick, NJ: Rutgers University Press, 2015).

83. Hume, "Voice in Kathy Acker's Fiction," 490. Of course, the threatened subject in Acker is most often female, and many critics have read Acker positioning such desire in resistance to power, as Susan Hawkins summarizes: "Acker's vehicle—blatantly desiring sexuality—affirms the possibility of a feminine subject capable of resisting patriarchal power, however temporarily, through various discursive practices." Hawkins, "All in the Family," 640. For examples of such approaches, see Martina Sciolino, "Kathy Acker and the Postmodern Subject of Feminism," *College English* 52, no. 4 (1990): 437–451; Karen Brennan, "The Geography of Enunciation: Hysterical Pastiche in Kathy Acker's Fiction," *boundary 2* 21, no. 2 (1994): 243–68.

84. Hume, "Voice in Kathy Acker's Fiction," 501.

85. Melinda Cooper, *Family Values*, 21. As Cooper reports, these activists had some success: "By the 1970s, then, the New Deal's major social insurance program, Social Security, had expanded in quantitative terms to include both women and African Americans—Fordism's non-normative subjects—and to keep pace with rising wages" (122). In a review of Cooper, Sarah Brouillette summarizes what Cooper sometimes tries to avoid saying: that Cooper is very much in favor of the welfare state but rejects "the restriction of its benefits to the Fordist white male breadwinner." Sarah Brouillette, "Couple Up: Review of 'Family Values: Between Neoliberalism and the New Social Conservatism,'" *boundary 2*, June 2, 2017, http://www.boundary2.org/2017/06/sarah-brouillette-couple-up-review-of-family-values-between-neoliberalism-and-the-new-social-conservatism/. Brouillette objects to Cooper because Brouillette sees the welfare state as bound not just to such restrictions, but to the ways in which the US welfare state depended on a global regime of resource extraction. While I agree with Brouillette along these lines, I join Cooper and Freeman in seeing some of the underlying *principles* of the welfare state as valuable.

86. Freeman, *Working-Class New York*, 256.

87. For an overview of such struggles, see Phillips-Fein, *Fear City*, 5–7. Phillips-Fein documents such struggles throughout her book.

88. Acker, *Toulouse Lautrec*, 217.

89. Ibid., 223.

90. Ibid., 274.

91. Robert Glück, "Long Note on New Narrative," in *Communal Nude: Collected Essays*, Semiotext(e) Active Agent Series (South Pasadena, CA: Semiotext(e), 2016), 21.

92. Acker, *Toulouse Lautrec*, 275.

93. Robert L. Heilbroner, *The Worldly Philosophers: The Lives, Times, and Ideas of the Great Economic Thinkers*, Revised edition (New York: Simon and Schuster, 1961), 168–70; Acker, *Toulouse Lautrec*, 276–77.

94. Acker, *Toulouse Lautrec*, 285.

95. Alworth, *Site Reading*, 120.

96. Kraus, *After Kathy Acker*, 147. "Neither a serial project nor a 'big novel,'" Kraus observes, "the book was composed from an assortment of fragments and outtakes written and saved since she moved to Solana Beach with Peter Gordon in 1973 and began writing prose" (145). Kraus notes that like Father, Gordon, in 1978, had begun dating another woman shortly after he and Acker married. In a 1986 interview, Acker notes "The most autobiographical part is the first bit about my husband which I made into her father; I just thought I'd change it." Kathy Acker et al., An Informal Interview with Kathy Acker on the 23rd April, 1986, *Over Here* 6:2, April 23, 1986, 10. In the same interview, Acker describes her early work, including *Blood and Guts*, as "simply linked stories," though when writing *Blood and Guts* she "wanted an all-over narrative" so that the novel might sell (4).

97. Acker, *Blood and Guts*, 27.

98. These closed worlds might be violated, as happened when Anne Waldman showed up late one night at Bernadette Meyer's apartment while Acker was living there to yell at Meyer. But for the most part, Acker lived alone with men throughout the 1970s. In the 1980s and 1990s, she mostly lived alone.

99. Kraus, *After Kathy Acker*, 133.

100. Comparing Merida to Mexico in *On the Road*, Amy Nolan describes it as a "vivid, primordial universe—a place of ruin that still contains original mystery and beauty." Amy Nolan, "'A New Myth to Live By': The Graphic Vision of Kathy Acker," *Critique* 53 (2012): 203. The quotations following in this paragraph are from Acker, *Blood and Guts*, 16–17.

101. Moody, *From Welfare State to Real Estate*, 13.

102. Fitch, *The Assassination of New York*, 30.

103. Fredric Jameson, *Postmodernism, or, the Cultural Logic of Late Capitalism* (Durham, NC: Duke University Press, 1999), 50–54.

104. Acker, *Blood and Guts*, 44.

105. Ibid., 56.

106. Ibid., 57.

107. Kraus quotes Urizen books editor Michael Roloff: "What looked like the 'greening of America' in that neck of the woods metamorphosed into the wildest kind of neo-liberalism down in Tribeca and the East Village." Kraus, *After Kathy Acker*, 152.

108. Acker, *Blood and Guts*, 138.

109. Daniel Stedman Jones, *Masters of the Universe: Hayek, Friedman, and the Birth of Neoliberal Politics* (Princeton: Princeton University Press, 2012), 173. In *Family Values*, Melinda Cooper describes this moment as "white middle-class owners turn[ing] their allegiance away from the welfare state." Cooper, *Family Values*, 157.

110. Andrew Stein, "The Biggest Tax State," *New York Times*, July 28, 1978.

111. Acker, *Blood and Guts*, 27.

112. Ibid., 56.

113. It eventually became the vehicle of her grandest success: Kraus opines that "its aggressive charm and dizzying sweeps between high culture and low would turn Acker into a post-punk icon for the Bush/Thatcher years." Kraus, *After Kathy Acker*, 152.

114. Cooper, *Family Values*, 25.

115. Sergio Bologna, "Workerism: An Inside View. From the Mass-Worker to Self-Employed Labour," in *Beyond Marx: Theorising the Global Labour Relations of the Twenty-First Century*, ed. Marcel van der Linden and Karl Heinz Roth (Leiden, Netherlands: Brill, 2014), 133.

116. Brouillette, *Literature and the Creative Economy*, 39. The idea that all post-Fordist labor requires a blurring of self- and job-identity has become both widespread and controversial. In an article citing Virno, Negri, and other Italian philosophers, feminist Angela McRobbie notes that, for example, while flight attendants used to think of "caring" as a "role," they are now encouraged to think of their "care" as an extension of themselves. McRobbie, "Reflections on Feminism, Immaterial Labour and the Post-Fordist Regime," *New Formations*, no. 70 (Summer 2010): 60–76.

117. Brouillette, *Literature and the Creative Economy*, 43.

118. Paolo Virno and Michael Hardt, eds., *Radical Thought in Italy: A Potential Politics* (Minneapolis: University of Minnesota Press, 1996).

119. Sylvére Lotringer and Christian Marazzi, eds., *Autonomia: Post-Political Politics* (New York: Semiotext(e), 1980), 8.

120. Lotringer and Marazzi, *Autonomia*, 70.

121. Cusset, *French Theory*, xi.

122. Ibid., xiv.

123. Sylvère Lotringer and Sande Cohen, eds., *French Theory in America* (New York: Routledge, 2001), 133.

124. Schwarz and Balsamo, "Under the Sign of Semiotext(e)," 204.

125. Kathy Acker, *Bodies of Work: Essays* (New York: Serpent's Tail, 1997), 86.

126. Ibid., 85.

127. Bradway, *Queer Experimental Literature*, 110.

128. Acker, *Bodies of Work*, 85.

Chapter 4

1. Mele, *Selling the Lower East Side*, 238.

2. Zukin, *Loft Living*, xx.

3. Ibid., xiv–xv.

4. Mele, *Selling the Lower East Side*, 238.

5. On gentrification as New York City's official housing policy, see Neil Smith, *Uneven Development: Nature, Capital, and the Production of Space*, 3rd ed. (Athens, GA: University of Georgia Press, 2008), 230.

6. The literature on artists as ideal workers is broad. For keystone examples with very different valences, see Boltanski and Chiapello, *The New Spirit of Capitalism*, especially 38–40 and 84–195; and Richard L. Florida, *The Rise of the Creative Class, Revisited* (New York: Basic Books, 2012). The Italian Autonomists, whom I mention at the end of chapter 3, have provided a rich source of frameworks for the artist as worker. See, for example, Paolo Virno, "The Dismeasure of Art: An Interview with Paolo Virno," in *Being an Artist in Post-Fordist Times*, ed. Pascal Gielen and Paul de Bruyne (New York: Distributed Art Publishers, 2009), 17–44; Paolo Virno, *A Grammar of the Multitude: For an Analysis of Contemporary Forms of Life* (Cambridge, MA: Semiotext(e), 2004); and Maurizio Lazzarato, "Immaterial Labor," in *Radical Thought in Italy: A Potential Politics*, ed. Paolo Virno and Michael Hardt (Minneapolis: University of Minnesota Press, 1996), 142–57. For suggestive accounts of how literature reflects and refracts this notion, see Brouillette, *Literature and the Creative Economy*, and Bernes, *The Work of Art in the Age of Deindustrialization*.

7. Lynne Tillman, "Downtown's Room in Hotel History," in *What Would Lynne Tillman Do?* (New York: Red Lemonade, 2014), 233–37.

8. Boltanski and Chiapello, *The New Spirit of Capitalism*, 164.

9. Boltanski and Chiapello, *The New Spirit of Capitalism*, 190. For an overview of the artistic critique, see 38–40, and for a detailed account of the history I mention here, see 184–95. When members of counterculture turned their attention to the workplace, Boltanski and Chiapello argue, they saw "paternalism, authoritarianism, compulsory work schedules, prescribed tasks, the Taylorist separation between design and execution, and, more generally, the division of labour" (185). Workers influenced by the counterculture came to demand "autonomy and self-management, and the promise of an unbounded liberation of human creativity" (187), all characteristics associated with the artist.

10. See Smith, *The New Urban Frontier*, 19. For overviews of research on artist-led gentrification, including its complications, see Vanessa Mathews, "Aestheticizing Space: Art, Gentrification and the City," *Geography Compass* 4, no. 6 (2010): 660–75; Carl Grodach, Nicole Foster, and James Murdoch, "Gentrification and the Artistic Dividend: The Role of the Arts in Neighborhood Change," *Journal of the American Planning Association* 80, no. 1 (2014): 21–35.

11. Jason Hackworth and Neil Smith, "The Changing State of Gentrification," *Tijdschrift Voor Economische En Sociale Geografie* 92, no. 4 (2001): 464–77.

12. Mathews, "Aestheticizing Space," 672.

13. Jane Jacobs, *The Death and Life of Great American Cities* (New York: Modern Library, 2011), 194.

14. Sharon Zukin, *The Cultures of Cities* (Cambridge, MA: Blackwell, 1995), 119.

15. See Justin O'Connor, "The Cultural and Creative Industries: A Critical History," *EKONOMIAZ. Revista Vasca de Economía* 78, no. 3 (2011): 37; Sharon Zukin, *Naked City: The Death and Life of Authentic Urban Places* (Oxford, UK:

Oxford University Press, 2011); Zukin, *The Cultures of Cities*; Suleiman Osman, "The Decade of the Neighborhood," in *Rightward Bound: Making America Conservative in the 1970s*, ed. Bruce J. Schulman and Julian E. Zelizer (Cambridge, MA: Harvard University Press, 2008), 106–27; Suleiman Osman, *The Invention of Brownstone Brooklyn: Gentrification and the Search for Authenticity in Postwar New York* (Oxford, UK: Oxford University Press, 2011).

16. Marvin J. Taylor, ed., *The Downtown Book: The New York Art Scene, 1974–1984* (Princeton, NJ: Princeton University Press, 2006), 68.

17. Tillman, "Downtown's Room in Hotel History," 236. Articles that praised the scene include Ricard, "The Pledge of Allegiance"; Ricard, "The Radiant Child"; Nicholas A. Moufarrege, "Another Wave, Still More Savagely than the First, Lower East Side 1982," *Arts Magazine* 57, no. 1 (1982): 69–73; Robinson and McCormick, "Slouching Toward Avenue D."

18. "Artists' Space Show," *The East Village Eye*, January 1982, 43.

19. "Introduction," in *Recodings: Art, Spectacle, Cultural Politics* (Port Townsend, WA: Bay Press, 1985), 35. See also Owens, "The Problem with Puerilism"; Craig Owens and Scott Stewart Bryson, *Beyond Recognition: Representation, Power, and Culture* (Berkeley, CA: University of California Press, 1992); Deutsche and Gendel Ryan, "The Fine Art of Gentrification."

20. Bernes, *The Work of Art in the Age of Deindustrialization*, 10.

21. Mathews, "Aestheticizing Space," 665.

22. Alison L. Bain, "Constructing Contemporary Artistic Identities in Toronto Neighbourhoods," *The Canadian Geographer/Le Géographe Canadien* 47, no. 3 (2003), 316.

23. Originating with Henri Lefebvre, this notion has become highly influential among urban theorists. For summaries of this idea, see, for example, David Harvey, *Rebel Cities: From the Right to the City to the Urban Revolution* (London: Verso, 2013); Don Mitchell, *The Right to the City: Social Justice and the Fight for Public Space* (New York: Guilford Press, 2003).

24. A prominent article in *The New York Times Magazine* featuring Basquiat on the cover helped solidify the scene's visibility. See Cathleen McGuigan, "New Art, New Money: The Marketing of An American Artist," *The New York Times Magazine*, February 10, 1985.

25. Gary Indiana, *I Can Give You Anything but Love* (New York, NY: Rizzoli Ex Libris, 2015), 53, 133.

26. Pierre Bourdieu, *The Rules of Art: Genesis and Structure of the Literary Field*, trans. Susan Emanuel (Palo Alto, CA: Stanford University Press, 1996), 56.

27. Sianne Ngai, *Our Aesthetic Categories: Zany, Cute, Interesting* (Cambridge, MA: Harvard University Press, 2012), 233.

28. Ibid., 11.

29. Gary Indiana, "Triumph of the Cute," *The Village Voice*, March 24, 1987.

30. Ngai, *Our Aesthetic Categories*, 239.

31. Gary Indiana, "Banks of America," *The Village Voice*, August 6, 1985.
32. Gary Indiana, "Slice of Life," *The Village Voice*, September 17, 1985.
33. Gary Indiana, "Living with Contradictions," *The Village Voice*, March 3, 1985.
34. Pearlman, *Unpackaging Art of the 1980s*.
35. Gary Indiana, "Art Objects," *The Village Voice*, 29 1985.
36. Indiana, "Imitation and Its Double."
37. Gary Indiana, "Quarterly Dividends," *The Village Voice*, October 8, 1985.
38. Florida, *The Rise of the Creative Class, Revisited*, 7.
39. Indiana, "Art Objects."
40. Gary Indiana, "Apotheosis of the Non-Moment," *The Village Voice*, May 6, 1986.
41. Gary Indiana, "Model Prisons," *The Village Voice*, January 27, 1987.
42. Indiana, "Imitation and Its Double."
43. Gary Indiana, "Framing Creatures," *The Village Voice*, May 7, 1985. Emphasis mine.
44. Gary Indiana, "Just Add Milk," *The Village Voice*, October 1, 1986. Emphasis mine.
45. Gary Indiana, "Cancelled Texts," *The Village Voice*, June 6, 1986.
46. Indiana, *I Can Give You Anything but Love*, 177.
47. Richard Serra, "Richard Serra's Urban Sculpture," interview by Douglas Crimp, in *Writings/Interviews* (Chicago: University of Chicago Press, 1994), 124.
48. Douglas Crimp, "Redefining Site Specificity" in Hal Foster, Gordon Hughes, and B. H. D. Buchloh, eds., *Richard Serra* (Cambridge, MA: MIT Press, 2000), 149.
49. Gary Indiana, "Debby with Monument: A Dissenting Opinion," *The Village Voice*, April 16, 1985.
50. Ibid.
51. Harriet F. Senie, *The Tilted Arc Controversy: Dangerous Precedent?* (Minneapolis: University of Minnesota Press, 2002).
52. Senie, *The Tilted Arc Controversy*.
53. Ibid., 42.
54. Ibid., 94.
55. Katz, *The Undeserving Poor*, 230.
56. Clara Weyergraf-Serra and Martha Buskirk, eds., *The Destruction of Tilted Arc: Documents* (Cambridge, MA: MIT Press, 1991), 92.
57. Ibid., 82.
58. Ibid., 74.
59. Crimp, *Before Pictures*, 12.
60. Ibid., 32.
61. Indiana, "Debby with Monument." Madhu Dubey makes a similar point when she observes, "African-Americans are fetishized as the guarantors of everything

that is felt to be at risk in the postmodern era—bodily presence, palpable reality, political intentionality." *Signs and Cities: Black Literary Postmodernism* (Chicago: University of Chicago Press, 2003), 8.

62. Siegle, *Suburban Ambush*, 165.

63. Freeman, *Working-Class New York*, 293.

64. Rosalyn Deutsche, *Evictions: Art and Spatial Politics* (Chicago: Graham Foundation for Advanced Studies in the Fine Arts; Cambridge, MA: MIT Press, 1998), 291.

65. Pearlman, *Unpackaging Art of the 1980s*, 21.

66. Gregory Sholette, "Nature as an Icon of Urban Resistance: Artists, Gentrification and New York City's Lower East Side, 1979–1984," *Afterimage* 25, no. 2 (1997): 17–20.

67. Ibid., 26.

68. Lynne Tillman, "Lynne Tillman with Jarrett Earnest," The Brooklyn Rail, November 2016, https://brooklynrail.org/2016/11/art/lynne-tillman-with-jarrett-earnest. See also Siegle, *Suburban Ambush*, 163–69.

69. Stephen Westfall, "Surrealist Modes Among Contemporary New York Painters," *Art Journal* 45, no. 4 (1985): 315. Admittedly, Scharf was influenced by graffiti.

70. Ibid., 318.

71. Lynne Tillman, "The Sick and the Well," *Guernica*, July 1, 2011, https://www.guernicamag.com/lynne_tillman_7_1_11/.

72. Jacques Rancière, *The Emancipated Spectator*, trans. Gregory Elliott (Verso Books, 2011), 13.

73. Jacques Rancière, "The Politics of Art: An Interview with Jacques Rancière," *Verso* (blog) accessed June 22, 2018, https://www.versobooks.com/blogs/2320-the-politics-of-art-an-interview-with-jacques-ranciere.

74. Lynne Tillman, M. G. Lord, and Andrew Durbin, *The Complete Madame Realism and Other Stories* (South Pasadena, CA: Semiotext(e), 2016), 19.

75. Tillman et al., *The Complete Madame Realism*, 30.

76. Tillman told Siegle, "If you're teaching writing in a small town, the experience around you is going to be very different from living on East Tenth Street." Quoted in Siegle, *Suburban Ambush*, 157.

77. Weeks, *The Problem with Work*, 103.

78. Tillman et al., *The Complete Madame Realism*, 23.

79. Ibid., 70.

80. Ibid., 42.

81. Ibid., 49.

82. Ibid., 44.

83. Hal Foster, "Between Modernism and the Media," in *Recodings: Art, Spectacle, Cultural Politics* (Port Townsend, WA: Bay Press, 1985), 49.

84. Tillman et al., *The Complete Madam Realism*, 75.

85. Foster, "Between Modernism and the Media," 37.
86. Brouillette, *Literature and the Creative Economy*, 13.
87. Dodie Bellamy and Kevin Killian, *Writers Who Love Too Much: New Narrative Writing 1977–1997* (New York: Nightboat Books, 2017), 495.
88. Halpern, "Realism and Utopia," 89. See also Bellamy and Killian, *Writers Who Love Too Much*, xi–xii.
89. Halpern, "Realism and Utopia," 83.
90. Quoted in Siegle, *Suburban Ambush*, 158.
91. Lorey, *State of Insecurity*, 75.
92. Lazzarato, "Immaterial Labor," 135.
93. Brouillette, *Literature and the Creative Economy*, 85.
94. Brandon Stosuy, "Introduction," in *Up Is Up, But So Is Down: New York's Downtown Literary Scene, 1974–1992*, ed. Brandon Stosuy (New York: New York University Press, 2006), 15.
95. Ron Magliozzi and Sophie Cavoulacos, eds., *Club 57: Film, Performance, and Art in the East Village, 1978–1983* (New York: The Museum of Modern Art, 2017), 11.
96. Alan Moore and Jim Cornwell, "Local History," in *Alternative Art, New York, 1965–1985: A Cultural Politics Book for the Social Text Collective*, ed. Julie Ault, Social Text Collective, and Drawing Center (New York, N.Y.) (Minneapolis: University of Minnesota Press, 2002), 323.
97. Randy Rosen, "Moving into the Mainstream," in Randy Rosen, Catherine Coleman Brawer, and Cincinnati Art Museum, eds., *Making Their Mark: Women Artists Move into the Mainstream, 1970–85* (New York: Abbeville Press, 1989), 21.
98. Siegle writes, "Given secondary and dependent gender roles [these women] find themselves not liberated into utopic freedom but empty, listless, occasionally even nostalgic." Siegle, *Suburban Ambush*, 195.
99. Lynne Tillman, *Haunted Houses* (New York: Poseidon Press, 1987), 154.
100. Reagan, "Capital City," 75.
101. Cooper, *Family Values*, 97.
102. See the introduction to Justin O'Connor and Derek Wynne, eds., *From the Margins to the Centre: Cultural Production and Consumption in the Post-Industrial City* (Aldershot, UK: Arena; Brookfield, VT: Ashgate, 1996).
103. Tillman, *Haunted Houses*, 77.
104. Ibid., 124.
105. Ibid., preceding quotations from 57, 70, and 57, respectively.
106. Siegle, *Suburban Ambush*, 180.
107. Ibid., 2.
108. Boltanski and Chiapello, *The New Spirit of Capitalism*, 109.
109. Diarmuid Hester, "Humor, Gentrification, and the Preservation of Downtown New York in Lynne Tillman's *No Lease on Life*," in *Transgressive Humor*

of American Women Writers, ed. Sabrina Fuchs-Abrams (London: Palgrave Macmillan, 2017), 135–53.

110. Lynne Tillman, *No Lease on Life* (New York: Harcourt Brace, 1998), 10, 11.

111. Ibid., 51.

112. Ibid., 132.

113. Hester, "Humor, Gentrification," 145.

114. Bruce Boone, *Century of Clouds* (Callicoon, NY: Nightboat Books, 2009), 31.

115. Sarah Brouillette, "Couple Up."

116. Tillman, *No Lease on Life*, 121.

117. Gary Indiana, "Just an Opinion," *The Village Voice*, June 25, 1985.

118. Gary Indiana, "It's a Pleasure to Serve You," *The Village Voice*, February 24, 1987.

119. Gary Indiana, "The Physiology of Taste," *The Village Voice*, January 7, 1986; Gary Indiana, "The Wages of Angst," *The Village Voice*, July 15, 1985.

120. Indiana published excerpts from the novel (titled *Burma* at the time) in *Bomb* and other publications starting in 1986.

121. Gary Indiana, *Horse Crazy*, 6. Max Blagg, Betsy Sussler, and Gary Indiana, "Gary Indiana," *BOMB*, no. 28 (1989): 32–33.

122. Indiana, "Apotheosis of the Non-Moment."

123. Gary Indiana, *Horse Crazy* (New York: Grove Press, 1989), 48.

124. Ibid., 59, 218.

125. Ibid., 121.

126. Ibid., 95–96.

127. Ibid., 95, 97.

128. Ibid., 118.

129. Muñoz, *Cruising Utopia*, 176.

130. Ibid.

131. Ahmed, *Willful Subjects*, 136.

132. Ibid., 133.

133. Indiana, *Horse Crazy*, 60.

134. Ibid., 19, 128.

135. Richard Canning, *Hear Us Out: Conversations with Gay Novelists* (New York: Columbia University Press, 2003), 22.

136. Jacques Rancière, *Dissensus: On Politics and Aesthetics* (New York: Bloomsbury Academic, 1975), 120.

137. Gary Indiana, "The Hollow," *The Village Voice*, October 10, 1985.

138. Ibid.

139. Ahmed, *Willful Subjects*, 169–70.

140. Indiana, *Horse Crazy*, 98.

Chapter 5

1. Siegle, *Suburban Ambush*, 273.
2. For a summary of such policies and their influence, see chapter 13 of Phillips-Fein, *Fear City*.
3. Mele, *Selling the Lower East Side*, 250. See also chapter 1 of Smith, *The New Urban Frontier*.
4. Mele, *Selling the Lower East Side*, 250.
5. Lefebvre, *The Production of Space*, 416–17.
6. Smith, *The New Urban Frontier*.
7. Joel Rose, *Kill the Poor* (New York: Atlantic Monthly Press, 1988), 33.
8. McGurl, *The Program Era*, 32. Admittedly, McGurl's paradigm—that, in some sense, the Program is everywhere—can apply, in its widest sense, to *Between C & D*. Of Ronald Sukenik, for example, McGurl writes, "The [underground] is at once a state of mind and an urban space, and while it stands opposed to the campus it, too, is the scene of research, a place where 'researchers in the risky discipline of living in contact with the deepest impulses' (7) can share their feelings," 325.
9. McGurl's third category, "lower-middle-class modernism," refers to the minimalism of Raymond Carver and his acolytes. This category hardly appears at all in *Between C & D*. In the introduction to the Penguin anthology, Rose and Texier indicate why, explicitly positioning their journal as aimed at writers who "didn't feel any affinity for the school of 'dirty realism' or weren't writing 'sensitive' narration teeming with believable characters a reader could care for throughout the length of the novel." Rose and Texier, "Introduction," ix.
10. Mark Leyner to Joel Rose, n.d., Between C & D, box 1, folder 37, Fales Library and Special Collections, New York University.
11. Catherine Liu, *Oriental Girls Desire Romance*, Revised edition (New York: Kaya Press, 2012), 227.
12. Dennis Cooper to Joel Rose and Catherine Texier, n.d., Between C & D, box 1, folder 18, Fales Library and Special Collections, New York University.
13. Catherine Texier to Andrew Strombeck, "Researcher working on Love Me Tender & Between C & D," August 21, 2017. Texier recalls, "Both the magazine and *Love Me Tender* were shaped by our moving into the neighborhood in that very special time. At the same moment all the small art galleries were opening in the neighborhood, and musicians, artists and writers were pouring in because it was really cheap to live here and the cross-pollination of viewpoints and talents was amazing, incredibly stimulating and heady. We gave readings in the neighborhood (ABC No Rio, Madame Rosa, Nuyorican Poet's Café), we went to the art openings, we worked not only with writers, but also with artists who wished to contribute to the magazine."
14. Joel Rose to Andrew Strombeck, "Between C & D," October 6, 2016. Mele, Mario Maffi and others have documented similar cases in the Lower East

Side of the era. These are sometimes characterized as "homesteading." Famously, the Lower East Side was also the site of "squatting," whereby individuals and groups took over buildings and renovated them without contacting city or landlord.

15. Rose had historical ties to the neighborhood. His mother had grown up there, and, in fact, had babysat in that very apartment: Rose reports that she could still "smell the boiled eels" when she visited in the 1980s.

16. Rose to Strombeck, "Between C & D."

17. Mele, *Selling the Lower East Side*, 182.

18. Phillips-Fein, *Fear City*, 3.

19. Mele, *Selling the Lower East Side*, 189, 191.

20. Ibid., 192.

21. Catalina Neculai, *Urban Space and Late Twentieth-Century New York Literature: Reformed Geographies* (New York: Palgrave Macmillan, 2014), 122.

22. This point is implicit throughout *The Program Era*, but perhaps comes through clearest in McGurl's discussion of a bus in Robert Olen Butler's *Mr. Spaceman*, which "carries a group roughly the size of a seminar enrollment" and represents one of the "analogical small groups and *small group meetings* that can help us understand the workshop as a social form" (385).

23. The question of whether housing counts as infrastructure is a lively one. As it has taken shape in literary studies, attention to infrastructure has generally referred to what Michael Rubenstein calls "public works": sewers, electrical grids, roadways, and so on (see Michael Rubenstein, *Public Works: Infrastructure, Irish Modernism, and the Postcolonial* (Notre Dame, IN: University of Notre Dame Press, 2010)). But a range of organizations—particularly those concerned with affordable housing—have argued for the importance of thinking of including housing as infrastructure. The Campaign for Housing and Community Development Funding, for example, has recently made this point in the context of 2017 discussions of a governmental infrastructure initiative. See Campaign for Housing and Community Development Funding, "Affordable Housing Infrastructure," n.d., http://nlihc.org/sites/default/files/Housing_as_Infrastructure_CHCDF.pdf; Will Fischer, "Infrastructure Plans Should Invest in Affordable Housing," Center on Budget and Policy Priorities, January 31, 2018, https://www.cbpp.org/research/housing/infrastructure-plans-should-invest-in-affordable-housing.

24. Kate Marshall, *Corridor: Media Architectures in American Fiction* (Minneapolis: University of Minnesota Press, 2013), 9.

25. Ibid., 24.

26. Quoted in Siegle, *Suburban Ambush*, 274. Describing the same moment, Rose wrote to me that "the streets were talking back." Rose to Strombeck, "Between C & D."

27. Catherine Texier, "The Red High Heels," *Between C & D* 1, no. 1 (1983): 3.

28. Friedrich A. Kittler, *Gramophone, Film, Typewriter* (Stanford, CA: Stanford University Press, 1999).

29. Matthew G. Kirschenbaum, *Track Changes: A Literary History of Word Processing* (Cambridge, Massachusetts: The Belknap Press of Harvard University Press, 2016), 52–53. As Kirschenbaum details, such systems hardly eliminated all the challenges of writing with computers. For one, no fewer than three dozen different word processing programs were on the market in 1983, two years after Rose started using the Epson (53).

30. Rose to Strombeck, "Between C & D." Rose continues "The idea just came to me. I made 25 copies, hand drew each one, brought them to Saint Mark's Bookstore and East Side Books and by the time I got home they were on the phone asking for more." Kirschenbaum calls Rose and Texier "prescient" for realizing the "potential for publishing and distribution." *Track Changes*, 196.

31. Texier to Strombeck, "Love Me Tender & Between C & D."

32. Catherine Liu: "Meanwhile, I kept up with Freud, Nietzsche, and Benjamin, mixing and matching my hits with an expert eye. I shot up speedballs of Kafka, Henry James, and Proust for my doses of fiction." *Oriental Girls Desire Romance*, 186–87.

33. Kirschenbaum, *Track Changes*, 37.

34. Corey Sandler, "Dot Matrix and the Printed Word," *PC Magazine*, November 1982. Kirschenbaum positions such anxieties more widely as a sense that using word processors entailed writers "cutting corners" (37). See *Track Changes*, 36–41.

35. The index of Jussi Parikka's *What is Media Archeology?* (Malden, MA: Polity Press, 2012), an overview of the field, has no entries for printers but plenty for consoles, software, protocols, and so on.

36. See R. E. Jackson, "Microprocessor Control for a High-Speed Serial Printer," *Proceedings of the IEEE* 64, no. 6 (June 1976): 960–65.

37. Rose to Strombeck, "Between C & D."

38. Foster Wallace cold submitted the manuscript to Rose and Texier.

39. This is how Kirschenbaum theorizes the word processor, as "a combination of the indefinite suspension of inscription *and* the allure of real-time editorial intervention—in stark contrast to the typewriter, where writing and editing were necessarily separate operations." Kirschenbaum, *Track Changes*, 47.

40. For overviews of these publications, see Stosuy, *Up Is Up*, 457–62.

41. This is the literary culture that Daniel Kane documents in *All Poets Welcome*. This DIY legacy inspired Rose and Texier, who saw *Between C & D* as "one of a long line of magazines a little bit more alternative and on the edge." Kane, *All Poets Welcome*, 57–64. Rose quotation is from Siegle, *Suburban Ambush*, 313.

42. See Owens, "The Problem with Puerilism"; Deutsche and Gendel Ryan, "The Fine Art of Gentrification." Mele covers the art scene and redevelopment in chapter 7 of *Selling the Lower East Side*.

43. "Cracked Mirror," Special Issue, *Redtape* 1, no. 6 (1986). Both Stosuy and Siegle point to this issue as emblematic of what Stosuy characterizes as a depiction of the "darker side of the era," and what Siegle calls "an experience of the city at

its most apocalyptic" with "images of city life, urban decay, or performances full of violence and amok sexuality." Stosuy, *Up Is Up*, 458; Siegle, *Suburban Ambush*, 328. Perhaps knowingly, Rose begins *Kill the Poor* with a reference to a brand of heroin called Red Tape, though given that that novel has wide concerns with building redevelopment, this may also be a joke about the regulations Rose encountered in redoing, for example, the building's boiler. *Kill the Poor*, 1.

44. Philip Pocock and Gregory Battcock, eds., *The Obvious Illusion: Murals from the Lower East Side* (New York: George Braziller, in association with The Cooper Union for the Advancement of Science and Art, 1980).

45. As chapter 3 notes, while the Lower East Side art scene was diverse in style, it was neo-Expressionism that often came to symbolize the scene's worst impulses.

46. Hollander writes, "there is also a pride of place within this writing, an understanding of the neighborhood's contested history. There is, therefore, no need for writers to caricature their surroundings, no need to sensationalize something that is already quite meaningful, and no need to distort local reality beyond recognition so that it conforms to a 'universal' narrative (such as Slumming Realism)." Kurt Hollander, "Introduction," in *Low Rent: A Decade of Prose and Photographs from the Portable Lower East Side* (New York: Grove Press, 1994), xiv.

47. Patrick McGrath, "The Gazebo," *Redtape* 1, no. 6 (1986): 3.

48. Ibid.

49. Holly Anderson, "Lower East Side Mesostics 81–82," *Redtape* 1, no. 6 (1986): 10.

50. Kathy Acker, "Two Inserts from Don Quixote," *Redtape* 1, no. 6 (1986): 22. In her submitted manuscript, Acker suggested that Carter add a note saying, "The editors do not consider this last to be intended as a slur upon the Arab people, rather, an experiment in pushing the borders of rhetoric i.e. the license to lie." Kathy Acker to Michael Carter, n.d., Redtape Archives, box 1, folder 2, Fales Library and Special Collections, New York University.

51. David Wojnarowicz, "Monologue by David Wojnarowicz," *Redtape* 1, no. 6 (1986): 25.

52. Smith, *The New Urban Frontier*, 8.

53. Ibid., 18.

54. Anthony Bourdain, "FAO," *Between C & D* 2, no. 1 (1985): 10–20. "FAO" refers to the brand of heroin purchased, named after the New York toy store FAO Schwartz.

55. In deploying the term "postmodernism," I understand it as both a historical phenomenon and a set of aesthetic techniques that circulated widely in the 1970s and 1980s. For useful discussions of the end of postmodernism, see the Fall 2007 issue of *Twentieth Century Literature* on "After Postmodernism" edited by Andrew Hoberek.

56. Concluding *The Program Era*, McGurl opines that literary production is like technology or sports where "systematic investments of capital over time have

produced a continual elevation of performance" leading to a "system-wide rise in the excellence of American literature in the postwar period" (409).

57. It's true that *Between C & D* traded, at times, in themes of danger, risk, decay, and other tropes of downtown. The flyer for the 1988 *Between C & D* anthology describes "the spirit of the magazine" as "gritty, urban, sometimes ironic, sometimes gutsy, erotic, violent, deadpan, unsentimental, playing with form but clearly narrative in intention." "New Writing from the Lower East Side," n.d., Between C & D, box 11, folder 14, Fales Library and Special Collections, New York University.

58. Yolande Villemaire, "Rrose Selavy, New York, 1921," *Between C & D* 2, no. 2 (1985): 3–8; Reinaldo Povod, "Things to Do Today," *Between C & D* 2, no. 2 (1985): 9–14; Normandi Ellis, "Rose of Anger," *Between C & D* 2, no. 2 (1985): 15–16; Darius James, "Negrophobia," *Between C & D* 2, no. 2 (1985): 17–21; Catherine Texier, "Scenes of New York Life #3," *Between C & D* 2, no. 2 (1985): 22–27; Gary Indiana, "From Burma," *Between C & D* 2, no. 2 (1985): 28–30; Peter Cherches, "Woodpeckers," *Between C & D* 2, no. 2 (1985): 32–34; Eileen Myles, "Mal Maison," *Between C & D* 2, no. 2 (1985): 44–48; Nina Zivancevic, "Mal Maison," *Between C & D* 2, no. 2 (1985): 49–50.

59. Maffi, *Gateway to the Promised Land*, 43.

60. Rose and Texier, "Introduction," xi.

61. David Wojnarowicz and Marion Scemama, "Collaborative Wall-Size Poster Ready for Hanging," *Between C & D* 1, no. 4 (1985).

62. Dennis Cooper, "Wrong," *Between C & D* 1, no. 4 (1985): 3–8.

63. Tom Ho to Joel Rose, n.d., Between C & D, box 1, folder 37, Fales Library and Special Collections, New York University.

64. David France, "Ed Koch and the AIDS Crisis: His Greatest Failure," The Daily Intelligencer, February 1, 2013, http://nymag.com/daily/intelligencer/2013/02/koch-and-the-aids-crisis-his-greatest-failure.html.

65. Darius James, *Negrophobia* (New York: Carol Pub. Group, 1992).

66. Charles H. Rowell and Brent Hayes Edwards, "An Interview with Brent Hayes Edwards," *Callaloo* 22, no. 4 (1999): 788.

67. Ronald A. T. Judy, "Irony and the Asymptotes of the Hyperbola," *boundary 2* 25, no. 1 (Spring 1998): 173.

68. Quoted in Judy, 169.

69. Esther B. Fein, "A Black Writer's Book Cover Raises Black Hackles.," *New York Times*, June 17, 1992.

70. Judy, "Irony and the Asymptotes of the Hyperbola," 171.

71. Ibid., 168. In an article that extends this point, Roland Murray describes a similar strain of writing as "black literature that neither pines ambivalently for the nationalist past nor positions art as a proxy for a communal wholeness that is nationalism in another guise." "Black Crisis Shuffle: Fiction, Race, and Simulation," *African American Review* 42, no. 2 (2008): 215.

72. In *On Edge: Performance at the End of the Twentieth Century,* Cynthia Carr documents one such performance, in which a "screeching" James read alongside the white poet Erl Kimmich. In what was surely a discomfiting moment, James spoke of the racism he'd encountered in New Orleans, and how this contrasted with a Lower East Side where "we keep our white folks in place." Cynthia Carr, *On Edge: Performance at the End of the Twentieth Century* (Wesleyan University Press, 1993), 114.

73. Catherine Liu, "Preface: Periodizing the '80s," in *Oriental Girls Desire Romance*, Revised edition (New York: Kaya Press, 2012), ix.

74. Ibid. Writing in *Lambda Book Report*, Sarah Schulman called *Oriental Girls Desire Romance* "the beginning of a new genre." Sarah Schulman, "Chairman Mao's Bad Daughter," *Lambda Book Report* 6, no. 5 (1997): 9.

75. Catherine Liu, "Monday in the Park with Brian," *Between C & D* 3, no. 2 (1987): 35–40. "Monday in the Park with Brian" is the first chapter of *Oriental Girls Desire Romance*, but the version that appears in the novel is much more realistic and structured than the version in *Between C & D*. "The Fat Man" appears as chapter 5, also in a more developed and realistic form. See *Oriental Girls Desire Romance* 1–24 and 127–151.

76. Catherine Liu, "Fat Man," *Between C & D* 4, no. 3 (1988): 53–57.

77. Liu, *Oriental Girls Desire Romance*, 300.

78. Ibid., 134.

79. Ibid., 8.

80. "Our love: the manuscript piling near our computers, reading each other's pages every day." Catherine Texier, *Breakup: The End of a Love Story* (New York: Doubleday, 1998), 3.

81. Rose, *Kill the Poor*, 26. This history resurfaces on 76, 97, and 209–10, among other places.

82. Ibid., 24.

83. Ibid.

84. Ibid., 109.

85. In her own reading of *Kill the Poor*, Neculai notes that the novel disrupts what otherwise might seem like a utopian activity of homesteading, as "a populist, more palatable form of gentrification," one seemingly more accommodating to existing populations. *Urban Space*, 132.

86. Rose, *Kill the Poor*, 97.

87. Ibid., 290.

88. Catherine Texier, *Love Me Tender* (New York: Penguin Books, 1987), 6.

89. In *The New Spirit of Capitalism*, Luc Boltanski and Eve Chiapello assert that the project is the fundamental form of social life for middle-class workers under post-Fordism: "The *project* . . . temporarily assembles a very disparate group of people, and presents itself as a *highly activated section of network* for a period of time that is relatively short, but allows for the construction of more enduring links that will be put on hold while remaining available" (104).

90. Texier, *Love Me Tender*, 95.
91. Ibid., 13, 143.
92. Ibid., 87, 139.
93. Ibid., 82.
94. Brouillette covers the relationship between diversity and the creative economy in chapter 5 of *Literature and the Creative Economy*.
95. Texier, *Love Me Tender*, 79, 82.
96. Ibid., 6.
97. Ibid., 149, 150, 152.
98. Ibid., 150.
99. Ahmed, *Willful Subjects*, 47.
100. Stosuy, "Introduction," in *Up Is Up*, 16.
101. Samuel G. Freedman, "The New New Yorkers," *New York Times Magazine*, November 3, 1985.
102. See William Sites, *Remaking New York*, 69–100.
103. Liu, "Monday in the Park with Brian," 37.
104. Cooper, "Wrong"; Patrick McGrath, "Lush Triumphant," *Between C & D* 3, no. 3 (1987): 31–39.
105. Rachel Kushner, *The Flamethrowers: A Novel* (New York: Simon and Schuster, 2014). For a reading of *The Flamethrowers* in terms of Occupy Wall Street, see Konstantinou, *Cool Characters*, 276–80. I take up *The Flamethrowers* in terms of the 1975 fiscal crisis in "The Post-Fordist Motorcycle: Rachel Kushner's *The Flamethrowers* and the 1970s Crisis in Fordist Capitalism," *Contemporary Literature* 56, no. 3 (2015): 450–75.
106. Rachel Kushner, "Insurrection: An Interview with Rachel Kushner," interview by Jesse Barron, *The Paris Review*, April 3, 2013.
107. Saskia Sassen, "The Informal Economy," in *Dual City: Reconstructing New York*, ed. Manuel Castells and John H. Mollenkopf (New York: Russell Sage Foundation, 1992), 86.
108. Ibid., 87–88.
109. Ibid., 15.
110. Texier, *Breakup*, 3.
111. Jasper Bernes, "The Poetry of Feedback," *e-flux*, May 2017, https://www.e-flux.com/journal/82/127862/the-poetry-of-feedback/.
112. Texier, *Love Me Tender*, 182.
113. Boltanski and Chiapello, *The New Spirit of Capitalism*, 75.

Afterword

1. David Wojnarowicz, *Close to the Knives: A Memoir of Disintegration* (New York: Vintage Books, 1991), 166.

2. Ibid., 166.

3. Schulman, *The Gentrification of the Mind*, 71–72.

4. Wojnarowicz, *Close to the Knives*, 70.

5. Ibid., 121, 122.

6. Deborah B. Gould, *Moving Politics: Emotion and ACT UP's Fight against AIDS* (Chicago: University of Chicago Press, 2009), 256, 5.

7. Leslie J. Wood and Kelly Moore, "From ACT UP to the WTO," in *From ACT UP to the WTO: Urban Protest and Community Building in the Era of Globalization*, ed. Benjamin Heim Shepard and Ronald Hayduk (New York: Verso, 2002), 36.

8. Wojnarowicz, *Close to the Knives*, 78–79.

9. In a letter to Marion Scemama, Wojnarowicz describes "people to call and bills to pay and people to write angry letters to and lawyers I worry are fucking me with their lawyer routines and landlords paying off buildings inspectors." 1990, Wojnarowicz Papers, box 3, folder 27, Fales Library and Special Collections, New York University.

10. Schulman, *The Gentrification of the Mind*, 27.

11. Roberts, *Revolutionary Time and the Avant-Garde*; Sholette, *Dark Matter*.

12. Sholette, *Dark Matter*, 7.

13. Wojnarowicz, *Close to the Knives*, 151.

14. Kelley, *Freedom Dreams*, 10, 9.

Works Cited

Abbott, Steve. "Notes on Boundaries/New Narrative." In *Writers Who Love Too Much: New Narrative Writing 1977–1997*, edited by Dodie Bellamy and Kevin Killian, 211–21. New York: Nightboat Books, 2017.
Acker, Kathy. *The Adult Life of Toulouse Lautrec*. In *Portrait of an Eye: Three Novels*, 185–310. New York: Grove Press, 1998.
———. *Blood and Guts in High School*. New York: Grove Press, 1984.
———. *Bodies of Work: Essays*. New York: Serpent's Tail, 1997.
———. 1974. Kathy Acker Notebooks. Fales Library and Special Collections, New York University Libraries.
———. "Letter from Kathy Acker to Ron Silliman," 1975. Ron Silliman Papers. Special Collections & Archives, UC San Diego Library.
———. Letter to Michael Carter, n.d. Redtape Archives, box 1, folder 2. Fales Library and Special Collections, New York University.
———. "Memory Experiments II," May 1974. Kathy Acker Notebooks 1968–1974, box 3, folder 9. Fales Library and Special Collections, New York University.
———. "Two Inserts from Don Quixote." *Redtape* 1, no. 6 (1986): 22.
Acker, Kathy, and Sylvère Lotringer. "Devoured by Myths." In *Hannibal Lecter, My Father*, 1–24. Semiotext(e) Native Agents Series. New York: Semiotext(e), 1991.
Acker, Kathy, R. J. Ellis, Caroline Bird, Dawn Curwen, Ian Mancor, Val Ogden, and Charles Patrick. An Informal Interview with Kathy Acker on the 23rd April, 1986. *Over Here* 6, no. 2 (1986): 1–13.
Ahmed, Sara. *Willful Subjects*. Durham, NC: Duke University Press, 2014.
Algarín, Miguel. "Nuyorican Literature." *MELUS* 8, no. 2 (1981): 89–92.
———. "Volume and Value of the Breath in Poetry." In *Talking Poetics from Naropa Institute: Annals of the Jack Kerouac School of Disembodied Poetics*, edited by Anne Waldman and Marilyn Webb, 325–45. Boulder, Colorado: Shambhala Publications, Inc, 1978.
Algarín, Miguel, and Bob Holman, eds. *Aloud: Voices from the Nuyorican Poets Cafe*. New York: H. Holt, 1994.

Algarín, Miguel, and Miguel Piñero, eds. *Nuyorican Poetry: An Anthology of Puerto Rican Words and Feelings*. New York: Morrow, 1975.

Alworth, David J. *Site Reading: Fiction, Art, Social Form*. Princeton, NJ: Princeton University Press, 2016.

Anderson, Fiona. "Cruising the Queer Ruins of New York's Abandoned Waterfront." *Performance Research* 20, no. 3 (2015): 135–44.

Anderson, Holly. "Lower East Side Mesostics 81–82." *Redtape* 1, no. 6 (1986): 10.

Armijo, Richard. "Artists' Space Show." *The East Village Eye*, January 1982, 43.

Ault, Julie. "Martin Wong Was Here." In *Martin Wong: Human Instamatic*, edited by Antonio Sergio Bessa, 83–96. London: Black Dog Publishing, 2015.

Bain, Alison L. "Constructing Contemporary Artistic Identities in Toronto Neighbourhoods." *The Canadian Geographer/Le Géographe Canadien* 47, no. 3 (2003): 303–17.

Banfield, Edward C. *The Unheavenly City Revisited*. Boston: Little, Brown, 1974.

Barnes, Clive. "Theater: 'Short Eyes,' Prison Drama." *New York Times*, March 14, 1974.

Barnhisel, Greg. *Cold War Modernists: Art, Literature, and American Cultural Diplomacy, 1946–1959*. New York: Columbia University Press, 2015.

Bauman, Zygmunt. *Liquid Modernity*. Cambridge, UK: Polity Press, 2000.

Beal, Sophia. *Brazil under Construction: Literature and Public Works*. New York: Palgrave Macmillan, 2013.

Bellamy, Dodie, and Kevin Killian, eds. *Writers Who Love Too Much: New Narrative Writing 1977–1997*. New York: Nightboat Books, 2017.

Berlant, Lauren Gail. *Cruel Optimism*. Durham, NC: Duke University Press, 2011.

Berman, Marshall. *All That Is Solid Melts into Air: The Experience of Modernity*. New York: Simon and Schuster, 1982.

Bernes, Jasper. "The Poetry of Feedback." *e-flux*, May 2017. https://www.e-flux.com/journal/82/127862/the-poetry-of-feedback/.

———. *The Work of Art in the Age of Deindustrialization*. Stanford, CA: Stanford University Press, 2017.

Best, Stephen, and Sharon Marcus. "Surface Reading: An Introduction." *Representations* 108, no. 1 (2009): 1–21.

Birns, Nicholas. *Theory after Theory: An Intellectual History of Literary Theory from 1950 to the Early Twenty-First Century*. Buffalo, NY: Broadview Press, 2010.

Blagg, Max, Betsy Sussler, and Gary Indiana. "Gary Indiana." *BOMB*, no. 28 (1989): 32–33.

Bologna, Sergio. "Workerism: An Inside View. From the Mass-Worker to Self-Employed Labour." In *Beyond Marx: Theorising the Global Labour Relations of the Twenty-First Century*, edited by Marcel van der Linden and Karl Heinz Roth, 121–43. Leiden, Netherlands: Brill, 2014.

Boltanski, Luc, and Eve Chiapello. *The New Spirit of Capitalism*. New York: Verso, 2007.

Boone, Bruce. *Century of Clouds*. Callicoon, NY: Nightboat Books, 2009.

Bourdain, Anthony. "FAO." *Between C & D* 2, no. 1 (1985): 10–20.
Bourdieu, Pierre. *The Rules of Art: Genesis and Structure of the Literary Field*. Translated by Susan Emanuel. Palo Alto, CA: Stanford University Press, 1996.
Bradway, Tyler. *Queer Experimental Literature: The Affective Politics of Bad Reading*. New York: Palgrave Macmillan, 2017.
Brennan, Karen. "The Geography of Enunciation: Hysterical Pastiche in Kathy Acker's Fiction." *boundary 2* 21, no. 2 (1994): 243–68.
Brouillette, Sarah. "Couple Up: Review of 'Family Values: Between Neoliberalism and the New Social Conservatism.'" *boundary 2*, June 2, 2017. http://www.boundary2.org/2017/06/sarah-brouillette-couple-up-review-of-family-values-between-neoliberalism-and-the-new-social-conservatism/.
———. *Literature and the Creative Economy*. Stanford, CA: Stanford University Press, 2014.
Buchloh, Benjamin H. D. "Detritus and Decrepitude: The Sculpture of Thomas Hirschhorn." *Oxford Art Journal* 24, no. 2 (2001): 41–56.
Cameron, Dan. "Outside Looking In: Martin Wong and New York in the 1980s." In *Martin Wong: Human Instamatic*, edited by Antonio Sergio Bessa, 103–8. London: Black Dog Publishing, 2015.
Campaign for Housing and Community Development Funding. "Affordable Housing Infrastructure," n.d. http://nlihc.org/sites/default/files/Housing_as_Infrastructure_CHCDF.pdf.
Canning, Richard. *Hear Us Out: Conversations with Gay Novelists*. Between Men—Between Women. New York: Columbia University Press, 2003.
Carr, Cynthia. *Fire in the Belly: The Life and Times of David Wojnarowicz*. New York: Bloomsbury, 2012.
———. *On Edge: Performance at the End of the Twentieth Century*. Wesleyan University Press, 1993.
Certeau, Michel de. *The Practice of Everyday Life*. Berkeley, CA: University of California Press, 1988.
Cherches, Peter. "Woodpeckers." *Between C & D* 2, no. 2 (1985): 32–34.
Clines, Francis X. "'Blighted Areas' Use Is Urged by Rohatyn: Rohatyn Urges a City Plan for Industry." *New York Times*, March 16, 1976.
Clune, Michael W. *American Literature and the Free Market, 1945–2000*. Cambridge Studies in American Literature and Culture. Cambridge, UK: Cambridge University Press, 2010.
Cooke, Lynne, and Douglas Crimp, eds. *Mixed Use, Manhattan*. Cambridge, MA: MIT Press, 2010.
Cooper, Dennis. Letter to Joel Rose and Catherine Texier, n.d. Between C & D, box 1, folder 18. Fales Library and Special Collections, New York University.
———. "Wrong." *Between C & D* 1, no. 4 (1985): 3–8.
Cooper, Melinda. *Family Values: Between Neoliberalism and the New Social Conservatism*. Cambridge, MA: MIT Press, 2017.

"Cover." *The Quality of Life in the Lower East Side* 8, no. 1 (February 1985): 1.

"Cracked Mirror." Special Issue. *Redtape* 1, no. 6 (1986).

Crimp, Douglas. "Alvin Baltrop: Pier Photographs, 1975–1986." *Artforum* 46, no. 6 (2008): 262–73.

———. *Before Pictures*. New York: Dancing Foxes Press; Chicago: University of Chicago Press, 2016.

———. "Redefining Site Specificity." In *Richard Serra*, edited by Hal Foster, Gordon Hughes, and B. H. D. Buchloh, 147–74. Cambridge, MA: MIT Press, 2000.

Cusset, François. *French Theory: How Foucault, Derrida, Deleuze, & Co. Transformed the Intellectual Life of the United States*. Minneapolis: University of Minnesota Press, 2008.

Delany, Samuel R. *Times Square Red, Times Square Blue*. Sexual Cultures. New York: New York University Press, 1999.

Deleuze, Gilles, and Félix Guattari. *Anti-Oedipus: Capitalism and Schizophrenia*. Minneapolis: University of Minnesota Press, 1983.

Demers, Jason. *The American Politics of French Theory: Derrida, Deleuze, Guattari, and Foucault in Translation*. Toronto: University of Toronto Press, 2019.

Deutsche, Rosalyn. *Evictions: Art and Spatial Politics*. Graham Foundation/MIT Press Series in Contemporary Architectural Discourse. Chicago: Graham Foundation for Advanced Studies in the Fine Arts; Cambridge, MA: MIT Press, 1998.

———. "The Threshold of Democracy." In *Urban Mythologies: The Bronx Represented since the 1960s*, edited by John Alan Farmer, 94–101. New York: Bronx Museum of the Arts, 1999.

Deutsche, Rosalyn, and Cara Gendel Ryan. "The Fine Art of Gentrification." *October* 31 (1984): 91–111.

Diserens, Corinne, ed. *Gordon Matta-Clark*. New York: Phaidon Press, 2006.

Dubey, Madhu. *Signs and Cities: Black Literary Postmodernism*. Chicago: University of Chicago Press, 2003.

Elden, Stuart. *Foucault's Last Decade*. Malden, MA: Polity Press, 2016.

Ellis, Normandi. "Rose of Anger." *Between C & D* 2, no. 2 (1985): 15–16.

Esteves, Sandra Maria. *Yerba Buena: Dibujos y Poemas*. Greenfield Review Chapbook no. 47. New York: Greenfield Review, 1980.

Federici, Silvia, and Arlen Austin, eds. *The New York Wages for Housework Committee 1972–1977: History, Theory and Documents*. New York: Autonomedia, 2017.

Federici, Silvia, and Arlen Austin, eds. "Women and Welfare." In *The New York Wages for Housework Committee 1972–1977: History, Theory and Documents*, 101–4. New York: Autonomedia, 2017.

Fein, Esther B. "A Black Writer's Book Cover Raises Black Hackles." *New York Times*, June 17, 1992.

Felski, Rita. *The Limits of Critique*. Chicago: University of Chicago Press, 2015.

Fields, Desiree. "Contesting the Financialization of Urban Space: Community Organizations and the Struggle to Preserve Affordable Rental Housing in New York City." *Journal of Urban Affairs* 37, no. 2 (2015): 144–65.

Fischer, Will. "Infrastructure Plans Should Invest in Affordable Housing." Center on Budget and Policy Priorities, January 31, 2018. https://www.cbpp.org/research/housing/infrastructure-plans-should-invest-in-affordable-housing.
Fitch, Robert. *The Assassination of New York*. New York: Verso, 1996.
Flood, Joe. "Why the Bronx Burned." *New York Post*, May 16, 2010. https://nypost.com/2010/05/16/why-the-bronx-burned/.
Flores, Juan. *Divided Borders: Essays on Puerto Rican Identity*. Houston: Arte Público Press, 1993.
Florida, Richard L. *The New Urban Crisis: How Our Cities Are Increasing Inequality, Deepening Segregation, and Failing the Middle Class—and What We Can Do about It*. New York: Basic Books, 2017.
———. *The Rise of the Creative Class, Revisited*. New York: Basic Books, 2012.
"Flyer for Between C & D: New Writing from the Lower East Side," n.d. Between C & D, box 11, folder 14. Fales Library and Special Collections, New York University.
Foster, Hal. "Between Modernism and the Media." In *Recodings: Art, Spectacle, Cultural Politics*, 33–58. Port Townsend, WA: Bay Press, 1985.
———. "Introduction." In *Recodings: Art, Spectacle, Cultural Politics*, 1–10. Port Townsend, WA: Bay Press, 1985.
Foster, Hal, Gordon Hughes, and B. H. D. Buchloh, eds. *Richard Serra*. October Files 1. Cambridge, MA: MIT Press, 2000.
Foucault, Michel. "Le Grand Enfermement." In *Dits et Écrits, Vol. I, 1954–1975*, 1170–71. Paris: Gallimard, 2001.
———. *The History of Sexuality*. New York: Pantheon Books, 1978.
———. "Lives of Infamous Men." In *Essential Works of Foucault, 1954–1988: Power*, edited by Paul Rabinow, 3:161–62. New York: New Press, 1997.
———. "We Are Not Repressed." In *Schizo-Culture: The Event*, edited by Sylvère Lotringer and David Morris, 144–60. New York: Semiotext(e), 2013.
France, David. "Ed Koch and the AIDS Crisis: His Greatest Failure." The Daily Intelligencer, February 1, 2013. http://nymag.com/daily/intelligencer/2013/02/koch-and-the-aids-crisis-his-greatest-failure.html.
Freedman, Samuel G. "The New New Yorkers." *New York Times Magazine*, November 3, 1985.
Freeman, Joshua Benjamin. *Working-Class New York: Life and Labor since World War II*. New York: New Press, 2000. Distributed by W. W. Norton.
Fried, Joseph P. "City's Housing Administrator Proposes 'Planned Shrinkage' of Some Slums." *New York Times*, February 3, 1976.
Garcia, Carlos. "Saving Preservation Stories: Diversity and the Outer Boroughs: The Reminiscences of Carlos 'Chino' Garcia." Interview by Layla Vural. New York Preservation Archive Project, November 3, 2017. http://www.nypap.org/wp-content/uploads/2017/12/Garcia_Chino_20171113.pdf.
Glück, Robert. "Long Note on New Narrative." In *Communal Nude: Collected Essays*, 13–26. Semiotext(e) Active Agent Series. South Pasadena, CA: Semiotext(e), 2016.

Glueck, Grace. "A Gallery Scene That Pioneers In New Territories." *New York Times*, June 26, 1983.
Gould, Deborah B. *Moving Politics: Emotion and ACT UP's Fight against AIDS*. Chicago: University of Chicago Press, 2009.
Graeber, David. *Direct Action: An Ethnography*. Oakland, CA: AK Press, 2009.
Greenbaum, Susan D. *Blaming the Poor: The Long Shadow of the Moynihan Report on Cruel Images about Poverty*. New Brunswick, NJ: Rutgers University Press, 2015.
Grodach, Carl, Nicole Foster, and James Murdoch. "Gentrification and the Artistic Dividend: The Role of the Arts in Neighborhood Change." *Journal of the American Planning Association* 80, no. 1 (2014): 21–35.
Guattari, Félix. "Gangs of New York." In *Chaosophy: Text and Interviews 1972–1977*, edited by Sylvère Lotringer, translated by Taylor Adkins, 291–95. Semiotext(e) Foreign Agents Series. New York: Semiotext(e), 2009.
———. "Molecular Revolutions and Q&A." In *Schizo-Culture: The Event*, edited by Sylvère Lotringer and David Morris, 184–95. New York: Semiotext(e), 2013.
Hackworth, Jason, and Neil Smith. "The Changing State of Gentrification." *Tijdschrift Voor Economische en Sociale Geografie* 92, no. 4 (2001): 464–77.
Halberstam, Judith. *In a Queer Time and Place: Transgender Bodies, Subcultural Lives*. Sexual Cultures. New York: New York University Press, 2005.
Halpern, Rob. "Realism and Utopia: Sex, Writing, and Activism in New Narrative." *Journal of Narrative Theory* 41, no. 1 (2011): 82–124.
Harris, K. P. "Avant-Garde Interrupted: A New Narrative after AIDS." *Contemporary Literature* 52, no. 4 (2011): 630–57.
———. "New Narrative and the Making of Language Poetry." *American Literature* 81, no. 4 (2009): 805–32.
Harvey, David. *A Brief History of Neoliberalism*. New York: Oxford University Press, 2005.
———. *Rebel Cities: From the Right to the City to the Urban Revolution*. London: Verso, 2013.
Hassell, Malve von. "Names of Hate, Names of Love: Contested Space and the Formation of Identity on Manhattan's Lower East Side." *Dialectical Anthropology* 23, no. 4 (1998): 375–413.
———. *Homesteading in New York City, 1978–1993: The Divided Heart of Loisaida*. Westport, CT: Bergin & Garvey, 1996.
Hawkins, Susan E. "All in the Family: Kathy Acker's Blood and Guts in High School." *Contemporary Literature* 45, no. 4 (2004): 637–58.
Heilbroner, Robert L. *The Worldly Philosophers: The Lives, Times, and Ideas of the Great Economic Thinkers*. Revised ed. New York: Simon and Schuster, 1961.
Heise, Thomas. *Urban Underworlds: A Geography of Twentieth-Century American Literature and Culture*. New Brunswick, N.J: Rutgers University Press, 2011.

Hernández, Carmen Dolores, ed. *Puerto Rican Voices in English: Interviews with Writers*. Westport, CT: Praeger, 1997.
Hester, Diarmuid. "Humor, Gentrification, and the Preservation of Downtown New York in Lynne Tillman's *No Lease on Life*." In *Transgressive Humor of American Women Writers*, edited by Sabrina Fuchs-Abrams, 135–53. London: Palgrave Macmillan, 2017.
Ho, Tom. Letter to Joel Rose, n.d. Between C & D, box 1, folder 37. Fales Library and Special Collections, New York University.
Hoberek, Andrew, ed. "After Postmodernism." *Twentieth Century Literature* 53, no. 3 (2007): 233–47.
Hollander, Kurt. *Low Rent: A Decade of Prose and Photographs from the Portable Lower East Side*. New York: Grove Press, 1994.
———. "Introduction." In *Low Rent: A Decade of Prose and Photographs from the Portable Lower East Side*, xi–xvi. New York: Grove Press, 1994.
Houen, Alex. *Powers of Possibility: Experimental American Writing Since the 1960s*. Oxford, UK: Oxford University Press, 2012.
Houle, Karen. "Micropolitics." In *Gilles Deleuze: Key Concepts*, edited by Charles J. Stivale, 2nd ed., 103–15. Montreal: McGill-Queen's University Press, 2011.
Hume, Kathryn. "Voice in Kathy Acker's Fiction." *Contemporary Literature* 42, no. 3 (2001): 485–513.
Indiana, Gary. "Apotheosis of the Non-Moment." *The Village Voice*, May 6, 1986.
———. "Art Objects." *The Village Voice*, May 21, 1985.
———. "Banks of America." *The Village Voice*, August 6, 1985.
———. "Cancelled Texts." *The Village Voice*, June 6, 1986.
———. "Debby with Monument: A Dissenting Opinion." *The Village Voice*, April 16, 1985.
———. "Framing Creatures." *The Village Voice*, May 7, 1985.
———. "From Burma." *Between C & D* 2, no. 2 (Fall 1985): 28–30.
———. "The Hollow." *The Village Voice*, October 10, 1985.
———. *Horse Crazy*. New York: Grove Press, 1989.
———. *I Can Give You Anything but Love*. New York: Rizzoli Ex Libris, 2015.
———. "Imitation and Its Double." *The Village Voice*, February 24, 1987.
———. "It's a Pleasure to Serve You." *The Village Voice*, February 24, 1987.
———. "Just Add Milk." *The Village Voice*, October 1, 1986.
———. "Just an Opinion." *The Village Voice*, June 25, 1985.
———. "Living with Contradictions." *The Village Voice*, March 3, 1985.
———. "Model Prisons." *The Village Voice*, January 27, 1987.
———. "The Physiology of Taste." *The Village Voice*, January 7, 1986.
———. "Quarterly Dividends." *The Village Voice*, October 8, 1985.
———. "Slice of Life." *The Village Voice*, September 17, 1985.
———. "Triumph of the Cute." *The Village Voice*, March 24, 1987.

———. "The Wages of Angst." *The Village Voice*, July 15, 1985.
Institute for Art and Urban Resources, Stephen Alexander, Eugenie Diserio, and P.S. 1 (Gallery), eds. *Rooms, P. S. 1: [Exhibition] June 9–26, 1976*. New York: The Institute, 1977.
Jackson, R. E. "Microprocessor Control for a High-Speed Serial Printer." *Proceedings of the IEEE* 64, no. 6 (June 1976): 960–65.
Jacobs, Jane. *The Death and Life of Great American Cities*. New York: Modern Library, 2011.
James, Darius. "Negrophobia." *Between C & D* 2, no. 2 (1985): 17–21.
———. *Negrophobia*. New York: Carol Pub. Group, 1992.
Jameson, Fredric. *Postmodernism, or, the Cultural Logic of Late Capitalism*. Post-Secondary Interventions. Durham, NC: Duke University Press, 1999.
Jones, Daniel Stedman. *Masters of the Universe: Hayek, Friedman, and the Birth of Neoliberal Politics*. Princeton, NJ: Princeton University Press, 2012.
Judy, Ronald A. T. "Irony and the Asymptotes of the Hyperbola." *boundary 2* 25, no. 1 (1998): 161–90.
Kane, Daniel. *All Poets Welcome: The Lower East Side Poetry Scene in the 1960s*. Berkeley, CA: University of California Press, 2003.
———. *"Do You Have a Band?": Poetry and Punk Rock in New York City*. New York: Columbia University Press, 2017.
Katz, Michael B. *The Undeserving Poor: America's Enduring Confrontation with Poverty*. 2nd ed. Oxford, UK: Oxford University Press, 2013.
Kelley, Robin D. G. *Freedom Dreams: The Black Radical Imagination*. Boston: Beacon Press, 2003.
Kindley, Evan. *Poet-Critics and the Administration of Culture*. Cambridge, MA: Harvard University Press, 2017.
Kirschenbaum, Matthew G. *Track Changes: A Literary History of Word Processing*. Cambridge, MA: The Belknap Press of Harvard University Press, 2016.
Kirwin, Elizabeth Seton. "It's All True: Imagining New York's East Village Art Scene of the 1980s." PhD diss., University of Maryland, 1999.
Kittler, Friedrich A. *Gramophone, Film, Typewriter*. Stanford, CA: Stanford University Press, 1999.
Konstantinou, Lee. *Cool Characters: Irony and American Fiction*. Cambridge, MA: Harvard University Press, 2016.
Kosuth, Joseph. "No Exit." *Artforum* 26, no. 7 (1988): 112–15.
Kramer, Jane. "Whose Art Is It?" *The New Yorker*, December 21, 1992, 80–109.
Kraus, Chris. *After Kathy Acker: A Literary Biography*. Semiotext(e) Active Agents Series. South Pasadena, CA: Semiotext(e), 2017.
Krauss, Rosalind. "Notes on the Index: Seventies Art in America. Part 2." *October* 4 (1977): 58–67.
Kronsky, Betty. "Betty Kronsky to Organizers of the Schizo-Culture Conference," November 18, 1975. Lotringer and Semiotext(e) Archive, series 2A, box 9, folder 32. Fales Library and Special Collections, New York University.

Kushner, Rachel. *The Flamethrowers: A Novel.* New York: Simon and Schuster, 2014.

———. "Insurrection: An Interview with Rachel Kushner." Interview by Jesse Barron. *The Paris Review*, April 3, 2013.

La Berge, Leigh Claire. *Scandals and Abstraction: Financial Fiction of the Long 1980s.* Oxford, UK: Oxford University Press, 2015.

———. *Wages Against Artwork: Decommodified Labor and the Claims of Socially Engaged Art.* Durham, NC: Duke University Press, 2019.

Latour, Bruno. *An Inquiry into Modes of Existence: An Anthropology of the Moderns.* Cambridge, MA: Harvard University Press, 2013.

———. *Reassembling the Social: An Introduction to Actor-Network-Theory.* Clarendon Lectures in Management Studies. Oxford, UK: Oxford University Press, 2005.

Lazzarato, Maurizio. "Immaterial Labor." In *Radical Thought in Italy: A Potential Politics*, edited by Paolo Virno and Michael Hardt, 142–57. Theory out of Bounds, v. 7. Minneapolis: University of Minnesota Press, 1996.

Lefebvre, Henri. *The Production of Space.* Translated by Donald Nicholson-Smith. Oxford, UK: Blackwell, 1991.

Levine, Caroline. *Forms: Whole, Rhythm, Hierarchy, Network.* Princeton, NJ: Princeton University Press, 2015.

Leyner, Mark. Letter to Joel Rose, n.d. Between C & D, box 1, folder 37. Fales Library and Special Collections, New York University.

Lipietz, Alain. *Towards a New Economic Order: Postfordism, Ecology, and Democracy, Europe and the International Order.* New York: Oxford University Press, 1992.

Lippard, Lucy. "Passenger on the Shadows." In *David Wojnarowicz: Brush Fires in the Social Landscape*, edited by Lucy Lippard, 2nd ed., 6–25. New York: Aperture, 2015.

Liu, Catherine. "Fat Man." *Between C & D* 4, no. 3 (1988): 53–57.

———. "Monday in the Park with Brian." *Between C & D* 3, no. 2 (1987): 35–40.

———. *Oriental Girls Desire Romance.* Revised ed. New York: Kaya Press, 2012.

———. "Preface: Periodizing the '80s." In *Oriental Girls Desire Romance*, Revised ed., ix–xii. New York: Kaya Press, 2012.

Lorey, Isabell. *State of Insecurity: Government of the Precarious.* Futures. London: Verso, 2015.

Lotringer, Sylvère. "Introduction: The French Connection." In *Schizo-Culture: The Event*, edited by Sylvère Lotringer and David Morris, 43–49. New York: Semiotext(e), 2013.

———. "Introduction to Schizo-Culture." In *Schizo-Culture: The Event*, edited by Sylvère Lotringer and David Morris. New York: Semiotext(e), 2013.

Lotringer, Sylvère, and Christian Marazzi, eds. *Autonomia: Post-Political Politics.* Semiotext(e) v. 3, no. 3. New York: Semiotext(e), 1980.

Lotringer, Sylvère, and David Morris, eds. "Anti-Psychiatry Workshop." In *Schizo-Culture: The Event*, 100–106. New York: Semiotext(e), 2013.

———. *Schizo-Culture: The Event.* New York: Semiotext(e), 2013.

Lotringer, Sylvère, and Sande Cohen, eds. *French Theory in America*. New York: Routledge, 2001.

Lukács, György. *Realism in Our Time: Literature and the Class Struggle*. New York: Harper & Row, 1964.

Maffi, Mario. *Gateway to the Promised Land: Ethnic Cultures on New York's Lower East Side*. New York: New York University Press, 1995.

Magliozzi, Ron, and Sophie Cavoulacos, eds. *Club 57: Film, Performance, and Art in the East Village, 1978–1983*. New York: The Museum of Modern Art, 2017.

Manges, Dayle. "Nuyorican Poetry (Book Review)." *LJ: Library Journal* 101, no. 6 (1976): 819.

Marshall, Kate. *Corridor: Media Architectures in American Fiction*. Minneapolis: University of Minnesota Press, 2013.

Martinez, Miranda J. *Power at the Roots: Gentrification, Community Gardens, and the Puerto Ricans of the Lower East Side*. Lanham, MD: Lexington Books, 2010.

Mathews, Vanessa. "Aestheticizing Space: Art, Gentrification and the City." *Geography Compass* 4, no. 6 (2010): 660–75.

McClanahan, Annie. *Dead Pledges: Debt, Crisis, and Twenty-First-Century Culture*. Post 45. Stanford, CA: Stanford University Press, 2017.

McGrath, Patrick. "Lush Triumphant." *Between C & D* 3, no. 3 (1987): 31–39.

———. "The Gazebo." *Redtape* 1, no. 6 (1986): 3.

McGuigan, Cathleen. "New Art, New Money: The Marketing of An American Artist." *New York Times Magazine*, February 10, 1985.

McGurl, Mark. *The Program Era: Postwar Fiction and the Rise of Creative Writing*. Cambridge, MA: Harvard University Press, 2009.

McRobbie, Angela. "Reflections on Feminism, Immaterial Labour and the Post-Fordist Regime." *New Formations*, no. 70 (Summer 2010): 60–76.

Mele, Christopher. *Selling the Lower East Side: Culture, Real Estate, and Resistance in New York City*. Globalization and Community, vol. 5. Minneapolis: University of Minnesota Press, 2000.

Mendez, Sergio. "Lower East Side Memories." *The Quality of Life in the Lower East Side* 10, no. 2 (1987): 16, 21.

Merrifield, Andy. *Henri Lefebvre: A Critical Introduction*. New York: Routledge, 2006.

Mitchell, Don. *The Right to the City: Social Justice and the Fight for Public Space*. New York: Guilford Press, 2003.

Moody, Kim. *From Welfare State to Real Estate: Regime Change in New York City, 1974 to the Present*. New York: New Press, 2007. Distributed by W. W. Norton & Co.

Moore, Alan, and Jim Cornwell. "Local History." In *Alternative Art, New York, 1965–1985: A Cultural Politics Book for the Social Text Collective*, edited by Julie Ault, Social Text Collective, and Drawing Center (New York, N.Y.), 321–65. Minneapolis: University of Minnesota Press, 2002.

Moore, Alan, and Marc H. Miller, eds. *ABC No Rio Dinero: The Story of a Lower East Side Art Gallery*. New York: ABC No Rio, 1985.
Morgan, Ted. *Literary Outlaw: The Life and Times of William S. Burroughs*. New York: W. W. Norton & Company, 2012.
Moufarrege, Nicholas A. "Another Wave, Still More Savagely than the First, Lower East Side 1982." *Arts Magazine* 57, no. 1 (1982): 69–73.
Moynihan, Daniel P., and American Academy of Arts and Sciences, eds. *On Understanding Poverty: Perspectives from the Social Sciences*. Perspectives on Poverty 1. New York: Basic Books, 1969.
Muñoz, José Esteban. *Cruising Utopia: The Then and There of Queer Futurity*. Sexual Cultures. New York: New York University Press, 2009.
Murray, Rolland. "Black Crisis Shuffle: Fiction, Race, and Simulation." *African American Review* 42, no. 2 (2008): 215–33.
Muth, Katie R. "Postmodern Fiction as Poststructuralist Theory: Kathy Acker's Blood and Guts in High School." *Narrative* 19, no. 1 (2011): 86–110.
Myles, Eileen. "Mal Maison." *Between C & D* 2, no. 2 (1985): 44–48.
Neculai, Catalina. *Urban Space and Late Twentieth-Century New York Literature: Reformed Geographies*. American Literature Readings in the 21st Century. New York: Palgrave Macmillan, 2014.
Ngai, Sianne. *Our Aesthetic Categories: Zany, Cute, Interesting*. Cambridge, MA: Harvard University Press, 2012.
Noel, Urayoán. *In Visible Movement: Nuyorican Poetry from the Sixties to Slam*. Contemporary North American Poetry Series. Iowa City: University of Iowa Press, 2014.
Nolan, Amy. "'A New Myth to Live By': The Graphic Vision of Kathy Acker." *Critique* 53 (2012): 201–13.
North, Joseph. *Literary Criticism: A Concise Political History*. Cambridge, MA: Harvard University Press, 2017.
O'Connor, Justin. "The Cultural and Creative Industries: A Critical History." *EKONOMIAZ. Revista Vasca de Economía* 78, no. 3 (2011): 24–47.
O'Connor, Justin, and Derek Wynne, eds. *From the Margins to the Centre: Cultural Production and Consumption in the Post-Industrial City*. Popular Cultural Studies 10. Aldershot, UK: Arena; Brookfield, VT: Ashgate, 1996.
Ortega, Eliana. "Sandra María Esteves' Poetic Work: Demythicizing Puerto Rican Poetry in the U.S." In *The Commuter Nation: Perspectives on Puerto Rican Migration*, edited by Carlos Antonio Torre and William Burgos, 329–42. Río Piedras, PR: Editorial de la Universidad de Puerto Rico, 1994.
Osman, Suleiman. "The Decade of the Neighborhood." In *Rightward Bound: Making America Conservative in the 1970s*, edited by Bruce J. Schulman and Julian E. Zelizer, 106–27. Cambridge, MA: Harvard University Press, 2008.
———. *The Invention of Brownstone Brooklyn: Gentrification and the Search for Authenticity in Postwar New York*. Oxford, UK: Oxford University Press, 2011.

Owens, Craig. "The Problem with Puerilism." *Art in America* 72, no. 6 (1984): 162–63.
Owens, Craig, and Scott Stewart Bryson. *Beyond Recognition: Representation, Power, and Culture.* Berkeley, CA: University of California Press, 1992.
Parikka, Jussi. *What Is Media Archaeology?* Malden, MA: Polity Press, 2012.
Pearlman, Alison. *Unpackaging Art of the 1980s.* Chicago: University of Chicago Press, 2003.
Pendakis, Andrew, ed. *Contemporary Marxist Theory: A Reader.* New York: Bloomsbury Academic, 2014.
Pérez, Roy. "The Glory That Was Wrong: El 'Chino Malo' Approximates Nuyorico." *Women & Performance: A Journal of Feminist Theory* 25, no. 3 (2015): 277–97.
Phillips-Fein, Kim. *Fear City: New York's Fiscal Crisis and the Rise of Austerity Politics.* New York: Metropolitan Books, 2017.
Piñero, Miguel. *Outlaw: The Collected Works of Miguel Piñero.* Houston: Arte Publico Press, 2010.
Pocock, Philip, and Gregory Battcock, eds. *The Obvious Illusion: Murals from the Lower East Side.* New York: George Braziller, in association with The Cooper Union for the Advancement of Science and Art, 1980.
Postone, Moishe. "The Current Crisis and the Anachronism of Value: A Marxian Reading." *Continental Thought & Theory* 1, no. 4 (2017): 38–54.
———. *Time, Labor, and Social Domination: A Reinterpretation of Marx's Critical Theory.* New York: Cambridge University Press, 1993.
Povod, Reinaldo. "Things to Do Today." *Between C & D* 2, no. 2 (1985): 9–14.
"P.S. 64/El Bohio (Former)." Place Matters. Accessed March 31, 2020. https://placematters.net/census/detail.php?id=499.
Ramirez, Yasmin. "La Vida: The Life and Writings of Miguel Piñero in the Art of Martin Wong." In *Sweet Oblivion: The Urban Landscape of Martin Wong*, edited by Amy Scholder, 33–44. New Museum Books. New York: Rizzoli, 1998.
Rancière, Jacques. *Dissensus: On Politics and Aesthetics.* New York: Bloomsbury Academic, 1975.
———. *The Emancipated Spectator.* Translated by Gregory Elliott. Verso Books, 2011.
———. *The Politics of Aesthetics: The Distribution of the Sensible.* Translated by Gabriel Rockhill. London: Bloomsbury Academic, 2013.
———. "The Politics of Art: An Interview with Jacques Rancière." *Verso* (blog), November 9, 2015. https://www.versobooks.com/blogs/2320-the-politics-of-art-an-interview-with-jacques-ranciere.
Reagan, Michael. "Capital City: New York in Fiscal Crisis, 1966–1978." PhD diss., University of Washington, 2017.
Reed, Anthony. *Freedom Time: The Poetics and Politics of Black Experimental Writing.* Callaloo African Diaspora Series. Baltimore: Johns Hopkins University Press, 2014.

Ricard, Rene. "The Pledge of Allegiance." *Artforum* 21, no. 3 (1982): 42–49.
———. "The Radiant Child." *Artforum* 20, no. 4 (1981): 35–43.
Rivas, Bittman (Bimbo). "Benito Y Vas Con Pique." 1987. The Records of CHARAS, Inc., box 6. Center for Puerto Rican Studies Library and Archives, Hunter College, CUNY.
———. "Winos." n.d. The Records of CHARAS, Inc., box 6. Center for Puerto Rican Studies Library and Archives, Hunter College, CUNY.
Robbins, Bruce. *Upward Mobility and the Common Good: Toward a Literary History of the Welfare State*. Princeton, NJ: Princeton University Press, 2007.
Roberts, John. *Revolutionary Time and the Avant-Garde*. New York: Verso, 2015.
Robinson, Walter, and Carlo McCormick. "Slouching Toward Avenue D." *Art in America* 72, no. 6 (1984): 134–61.
Rohatyn, Felix G. "Indeed, 'the Moral Equivalent of War.'" *New York Times*, August 21, 1977.
Ronda, Margaret. "The Social Forms of Speculative Poetics." *Post45*, April 26, 2019. http://post45.research.yale.edu/2019/04/the-social-forms-of-speculative-poetics/.
Rose, Joel. *Kill the Poor*. New York: Atlantic Monthly Press, 1988.
———. Letter to Andrew Strombeck. "Between C & D." October 6, 2016.
Rose, Joel, and Catherine Texier. "Introduction." In *Between C & D: New Writing from the Lower East Side Fiction Magazine*, edited by Joel Rose and Catherine Texier, ix–xi. New York, N.Y: Penguin Books, 1988.
Rosen, Randy. "Moving into the Mainstream." In *Making Their Mark: Women Artists Move into the Mainstream, 1970–85*, edited by Randy Rosen, Catherine Coleman Brawer, and Cincinnati Art Museum, 7–26. New York: Abbeville Press, 1989.
Rosen, Randy, Catherine Coleman Brawer, and Cincinnati Art Museum, eds. *Making Their Mark: Women Artists Move into the Mainstream, 1970–85*. New York: Abbeville Press, 1989.
Rotella, Carlo. *October Cities: The Redevelopment of Urban Literature*. Berkeley, CA: University of California Press, 1998.
Rowell, Charles H., and Brent Hayes Edwards. "An Interview with Brent Hayes Edwards." *Callaloo* 22, no. 4 (1999): 784–97.
Rubenstein, Michael. *Public Works: Infrastructure, Irish Modernism, and the Postcolonial*. Notre Dame, IN: University of Notre Dame Press, 2010.
Russell, John. "Gallery View: An Unwanted School in Queens Becomes an Ideal Art Center." *New York Times*, June 20, 1976.
Sagalyn, Lynne B. *Times Square Roulette: Remaking the City Icon*. Cambridge, MA: MIT Press, 2001.
Salaam, Yusef A. "Winos: Dramatic Tale of Drunks, Drugs, and Dreams." *New York Amsterdam News*, December 5, 1981.
Sandler, Corey. "Dot Matrix and the Printed Word." *PC Magazine*, November 1982.

Saralegui, Tee. "How Would You Handle a Rent Strike?" 1978. The Records of CHARAS, Inc. Center for Puerto Rican Studies Library and Archives, box 6. Hunter College, CUNY.

Sassen, Saskia. "The Informal Economy." In *Dual City: Reconstructing New York*, edited by Manuel Castells and John H. Mollenkopf, 79–102. New York: Russell Sage Foundation, 1992.

Schulman, Sarah. "Chairman Mao's Bad Daughter." *Lambda Book Report* 6, no. 5 (1997): 9.

———. *The Gentrification of the Mind: Witness to a Lost Imagination*. Berkeley, CA: University of California Press, 2012.

Schwarz, Henry, and Anne Balsamo. "Under the Sign of Semiotext(e): The Story According to Sylvere Lotringer and Chris Kraus." *Critique: Studies in Contemporary Fiction* 37, no. 3 (1996): 205–20.

Sciolino, Martina. "Kathy Acker and the Postmodern Subject of Feminism." *College English* 52, no. 4 (1990): 437–45.

Senie, Harriet F. *The Tilted Arc Controversy: Dangerous Precedent?* Minneapolis: University of Minnesota Press, 2002.

Serra, Richard. "Richard Serra's Urban Sculpture." Interview by Douglas Crimp. In *Writings/Interviews*, 125–40. Chicago: University of Chicago Press, 1994.

Ševčenko, Liz. "Making Loisaida: Placing Puertorriqueñidad in Lower Manhattan." In *Mambo Montage: The Latinization of New York City*, 293–318. New York: Columbia University Press, 2001.

Sholette, Gregory. *Dark Matter: Art and Politics in the Age of Enterprise Culture*. London: Pluto Press, 2010.

———. "Nature as an Icon of Urban Resistance: Artists, Gentrification and New York City's Lower East Side, 1979–1984." *Afterimage* 25, no. 2 (1997): 17–20.

Siegle, Robert. *Suburban Ambush: Downtown Writing and the Fiction of Insurgency*. Parallax: Re-Visions of Culture and Society. Baltimore: Johns Hopkins University Press, 1989.

Sites, William. *Remaking New York: Primitive Globalization and the Politics of Urban Community*. Globalization and Community, vol. 12. Minneapolis: University of Minnesota, 2003.

Smith, Neil. *The New Urban Frontier: Gentrification and the Revanchist City*. New York: Routledge, 1996.

———. *Uneven Development: Nature, Capital, and the Production of Space*, 3rd ed. Athens, GA: University of Georgia Press, 2008.

Snyder, Robert W. *Crossing Broadway: Washington Heights and the Promise of New York City*. Ithaca, NY: Cornell University Press, 2015.

"Stage: 'Conga Mania': Play in Nuyorican Fete Is Set in Pocket Park." *New York Times*, February 19, 1975.

Starecheski, Amy. *Ours to Lose: When Squatters Became Homeowners in New York City*. Chicago: University of Chicago Press, 2016.

"Start Your Own Agency." *The Quality of Life in the Lower East Side* 8, no. 1 (February 1985): 11.

Stein, Andrew. "The Biggest Tax State." *New York Times*, July 28, 1978.

Stosuy, Brandon, ed. *Up Is Up, But So Is Down: New York's Downtown Literary Scene, 1974–1992*. New York: New York University Press, 2006.

———. "Introduction." In *Up Is Up, But So Is Down: New York's Downtown Literary Scene, 1974–1992*, edited by Brandon Stosuy, 15–30. New York: New York University Press, 2006.

Strombeck, Andrew. "The Post-Fordist Motorcycle: Rachel Kushner's *The Flamethrowers* and the 1970s Crisis in Fordist Capitalism." *Contemporary Literature* 56, no. 3 (2015): 450–75.

Subcommittee on Economic Stabilization of the Committee on Banking, Finance and Urban Affairs, H. of Rep., 95th Cong., 1st S. "Securities and Exchange Commission Staff Report on Transactions in Securities of the City of New York." August 1977. https://www.sec.gov/info/municipal/staffreport0877.pdf.

Sugrue, Thomas J. *The Origins of the Urban Crisis: Race and Inequality in Postwar Detroit—Updated Edition*. Princeton, NJ: Princeton University Press, 2014.

Sullivan, Ronald. "Bronx Drug Program Called a 'Ripoff': Political Controversies Reported Auditors Uncover Abuses Strong Action Opposed." *New York Times*, November 28, 1978.

Tabb, William K. *The Long Default: New York City and the Urban Fiscal Crisis*. New York: Monthly Review Press, 1982.

Taylor, Marvin J., ed. *The Downtown Book: The New York Art Scene, 1974–1984*. Princeton, NJ: Princeton University Press, 2006.

Texier, Catherine. *Breakup: The End of a Love Story*. New York: Doubleday, 1998.

———. Letter to Andrew Strombeck. "Love Me Tender & Between C & D." August 21, 2017.

———. *Love Me Tender*. New York: Penguin Books, 1987.

———. "Scenes of New York Life #3." *Between C & D* 2, no. 2 (1985): 22–27.

———. "The Red High Heels." *Between C & D* 1, no. 1 (1983): 3–5.

Thomas, Lorrin. *Puerto Rican Citizen: History and Political Identity in Twentieth-Century New York City*. Chicago: University of Chicago Press, 2010.

Tillman, Lynne. "Downtown's Room in Hotel History." In *What Would Lynne Tillman Do?*, 233–37. New York: Red Lemonade, 2014.

———. *Haunted Houses*. New York: Poseidon Press, 1987.

———. "Lynne Tillman with Jarrett Earnest." Interview by Jarrett Earnest. The Brooklyn Rail, November 2016. https://brooklynrail.org/2016/11/art/lynne-tillman-with-jarrett-earnest.

———. *No Lease on Life*. New York: Harcourt Brace, 1998.

———. "The Sick and the Well." Interview by Elizabeth Koch. *Guernica*, July 1, 2011. https://www.guernicamag.com/lynne_tillman_7_1_11/.

Tillman, Lynne, M. G. Lord, and Andrew Durbin. *The Complete Madame Realism and Other Stories*. Semiotext(e) Native Agents Series. South Pasadena, CA: Semiotext(e), 2016.

Tuck, Eve, and K. Wayne Yang. "Decolonization Is Not a Metaphor." *Decolonization: Indigeneity, Education & Society* 1, no. 1 (2012): 1–40.

Tucker-Abramson, Myka. "Make Literary Criticism Great Again (Review of David Alworth's Site Reading: Fiction, Art, Social Form)." *boundary 2*, September 26, 2018. https://www.boundary2.org/2018/09/myka-tucker-abramson-make-literary-criticism-great-again-review-of-david-alworths-site-reading-fiction-art-social-form/.

Vega Yunqué, Edgardo. "City Lit: Yanqui Doodle." *City Limits,* September 1, 1998. https://citylimits.org/1998/09/01/city-lit-yanqui-doodle/.

———. *The Lamentable Journey of Omaha Bigelow into the Impenetrable Loisaida Jungle*. Woodstock, NY: Overlook Press, 2004.

Villemaire, Yolande. "Rrose Selavy, New York, 1921." *Between C & D* 2, no. 2 (1985): 3–8.

Virno, Paolo. "The Dismeasure of Art: An Interview with Paolo Virno." In *Being an Artist in Post-Fordist Times*, edited by Pascal Gielen and Paul de Bruyne, 17–44. New York: Distributed Art Publishers, 2009.

———. *A Grammar of the Multitude: For an Analysis of Contemporary Forms of Life*. Semiotext(e) Foreign Agents Series. Cambridge, MA: Semiotext(e), 2004.

Virno, Paolo, and Michael Hardt, eds. *Radical Thought in Italy: A Potential Politics*. Theory out of Bounds, v. 7. Minneapolis, MN: University of Minnesota Press, 1996.

Wacquant, Loïc J. D. *Punishing the Poor: The Neoliberal Government of Social Insecurity*. English language ed. Politics, History, and Culture. Durham, NC: Duke University Press, 2009.

———. *Urban Outcasts: A Comparative Sociology of Advanced Marginality*. Cambridge, MA: Polity, 2008.

Wagner, Anne M. "Splitting and Doubling: Gordon Matta-Clark and the Body of Sculpture." *Grey Room* 14 (Winter 2004): 26–45.

Wark, McKenzie. *The Beach Beneath the Street: The Everyday Life and Glorious Times of the Situationist International*. New York: Verso, 2011.

Warner, Michael, and Lauren Berlant. "Sex in Public." In *Publics and Counterpublics*, 187–208. New York: Zone Books, 2002.

Washington, Father Jack. "Do-It-Yourself-Banking." *The Quality of Life in the Lower East Side* 8, no. 1 (February 1985): 7.

Watson, Jini Kim. *The New Asian City: Three-Dimensional Fictions of Space and Urban Form*. Minneapolis: University of Minnesota Press, 2011.

Weeks, Kathi. *The Problem with Work: Feminism, Marxism, Antiwork Politics, and Postwork Imaginaries*. Durham, NC: Duke University Press, 2011.

Westfall, Stephen. "Surrealist Modes Among Contemporary New York Painters." *Art Journal* 45, no. 4 (1985): 315–18.
Weyergraf-Serra, Clara, and Martha Buskirk, eds. *The Destruction of Tilted Arc: Documents*. Cambridge, MA: MIT Press, 1991.
Williams, Jeffrey J. "The Little Magazine and the Theory Journal: A Response to Evan Kindley's 'Big Criticism.'" *Critical Inquiry* 39, no. 2 (2013): 402–11.
———. "The Rise of the Theory Journal." *New Literary History* 40, no. 4 (2009): 683–702.
Williams, Raymond. *The Country and the City*. Oxford, UK: Oxford University Press, 1975.
Wilson, William J. *The Truly Disadvantaged: The Inner City, the Underclass, and Public Policy*. 2nd ed. Chicago: University of Chicago Press, 2012.
Wojnarowicz, David. *Close to the Knives: A Memoir of Disintegration*. New York: Vintage Books, 1991.
———. *In the Shadow of the American Dream: The Diaries of David Wojnarowicz*. Edited by Amy Scholder. New York: Grove Press, 1999.
———. Letter to Marion Scemama. 1990. Wojnarowicz Papers, box 3, folder 27. Fales Library and Special Collections, New York University.
———. *Memories that Smell like Gasoline*. San Francisco: Artspace Books, 1992.
———. "Monologue by David Wojnarowicz." *Redtape* 1, no. 6 (1986): 25.
———. *The Waterfront Journals*. Edited by Amy Scholder. New York: Grove Press, 1996.
Wojnarowicz, David, and Marion Scemama. "Collaborative Wall-Size Poster Ready for Hanging." *Between C & D* 1, no. 4 (1985).
Wong, Martin. "Chino-Latino: The Loisaida Interview." Interview by Yasmin Ramirez. In *Martin Wong: Human Instamatic*, edited by Antonio Sergio Bessa, 109–24. London: Black Dog Publishing, 2015.
Wood, Leslie J., and Kelly Moore. "From ACT UP to the WTO." In *From ACT UP to the WTO: Urban Protest and Community Building in the Era of Globalization*, edited by Benjamin Heim Shepard and Ronald Hayduk, 21–34. New York: Verso, 2002.
Yau, John. "All the World's a Stage: The Art of Martin Wong." In *Martin Wong: Human Instamatic*, edited by Antonio Sergio Bessa, 37–62. London: Black Dog Publishing, 2015.
"You Can Do It: Artist Housing Issue Defeated." *The Quality of Life in the Lower East Side* 6, no. 12 (April 1983): 5.
Young Lords Party and Michael Abramson, eds. *Palante: Young Lords Party*. New York: McGraw-Hill, 1971.
Zamora, Daniel, and Michael C. Behrent, eds. *Foucault and Neoliberalism*. Malden, MA: Polity Press, 2016.
Zivancevic, Nina. "Mal Maison." *Between C & D* 2, no. 2 (1985): 49–50.

Zukin, Sharon. *The Cultures of Cities*. Cambridge, MA: Blackwell, 1995.
———. *Loft Living: Culture and Capital in Urban Change*. 25th anniversary ed. New Brunswick, NJ: Rutgers University Press, 2014.
———. *Naked City: The Death and Life of Authentic Urban Places*. Oxford, UK: Oxford University Press, 2011.

Index

ABC No Rio, 7
Acker, Kathy: 2, 4, 18, 114–15; and apartments, 102, 104, 105, 107–108, 110–11; and appropriation, 99, 100, 105, 111, 115; and appropriation of Marxist critics, 105; and Autonomia, 115; and Fordism, 111–12; and literary form, 10; and Post-Fordism, 114–15; and poverty, 102, 104, 108–109; and scale, 107–109; and the welfare state, 110; and the underclass, 98–99; *Blood and Guts in High School*, 4, 24, 107–12; in *Between C & D*, 160; in *Redtape*, 162; journals, 101; living circumstances, 8, 99, 103; *The Adult Life of Toulouse Lautrec*, 99, 102–106; writing method, 100–101
ACT UP, 7, 180–83, 185
activist organizations: ACT UP, 180–83, 185; Adopt-a-Building, 70; Charas, 15, 70–71; Dynamite Brothers, 2, 63; Green Guerillas, 67; Real Good Society, 61; The Young Lords, 61, 94–95; and housing, 55–56, 62–64
Actor Network Theory (Bruno Latour), 47, 52, 77–78
Adopt-a-Building, 70
African-American literature, 166

Ahearn, John, 45
Ahmed, Sara, 50, 53, 147, 149
AIDS: 7, 20, 146, 147, 148, 149, 150, 165, 179–83; and art, 149–50; and David Wojnarowicz, 179–83; and hospitals 147, 149, 165; and Gary Indiana 147, 149–50
Algarín, Miguel: 2, 3, 57–64, 65, 66, 73, 75, 77, 80, 82, 83, 102; and rebuilding Lower East Side, 62–64; and representations of Lower East Side, 69–70; as responding to "outlaw" stereotype Puerto Ricans, 65–66; and space/spatiality, 59
Alphabet City. *See* Lower East Side
Alworth, David, 23, 106–107
Anderson, Fiona, 34
anti-taxation movements, 31, 110–11
apartments: and artists, 78; and *Between C & D*, 151–53, 154–57; and Catherine Texier, 151–53, 154–57; community gardens providing respite from, 68; and David Wojnarowicz, 183–84; diversity in, 152; and Edgardo Vega Yunqué, 76–77; and Gary Indiana, 146; and Joel Rose, 151–53, 154–57; and Kathy Acker, 102, 104, 105, 107–108, 110–11; and literary production, 10, 23, 61, 154–57;

245

apartments *(continued)*
    literary representations of, 77, 98, 107–108, 110–11, 134, 142, 146, 183–84; and Lynne Tillman, 141–42; and Nuyorican Poets Cafe, 61; and writers, 3–4, 46, 100, 102, 104, 105, 110, 111, 123, 129, 152; rundown, 64
appropriation: and artists, 144; and writers, 99, 100, 111
architecture: and literary form, 155–57; and literary production, 155–57
art: and AIDS, 149–50; and death, 149–50; and finance, 124–25, 132; and gentrification, 7, 8, 19–20, 30, 39, 42, 56, 129–31, 135–36, 140–42, 146, 148, 150; and identity, 81, 119; and Lower East Side, 18–20; and the spectator, 129–30, 132–35; and the underclass, 121, 134–35; found, 173; Neo-Expressionist, 125; of institutional critique, 125–26; second economy of, 18, 52; Simulationist, 131; site-specific, 36–37, 52; Surrealist, 132
art collectives: Colab, 7, 180, 187; Group Material, 7, 10, 131, 180, 187; Political Art Documentation/Distribution (PAD/D), 131, 187
art criticism: and Gary Indiana, 122–29; literary representations of, 147–48
art exhibitions: *Art of the Evicted* (PAD/D), 131; *Out of Place* (PAD/D), 131; *People's Choice* (Group Material), 131; *Real Estate Show* (Colab), 7, 131; at Chase Manhattan Bank, 124; *Rooms*, 3, 36; *Zero or Not*, 126
Art in America, 130, 131, 134, 160, 161
Artforum, 160

artists: 3; and activism, 7; and gentrification, 19–20; and poverty, 18; and the 1975 fiscal crisis, 30–31, 35; and writers, 19–20; as ideal workers, 19; female, literary representations of, 140–41; literary representations of, 140, 144–46, 144–48, 170; networks of, 36
Artists' Homeownership Plan, 19, 75, 117, 118, 152
Asian-American literature, 167
austerity: 1–2, 5, 8, 11, 70, 97, 99, 151; and critical theory, 86; and CUNY, 91; and Puerto Ricans, 62; and schools, 37; protests against, 96; resistance to, 93
authenticity: 176; and literature, 137, 153, 163; and real estate, 49; desire for, 49; lack of, 118
Autonomia (issue of *Semiotext(e)*), 112–14
Autonomia (social movement), 115; and gentrification, 113–14; and precarity, 114

Baltrop, Alvin, 40
bankers: and 1975 fiscal crisis, 15, 93, 103, 139; and art exhibits, 124; and female-headed households, 139; and poverty, 103, 124
Basquiat, Jean-Michel, 18, 42
Baudrillard, Jean, 19, 85, 97, 98, 115
Bauman, Zygmunt, 4, 10
benefits. *See* welfare state
Benzene (journal), 122, 160
Berlant, Lauren, 6, 34, 48
Berman, Marshall, 27–28
Bernes, Jasper, 7, 19
Between C & D: 151–67; and aesthetics of downtown New York, 160–67; and apartments, 154–57; and art, 173; and buildings, 154–57;

as documenting neighborhood, 164; and dot-matrix printer, 157–60; and drugs, 163; and gentrification, 161; history of, 154–56; outsider sensibility, 154; print runs of, 159; process, as represented in *Kill the Poor*, 168; process, as represented in *Love Me Tender*, 169; taglines, 158; and windows, 157, 163; and Ziploc bags, 158, 163

Between C & D: New Writing from the Lower East Side Fiction Magazine (collection), 10

Beuys, Joseph, 131

Boltanski, Luc and Chiapello, Eve: 30, 43, 138, 176; and "artistic critique," 118

Bomb (journal), 122

Boone, Bruce, 143

Bradway, Tyler, 12, 114, 115

Brouillette, Sarah, 19, 112, 136, 143

buildings of the Lower East Side: 12–14; as abandoned, 14, 70, 155; and *Between C & D*, 154–57; as decayed, 3, 13, 14, 15, 29, 110; burning of, 169

built environment: and identity, 64, 67, 75; and literary production, 10, 23, 61, 154–57

Burroughs, William, 97

Carr, Cynthia, 32, 43, 46, 47, 49, 51

Carter, Michael, 161

Chunn, Nancy, 126

city landscape: and literature, 12–13

Colab, 7, 131, 180, 187; The Real Estate Show, 7

Columbia University, 85, 86

community buildings: El Bohío 72–73; literary representations of, 67–69, 75

community gardens, 67–69

Cooper, Dennis: 154; in *Between C & D*, 165

Cooper, Melinda, 33, 89, 104, 139

Cover (journal), 160

creative class: 125, 167, 171; as "productive," 70

creative economy, 19–20, 40, 109, 147, 150

Crimp, Douglas, 40, 127

Crisis, Fordist, 53

CUNY: 1, 166; and literary representations of universities, 74; and micropolitical theory of universities, 91; and resistance to tuition hikes, 112

de Certeau, Michel, 14, 24

Delany, Samuel, 18, 34–35

Deleuze, Gilles, 2, 85, 87, 88, 94, 115

Deutsche, Rosalind, 18, 39, 130

do-it-yourself: 5–7; and activism, 70–72; and *Between C & D*, 174; and Charas, 71; and housing rehabilitation, 63–64; and literary form, 9–10; and literature, 9; as political intervention, 7; and Semiotext(e) (collective), 87; as utopian desire, 8–9; issue of *The Quality of Life in Loisaida*, 70–72; utopian possibilities of, 188

dot-matrix printer: 157–60; aesthetics of, 163; and literary form, 161; and literary production, 157–60; and media studies, 157–60; memory buffer, 158–59; and typewriter, 158–59

East Village. *See* Lower East Side

East Village Eye, The (journal), 118, 120

El Bohío, 70, 73

Emergency Financial Control Board, 2, 7, 55–56, 31–32, 63–64, 88, 119, 181

Esteves, Sandra Maria: 60, 65, 66–67, 82; "a pile of wood," 67; "i look for peace great graveyard," 66

Federal Plaza, 127–29
Federici, Sylvia, 96
feminism: and space, 48
fires: literary representations of, 169; and Martin Wong, 83
fiscal crisis, 1966, 103
fiscal crisis, 1975: 1, 15, 31–32, 55, 57, 88, 105, 150, 151; and literary imagination, 24
fiscal crisis, 2008: 1; and Marxist theory, 21
fiscal policy: after 1975 crisis, 1–2
Flores, Juan, 64
Florida, Richard, 5, 125
Ford, Gerald, 31, 88
Fordism, 8, 19, 30, 33, 64, 89, 99, 104, 110, 118, 140; and Lynne Tillman, 140; and family, 140
Foster, Hal, 121, 123, 125, 126, 132, 135
Foucault, Michel: 2, 85, 87, 88, 91, 115; and criminality, 91; *The History of Sexuality Volume 1*, 91; "Lives of Infamous Men," 50; and neoliberalism, 96–97; and repression, 91; and theory of micropower, 91

galleries of Lower East Side: 5, 6, 7, 15, 17, 18, 19, 47, 52, 119, 124, 125, 126, 131, 132, 133, 134: overview of, 18–20; and Lynne Tillman, 129–30; literary depictions of, 129–30
Gans, Herbert, 49
Garcia, T. C., 65
gentrification: 4, 7–9, 12, 16, 19–20, 22, 30, 39, 40, 42, 56, 59, 71, 75–77, 113–14, 115, 119–22, 129–31, 134–36, 140, 141–42, 146, 148, 150, 152, 169, 171, 180, 185; and *Between C & D*, 161; and David Wojnarowicz, 183–84; literary representations of, 169, 171, 180; and literature, 183–84; resistance to, 75; and Sarah Schulman, 185
graffiti: 81, 168; and art, 17, 80, 121, 125; and underclass, 17
Greenspan, Alan, 88
Group Material (artist collective), 7, 10, 131, 180, 187
Grove Books, 111
Guattari, Félix: 2, 85, 87, 88, 90–91, 115; "Gangs of New York" essay, 93–96; and micropolitical theory of universities, 91; and rejection of class-based struggle, 98

Halberstam, Jack, 33–34
Halpern, Rob, 11
Halt Catch Fire (AMC series), 158
Haring, Keith, 18, 42, 72, 78, 132, 147
Harlem, 93: as "schizo-city," 91–92
Harris, Kaplan, 11
Heilbroner, Robert, 105
Heise, Thomas, 13, 62
Heiss, Alanna, 3
Helmsley, Leona, 173
High Line (New York park), 53
Hirschhorn, Thomas, 53
Hollander, Kurt, 162
Holzer, Jenny, 111, 114
homelessness, 16, 20, 46, 126, 127, 128, 129, 134, 142, 170
homesteading: 63–64; and identity, 64; and Nuyorican poetry, 63
hospitals: 86; and AIDS, 147, 149, 165; and Gary Indiana, 147, 149; and Kathy Acker, 98; Lincoln Hospital, occupation of, 94–95

Houen, Alex, 12, 99
housing: and activism, 55–56, 62–64, 70–72; and homelessness, 128; and Lynne Tillman, 140
housing activists, 118
housing projects, 38, 53, 76
housing rehabilitation: 71, 155; literary representations of, 67, 167–68
Hujar, Peter, 180, 181, 182, 183, 184

identity: and art, 81, 119; and the built environment, 64, 67, 75; and homesteading, 64; and institutions, 60; and literature, 5, 12, 60, 61, 66, 83, 119, 137, 163, 167; and social movements, 81, 114, 153; Nuyorican, 64
impoverished. *See* underclass
Indiana, Gary: 14, 18, 98; and AIDS, 147, 149–50; and art of institutional critique, 125–26; in *Between C & D*, 160, 164, 172; and death, 149–50, 149–50; and disgust, 124; and the cute, 124; art criticism, 122–29; *Horse Crazy*, 18, 144–49; *I Can Give You Anything but Love*, 111, 123; literary representations of art criticism in, 147–48; living circumstances, 123; *Village Voice* columns, 122–29, 144
industrial economy. *See* Fordism
institutions: and identity, 60; literary, 83

Jacobs, Jane, 34, 37, 44, 48, 49, 120
James, Darius: 160, 163, 165–66; in *Between C & D*, 164; *Negrophobia*, 165–66
jobs: loss of, 1, 40, 64, 88, 95; management of, as theorized by Loïc Wacquant, 89; and "Schizo-Culture" conference, 92

journals: *Art in America*, 130, 131, 134, 160, 161; *Artforum*, 160; *Benzene*, 122; *Between C & D*, 154–56, 157–60, 160–67; *Bomb*, 122; *The East Village Eye*, 118, 120; of literary theory, 86; *New Literary History*, 86; *New York Native*, 165; *October*, 124, 128, 129, 161; *The Quality of Life in Loisaida*, 6, 56, 71–72; *Redtape*, 161–63; *Semiotext(e)*, 86, 87, 112–14; *The Floating Bear*, 161; *The Village Voice*, 14, 98, 122–29, 144, 145, 170

Katz, Michael, 127
Kelley, Robin D. G., 59, 187
Kirschenbaum, Matthew, 157
Kittler, Friedrich, 157
Koch, Edward, 19, 117, 130
Konstantinou, Lee, 99–100
Koons, Jeff, 18, 131, 132
Kosuth, Joseph, 3, 36, 126
Kraus, Chris, 98, 107, 111; *After Kathy Acker*, 101
Krauss, Rosalind, 52, 128
Kruger, Barbara, 158
Kushner, Rachel, 174

labor market, 89, 130, 173; and the Young Lords, 95
landlords, 83
abandoning buildings, 55
Latour, Bruno, 22–24, 46, 47, 56, 77–78
Lefebvre, Henri, 8, 14, 22, 24, 30, 40, 53, 56, 60, 67, 69, 152, 168
Levine, Sherri, 114
Leyner, Mark, 153
Lincoln Detox clinic, 94
literary canon: and Lower East Side writers, 10
literary experimentation, 11, 10–12; and New Narrative, 11, 136–37

literary form: 4, 9, 100–101; and
David Wojnarowicz, 46, 48; and
do-it-yourself, 9–10; and dot-matrix
printer, 159–60; and Gary Indiana,
120; and Kathy Acker, 101–102;
and Lynne Tillman, 120; and New
Narrative, 11, 119, 136–37, 140,
141, 144
literary institutions: El Bohío, 72–73;
Nuyorican Poets Cafe, 57–59, 61,
183
literary production: and apartments,
61; and architecture, 155–57; and
space/spatiality, 23
literary theory: 85–97; and Marxism,
21; as benefiting from welfare state,
86; in U.S. academy, 96–97. *See also*
poststructuralism
literature: and apartments, 154–57;
and buildings, 154–57; and canon,
10; and fiscal crisis, 2, 3–4; and
gentrification, 152, 169, 171, 180;
and identity, 5, 12, 61, 66, 83, 119,
137, 163, 167; and imagination, 24;
as produced in apartments, 151–53;
as recording post-crisis conditions, 2,
4–5, 9–10
Liu, Catherine: 154, 166–67; *Oriental
Girls Desire Romance*, 154
Loisaida (as name for Lower East
Side), 5, 17, 56, 60, 61, 62, 63, 65,
71, 72, 73, 74, 75, 76, 78, 155,
162
Lorey, Isabell, 6, 137
Lotringer, Sylvère, 2, 85, 87–88, 89,
90, 97, 114
Lower East Side: community gardens
of, 67–69; as frontier, 49, 62,
65–66, 81, 141, 152, 161, 162–63,
164; geography of, 5; literary
representations of, 107–109;
oppositional cultures of, 24, 27,
55–57, 59, 60, 63–64, 68, 70–72,
185; aesthetic representations of,
135; as utopian space, 118
Lukács, György, 12, 106
Lyotard, Jean-François, 85

Maffi, Marlo, 13, 71, 164
manufacturing, decline of, 30
mapping: and David Wojnarowicz,
51; and Kathy Acker, 107–109; and
literature, 23
Marazzi, Christian, 113
Marshall, Kate, 156
Marxism: 21; and Autonomia, 114–15;
and Kathy Acker, 105
Matta-Clark, Gordon: 30, 35–40;
Day's End, 3, 53; *Fake Estates*, 38;
and New York piers, 40; in *Rooms*
exhibition, 37; and real estate
development, 39–40; and scale,
37–40; and space/spatiality, 37–38;
Window Blow Out, 38–39
McCormick, Carlo, 120, 130
McGrath, Patrick, 145, 162, 174
McGurl, Mark: 12; and Cold War
university, 10; and space, 156; and
"high cultural pluralism," 153;
Program Era in American literature,
3, 153, 163, 173, 176; and
"technomodernism," 153
media studies; and dot-matrix printer,
157–60
Mele, Christopher, 13, 42, 60, 155,
168
Meléndez, Jesús Papoleto, 69
micropolitics, theory of (associated
with Gilles Deleuze, Michel
Foucault, and Félix Guattari):
85–86, 90, 91–92, 100; and 1975
fiscal crisis, 87–88; and criminality,
91; and hospitals, 94–95; and
residents of Harlem, 93; and

schools, 89; and The Young Lords, 94–95; and universities, 90–91
Moses, Robert, 34
Municipal Assistance Corporation, 1–2, 7, 31–32, 55–56, 63–64, 88, 111, 119, 181
Muñoz, José, 33, 48, 82, 147
Myles, Eileen: in *Between C & D*, 164

Neculai, Catalina, 153, 155, 156
Negri, Antonio, 112, 113
Neo-Expressionism, 125
networks: and art galleries, 19; of artists, 20, 36, 40; and *Between C & D*, 151, 154, 176; between white bohemians and Puerto Ricans, 171; breakdown of, 6, 29; building of, 183; and capital, 62; and discipline, 90; and disconnection, 170; and Fordist crisis, 53; of Fordist era, 4, 29; and homesteading, 63–64; as immobilizing, 146; and job-hunting, 35; literary representations of, 186; of Lower East Side, 23, 78, 106, 151, 167, 172, 183; and Martin Wong, 78; micropolitical theory of, 90; of New York City, 65; and Nuyorican literature, 55–57; and post-crisis conditions, 3, 186; and Post-Fordism, 119, 150, 176; and Puerto Rican literature, 17, 82–83; and Puerto Ricans, 172; of real estate development, 155; of Times Square porn theaters, 35; theory of, 22; and welfare state, 180; and work, 170
New Literary History (journal), 86
New Narrative (literary movement): 11, 105, 119, 136–37, 140, 141, 143; and Post-Fordism, 136–37
New York City: as "capital of French philosophy," 88; government, 39; and austerity, 1–2; post-crisis, 100, 174; as site for aesthetic experimentation, 19
Ngai, Sianne, 123
North, Joseph, 96
Nuyorican: as identity, 64; origins of term, 60
Nuyorican poetry: and "outlaw" trope in Puerto Rican literature, 65–66; and rebuilding, 66–67; and space/spatiality, 55–57, 60
Nuyorican Poetry (anthology), 61–62, 61–70
Nuyorican Poets Cafe: 57–59, 183; founding of, 61

October (journal), 124, 128, 129, 161
Owens, Craig, 19, 121, 123, 125, 126, 130, 131, 132, 135

P.S. 64. *See* El Bohío
Pérez, Roy, 81
Phillips-Fein, Kim, 24, 155
piers, New York, 34, 39–40, 43
Pietri, Pedro, 60
Piñero, Miguel: 57, 59, 60, 61, 66, 75, 77, 78, 80, 82, 101, 159, 169, 172, 176; in *Between C & D*, 160; as character in *Kill the Poor* (Joel Rose), 169; as depicted by Martin Wong, 57; "The Book of Genesis According to Saint Miguelito," 69; "A Poem for Joey's Mami's Struggle," 64–65; Short Eyes (play), 61, "Twice a Month Is Mother's Day," 64
police: and Real Estate Show, 7; literary representations of, 44, 46, 75; theorized as surveillance system, 90, 94
Political Art Documentation/Distribution (PAD/D), 131

Post-Fordism: 7, 9, 19, 20, 30, 82, 100, 112, 118, 119, 122, 123, 125, 136, 137, 142, 148, 150, 174–76, 177; and Samuel Delany, 35; and the family, 111–12
post-industrial economy. *See* Post-Fordism
postmodernism: 10–11, 52; and art, 125; and *Between C & D*, 153, 163; as divided from identity literature, 12; and Kathy Acker, 99; limitations of, 115; and New Narrative, 11, 137
Postone, Moishe, 8, 22
poststructuralism: 85–86, 87–91; and New Narrative, 138; at "Schizo-Culture" conference, 87–91
poverty: and and David Wojnarowicz, 42, 46, 51; and Kathy Acker, 103–105; literary representations of, 64–65, 103–105, 109–10; and Nuyorican poetry, 64–65
Povod, Reinaldo: 17, 160, 164, 173; in *Between C & D*, 164
precarity: 18, 48, 50, 52, 53, 76, 89, 112, 138, 141, 175, 176, 179, 180, 181, 182, 183–84, 185, 188; and art, 52; and Autonomia (social movement), 114
Prince, Richard, 114, 144
prisons: and David Wojnarowicz, 50; and Nuyorican literature, 66; and "Schizo-Culture" conference, 89, 90; and Sylvère Lotringer, 89, 90; literary representations of, 50, 66
Proposition 13 (anti-taxation law), 31
Puerto Rican literature: 5, 57–59, 60–70, 73–77, 82–83, 160, 164; as anthologized, 62; and gentrification, 20; and "outlaw" trope, 66; and networks, 17
Puerto Ricans: 60–64, 60–70, 78; as adaptive, 70; and abandoned buildings, 64, 69–70; and activism, 95; and austerity, 62; and community gardens, 69; and graffiti art, 121; and homesteading, 63–64; literary representations of, 76–77, 109, 157, 167, 169–70, 171–72; in Lower East Side, 56; perceptions of, 74; and real estate development, 60; and resistance to gentrification, 75; and space/spatiality, 55–57, 83; and space/spatiality, 62; and "underclass" narrative, 65
Purple, Adam, 3

Quality of Life in Loisaida, The (journal), 6, 56, 71–72, 71–72
queer writing: in *Between C & D*, 165
queerness: and AIDS, 181–82; and art criticism, 129; and cruising, 49; and Gary Indiana, 129, 147; and Martin Wong, 81; and poverty, 33–34; and proximity (Roy Pérez concept), 81; and space/spatiality, 33, 35, 147; and time, 33–34; and utopian possibility, 48, 82

Rajchman, John, 90
Rancière, Jacques, 78, 132, 133, 134, 149, 150
Reagan, Michael, 103, 139, 198
real estate development: 30, 34, 42, 56, 62, 76, 81, 130, 152, 173, 174; and art, 37, 42, 53; and David Wojnarowicz, 42; and "East Village" as name for Lower East Side, 5; and Gordon Matta-Clark, 39–40; and the High Line, 53; and homesteading, 63–64; literary representations of, 76, 169; and literature, 13; and Lower East Side, 162–63; and manufacturing, 32, 55; and Nuyorican poetry, 60, 66–67;

resistance to, 43; and Times Square, 35, 49
Redtape (journal): 160; as romanticizing danger of Lower East Side, 161–63
Reich, Robert, 176
Rivas, Bittman John "Bimbo": 6, 17, 56, 72–77, 82; *Benito y Vasconpique*, 75; *El Piraguero de Loisaida*, 76; *Don Quixote de Loisaida*, 72; *Winos*, 73–74
Roberts, John, 18, 23, 24, 52, 185, 187
Rohatyn, Felix, 32, 55, 79
Rooms (exhibit), 3, 36
Rose, Joel: 6, 17, 168–70; and apartments, 154–57; and *Between C & D*, 151–67; and *Between C & D* history, 154–56; and dot-matrix printer, 157–60; *Kill the Poor*, 17, 152, 156, 167–69
Rosenthal, Mel, 44–45
Rotella, Carlo, 13, 24
Rumsfield, Donald, 88

Salle, David, 26, 125, 145, 170
Sassen, Saskia, 174–75
scale: and activism, 7; and Actor Network Theory (Bruno Latour), 22; and *Between C & D* 160; and Charas, 70–71; in David Wojnarowicz *The Waterfront Journals*, 48, 50, 52, 53, 56; in Kathy Acker *Blood and Guts in High School*, 107–109, 110; and Nuyorican poetry, 69–70; and manufacturing, 175; and production of space (Henri Lefebvre concept), 15; and post-crisis landscape, 25, 35, 44; and identity, 37–40
Schnabel, Julian, 26, 117, 125
schools: literary representations of, 76; P.S. 1 (First Ward School Queens), 3, 36–37; P.S. 164 (El Bohío), 71; theorized in terms of micropolitics, 89, 90–91
Schulman, Sarah, 9, 180, 185, 186
Semiotext(e) (collective): 87; and crisis-era New York, 87–88; and Harlem, 91–92; and poverty, 92; and underclass, 86; legacy of, 97; limitations of, 113; "Schizo-Culture" conference, 21, 85–86
Semiotext(e) (journal), 86, 87, 112–14
Serra, Richard: 36; *Tilted Arc*, 127–29, 145–46
Sholette, Gregory, 131, 185
Siegle, Robert, 5, 9, 130, 137, 138, 141, 151, 153, 156, 186, 198
Silliman, Ron, 101, 102
Simon, William, 15
site-specific art: 35–37, 52; *Tilted Arc*, 127–29
Smith, Kiki, 78, 131, 158
Smith, Neil, 15, 24, 49, 55, 62, 119, 152, 168
social classes; and criminality, 90; conflict between, 118, 127, 153; contact between, 18, 20, 22, 34, 35, 73–74, 98–99, 104, 114, 152, 154, 160, 161, 162, 166, 167, 185, 187; in Kathy Acker, 109; literary representations of, 171–72; managing discontent between, 89
social movements; and identity, 114, 153
South Bronx, 44, 98
space and spatiality: 16; and David Wojnarowicz, 43–44, 46, 48–49, 183–84; and Fordism, 138–40, 140; and Gary Indiana, 147; and Gordon Matta-Clark, 37–38; and Joseph Kosuth, 126; and Kathy Acker, 107–109, 112; and Lynne Tillman, 138, 140; negative depictions of, 62,

space and spatiality *(continued)* 65–66; and Nuyorican literature, 55–57, 60, 62, 65–66, 69–70, 77; and Puerto Ricans, 55–57, 62, 83; and Thomas Hirschorn, 53; and art, 52–53, 120–21, 127–29, 135; and creative writing, 12; and literature, 13; in literature, 147; and poverty, 98; and queerness, 33–34; theories of, 8, 14–15, 22, 23, 30–31, 50, 60, 67, 106–107, 149, 152
Spiegelman, Art, 158
St. Mark's Bookstore, 98
Starr, Roger, 1, 52
suburbanization: and "artistic critique" (Boltanski and Chiapello concept), 138; and desire for authenticity, 48–49; form of life under, 182; literary representations of, 11, 138, 140, 141, 143, 182; and "ONE TRIBE NATION" (David Wojnarowicz concept), 182; resistance to, 9; as site of income inequality, 5; and "suburban ambush" (Robert Siegle concept), 9, 138, 143, 186
surface reading (literary critical method), 21, 22
Sweezy, Paul, 105

Texier, Catherine: 6, 146, 170–73; and *Between C & D*, 151–67; and *Between C & D* history, 154–56; and dot-matrix printer, 157–60; *Love Me Tender*, 18, 168, 170–72, 175; and Puerto Rican characters, 157, 171–72; and apartments, 154–57
Tillman, Lynne: 145, 129–35, 138–43; in *Between C & D*, 160; and the female artist, 140–41, 142–43; and Fordism, 138–40; and gentrification, 141–42; *Haunted Houses*, 4, 138–43; Madame Realism essays, 129–35; *No Lease on Life*, 4, 141–42; and space/spatiality, 135, 138–40; and the spectator, 129–30, 132–35; and suburbanization, 138–40
Times Square, 35, 49
Tompkins Square Park: literary representations of, 73–74
Tompkins Square Riot, 156
Trump, Donald: 173, 187; and Trump Tower (1983), 130

underclass: 29–32, 47, 62, 65; and David Wojnarowicz, 32–33; and graffiti art, 121, 134–35; and homelessness, 128; and Kathy Acker, 98–99; and Michel Foucault, 93; and Puerto Ricans, 70; as irredeemable, 32; literary representations of, 168; overview of term, 16–17
unions, 4, 32, 56, 89, 98, 105–106
utopian possibility: and do-it-yourself, 188; and queerness, 48

Village Voice, The, 14, 98, 122–29, 144, 145, 170
Villemaire, Yolande; in *Between C & D*, 164
Virno, Paulo, 112, 137, 147, 148

Wacquant, Loïc, 33, 42, 89, 90
Wages for Housework movement, 96, 139
Wark, McKenzie, 14
Warner, Michael, 34
Washington Heights, 98
Watson, Jini Kim, 12
Webster, Meg, 149

Weeks, Kathi, 9
welfare state: 1–2, 31, 47, 87; attacks on, 3, 16–17, 31, 32, 34, 55, 62, 88, 107, 109–10, 173; decline of, 4, 29, 30, 86, 97, 138, 143; and do-it-yourself, 6, 7; and literary theory, 86; and writers, 104; support for, 93, 104, 112, 127; withdrawal of, 7
Wilson, William Julius, 16, 33–34
windows: and art, 38–39; and *Between C & D*, 157; and Gordon Matta-Clark, 38–39
Wojnarowicz, David: 18, 29, 32–33, 40–52, 144; and AIDS, 179–83; *Close to the Knives*, 183–84; *Fuck You Faggot Fucker*, 51; *Junk Triptych*, 42; and literary form, 10, 49; living circumstances, 8; and poverty, 42, 46, 51; and queer space, 34–35; and queer time, 33–34; and queerness, 181–82; and real estate development, 42, 48–49; and scale, 41, 48, 53; and space/spatiality, 43–44, 46, 48–49; *The Waterfront Journals*, 29, 32–33, 43–51, 111; *What is this little guy's job in the world?*, 42

Wong, Martin: 9, 77–82; *Attorney St. Handball Court*, 80; *The Flood*, 83; *It's Not What You Think, What Is it Then?*, 79; *My Secret World*, 81; *No Es Lo Que Has Pensado*, 80; *Portrait of Mickey Piñero at Ridge Street and Stanton*, 57; *Stanton Near Forsyth*, 83; *Sweet Oblivion*, 83
work: and do-it-yourself, 8–9; informal, 174–75; nature of, 7, 8, 19, 20, 30, 33, 82, 89, 100, 112, 118, 119, 122, 125, 136, 137, 148, 150, 174–76, 177; resistance to, 8–9, 33, 43, 134, 142
writers: as archeologists, 164; and apartments, 151–53, 154–57; and appropriation, 9, 11; and artists, 19–20; and buildings, 154–57; living circumstances of, 3–4, 7–8, 102–103; as sociologists, 47

Young Lords, The, 61, 90, 94–95
Yunqué, Edgardo Vega: 66, 76–77; *The Lamentable Journey of Omaha Bigelow*, 76–77

Zukin, Sharon, 68, 119

www.ingramcontent.com/pod-product-compliance
Lightning Source LLC
Chambersburg PA
CBHW020645230426
43665CB00008B/320